COMPLEX SOVEREIGNTY:
RECONSTITUTING POLITICAL AUTHORITY
IN THE TWENTY-FIRST CENTURY

EDITED BY
EDGAR GRANDE AND LOUIS W. PAULY

Complex Sovereignty: Reconstituting Political Authority in the Twenty-first Century

UNIVERSITY OF TORONTO PRESS
Toronto Buffalo London

Library and Archives Canada Cataloguing in Publication

Complex sovereignty : reconstituting political authority in the
twenty-first century / edited by Edgar Grande and Louis Pauly.

Includes bibliographical references and index.
ISBN 0-8020-3881-6

1. Sovereignty.   2. International organization.   3. World politics –
21st century.   4. International relations.   I. Grande, Edgar, 1956–
II. Pauly, Louis W.

JZ4034.C64 2005   320.1'5   C2005-901240-4

University of Toronto Press acknowledges the financial assistance to its
publishing program of the Canada Council for the Arts and the Ontario
Arts Council.

University of Toronto Press acknowledges the financial support for its
publishing activities of the Government of Canada through the Book
Publishing Industry Development Program (BPIDP).

Contents

Acknowledgments

This book originated in the beautiful garden of the Munk Centre for International Studies at the University of Toronto, during the time that Edgar Grande held the DAAD Distinguished Visiting Professorship in German and European Studies.

In the spring of 2002 colleagues from both sides of the Atlantic were invited to join the editors in developing the idea of 'complex sovereignty.' Most of us met again half a year later in Munich. A lengthy process of writing and revising chapters under the guidance of the editors and two anonymous referees followed.

As the book evolved, the Munk Centre lived up to its reputation as an incubator of collaborative scholarship. The Technical University of Munich, where Edgar Grande was then based, provided a congenial venue for our second meeting. Our meetings were made possible by the German Academic Exchange Service/Deutscher Akademischer Austausch Dienst (DAAD), the Centre for International Studies at the University of Toronto, and the Chair for Political Science at the Institute for Social Science, Technical University of Munich.

Peter Katzenstein and Janice Stein attended the Toronto meeting and helped considerably in opening the path to new research and writing. For organizational assistance and copy-editing, we thank Tina Lagopoulos, Kate Baltais, and Harold Otto. Joanna Langille enthusiastically helped us move the project to its concluding stage and, among other things, compiled the list of acronyms. Nisha Shah made fundamental contributions over many months to the preparation of the final manuscript; we look forward to watching her own promising scholarship in this field develop in the years ahead. Finally, we thank Virgil Duff,

Stephen Kotowych, and Anne Laughlin of the University of Toronto Press for their enthusiasm and encouragement. On behalf of all the contributors, we dedicate this book to our students.

EDGAR GRANDE
LOUIS W. PAULY

Abbreviations

APEC	Asia-Pacific Economic Cooperation
ARENA	Asian Regional Exchange for New Alternatives
BCBS	Basel Committee on Banking Supervision
BSP	Biosafety Protocol
CAC	Codex Alimentarius Commission
CAP	Common Agricultural Policy
CBD	Convention on Biological Diversity
CCT	Consultative Committee for Telecommunications
CEER	Council of European Energy Regulators
CEN	European Committee for Standardization
CHIPS	Clearing House Inter-bank Payments System
COP	Conference of Parties
CPGR	Commission on Plant Genetic Resources
CPSS	Committee on Payment and Settlement Systems
CRMPG	Counterparty Risk Management Group
CSCE	Council for Security and Cooperation in Europe
CTG	Committee on Trade in Goods
CUFTA	Canada–U.S. Free Trade Agreement
DFAIT	Department of Foreign Affairs and International Trade, Government of Canada
EC	Commission of the European Union
EEC	European Economic Community
ECOSOC	Economic and Social Council, U.N.
EEA	European Environmental Agency
EMEA	European Agency for the Evaluation of Medicinal Products
EU	European Union

FAO	Food and Agriculture Organization, U.N.
FATF	Financial Action Task Force, FSF
FDA	Food and Drug Administration, U.S.
FSF	Financial Stability Forum
G-7	Group of Seven
G-8	Group of Eight
G-10	Group of Ten
G-20	Group of Twenty
G-22	Group of Twenty-Two
GAAP	Generally Accepted Accounting Principles
GAO	General Accounting Office, U.S.
GATT	General Agreement on Tariffs and Trade
GMO	genetically modified organism
IAIS	International Association of Insurance Supervisors
IASB	International Accounting Standards Board
IATRC	International Agricultural Trade Research Consortium
ICANN	Internet Corporation for Assigned Names and Numbers
ICSID	International Convention on the Settlement of Investment Disputes
IFAC	International Federation of Accountants
IJC	International Joint Commission
ILO	International Labour Organization
IMF	International Monetary Fund
INGO	international non-governmental organization
IOSCO	International Organization of Securities Commissions
IPPC	International Plant Protection Convention
ISO	International Organization for Standardization
LTSC	Land Transportation Sub-committee
MCC	Millennium Challenge Corporation
NAEWG	North American Energy Working Group
NAFTA	North American Free Trade Agreement
NIEO	New International Economic Order
NORAD	North American Air Defense Command
ODA	official development assistance
OECD	Organization for Economic Co-operation and Development
OIE	Organisation Internationale des Épizooties
ONP	open network provision
PCT	Patent Cooperation Treaty
PPBS	Planning, Programming, and Budgeting System

PPP	public-private partnership
PPPN	public-private policy network
PRSP	Poverty Reduction Strategy Paper
ROSC	Report on the Observance of Standards and Codes
SICE	Foreign Trade Information System
SPS	Sanitary and Phytosanitary
TRIPS	Trade-Related Aspects of Intellectual Property Rights
TSSC	Telecommunications Standards Sub-committee
UNA-USA	U.N. Association of the U.S.A.
UNCED	United Nations Conference on Environment and Development
UNCITRAL	United Nations Commission on International Trade Law
UNCTAD	United Nations Conference on Trade and Development
UNDP	United Nations Development Program
UNESCO	United Nations Educational, Scientific, and Cultural Organization
UNHCR	United Nations High Commissioner for Refugees
UPOV	International Union for the Protection of New Plant Varieties
USAID	U.S. Agency for International Development
USDA	U.S. Department of Agriculture
USDOT	U.S. Department of Transport
WCD	World Commission on Dams
WIPO	World Intellectual Property Organization
WTO	World Trade Organization

COMPLEX SOVEREIGNTY

1 Reconstituting Political Authority: Sovereignty, Effectiveness, and Legitimacy in a Transnational Order

LOUIS W. PAULY AND EDGAR GRANDE

How distant seems the year 1989, when historic and surprising events stirred many dreams of a new and more tranquil world order. The sudden end of the Cold War, as well as recent progress towards economic integration among countries in various regions, revolutionary advances in communications technologies, and the rapid emergence of myriad global social networks sparked a revival of idealistic thought. Europe was moving unexpectedly quickly from enlarging its common market to deepening monetary integration among the member-states of the European Union. These developments gave tangible expression to underlying processes that were widely deemed to have vast transformative potential. Scholarly debates focused less on whether such processes existed than on the desirability and durability of particular outcomes.[1] In such a context, the stubborn insistence of nativist Americans, embattled Israelis, and newly assertive developing countries on upholding the sanctity of state sovereignty – and the political independence of the nation – somehow appeared anachronistic. It seemed certain that, eventually, they would get over it.

Then Osama bin Laden's followers destroyed the World Trade Center and a section of the Pentagon. The ensuing war against Afghanistan's Taliban government, followed in 2003 by the invasion of Iraq, seemed to be evidence that the classical sovereign state was back. The United States mobilized against Iraqi President Saddam Hussein, while some of its key allies pointedly withheld their support. Such actions seemed to constitute further evidence that the security state, whose origins lie in the world of seventeenth-century Europe, had re-emerged from out of the dusky shadows. Nevertheless some observers called for deeper reflection. Could it be that al-Qaida's very success was a portent, in a world of asymmetrical threats and capabilities, where as an institution sovereign statehood was ill-adapted to respond effectively to citizens' fundamental demands for protection? Could it be that the monstrous postwar challenges of remaking failed states like Afghanistan and Iraq were demonstrations of the impossibility of actually solving pressing global problems in the absence of some new kinds of instruments for coordinating political activities across traditional territorial and functional borders? Moreover, could it be that the nature of other dramatic challenges to the prosperity and very survival of human life on earth – from viral pandemics to deterioration of the environment – pointed in a direction away from the historical doctrine of state sovereignty?

The tension between the reassertion of political authority by sovereign states and the emergence of dilemmas that cannot be resolved by radically decentralized decision-making structures forms the backdrop for this book. This collaborative study crosses the disciplines of political science, international relations, sociology, and political economy. The contributors have joined together in a systematic effort to understand and assess the character and likely future trajectory of political authority as it is being reconstituted at the global level. Together, they argue that we are living in a world where the levers of political control are no longer entirely clear. Nevertheless, they also contend that we are not, at least not yet, living in a situation that can be adequately described by the word 'chaos.' Instead, they describe a fascinating and vitally important struggle to give coherence to a complicated system of multiple and overlapping hierarchies. The idea that is currently at the core of that struggle to construct global political authority we call *complex sovereignty*.

Background

After years of intense scholarly debate, there is now widespread consensus that, despite increasing economic, social, and political pressures, the modern nation-state is not yet headed for the dustbin of history. This form of polity has not mutated into some kind of 'virtual' condition.[2] In most parts of the world, states seem to be more important than ever for the production of public goods such as security and welfare. Where states have failed, it seems quite clear that it is certain specific structures of the state that have failed, rather than the idea of the state itself.[3]

Nevertheless, there is now also a reasonably robust consensus that such conclusions should not be extrapolated to the point of arguing that the long historical evolution of the core structures of political authority in the form of the territorial state has reached its end. In fact, we can observe a *complex and partly contradictory transformation* of authority, until now centred in the state. This transformation affects the basic institutions, principles, norms, and procedures of contemporary policymaking.

We contend that this transformation is a *multi-dimensional and multi-scalar process*. It affects all aspects of public authority, in particular the distribution of political decision-making power across territorial levels, the relation between public and private actors, and the definition of public functions. The contributors to this book, in dialogue with one another across their various chapters, observe a redistribution of responsibilities for the production of common goods among public and private actors, the emergence of new forms of private interest government (i.e., the private production of public goods), and new modes of cooperation between public and private actors (e.g., policy networks and public-private partnerships). They do depict a world where new institutional forms of public policy-making at various geographical and functional levels (sometimes integrating different levels) are emerging. They assess multi–level systems of governance, international regimes, policy networks, and transnational policy spaces within which unique types of governing arrangements are evolving.

These new forms of governance have not replaced the modern nation-state, and there are good reasons to assert that they will not do so unambiguously in the near future. In most of them, national governments still play an important, even indispensable, role. But nation-states, as David Held and his colleagues put it in a well-known formulation, 'have gradually become enmeshed in and functionally part of a larger pattern of global transformations and flows.'[4] In an increasing number of domains, they can no longer simply dictate the rules of the game.

With the rise to international leadership of states that rest on democratic principles, legitimate political authorities have found themselves drawn increasingly to non-hierarchical and non-majoritarian modes of conflict resolution. Except during war-time emergencies, states have more often than in past centuries resorted to soft policy instruments to achieve their goals. In short, nation-states negotiate with one another as well as with an expanding array of other actors, as they seek collectively binding decisions and new kinds of public goods. Our working hypothesis in this book is that such developments suggest a fundamental transformation in the organization of political authority in modern societies. Across much of the world, and certainly among the most powerful societies, state sovereignty is not obsolete; it is, however, being reconstituted.

Political Authority, States, and Sovereignty

Considerable conceptual confusion surrounds contemporary debate on the nature and implications of new forms of governance and their institutionalization. In the wake of intensifying arguments about globalization, de-territorialization, and the possible end of the nation-state, John Ruggie made the astute observation 'that [international relations scholars] are not very good ... at studying the possibility of fundamental discontinuity in the international system; that is, at addressing the question of whether the modern system of states may be yielding in some instances to postmodern forms of configuring political space. We lack even an adequate vocabulary; and what we cannot describe, we cannot explain.'[5] Although substantial efforts have been made in recent years to produce some conceptual clarity, a common understanding about the form, extent, scope, and consequences of the ongoing changes in political authority remains to be achieved.[6] Consequently, we can find a variety of different hypotheses and arguments both on the foundations, development, and future of modern states and on the role of sovereignty in this regard. Our starting point in this book is a distinction between three basic concepts: political authority, statehood, and sovereignty. Each of these concepts needs to be viewed in its proper historical context.

We are not witnessing the end of sovereignty with the advent of some postmodern kind of political authority. That said, it is not plausible to maintain that sovereignty has remained what it once was. We are living through a time when changes are occurring in both the internal and external dimensions of state sovereignty, as it has classically been understood. These changes, we argue in this book, have contributed to a significant *deepening in the complexity of sovereignty*. In the following chapters, these complexities will be explored in detail.

The modern state is a historically specific expression of political authority, with sovereignty as one of its defining characteristics. A key question being asked across many fields today is whether the 'modern' period itself has come to an end. As compared with statehood and sovereignty, *political authority* (politische Herrschaft) is defined most broadly. Max Weber famously asserted that political authority is 'the probability that a command with a given specific content will be obeyed by a group of persons.'[7] He took probability to be a measure of legitimacy: the double-sided belief that the giver of such a command is entitled to do so *and* that the subjects of such a command have an obligation to obey.[8] Empires, leagues, tribes, and kinship groups all embodied such expectations in the premodern period. In modernity, however, the key locus of political authority became the state.[9]

In historical terms, states are a recent innovation in governance. They originated in discrete European monarchies, and in a distinct process of state building and adaptation that stretched from tenth-century Europe to an eighteenth-century world remoulded by the extension of European state power.[10] Today, Europe is still at the centre of discussions about the state, but it is also the centre of discussions about the human potential for superseding traditional forms of state. In his remarkable history of the state in Europe, one that captures much contemporary thinking on this subject, Wolfgang Reinhard even goes so far as to argue that the modern state no longer exists there, but became extinct by the last third of the twentieth century.[11] We take a different view in this book.

What is the modern state and what are its basic features? Again, Max Weber's work provides a useful starting point. According to his widely adopted definition, the modern *state* can best be characterized by its 'monopoly of the legitimate use of physical force within a given territory.'[12] The most important, although often neglected, aspect of this definition is its claim regarding the state's coercive monopoly. Modern states were thus distinct from premodern forms of authority because of their ability to concentrate, institutionalize, and regulate the use of coercive force in a way not found in premodern societies. In brief, modern states restricted and civilized the use of coercion in society. This process of 'civilizing' coercive force can be delineated through four principles, which are – explicitly or implicitly – essential parts of Weber's conception:

1 *The principle of sovereignty.* Sovereignty is implied by the 'monopoly' of legitimate coercion. Sovereignty concentrates legitimate coercive

powers within a society in the hands of public authorities, thereby excluding individuals, groups, and organizations from actively participating in legitimate means of exercising coercion.

2 *The principle of territoriality.* Territoriality circumscribes the exercise of authority within the territorial boundaries of the state. The coercive power of the state, thus, does not legitimately extend beyond its geographical borders, except in self-defence.

3 *The principle of rational legitimacy.* Rational legitimacy requires that political authority must necessarily (although not exclusively) be based on formal rules and a consistent, codified legal order, rather than on tradition or charisma;

4 *The principle of bureaucratic institutionalization.* Bureaucratic institutionalization guarantees that sovereign powers are exercised permanently, reliably, and uniformly within a given territory.

The modern state integrated these four principles in a distinctive way. This largely contributed to its competitive success and its stability. Furthermore, in the twentieth century, after the decline of colonial empires, the modern state became the only legitimate form of institutionalizing political authority. To be sure, other forms of governance persisted, but they were subordinated to the authority of the state. Moreover, the effectiveness and legitimacy of these other forms of political community depended on whether they were recognized by the state or by international organizations comprised of states.

If a fundamental transformation of the modern state is now taking place, we would expect these constitutive principles to be significantly affected. More precisely, the reconstitution of public authority should mean the erosion, transformation, and reconfiguration of the observable ways in which these basic principles of modern statehood are expressed.

Obviously, transformations of particular states can vary in scope and extent. First, such transformations can either be limited to one of these four principles or involve all of them at the same time. Second, we can think of at least two types of changes: (1) internal changes of basic principles of modern statehood or (2) their replacement by some other principle of political authority. Changes of the first type would suggest the transformation of recognizable forms of state and most likely would be of an incremental nature.[13] Changes of the latter type would indicate the transition to some postmodern configuration of political authority.[14]

Complexities of Sovereignty: Historical Perspective

Although there is widespread agreement that sovereignty remains an indispensable attribute of the modern state, and that it is absent in pre-modern forms of political authority, the exact relationship between the state and sovereignty is highly contested. Our preferred conceptualization takes sovereignty and the state to be two sides of the same coin. Sovereignty is what distinguishes the modern state from its premodern, feudal predecessor and also from emerging postmodern forms of political authority.[15] An alternative theory might suggest that sovereignty is associated with all forms of political organization – whether empires, feudal systems, polities of states, absolutist states, or modern states.[16] In such a typology, the distinguishing feature of the modern state would be its close association with the idea of a nation, a sentiment crystallized in political ideology since the eighteenth century. But this risks confusing a defining attribute with a legitimating ideology. More generally, recent analyses of the modern state, sovereignty, and governance have been susceptible to two shortcomings. They have tended either to conceptualize sovereignty in zero-sum terms (i.e., as fully present or entirely absent from a given political structure) or to treat modern states as fully evolved *entities* (where the state-sovereignty linkage is invariable and any evidence of change must be associated with state decline).[17]

These approaches ignore what must reasonably be seen as the historical ambiguities of sovereignty. As a consequence, they make it more difficult to observe and assess the very essence of the putative transformation of public authority in the contemporary world. To avoid such shortcomings, it is crucial to keep the concept of sovereignty in its proper evolutionary and comparative-historical context. The practices, expression, and even theoretical conceptualization of sovereignty have changed over time, and we argue in this book that they continue to change. By way of previewing the main analytical themes in the chapters below, we can observe several transformations of the concept of sovereignty both in scholarly writings and in its common usage.[18]

In 1576, Jean Bodin famously conceived of sovereignty as both *absolute* and *exclusive*.[19] In his view, the acceptance of any additional authority within the same territory would necessarily destroy the effectiveness of sovereignty. Such a conception, however, was unrealistic from the outset, since even in absolutist states there was typically a division of labour in the making and execution of laws. Bodin tried to solve this problem by distinguishing between sovereignty-in-principle concentrated in the hands – or, more precisely, in the person – of the emperor, and government, and the actual division and organization of sovereignty-in-practice.

Bodin's rigid conceptualization has long been the subject of much critical debate and significant reformulation.[20] Most importantly, with the replacement of the absolutist state by the constitutional state, and later on, by the democratic state, sovereignty-in-practice has mutated over time. Indeed, discursive development and the empirical emergence of new forms of state have proceeded in a dialectical fashion. The English idea of parliamentary sovereignty,[21] Rousseau's concept of popular sovereignty (which shifts the locus of authority from the emperor to the people), and the Weberian concept of 'state sovereignty,' (which attributes sovereignty neither to an emperor nor to the people but to the state itself) all helped to construct the ideological foundations for discrete modern states.

Changes in the internal organization of political authority did not render the sovereignty of actual states more or less relevant or consequential. In many respects, as we discuss further below, these internal changes were necessary for states to retain as much scope as possible for the external dimension of sovereignty. Different forms of government turned out to be entirely compatible with the idea of sovereignty appropriately softened for the post-Bodin era. One might justifiably claim, moreover, that this softening became more and not less obvious around the time of the 1648 Peace of Westphalia, which has conventionally been viewed to be a decisive moment in the definition of state sovereignty. Considerable historical evidence supports the contrary view, however, that the harder version of state sovereignty that is associated in the popular mind with Westphalia really only emerged after the French revolution and with the strengthening of nationalist ideologies during the industrial revolution of the nineteenth century. Studies of the Holy Roman Empire and its legacy in Europe suggest soft and porous boundaries around sovereign authority even in Bodin's day, their hardening some two centuries ago, and a gradual reversion to earlier norms after the world wars of the twentieth century.[22] Recent path-breaking constructivist studies of state sovereignty in general have moved suggestively along similar lines.[23]

There is, of course, the risk that analysts can push such thinking to an extreme position. Sovereignty cannot simply exist in the eye of the beholder, for the political dynamics of objective coercive capabilities and the mutual recognition of legitimate claims to rule have always been central to empirical processes of the building, decline, and transformation of the state. Precisely here is where the contribution of this book comes in. Collectively, we have not aspired to provide a detailed account of the history and evolution of sovereignty. The contemporary period of transformation is our focal point. Still, our collaborative research strongly suggests that state sovereignty has become both more abstract and more complex, since its inception.

Based on the assumption that modern states are in fact integrated within an encompassing system of states, we can develop a more refined concept of sovereignty that is based on the following four propositions:

1 Internal and external sovereignty must be distinguished. Internal sovereignty refers to the relationship between state and society (i.e., the state's autonomy from society), whereas external sovereignty refers to the state's external relations in the international system (i.e., the state's independence from other states). In both respects, sovereignty is not simply the product of coercive capacities, but the result of *mutual recognition*. It is important to differentiate these two sources of recognition: whereas internal sovereignty relies on domestic consensus, external sovereignty is premised on international recognition by other states. The criteria for recognition may vary considerably over time, and both dimensions of recognition do not necessarily coexist easily.[24] Many states have enjoyed international recognition without achieving domestic consensus (e.g., authoritarian regimes or failed states such as Somalia). There are also cases of political authorities that, despite having substantial domestic support, have not been recognized by other states (e.g., the early Communist government in Cuba and the Taliban regime in Afghanistan).

2 Sovereignty can be divided and transformed without losing its substance. On this ground, we can remain open to the possibility of an internal transformation of sovereignty, and the emergence of different institutional forms, both of which can be seen to be different stages in the development of modern states. Indeed, the idea that sovereignty can be divided and reconfigured is, arguably, one of the most important innovations in modern political philosophy. With respect to the state's internal sovereignty, the result has been that

new institutional arrangements for the horizontal and vertical division of political authority, such as the separation of constitutional powers and federalism, have come to be seen as legitimate expressions of sovereignty.
3 The two dimensions of sovereignty – internal and external – can develop separately from one another. This implies that there is no necessary correspondence between the different stages of their development.
4 Although internal and external sovereignty can have separate trajectories of development, the two dimensions nevertheless remain interdependent.

Because internal and external sovereignty can have separate, yet interdependent, trajectories of development, we can identify various empirical clusters in the historical development of sovereignty. These clusters include the following:

- The *absolutist state* (seventeenth and eighteenth century), characterized by the concentration and centralization of sovereign power and security functions
- The *constitutional state* (nineteenth century), characterized by the diffusion of sovereign power among governors, constitutions, and legal rules
- The *nation-state* (nineteenth century), characterized by the integration of domestic populations through ideas about common history, language, sociocultural beliefs, and doctrines concerning national security
- The *democratic state* (nineteenth and twentieth century), characterized by a shift in the locus of sovereignty from rulers to ruled – essentially, the emergence of popular sovereignty
- The *welfare state* (twentieth century), characterized by the extended functions of sovereign power, including much more broadly defined responsibility for the security of citizens.

Flowing out of these propositions, the central question of this book is whether recent transformations of public authority within some states have actually led us to a sixth form of modern statehood, which might bear labels such as the 'transnational cooperation state' or the 'networked state.' This new type of state might emerge, for example, from the interplay of tensions between, on the one hand, the insistence that all those who are meaningfully affected by decisions be somehow incorporated directly or indirectly into complex processes of decision-making and, on the other hand, the historical legacy of territorially based constructions of political and cultural identities.[25]

A similar, albeit less complicated development can be observed with respect to the external sovereignty of states. Histories of external sovereignty typically begin in the seventeenth century.[26] Even if one takes a more evolutionary approach, by the nineteenth century the doctrine of external sovereignty came to have three distinct elements:

1 States were defined as the basic units of the international system. Although other public and private authorities existed, they lacked sovereignty.
2 All states were considered to be legally equal, regardless of the size of their territory or the magnitude of their military power.
3 State sovereignty was understood to mean freedom from external interference. This was best understood as a prohibition on interference by one state in the internal affairs of another state.

Even from its inception, however, sovereignty has always been contested and challenged, in theory as well as in practice. The most significant transformation of any rigid conception of external sovereignty has been occurring since the Second World War, especially as can be seen in the emergence of a transnational human rights regime, whereby aspirations for individual rights have gradually been superseding the legitimacy of target states and their insistence on non-interference.[27] A similar dynamic appears incipient in the development and broadening acceptance of a 'responsibility to protect' vulnerable human beings, notwithstanding the resistance of local governmental authorities.[28] It requires little imagination to interpret such trends as part of a shift to *transnational sovereignty*. This type of sovereignty would differ from its doctrinal predecessor in at least two respects: First, it would in principle weaken the role of traditional states in international relations, and second, it would qualify, at times even suspend, the immunity of states from external influence. Accepting the notion that the earlier doctrine always masked actual hierarchies of power in the world, such a shift would also imply deeper potentialities in terms of global reordering.[29] Among scholars of international relations, the observation and analysis of such developments is central to key debates within the field.

For our present purposes, tracing the historical differentiation of sovereignty allows us to distinguish the main argument of this book from two competing hypotheses. The first, following Stephen Krasner, maintains that the model of sovereignty that is conventionally associated with Westphalia has been irrelevant for a long time and that it has long been nothing more than a system of 'organized hypocrisy.'[30] The second contends that current transformations of public authority are not unprecedented and thus not unique. We take a different view. The central thesis shared by the authors in this volume is that sovereignty exists and remains a relevant attribute of states and that recent changes in both the conceptualization and practice of sovereignty are unique and significant, even if their effects are variable. Earlier transformations in political authority can teach us all there is to know, but they can only provide rough analogies for explaining the present.

Read together, the chapters in this book make the case that contemporary transformations of the internal and external dimensions of the sovereignty of the state are constructing a new historical cluster of sovereign power. Ulrich Beck has proposed one formulation of this thesis; he calls this new cluster of sovereign power the *cooperation state*, a necessarily transnational polity that is based on a high degree of coordination, both internal and external.[31] At a time when the most powerful state in the international system appears to be reasserting hard-sovereignty aspirations, and when states that are still emerging from colonialism are energetically upholding the strict doctrine of sovereignty in defending their newly won political autonomy, Beck's is a bold and controversial formulation indeed. The other contributors to this volume debate Beck's specific formulation, and the debate remains as open as it is important. Furthermore, they do agree that the theoretical innovations and empirical evidence that they have surveyed strongly suggest a tendency in Beck's direction. As comparativists with a strong interest in international relations, the analyses by these authors highlight mounting pressures on the United States of America and other countries with apparently strong rhetorical attachments to unequivocal understandings of sovereignty, particularly to its external dimension. Collectively, they also outline key conceptual and empirical aspects of the political transformation that is purported to be unfolding in the contemporary world, a transformation suggestive of the potential emergence of new hierarchies of power and authority.

Transformations of Sovereignty: Dimensions of Change in the Actual Structures of Governance

The transformation of sovereignty is only one dimension of the change in political authority. We provide below a brief outline of the key dimensions of change in the reconstitution of public authority and, by extension, sovereignty. What is proffered here is a framework that goes beyond the usual internal-external understanding of sovereignty.

To reduce current processes of transformation to problems of internal sovereignty is highly misleading. It is true that problems of national sovereignty exist, and they are important. But such problems are only one aspect of a series of complex and ambiguous developments. Most importantly, the reconstitution of political authority in its fullest sense should be seen not only as a historical process, but also as a multi-dimensional phenomenon that comprises territorial, functional, and political aspects of the contemporary experience of governance. This reconstitution can be outlined in three steps:

1 Most importantly, the nation-state has lost its monopoly on collectively binding decision-making and on the production of public goods. In recent decades, we have witnessed the strengthening of international organizations; the establishment of new, regional levels of political decision-making; the emergence of new forms of governance and new types of interaction and cooperation between public and private actors; and the emergence of new roles for private actors in the production of public goods. Territoriality still matters, but the evident result of this intensifying interaction has been a substantial *spatial reconfiguration of public authority.*[32]
2 There is a continuous reassessment and redefinition of public functions. As a consequence of privatization, liberalization, deregulation, and re-regulation, the scope of the public sector has been changing, and the measures and instruments used to perform public functions have been adapting. At the same time, political dynamics have created new public functions for ameliorating environmental deterioration on a global scale and have both expanded and reinforced state security functions to protect citizens from global terrorism. This has resulted in a complex *functional reconstitution of public authority.*
3 Governance in industrially advanced societies has been confronted with new and unique *problems of democratic legitimacy.* This is partly because most of the new forms of governance with which they are

experimenting have serious shortcomings, particularly where participation, representation, and control are concerned.[33] These problems have been exacerbated by the process of globalization, which has created new political cleavages and intensified political conflicts. At the same time, new electronic media (e.g., global television networks and the Internet) have been changing profoundly not only the scope and intensity, but also the logics of political communication.

In sum, the idea of reconstituting public authority implicates the institutional form of state sovereignty, and its scope and content as well.

Although the hypothetical transformation of state sovereignty through such processes in the contemporary period would be vitally important, it can easily be rendered difficult to prove. Associated debates are excessively abstract. Only with the advantage of historical hindsight can such a transformation be assessed clearly. Like the steps leading to the emergence of the absolutist state and the democratic state, the policy decisions that brought about the welfare state seemed modest and incremental to those who lived through making and introducing them. But such an insight provides a clue for investigators trying to pierce through the fog of our own time. The contributors to this book are joined together in the conviction that systematic and comparative observation of contemporary changes in actual practices of governance can provide insight into the deeper transformation of state sovereignty. With one exception, these authors are based neither within the United States nor the United Kingdom, two states at the forefront of earlier transformations of state sovereignty. Marked by an obvious reluctance to question the doctrinal outcomes of those struggles, doctrines now embedded in constitutional forms and foreign policy traditions, it can be argued that policymakers and citizens in those particular two states are having the greatest difficulty in perceiving and adjusting to the ambiguities of transnational structures of authority. We believe that sensibilities shaped by experiences with the challenges of governance in both contemporary Canada and Germany contribute unique perspectives on the transformation of state sovereignty. The novelty of our collective project also is informed by our examination of these kinds of challenges across a range of public, private, and hybrid public-private regimes at the international, regional, and national levels of governance.

The selection of cases examined in this volume constitute a comprehensive heuristic device for defining and probing the research frontier on state sovereignty. As will be seen, each of the examples reveals:

1 The increasing importance of regional and international levels of governance
2 An apparently increased significance and influence of private actors, both domestically and in the larger global system, with respect to the production of public goods
3 Increasing reliance on non-hierarchical and non-majoritarian methods of political conflict resolution at all levels – national, regional, and international.

This book is a contribution to the now rapidly deepening research on such matters. Do not assume, however, that every question on the research agenda is close to being answered definitively. The authors represented herein share the view that empirically based research can be a help in pushing away from polemics and towards understanding. Nevertheless, as some now commonly contend, while the world may be moving in the direction of 'cosmopolitanism,' 'globalism,' or 'empire,' systematic empirical assessment is essential to see the actual pathway.[34]

The Analytical Agenda

At the outset of this comparative exploration of the putative reconstitution of public authority, we freely admit that the very fact of the emergence of new forms of governance does not necessarily mean that they will become the dominant or exclusive forms in the twenty-first century. Nor does their emergence imply that they will be stable, effective, and ultimately legitimate. In truth diverging trends in approaches to governance are readily observable in the early years of this new century. This becomes perhaps especially apparent when public rhetoric surrounding doctrines of state sovereignty is contrasted and compared among various states around the world, including the United States, Russia, China, many developing countries, continental Europe, and Canada. Only in the latter cases are we now frequently hearing about the sharing or pooling of sovereignty. To be sure, such talk provokes reactions, even in those states. But on a range of issues traditionally viewed as being central to the autonomy and integrity of state authority – from deep economic and social reforms to military security – public rhetoric in Europe and Canada, for example, concerning the malleability of sovereignty appears to be matched by a historically unusual openness to *transnational coopera-tion*, a phenomenon now also apparently crossing formerly distinct boundaries between the 'public' sphere and the 'private.' It is worth putting the phenomenon of transnational cooperation under scrutiny and probing the reasons for differences in approaches to it around the world.

To arrive at such distinctions, the contributors to this volume exam-ine the ability and the willingness of private actors, interest groups, and transnational social movements to cooperate, but they focus more of their attention on the ability and willingness of states to cooperate. In the concluding chapter, we group states into one of four different categories: (1) those both able and willing to cooperate; (2) those able but unwilling to cooperate; (3) those unable to cooperate, although they would be willing to do so; and (4) those both unable and unwill-ing to cooperate.

Four issues guide the research presented in this book:

1 The institutionalization and the overall *institutional architecture* of new transnational forms of governance, in particular the relations between various differentially empowered organizations that pro-vide public goods
2 The *role of states* in these new transnational forms of governance, their ability and their willingness to cooperate in transnational arrangements of policymaking, their willingness to comply with transnational rules and norms, and their ability to implement such rules and norms
3 The organizational problems of *private actors* and their possible con-tribution to transnational governance
4 The *legitimacy* of new forms of governance, specifically the obstacles to democratic participation in transnational forums of decision-making.

The authors of this book explore these issues. In dialogue with one another, each provides insight and suggestions for addressing the com-plex dynamics of reconstituting political authority. Together, they con-clude that such an outcome is very demanding, highly contingent, and enmeshed in conflictual processes. In short, their minds remain open to the possibility that significant contemporary challenges to governance may be charting the road to new structures of sovereignty in a more complicated world. Mindful of past reversals in human progress, however, they also remain wary of predicting any such ultimate implications. It is accomplishment enough to identify and highlight new tendencies relevant to such reversals, as well as perhaps, new and hopeful legacies that raise the bar for future retrogression.

This book is organized as follows. The first three chapters provide overviews and applications of three promising approaches to the issues of reconstituting sovereignty, as addressed above. Ulrich Beck develops his theory of world risk society and applies it to some of the challenges that are confronting Europe and the United States today. Mathias Albert extends modern systems theory, as developed by Niklas Luhmann, to the analysis of international relations, and Guy Peters summarizes and provides examples of key concepts in modern organization theory as found in actual contexts of governance.

Specific examples of territorial and institutional adaptation in governance practices are examined in the chapters by William Coleman, Louis Pauly, Burkard Eberlein and Edgar Grande, and Stephen Clarkson (with his collaborators). These chapters are followed by two that explore the dynamic processes of governance innovation that are currently blurring the distinction between public and private authority. Tanja Börzel and Thomas Risse examine public-private partnerships at the international level, and Tony Porter offers a complementary analysis of norm generation by actors in the private sector.

Underlying all of these contributions is a concern about the legitimacy of governance beyond the nation-state. Grace Skogstad and Michael Greven both examine critical interventions that highlight the challenges and potential solutions to securing legitimacy in new and emerging structures of governance. The concluding chapter returns us to a consideration of the meaning and implications of the reconstitution of political authority early in the twenty-first century.

NOTES

1 See, e.g., Greven and Pauly (2000), which inspired this volume.
2 Arguments suggesting the erosion of sovereignty and of the nation-state as traditionally conceived are presented by Albrow (1996), Camilleri and Falk (1992), Ohmae (1995), Strange (1996), Rosecrance (1999), and Reinhard (2000), to mention only a few prominent authors.

3 This holds least for industrially advanced societies. On the failure of the postcolonial state in Africa, see Herbst (2000).

4 Held et al. (1999). On this theme, also see Slaughter (2004).

5 Ruggie (1993: 143f).

6 See, e.g., the concepts of sovereignty presented by Krasner (1999), Hall (1999), Philpott (1999) and Biersteker (2002). In this regard, we agree with Biersteker's view (p. 157): 'One of the most important analytical challenges for scholars of international relations is to identify different meanings of state, sovereignty and territory, and to understand their origins, comprehend their changes of meaning, analyze their interrelationships, and characterize their transformations.' Also see Biersteker and Weber (1996).

7 Weber (1978: 55).

8 'Legitimate authority,' according to Weber, is an authority which is obeyed, at least in part, 'because it is in some appreciable way regarded by the [subordinate] actor as in some way obligatory or exemplary for him' (Weber 1978: 31).

9 For more on premodern forms of political power and authority see Mann (1986). Spruyt (1994) provides a comprehensive discussion of alternatives to the nation-state.

10 Tilly (1990), Reinhard (2000: 15).

11 Reinhard (2000: 535).

12 Weber (1978: 78).

13 These are taken up in the chapters below that refer, e.g., to the theory of reflexive modernization (Beck, Giddens, and Lash, 1994; Beck 2002) or to the theories of post-Fordism (Jessop 1994).

14 Much recent work on notions of private authority tends in this direction. See, e.g., Cutler (2003), Hall and Biersteker (2002), and Cutler, Haufler, and Porter (1999). Also see Rosenau (2003).

15 For authoritative summaries of this position see Hinsley (1966) and Quaritsch (1970).

16 Held (1995).

17 In Krasner's (1999) work, we can find the most obvious strategies to reconcile a static concept of sovereignty with the ongoing transformations of political authority. Either the significance of the changes can be denied or the significance of the concept itself can be refuted. Krasner is an advocate of the latter position.

18 See Quaritsch (1970), Bartelson (1995).

19 This is what Keohane (2001: 6) has labelled 'unitary sovereignty.' See Bodin (1992).

20 See Hardt and Negri (2000: part 2).

21 To put it more precisely: of the 'king in parliament.'

22 Such an argument is well made by Osiander (2001).

23 Bartelson (1995). See also, Onuf (1989), Kratochwil (1989), Wendt (1999), Reus-Smit (1999), Hall (1999), Hurd (1999), Keene (2002).

24 Biersteker (2002).

25 Some authors argue that there has also been a reduction in state functions in the wake of a transition from the welfare state to a 'neo-liberal state' or to a 'workfare state' (Biersteker 2002; Jessop 1994). We see the transformation of political authority as less straightforward. Its result has been the functional reconfiguration of public authority rather than its reduction and a blurring of traditional territorial claims. On the reconceptualization of the latter, see Ruggie (1993) and Appadurai (1996).

26 Philpott (2001) presents a sophisticated analysis.

27 For a more detailed discussion see Held (1995) and Lyons and Mastanduno (1995).

28 Evans and Sahnoun (2002), Finnemore (2003).

29 Lake (2003) provides an excellent review of relevant literature. Also see Lake (1999).

30 Krasner (1999).

31 Beck (2002).

32 On territoriality, and specifically on the distinct matter of not changing boundaries by force, see Zacher (2001).

33 See, among others noted below, Greven and Pauly (2000), and Zürn (2000b).

34 Hardt and Negri's (2000) formulation has been highly suggestive, but it also demonstrates the difficulties of assessing dimensions of actual change.

2 World Risk Society and the Changing Foundations of Transnational Politics

ULRICH BECK

The prevailing attitude among intellectuals today involves a kind of flight from a world situation so contorted that familiar instruments of theory, traditional expectations of the future, and classical means of politics cease to operate.[1] I have tried to address this situation with a research program on a *second modernity,* or *reflexive modernization,* that requires not only new concepts but also a different social-scientific grammar in order to grasp and explain an explosive dynamic in a world that no longer corresponds to the image of actively self-reproducing its structures and system.[2] The theory of *world risk society,* developed in my earlier work, helps in examining how such a dynamic is changing transatlantic relations.[3] On the basis of this theory, my objective in this chapter is to put forward a number of hypotheses that are relevant to the overarching theme of reconstituting sovereignty and of this book as a whole. First, the chapter provides a theoretical orientation. Then it considers the contradictory perceptions of risk that prevail in the United States and in Europe and the extent to which these differing perceptions accounts for the contemporary drift between the two regimes. The chapter then outlines the distinctive logics of ecological, economic, and terrorist risks and the significance of world risk society for generating cooperative strategies of risk reduction in Europe and the United States. Finally, the chapter attempts to draw some theoretical and policy conclusions under the paradigmatic term, *cosmopolitan realism.*

World Risk Society: Outline of a Theory

Let us consider twelve theorems that distinguish new risks from old risks and suggest why the dynamic of conflict within world risk society should be seen in terms of a second, reflexive phase of radical modernization.

Theorem 1: Global Risks as a Social Construction

New risks are perceived to be transnational or global risks. Even when disaster strikes a particular place and produces a grim yet limited toll of dead and wounded, the risk is perceived as unlimited; in the end, it could affect anyone. In this sense, global risks should be differentiated from 'problems that know no frontiers' (e.g., illiteracy, poverty, and so on), because they universalize the likelihood of destructive effects.

We must clearly distinguish between the physical event of a disaster (or an ongoing process of destruction) and the *unlimited expectation* of such disasters to be a global risk. Whether a destructive event counts as a global risk depends not only on the number of dead and wounded or the scale of the devastation of nature, it is also the expression of how the event comes to be perceived. Environmental issues, for example, were once considered by some observers to be a German fad, but since the 1992 U.N. conference in Rio de Janeiro, few still seriously hold such a view. Now, those who deny the reality and urgency of environmental issues must justify themselves. The entire process of social recognition can be quite protracted, but it can also be sudden and dramatic. The terrorism risk, for example, acquired global recognition in one fell swoop, under the impact of the horrible television images of 11 September 2001, even though the urgency of the risk and its priority in the list of global problems remain hotly debated.

Theorem 2: Global Risk as Reflexive Globality

Global risks are an expression of global interdependence and render the latter more intense.[4] Unlike, say, global production chains, which may remain latent, global risks break into human consciousness by virtue of their physical and political explosiveness. One of their peculiar characteristics is the combination of actual interdependence with an awareness of that condition, which I call *reflexive globality*, meaning that, at least under certain circumstances, global risks generate a public. They attract the attention, and economic interests, of the mass media; they threaten everyone, converting the entire world into prisoners and voyeurs of disasters.

Theorem 3: Wars without War

Global risks have a destructive potential comparable to, or perhaps greater than, actual wars. With respect to environmental risks, for example, we effectively confront wars without war. These risks stem from the side-effects of modernization, which may not always be readily attributable to the state. Daase puts it like this:

> The paradigmatic security threat has not become obsolete since the end of the Cold War: there are still states which compete for territory and resources and pose a military threat to one another. But the dangers that have been more sharply perceived since the end of the East-West conflict are of quite a different kind, often lacking a clearly identifiable player, a hostile intent or a military potential. The danger is not direct, intentional and definite, but indirect, unintentional or indefinite. In short, it is a question not of threats but of risks ... What distinguishes security risks from security threats is the loss of certainty about the future when at least one element of the classical security calculation – player, intent or potential – becomes an unknown quantity. As a result, the security triangle gives way to a multiplicity of risk factors, and the number of potential dangers is increased.[5]

Theorem 4: Manufactured Uncertainty

In the first modernity, the international system was in principle predictable, because states held one another in check. In the second modernity, the international system is inherently *unpredictable*. We do not actually know whether and when a suicide bomber will destroy a railway station or fly an aircraft into a nuclear reactor which could trigger a full-scale disaster. We do not know when climate change will produce floods here and droughts there. We lack the help of probability calculations for such *unknown unknowns*.[6] The international system in the second modernity is beset with transnational dangers: 'International politics is primarily distinguished not by threats – and hence by the intention and capacity of various players to inflict significant damage on one another – but to an increasing extent by risks.'[7] Uncertainty manufactured in and through civilization does not remove, however, but actually increases the necessity of making decisions.[8]

Theorem 5: Uncertainty Enables Perception

The more apparent it becomes that global risks divest scientific methods of their predictive capacity, the greater is the influence acquired by risk perception. The distinction between actual risks and risk perception is becoming blurred.[9] The reasons that certain groups of people believe in a risk – or, in other words, sociological research into the cultural perception of risk – thus become more important than the possible scenarios conceived by experts.

Theorem 6: Blurred Lines of Conflict

Global risks open up a meta-power game involving the deconstruction and reconstruction of boundaries, rules, responsibilities, Us-and-Them identities, scope for action, and priorities of action. The paradox is that prevailing uncertainty about the definition of risk disrupts old certainties and creates new ones in their place, in particular, there is the comfortable certainty that one is apprised of the real global risk, whereas others' risk awareness is a paranoid, irrational, and highly dubious obfuscation of real interests. Different cultural perceptions generate secular-religious certainties of risk, whereby my risk is a clear priority overshadowing all others, and your risk stems from a betrayal of the ethos of Western rationality. The essence of the world changes with one's particular *risk religion*. Are you a climate disaster realist or a terrorism realist? Make no mistake: the choice of risk involves not only a choice among different risks but a choice among different world-views. These choices define who is guilty and who is innocent, who will be promoted and who will be demoted, military options or assertions of human rights, the logic of war or the logic of legal obligations. A perverse kind of apocalyptic 'beauty contest' ensues – to decide which risk represents the most terrible or senseless threat to civilization. Does the prize go to climatic trends or to al-Qaida? Or is the truly worst risk of human collapse still to be discovered in human genetics or nanotechnology?

Theorem 7: The Politics of Enablement

Recognized risks to civilization offer an exceptional, extra-democratic source of legitimacy. Counteraction across sovereign frontiers, even when it infringes on the norms of international law and democracy, can always invoke the need to ward off physical or moral dangers to humanity. This enablement politics can be seen in quite different forms among super-powerful, as well powerless players, and across both states and social movements. Nevertheless, such enablement, or self-enablement, is so fragile and risky, so controversial and yet so significant for the future of the world that it is necessary to examine its claims repeatedly, publicly, and in the most thorough manner.

Theorem 8: The Failure of National and International Regulatory Systems

The dynamic of world risk society thus becomes a perfect example of reflexive modernization: the national basis for the calculation and prevention of culturally manufactured uncertainty has been disintegrating. World risk society should be understood in a *post-social* sense, since neither national nor international politics and society have rules about how new risks should be handled, how urgently each of them should be addressed, and which political or military strategies should be adopted to confront them. Each conflict over a particular risk becomes the locus for a meta-power game over future rules for the handling of indeterminate and illimitable risks.

Theorem 9: The New Politics of Uncertainty

Global risks have a structure that is inherently ambivalent: these are uncontrollable second-order risks (because of the institutional failure), but at the same time (by virtue of their social construction) they are, in principle, controllable because they necessitate a new *politics* of uncertainty. They rest on a distinction between *inherent uncontrollability* and *actual lack of control*. They are precisely *not* dangers in the premodern or postmodern sense, because they rest on what Albert, in his chapter in this volume – following Luhmann, terms *decisions*.[10] Global risks, therefore, raise issues of attributability, or responsibility, and lead to conflicts over the distribution of guilt, costs, and justice. Global risks always necessitate political counteraction and, hence, what I have called *risk politics*.[11] There is no uncontrollable destiny, and this means that national and international politics (and *mutatis mutandis* transnational corporations) are freed of all constraints. The global public discourse of risk puts intense pressure on them however to justify themselves and to take appropriate action. National and international politics are, so to speak, condemned to counteraction.

This expectation of counteraction means that, even if all available solutions fail to produce results, a counterfactual belief will remain that the risks are controllable. To do nothing in the face of recognized risks is *politically* impossible – regardless of whether any action reduces or increases the risks or has any effect on them at all. The anonymity of uncontrollable risks must be broken: global risks, to be risks, need to have a face. Bin Laden's face, for example, is the face of the risk of terrorism. The manufactured uncertainty of recognized global risks, or *fortuna* in classical political theory, which is not susceptible to political control, is here translated into *virtù*, for which political instruments and institutions must be invented or overhauled. This gives rise to a hierarchy of political action, in which greater value attaches to proactive than to reactive forms.

Theorem 10: The Politics of Risk Construction and Risk Minimization

We must distinguish between two forms of risk politics: a politics of risk *construction* (involving the social construction of risks) and a politics of risk *minimization* (involving prevention, mitigation, and cross-border intervention). The latter presupposes the former: the construction of risk also defines the scope for action minimization of the risk. Both involve a definition of reality, cognitively in the former case and through political action, in the latter. Risk construction is typical of sociological constructivism, whereas risk minimization is more characteristic of realism in political science.

Theorem 11: Side-Effects of Side-Effects: The Paradoxes of Risk

Awareness of side-effects logically raises the question of which side-effects are or can be produced by the political construction of risks or by various strategies of risk minimization. The following risk paradoxes may be identified: (1) Side-effects of side-effects produce a public. The more extreme and the more damaging the consequences, the greater is the likelihood that, with varying degrees of distortion, these side-effects will become the subject of public reports and discussion. (2) Political action and decisions to reduce or avoid risks may, in accordance with the law of side-effects, actually maximize the dangers that they are intended to minimize.[12] (The 'war on terror' in Iraq, for example, has had the effect of making Iraq a happy hunting ground for trans-national terrorist networks.)

Theorem 12: Implications for the Social Sciences

World risk society poses novel challenges for politics and for everyday life, and for the social sciences as well. On the one hand, scholars must recognize that social interactions no longer are as clearly defined in space and time as was assumed when the nation-state defined the dominant paradigm. On the other hand, world risk society implies a model of global socialization which, in contrast to the usual image of positive integration on the basis of shared values and norms, rests upon conflict over *negative* values, namely, risks, crises, and the dangers of destruction. Risks are not increased, but *the limits are removed* on the uncontrollable risks of interdependence. This is true in three senses: spatial, temporal, and social.

Spatially, we find ourselves facing risks that pay no heed to national or other frontiers. Such risks include climate change, atmospheric pollution, and the ozone hole, and they concern all of us although not in equal measure. *Temporally*, the long latency period of global problems such those connected with nuclear waste or the effects of genetically modified food excludes them from the usual routines for handling industrial dangers. Moreover, *socially*, the allocation of a risk potential becomes problematic, as does any answer to the prisoner's dilemma. Determining who, in any legally significant sense, actually causes environmental pollution or a financial crisis, is difficult when these problems only arise through the combined activity of large numbers of individuals. Thus, dangers to civilization are posed as largely deterritorialized, and it is therefore hard to allocate responsibility for them and harder yet for the national state to control them.

Both the unbounded quality of the new risks and the fact that they are not subject to calculation have been the theme of numerous controversies, many of which are examined in this book. The culture of *merely residual risk* is still locked in a protracted public dispute with a *culture of uncertainty*. The sociologically significant aspect, however, is that such a culture seems more and more to be gaining the upper hand. Like the Chernobyl disaster or the bovine spongiform encephalopathy (BSE) crisis, the terrorist attacks of 11 September 2001 in New York and 11 March 2004 in Madrid show that the real issue is not the calculation of risks to the third or whatever decimal place. The real issue is the change in the *global public perception and construction* of risks. Not so long ago, especially in the perceptual horizons of the U.S. administration, it was still the case that a lack of preventive forethought helped to defuse the situation. Now, however, to minds shaken by catastrophe, a proactive approach seems to race ahead of the impending dangers and lends them a universal significance and political urgency that is relatively independent of any particular incidents.

The reasons for this lie in a two-pronged failure: the failure of our concepts and theories to grapple with the risks that terrorist attacks pose for civilization and the failure of national and international institutions that claim (and ostensibly take action) to be protecting citizens from dangers. This new aspect finally dawned on people in the wake of 9/11: they realized that today we face a *different kind* of risk, the full implications of which cannot be grasped by those living today. World political reactions were correspondingly hieratic and confused, and intellectuals expressed the same general sense of bewilderment. Not only had terrorist attacks cost several thousand human lives and brought home the new vulnerability of the American nation, they had also revealed a general conceptual inadequacy and disorientation. The idea of deterrence, on which the post-1945 military security system was built, is no longer applicable. Nevertheless, or for that very reason, some action or pretence of action must be taken. At every level of world risk society, in national and international politics, in jurisprudence, in science and economics, and in the everyday life of ordinary individuals, the problem now is to understand and tame the contradictions involved in the compulsion to control the uncontrollable.

Global Risk as a Product of Cultural Perceptions

The broad lines of conflict during the Cold War were openly political and owed their explosive potential to issues of national and international security. The geopolitical lines of conflict in world risk society run between different cultures of risk perception. We are, in fact, experiencing an invasion of politics by culture. The clearer it becomes that expert knowledge is unavailable or inadequate for the definition of the undefinable, and the more evident the failure of such knowledge in the face of *unknown unknowns*, the greater becomes the role that cultural perceptions play in deciding which giant risks to civilization are real and which unreal, what should be the priorities, and what political strategies should be pursued to tackle them.

What role, for example, have cultural perceptions played in ensuring that negotiations over how to deal internationally with the risks of climate change have up to now ended in failure?[13] It is well known that the United States and the European Union have proposed differing policy instruments for tackling the challenge of climate change. Yet, curiously, their interests would seem to be congruent.

Scientific findings about the regional effects in North America and Europe suggest that these regions will have to face considerable changes, even if they are less in danger than small island states, for example. Their economic activity and energy-intensive lifestyle mean that both are important players in the need for the international community as a whole to address the problem. Climate protection measures could also enable both regions to reduce their dependence on fuel imports and to occupy a leading position in environmental technology markets, since both have a high potential for innovation in this area. More crucial to the U.S.-EU policy divergences during international climate negotiations has been the way in which the risks of global climate change are perceived.[14]

Thus, although it is true that so-called *hard factors* such as economic-industrial benefits, strategic power benefits, oil supplies, and so on play a role, social-cultural factors have become critical in determining the differing perceptions of risk by different societies, cultures, and states.[15]

Grace Skogstad, in her chapter in this book, comes to a similar conclusion regarding the European-American trade conflict over the EU ban on imports of genetically modified food. Different approaches to regulation also played a role, of course, but the decisive factor appears to be the different perceptions of risk that prevail in the USA and Europe. Moreover, the expanded possibilities for democratic participation in the EU may have intensified the conflict, since the views of Europeans had a greater chance of being articulated and implementated institutionally.

Risk perception, in short, is drawing new boundaries. Groups, countries, cultures, and states that share the same definition of a threat form the *inside* of a *transnational risk community*, which develops its profile and institutional structure, comprised of national and international players and institutions, as a preventive defence against specific causes and sources of danger. Those who, for whatever reason, do not share in the definition of a threat are *outside* of the risk community. Even if they wish to remain 'neutral,' they can easily become part of the threat against which any ensuing fight is waged. In this way, lines of conflict take shape under the aegis of risk perception. Behind those lines, regions enter the terrain of world risk society carrying very different historically determined situations, experiences, and expectations.

Striking examples are the differing degrees of urgency, or indeed reality, that Europeans and Americans ascribe to the dangers of climate change and transnational terrorism. We should not, however, overlook the possibility of a sudden *change* in perception: the so-called *conversion effect*. Before 9/11, the two sides of the Atlantic held conflicting perceptions and evaluations of climate risk, but *not* of terrorist risk. Only through and after 9/11 did the United States abandon its general agnosticism concerning the 'collapse of civilization' scenarios, which mainly originated in Europe. After 9/11, the United States transformed itself – in relation to transnational terrorism – from an exporter of optimism to an exporter of pessimism. Thus, the asymmetry of risk perception, which played a significant role in later tensions and divergences between the United States and Europe, crystallized first on the basis of the radical and sudden change in risk perception by the United States, but not Europe.

This conversionlike change in perception, and the rejection of such perceptual change by Europeans, should be seen in the context of the pre-existing institutional structure that was specific to each region. (Or, to put it in sociological terms, a social-constructivist approach should be combined with a neo-institutionalist approach.) As Daase has shown, the conversion phenomenon in the United States rested not only on an overnight transformation that turned risk sceptics into risk believers, but also on the fact that the conversion broke through the 'reform blockage of the 1990s' that had stymied U.S. foreign and security policy: 'What appears to outsiders as a rapid and dramatic shift in American foreign policy is the result of impeded adaptation to a changed security situation. The decisive factor was that, for all the reform proposals and strategic recommendations, the national security architecture ... had remained fundamentally a product of the Cold War. The 11th of September overcame the bureaucratic and institutional hurdles and made it possible to implement a proactive strategy, thereby smoothing the way for a thoroughgoing risk politics.'[16]

In Europe, however, the September 2001 shock did not open the frequently invoked 'window of opportunity' to deploy ready-to-use plans for military reform.[17] On the contrary: recognition of the terrorist risk cut right across Europe's by now long-standing institutionalized peace mission, both internally and externally. An urgently expressed emphasis on climate change, conversely or perversely, is fully in line with such a mission. Inevitably, the crusading zeal with which the administration of George W. Bush embraced a doctrine of prevention using military means and intervention overseas was perceived to be an attack on the very premises of Europe's risk certainty, which has wagered on peaceful change in the world through institutional reforms that are linked, say, to climate risk on a global basis.

The September 2001 terrorist attack has restored to American military and foreign policy an image of the enemy, that had long been missing and that allows the United States to create a clear focus for the mobilization of support both at home and abroad, crossing the frontiers and camps of political parties and national states. With the construction of militarily oriented *global risk communities, coalitions against terror* can take shape by forcing all national states to decide whether they are for or against. In the process, the geopolitical landscape has been ploughed up. Traditional opponents, such as Russia or China, may become linked in an *alliance against terrorism*, while traditional allies of the United States, including France and Germany, mobilize international resistance to the war in Iraq and – in the eyes of Americans fighting for their very existence – exclude themselves from the alliance, or find themselves excluded.

The cultural perceptions of risk and threat in Europe and in the United States have been drifting ever further apart, and it is *because* they have been drifting further apart that it would now appear that Europeans and Americans live in different worlds. To Europeans, issues like climate change or even the dangers that gigantic financial flows can represent have a much greater role than does the threat posed by terrorism. In American eyes, Europe seems to suffer from environmental hysteria, whereas to many Europeans, Americans seem to be afflicted by terrorism hysteria. Their respective definitions of danger have given rise to differing images of the people *behind* and *responsible* for them, differing strategies for action, and not least, differing *antagonisms*, and therefore the drifting apart of the risk cultures that prevail on the two sides of the Atlantic threatens to result in a cultural break between the United States and Europe. The global character of world risk society is thus expressed in a contradictory dynamic: the concurrent experience of unity and disintegration.

The *common destiny of civilization*, which is a politically significant idea if ever there was one, fragments into questions about who shares what definitions of risk and how to confront the threats. The critical issue here is not concerned with how many terrorist attacks result in how many deaths, or with what disastrous climate (and associated social and political) changes are likely to creep up on us or suddenly undergo a dramatic escalation. What is really decisive is the extent to which the terrorist risk is shaping perceptions of international politics, and whether it is fostering a preventive military or preventive political view of the world. A change in perception that is mainly militarily driven would force Europe into the role of an outsider concerned with luxury issues. New conflicts and new alternatives are taking shape, and the least of the fault lines involve differing constructions, dimensions, and perceptions of potential sources of global risk.

The Diverse Logics of Ecological, Economic, and Terrorist Risks

At least three axes of conflict may be identified in world risk society: *ecological risk conflicts* that set up a global dynamic, struggle arising from *global financial risks* that initially appear to be isolated and national, and conflicts linked to *threats from terrorist networks* that are considered to be supported by particular states. To begin with ecological risks that carry a physical threat, we should distinguish between *wealth-related* destruction (such as the ozone hole or the greenhouse effect, which may essentially be laid at the door of the Western industrial world, even though their impact is obviously global) and *poverty-related* destruction (such as the loss of rainforest which is mostly limited to discrete parts of the world but is so massive as to have major consequences globally).

Global economic risks, those imponderables of money and financial markets have in recent years increasingly occupied public attention in world risk society. They, too, fit into the model of the new uncontrollable risks that are setting the contours of that society. As Pauly's chapter in this book suggests, it is in global economic risks that we see the full force of the contradictory distribution of *goods* and *bads* that result from taking risky decisions. Scarcely open to spatial or institutional containment, global economic risks demonstrate the limits of quantitative calculations of risk and of private insurance options. For, at least in their resulting costs, economic risks are largely deterritorialized, difficult to attribute to specific actors or causes, and less susceptible to national control.

Crises are as old as financial markets themselves. Certainly, at least since the worldwide crisis of 1929, it has been clear to everyone that financial crashes can have catastrophic consequences – especially at the political level. The Bretton Woods institutions, established in the aftermath of the Second World War were intended to provide global political answers to global economic problems. Their functioning was key to the development of the welfare state in Europe. Since the 1970s, however, those institutions have largely been replaced with the necessity and reality of successive ad hoc solutions, so that today we face a paradoxical situation: while markets are both more liberal and more global than ever, the global institutions that might keep their consequences under control have had their powers dramatically curtailed. Against this background, a worldwide financial disaster on the scale of 1929 cannot be ruled out.

In contrast to environmental and technological risks, whose physical effects first become sociologically important in, so to speak, their *externalities*, financial risks directly affect a social structure – the economy, or to be more precise, the guarantee of solvency that is indispensable to the normal functioning of the economy. Thus, the impact of financial risks is felt much more strongly in other social structures than is the impact of global ecological and physical risks. Therefore, it is easier to *individualize* or *nationalize* risk, which produces greater differences in the perceptions of risk. Moreover, global financial risks – not least with how they are perceived internationally (in statistical terms) – are also seen to be *national* risks to individual countries or regions. This in no way implies that the economic risks of interdependence are in any way decreased. Since all the sub-systems of modern society rely on the proper functioning of other sub-systems, a withdrawal from interdependence would prove to be catastrophic. No other functional system has such a prominent role in the modern world, as the economy, and therefore, the world economy is without a doubt a central dimension of world risk society.

We must further distinguish between ecological and financial dangers, on the one hand, and the threat from global terrorist networks, on the other. Ecological and economic conflicts can be conceptualized within a model of the *side-effects* of radical modernization: both result from the accumulation and distribution of *bads* that go together with the production of *goods*. In contrast, terrorist activities must be conceptualized within a model of *intentional* catastrophes. Effects which, in the model of ecological and economic risks, are unintentionally triggered as side-effects here become *deliberately planned effects*: the principle of deliberately exploiting the vulnerability of modern civil society replaces the principle of chance and accident. To produce a general sense of danger and even panic, terrorists only have to target what are called *residual risks* – and thus the civil consciousness of a highly complex and interdependent world.

In this light, it becomes necessary to take a fresh look at the link between trust and risk. As a general rule, the less trust exists, the greater the (perception of) risk. The terrorist threat must be understood precisely as an accelerated destruction of trust. If taken seriously, as a matter of life and death, the threat of terrorism replaces active trust with active distrust; and calls into question the trust that had hitherto been placed in neighbours and fellow citizens, strangers, and governments. The dissolution of trust increases the number of risks, and this turns the terrorist threat into a multiplication of risks because it releases every imaginable risk fantasy.

Terrorist networks are, so to speak, non-governmental organizations of violence. Whereas military attention used to be turned to military organizations in other countries, and to ways of resisting attack from them, now the whole world of national states is challenged by transnational threats coming from sub-state individuals and networks. As already discussed with regard to the cultural realm, we are now experiencing in the military realm the *death of distance* – and this at a high stage of civilization, where anything can become a lethal weapon in the hands of a determined fanatic. The peaceful symbols of civil societies can be turned into instruments of hell. This is not new, in principle. Today, however, it is omnipresent as a key experience.[18] The terrorist attacks of recent years have created a general awareness of the vulnerability of civilization itself. To varying degrees, we are insured against accidents of many kinds, yet we are completely defenceless in face of disasters that are planned by anonymous transnational terrorist networks. Their international manipulation of the susceptibility of civilization to chance and accident is aimed at plunging all humanity into the abyss of a self-crippling culture of fear. Preventive fantasies become unbound by actual probabilities, and thus they begin to erode the very foundations of freedom and democracy.

For all their differences, ecological, economic, and terrorist risks under conditions of interdependence have in common two key features. First, they all promote or compel a *politics of proactive counteraction*, which disrupts the basis of the existing structures and alliance systems of international politics, makes redefinition and reform unavoidable, and brings new political philosophies to the fore. The premises of what is *national* and what is *international*, of how they should be related to and demarcated from each other, must now be openly renegotiated in the framework of risk prevention and within the meta-power game of global and national security policies.

Second, neither ecological, economic, nor terrorist risks can simply be passed off as *external* threats. Rather, they must be understood to be the consequences of actions and uncertainties that has civilization manufactured. Therefore, the risks to civilization carry the potential to sharpen a global normative awareness and create a public and, per-haps, even a cosmopolitan vision of the world. In world risk society, as old certainties fall away, a new transnational public space might emerge. As various chapters in this book contend, such a space is now emerging in Europe through the clash of views about the causes and implications of global dangers. As risk perceptions and the associated debates evolve, it is not impossible to imagine that this space is going to extend beyond Europe.

European and Transnational Responses to New Global Risks

In asserting that civil society is less aroused by any decisions them-selves than by the dangers it perceives to be consequences of particular decisions, the theory of world risk society puts in question and replaces one of the fundamental premises of traditional political the-ory. Decisions as such remain a matter (or source) of indifference. Only the perception of – and communications about – problematic conse-quences is what makes people anxious and worked up, shaking them out of their apathy and egoism to produce the communal and social dimension of a transnational and postnational public space for action.[19] In other words, perceptions of danger, most importantly as constructed by the media, have their own side-effects; in particular, *they produce a public.*

Global risks, as underlined and amplified by the media, release an element of reflection and communication. Organizations and individu-als must identify the consequences of other people's actions that affect them; they must ascribe these to others and hence struggle for agree-ment about the nature of the problem and what is to be done to tackle it. There is also a political element to this process. For, in order to act politically, and hence to minimize the risks that endanger everyone, those who are affected have to organize politically across borders, in one way or another or they must bring about the necessary changes to established political institutions and players. Whether this promises to be successful matters not. No great new 'we' results, but the process does have a *transnational resonance* through which external perspectives become internal and the excluded are included. Global interdependence turns uninvited and even absent others into fellow inhabitants and neighbours. Acknowledged risks force people to build communicative bridges, where none or almost none existed before, between monological arenas and sectoral publics, across systemic and linguistic boundaries, and beyond conflicts of opinion, interest, class, nation, and religious denomination.

The forced, involuntary character of this *side-effects public* can mitigate or overcome the classical problems of deliberately created publics, namely, the lack of target groups, the difficulty of mobilizing people, and their unwillingness to cooperate. Global risk is infectious. It seeks out potential targets, opens up sections of the public, and compels attention as well as actual or symbolic cooperation. Global risk finds a way of getting through to publics and communication networks that are otherwise isolated within their specific policy fields.

We are talking here about the mobilization of affected groups not from above or below but through the power of unintended side-effects – and thus, in a sense, of an *involuntary* public that breaks through the system of compartmentalized responsibilities, criteria of relevance, and channels of communication that hitherto had been taken as axiomatic. Risk publics disaggregate and re-aggregate democracy. Risk public disprove the idea that democracy is possible only within the social container of the national state. Risk publics create a public space and reference framework in which the issues that are affecting people can be defined across frontiers, so that pressure for action can be brought to bear in appropriate ways. Precisely this is what has happened recently in Europe.

The political locus of world risk society is not the street, it is *television*, with the street being redefined as a television stage. Its political subjects are the transnational campaigning movements. In the current and impending scenarios of horror, they know how to stage in the media the cultural symbols that will raise latent threat to the level of consciousness. This is true in the case of *European* risk awareness, but less so regarding its counterpart, United States, where the state plays the role of staging the terrorist risk in the mass media.

In both Europe and America, global dangers have not intensified a overall sense of emptiness or meaninglessness. Rather, they have created a horizon of meaning that is dominated by avoidance, protection, and assistance and a moral climate that grows more intense as the scale of the perceived danger rises – but also a climate that can become so heated that it starts to breed pogroms. In such a hothouse of fear, the classical dramatic roles of hero and well-poisoner acquire new political meaning, so that xenophobic and anti-Semitic stereotypes and movements may experience a lethal revival. Perceptions of the world within the coordinates of a self-endangering civilization make a universal drama out of morality, religion, fundamentalism, hopelessness, tragedy, and tragicomedy that is interwoven with their opposites: salvation, help, and liberation. The established players – the state and the economy – are free to assume the role of villain and maker of poisons, but they can also slip into the role of hero or friend in need. This is the background against which global social movements are able to take the limelight through ruses of impotence. By astutely using the mass media, these movements practise a kind of *judo politics*, with the aim of turning the superior strength of sinners, be they corporations or governments, against themselves.

In such a context, traditional state structures can be weakened. In the European Union today, for example, the threat comes not from strong opposing states, but from weak states, from the breakdown of states, and even from a *failure* of the state. The EU no longer faces a rival military power with hostile intentions, persons, and institutions, whose names are known, who wear uniforms, hold identifiable positions, and can therefore be systematically spied on with the help of a network of secret services. Instead, the EU is confronted with the dangers of states whose own structures are no longer functioning.

The risk of state collapse is no longer confined to sub-Saharan Africa and other distant regions. This risk now affects virtually the entire European periphery, from the south to the southeast and even to the Middle East. Mass emigration, fundamentalist extremism, drug addiction, and organized crime on that periphery do not simply challenge Europe's humanitarian ideals: they now pose tangible security problems for Europe itself, a situation that European officials now regularly acknowledge.[20] When asked why German soldiers are on active service in Afghanistan, the German Ministry of Defence has repeatedly replied that it is because the security of Germany must now be defended on the Hindu Kush. This only makes sense if one thinks of

Europe in cosmopolitan terms. Then the question really does arise of Europe's possible role in controlling zones of insecurity that critically affect its own security interests. If such strategies in risk politics are to succeed, it is imperative that the zones of insecurity are perceived by the EU to be coextensive with the zones of insecurity that Washington has in mind. After initial deep differences over Bosnia, in the early 1990s, the United States and Europe found a common definition of risk so that they could act to stem the bloody conflicts in the Balkans in 1995 and 1999. Under U.S. leadership, NATO expanded to include the countries of Central Europe, with the goal of establishing peace and security in the zones of insecurity that were generated by the collapse of the Cold War order. Moreover, although Russia has not formally become a member-state, it has been *externally integrated* into a new quasi-member partnership with the new NATO. Europe has thus been made more democratic, peaceful, and secure (including on its external frontiers) than ever before in history.

For the first time since the Second World War – indeed, since the beginning of the twentieth century – neither Europeans nor Americans have to fear an outbreak of military conflict in Central Europe. This is not least the result of the success of transatlantic risk politics since the end of the Cold War. In 1995, the EU established a Euro-Mediterranean partnership that includes the twelve countries on the southern and eastern rim of the Mediterranean Sea.[21] In cooperation with NATO, the Conference on Security and Cooperation in Europe (CSCE) as well as other organizations, the European strategy to control zones of insecurity in North Africa has been directed at economic and political liberalization, the gradual construction of a free trade area, and extensive support for private enterprise. It is hoped that all this will improve conditions in the countries of North Africa, not only economically but also with regard to civil society and human rights.

But such a policy can become entangled in what we might call the *circle of globalization*. Good intentions – economic liberalization and the creation of a basis for democracy in civil society – can have the paradoxical effect of accelerating the breakdown of unstable states and thus of actually redoubling the security risks for Europe. As shown by various civil wars and humanitarian emergencies, unintended consequences can accompany interventions in Europe's peripheral areas and necessitate even deeper engagement. Security policy thus becomes trapped in a *negative risk paradox*.

European self-absorption can obscure such a paradox. Indeed, perhaps Europe has always made it difficult to see the extent to which the process of continental integration depends on a particular constellation of external factors. The threat from the Soviet Union and the military protection provided by the United States and allies like Canada had encouraged the countries of Western Europe to band together. That military shield created space for the convalescence of a Europe wounded by the two world wars and eventually for the building of a militarily weak community through economic harmonization, reconciliation, and democracy. The end of the Cold War dissolved these historical coordinates. Europeans have yet to come fully to grips with this reality. The collapse of the Soviet Union and the threat of smaller wars on all sides has sharpened tensions between the United States and Europe, as well as between various current and potential member-states of the European Union, whose respective security interests were no longer automatically perceived to be in harmony. Thus, it would be both ahistorical and unrealistic simply to project into the future the success story of European integration, for the writing on the wall is obviously in a different language. At present there is no single European view on the vital issues of war and peace, which means that *the experiment in European integration could end in failure*.

What is the very meaning of *integration* in the face of the unseeable enemies of world risk society? Or, to put it more strongly, what is the meaning of *Europe* amid the new risks to the world situation, where the old external stabilizers of integration have fallen away, where spatial and therefore substantive geostrategic frontiers are being expanded, and where there is the emergence of new kinds of global risk for which no one has answers? Today, Europe stands at a crossroads where debate on basic issues of political order in world risk society has become essential – issues on that go far beyond those to be addressed in a conceivable European constitution. Some suggestions for future directions could come out of what I call *cosmopolitan realism*.[22]

Cosmopolitan Realism and Transnational Politics

The conflicts in Afghanistan and Iraq are the first against global risk. For Americans, a new threat to humanity has fundamentally altered the security situation after 9/11. But Europeans consider the Americans to be overreacting, or even hysterical. Americans have now perceived the horror of terrorism staring them in the face, whereas for Europeans the horror has been of war. What happened in Iraq has demonstrated, for Europeans anyway, the paradoxical character of a proactive military politics of risk.

In the United States, the unilateral assertion of military power seemed essential. Across the Atlantic, this occasioned the writing of myriad revolutionary pamphlets about the necessity of mounting a European counterforce. Descriptively, as well as politically, both models rapidly became obsolete. Without underestimating the unparalleled military superiority of the United States, we can say that the dream or nightmare of ruling the world through military force has been refuted in Iraq. Joseph Nye is correct in stating that 'the United States has built an army that is good for smashing down doors, removing dictators and then going back home; it is not so good at the difficult imperial work of building a democratic order.'[23]

The experience in Iraq has caused Americans to doubt the proposition, held by many in the aftermath of 9/11, that war would create justice. Even Robert Kagan, who only a short while ago made much of the distinction between Europe and the United States in this regard, has come round to the view that national interests cannot be defined narrowly. The vague, yet significant question of *legitimacy in world politics* is essential, both for the projection of American power and for the response to global challenges.[24]

The idea that national interests must ultimately be subordinated to the cosmopolitan goals of democracy and freedom truly is a *realist* one. Many long years ago, Benjamin Franklin wrote: 'it is a common observation here that our cause is the cause of all mankind, and that we are fighting for their liberty in defending our own.'[25] This early and illuminating statement of cosmopolitan realism surely could remain relevant for the United States today. As suggested by Franklin, enduring power stems not only from the gun, but primarily from the legitimacy of power exercised in a principled interplay with all of humanity. Only when power is converted into international cooperation can it escape the dangers that increase when independent military initiative confronts global risks. From Iraq to North Korea, impulses towards radicalism have resulted in ever greater requirements for multilateral cooperation.

Similarly, in Europe, the initial impulses towards creating a counterpower to the United States soon collapsed, for they rested on four flawed premises: (1) not global risks but the unbridled lust for power motivated the United States after 9/11; (2) all threats to Europe that would require U.S. military protection have receded; (3) the sense of a

European 'we' could best be sharpened and secured in opposition to the United States; and (4) an integrationist vanguard akin to the original members of the European Community could and should move to regain Europe's capacity for action both internally and externally.[26] All of these quickly proved to be fantasies, first, because they ignored the dominance of global risks, and second, because they failed to see that such risks can be converted into an impetus for cooperation in a global political order that is properly legitimated.

Any attempt to build an expanded European Union on an anti-American basis threatens to divide Europe internally and to split the Atlantic alliance, on which Europe still depends externally. The power of the United States is not necessarily the root cause of the world's problems. American power can also constitute, or be turned into, the indispensable means for overcoming those problems. The megapower does not have to be countered. Rather, perhaps it can be channelled through setting common strategic objectives. Moreover, it is obvious that no American president, from whichever political party, is going to accept counterpower as the basis for cooperation with the United States.

The perspective commonly held by Americans also deserves to be criticized. Any power that fights the global risk of terrorism simply in the name of its own *national* security endangers the legitimacy and effectiveness of such action, even if it should have the military means to try to impose its will. To tackle global threats, the United States is in need of the legitimacy that Europe can provide. It must also be said that only when the European Union (and the United Nations) cooperate with the United States will they – and thus the whole world – stand a serious chance of reducing global risks.

Prospects for World Risk Society

In the past sixty years, a special instance of cosmopolitan realism – *the West* – took shape in the U.S.-led transatlantic relationship. This was a break with the traditional either-or logic of realism or neo-realism. All participating national states and governments were able thereby to experience for themselves that cooperation among states carries the political benefit of mutual sovereignty and the settlement of conflicts between nations. The renunciation of autonomy and the acquisition of sovereignty only appear to be a paradoxical combination. Cosmopolitan realism rests on the asymmetry of power and the egoisms of sovereignty balancing each other out through a kind of transnational social contract from which everyone involved stands to gain. This establishes a two-pronged self-restriction, that corresponds not to a fanciful idealism but to the realistic maximization of national interests.

The United States must forego the wielding of its hegemonic power for the sake of its own – properly understood – national interests. At the height of America's power after the Second World War, among its so-called greatest generation were cosmopolitan entrepreneurs in numbers never seen before. They helped European cosmopolitanism to its feet through a system of transnational alliances, organizations, and legislation. The United States is strong *because* it drew its power from cosmopolitan realism, that is, because it increased its strength by tying itself to transnational political coalitions, to an international legal framework, and to procedural consensus. National interests were thereby served on both sides of the Atlantic.

That postwar power asymmetries have not been overcome but were only carefully 'looked after' becomes apparent when we consider the exit option, which was and is available *only* to the hegemon. Associated costs virtually rule this option out for other members of the alliance, and herein lies a crucial difference between the transatlantic community and the European Union. In this sense, there is no real hegemon in the European Union. The exit option is equally an existential threat for *all* member-states and their governments. By contrast, America as hegemon has always the option of breaking loose and ignoring international treaties and institutions. As demonstrated by the administration of George W. Bush, the United States could even celebrate this as the exercise of inviolable national sovereignty or even as *liberation*. Historical experience teaches us that a common strategic goal makes power asymmetries bearable and even functional for all parties. This is precisely what the Bush administration has forgotten. In the end, the United States has scorned the basic idea behind the Atlantic alliance: the United States uses its power legitimately only when it acts in the name of others and for generalized objectives.

Nevertheless, the ecological, economic, and terrorist dangers to world risk society could, once again, give rise to new common strategies. In the post-9/11 world, the Middle East, in particular, has taken on a new and more dangerous significance. Indeed, its turmoil represents an acute problem even for Europe's *internal* security. One perceptive observer has stated:

To meet this challenge appropriately, the West needs something more than, and different from, a plan for military intervention. It needs an approach that faces up to the real roots of the problem and changes the dynamic that has produced monstrous regimes. Otherwise, the names of the terrorist groups and their protecting states may change, but the long-term threat will remain and grow more intense. The West must therefore develop a strategy that aims at more than managing the status quo of breakdown. It must actively seek to help the region to transform itself into a context of societies able to live in peace with one another, which no longer produce ideologies and terrorists geared to mass indiscriminate killing and increasingly in possession of the technological means to carry it out.[27]

Making a distinction between *political* and *military* risk politics is central to the construction of a common strategic goal across the Atlantic. The risk paradox applies to both. As noted above, the war in Iraq spawned more, not less terrorism. In its aftermath, we have also seen how political intervention increased the danger of contrary effects. The distinction between genuine and non-genuine cosmopolitanism is key to achieving any new understanding between the United States and Europe. This cosmopolitanism must include a serious, and not merely rhetorical, attempt to defuse and as far as possible pacify the barbaric conflict between Israelis and Palestinians, for example. Military means may need to be deployed to this strategic end, but if the point is to help countries to help themselves, then the decisive means must be political and economic. The West's real Achilles heel is not military in nature. Instead, it is political paralysis and inadequacy in imagining the containment of global risks, both of which must be overcome if a Muslim *and* democratic alternative is to be encouraged in the Arab world. Furthermore, it is precisely here that a cosmopolitan Europe can make a central contribution, for example, by pushing forward with Turkey's membership in the EU. This is no longer a question of identity, but a necessary contribution to the internal security of Europe.

The political goal to build bridges in the Middle East and help the Islamic world to modernize represents a European supplement, alternative or necessary corrective to the policy of the United States to try to change the world by military means. America's hegemonic power, even in the interests, of the United States, should no longer withhold recognition and support for such an outwardly directed European cosmopolitanism. To this end, expansion of the European Union would become an expansion of the common power to reduce global risks, in a different yet comparable form from that which the founding generation used to create the Western alliance.

With such a tangible objective in mind, cosmopolitan realism in contemporary transnational politics may be summed up under the following five points.

First, the theory of world risk society highlights the new historical realization that no nation can deal with its problems alone. This is no longer an idealist principle of utopian internationalism, or ivory-tower social theory, but a matter of practical politics.

Second, world problems create transnational commonalities. Survival is possible only through the cosmopolitan conception and practice of national politics. National states, whether weak or strong, no longer are the primary elements for the solution of even basic national problems. Interdependence is the precondition of the continued existence of humanity. Cooperation is no longer a means but the end. The more that globality is consciously embraced, and the more that cultures, countries, governments, regions, and religions are affected by it, the more ineffective it is going to be for states to act unilaterally. Effectiveness and legitimacy flow from the behaviour of transnational cooperation states.

Third, international organizations are not only the continuation of national politics by different means. They group together, transform, and *maximize* national interests. They give rise among states to positive-sum games that replace the negative-sum games of national autonomy. International organizations *change* and *convert* national interests into transnational interests and open up new transnational spaces of power and formative development.

Fourth, this is why two institutions that feel an affinity with one another – the European Union and the United Nations – are so important for the future of global risk politics. The refusal of the U.N. Security Council and some European countries (and Canada, for that matter) to act as rubber-stamps for U.S. military unilateralism has not, as some commentators had suspected it would, led to a situation of declining relevance for the EU and the United Nations. On the contrary, both institutions have gained in global credibility and enhanced their capacity to ensure effective and legitimate future interventions to reduce global risks.

Fifth, unilateralism has proven itself to be uneconomical. Policies informed by cosmopolitan realism, on the other hand, are *economical*.

They save on costs and redistribute their burden. Unilateral military action is far more expensive than are strategies of political prevention, and its cost rises exponentially as it loses legitimacy. Shared responsibility, indeed, shared sovereignty, means shared burdens. Moreover, transnational cooperation, which is not least of the components of cosmopolitan realism, is also good business.

NOTES

1   This chapter was translated from the original German by Patrick Camiller. Its themes are developed more fully in Beck and Grande (2004).
2   Beck, Bonß, and Lau (2001); Beck and Lau (2005); Beck (2005).
3   On the theory of world risk society, see Beck (1988, 1992, 1997a-c, 1999, 2004), Giddens (1994), Münch (1996), Adam and van Loon (2000), Bernstein (1996), Baker (2003), Bougen (2003), Ericson and Doyle (2003); Ewald (1993); and on its implications for international politics, Zürn (1998) and Daase, Feske, and Peters (2003).
4   See the discussion of 'globality' in Robertson (1992, 1998) and Albrow (1996), where a close link is made between global interdependence and global awareness of interdependence. In international relations theory too, the concept of global interdependence (originally developed in opposition to realism) is part of the theoretical canon, although for a long time it was one-sidedly geared to economic interdependence. See Cooper (1968), Keohane and Nye (1977), Spindler (2003); and, for empirical analysis, Held et al. (1999).
5   Daase (2002: 15f).
6   Beck (1999), Wehling (2002).
7   Daase, Fenske, and Peters (2003: 267).
8   Beck and Lau (2005).
9   Douglas and Wildavsky (1982), Hajer and Wagenaar (2003), Rayner (1992).
10   Luhmann (1991).
11   Beck (1988), Münch (1996).
12   Münch (1996), Daase (2002).
13   Tänzler (2002).
14   Ibid., 89.
15   See Daase, Feske, and Peters (2003: 269).
16   Daase (2002:115).
17   Kingdon (1995).
18   In the future, risk analysis will also have to address the malicious triggering

of disasters, a logic that instrumentalizes the discarded 'residual risk' of disaster in order to maximize its effect. This poses the dilemma that, while risk analysis must anticipate events and think the unthinkable, this good intention may actually open a Pandora's box and suggest possible new forms of terrorist attack. Risk analysis thus itself becomes risky, and this is based on the fact that imagining hitherto unimagined dangers can become an unintended form of midwifery.

19 Dewey (1996), Beck (2002).
20 Wolf (2002: 243).
21 Ibid.
22 Beck (2002, 2004).
23 Nye (2002: 160).
24 Kagan (2003 and 2004:8); Beck (2002).
25 Letter to Samuel Cooper, 1 May 1777.
26 On this theme, in the summer of 2003, Jacques Derrida and Jürgen Habermas gave prominence to a public debate over the concept of a *European core*.
27 Asmus (2003: 25).

3 Restructuring World Society: The Contribution of Modern Systems Theory

MATHIAS ALBERT

Globalizing processes are challenging central concepts in the fields of international relations, political theory, and sociology. They have complicated such basic concepts as state, territoriality, and political authority, thus rendering problematic the analytical legitimacy of what is conventionally called the Westphalian or 'international' paradigm. International relations scholars, political theorists, and sociologists alike thus find themselves at a juncture where many of their fundamental ideas must be questioned, re-evaluated, and perhaps even jettisoned.

A most intriguing and stimulating development in contemporary social and political analysis, as noted in Chapter 1, is that this questioning of what has long been known as the Westphalian system opens up a number of conceptual spaces and enables innovative conceptual frameworks that are interdisciplinary in nature and that address the prevailing dynamics of a globalizing era. Most prominently, older terms such as *international society*[1] are being re-examined, with newer terms like *global civil society*,[2] *world risk society*,[3] and *world society*[4] being employed to describe the emerging political context.[5]

These new concepts, for the most part, do not entail any far-reaching claims about the sudden emergence of new structural features for today's global social reality. Rather, they are best understood as fresh and comprehensive attempts to reconceptualize social and political theory against a new reality that problematizes both the assumption that political and social orders are circumscribed by the boundaries of national-territorial states and the interpretation of globalization as merely the transcendence of borders – an understanding that implicitly underscores rather than questions the analytical centrality of the state.

By challenging entrenched assumptions that take the national-territorial state, which is the hallmark of the Westphalian paradigm, as the
starting point of social inquiry, these new conceptualizations were
developed in efforts to overcome what Ulrich Beck in his earlier works,
calls 'methodological nationalism.'[6] (See Theorem 12 in Chapter 2 in
this book.)

The conceptual frameworks mentioned above imply divergent consequences for how the loci and models of political authority are to be
understood. In particular, they draw attention to the reconfiguration,
and indeed reconstitution, of political authority in a global context –
beyond the state – and the idea of a national *society* that accompanies
this political authority. Rather than offering a comprehensive overview
of the various new approaches, this chapter focuses on a conceptualization of world society that is inspired by modern systems theory. My
intention is to demonstrate that a radical shift in theoretical perspectives is necessary because taking the world beyond the nation-state to
be some kind of *international* system cannot adequately describe how
political authority in the twenty-first is constituted and exercised.

My argument is not that 'international' as a notion or that
approaches traditionally characteristic of the field of International
Relations (IR) should simply be abandoned outright.[7] My argument is
the following: conceptually, *international* can only partially account for
contemporary social reality, which increasingly is *global* in scale. Without redefining International Relations as a narrow sub-specialization of
some kind of 'global sociology,' the seemingly paradoxical claim will
be advanced, namely, that the discipline of International Relations is
particularly well suited to addressing the characteristics of political
authority in today's world society.[8] No wholesale deconstruction of
international in the context of a global sociological approach is
attempted here. My only aim is to relocate international within an analytical framework of a world society. My intent is to provide *one among
many possible tours d'horizon*, by focusing on how questions about the
constitution and reconstitution of political authority can be asked if
they are first disembedded from analytical frameworks that rely on
methodological nationalism which is subsequently re-embedded
within the structures of a world society theory.

This *tour d'horizon* will unfold in three steps. The *first step* provides a
brief outline some of the problems associated with *international*, the
principal concept of Westphalian politics. The main problem, I contend,
is that 'international' interpretations of politics beyond the state repro-

duce a world-view that analytically and ontologically relegates other forms of social relations to a secondary rank. That world-view is perpetuated by an understanding of the international *system* that relies on a highly unspecified (if not merely superficial) use of the concept 'system.' The difficulties that arise with both of these ideas are tied up with the constitution of political authority. Recent challenges to the meaning and deployment of these notions demonstrate that discussions about the constitution of political authority no longer can be phrased as questions about the loci of political authority – neither with respect to its legitimacy, nor its range. Such discussions must now emphasize the mode and function of political authority in a global context, as is particularly emphasized in the concluding chapter to this volume.

The *second step* proposes modern systems theory as *one* promising analytical framework for rethinking the constitution of political authority in a global context. The objective is not to advocate a wholesale adoption of this complex body of theory but to demonstrate that its vocabulary provides a theoretically rich understanding of both the concept of a social system and the conceptualization of political authority within the parameters of world society theory. Thus, the first step of the argument draws attention to some shortcomings in thinking about the constitution of political authority in international terms, while the second explores one possibility for re-embedding discussions of political authority in a theory framed in terms of an *internally differentiated* society rather than in terms of a sharp distinction between domestic and international political spaces, as assumed in Westphalian models of political authority.

The third step proposes that while such a systems-theoretical perspective can assist in reformulating questions about the constitution of political authority – and can therefore contribute to a rich understanding of the constitution of political authority in a decidedly *global* context – it can also benefit from the insights of more traditional forms of IR theorizing on reconfigurations of political authority beyond the nation-state.

Decentring the 'International'

It is commonly accepted that the word 'international' is unable to capture the totality of social relations that traverse the boundaries of nation-states. While certainly able to describe the political interactions among sovereign nation-states (the traditional realms of diplomacy and foreign policy), the increasing relevance of non-state actors (engaged in social interactions spanning state boundaries), the growing importance of regional and global structures, and the increased efficacy of international norms have resulted in terms such as 'transnationalism' and 'globalism.' These new terms are responses to the inadequacy of the 'international' to depict observed empirical phenomena, which makes the 'international' an unsatisfactory analytical (or indeed epistemological) category to describe *global* society. Thus understood, the 'international' might be seen as a description of social structures that have lost much of their relevance in face of their increasing denationalization through transnationalization or globalization. Alternatively, it might be seen as an analytical category or mode of thought that has been inadequate since its very inception (if seen from the vantage point of world systems theory, for example).

Yet despite the inadequacies of the 'international,' it is an idea that cannot be discarded easily as it forms an important part of contemporary *social discourse*. It shapes actors' perceptions, leaves its imprint on everyday as well as political and academic language, and provides a concept that might be transcended in numerous forms. Furthermore, the 'international' manages to command authority by forcing concepts such as the 'transnational' and the 'global' to at least partially *define themselves by the way in which they are not* (or at least not entirely) 'international.'

This persistence of the 'international' as a concept that shapes perceptions and academic vocabulary is, however, not only the result of its powerful epistemological connotations (a theme given extensive treatment in 'critical' IR scholarship over the last decade or so). It also reflects the fact that a significant amount of political, economic, and legal interaction takes places between sovereign states. Nevertheless, leaving arguments about the social construction of statehood aside, it seems that extant patterns of social and political interaction cannot be described strictly as interactions between states, or 'inter-national' relations. The evolution of new norms and legal forms, the structures and processes of the world economy and the interactions between so-called civil society actors point to a transcendence (or a violation) of the international system as understood in Westphalian terms. Even more, this transcendence seems to permeate into issues of security, which are usually seen as the exclusive domain of inter-state politics. Be it through the emergence of mature 'security communities'[9] or the blurring of the internal-external security distinction,[10] security in a globalizing world throws the Westphalian international paradigm into sharp relief.

Still, these observations do not necessarily lead to a wholesale rejection of the analytical value of the idea 'international relations.' Rather, an analytical rescue of the 'international' seems possible by adopting one of two strategies. On the one hand, it could be argued that the realm of international relations refers to one *specific* form of social relations – relations between states – that can legitimately be isolated from other forms of political interaction (this argument is compatible with a realist world-view). On the other hand, the 'international' world-view could be relaxed, without challenging some of its central assumptions. This strategy is common among approaches employing theories of governance beyond the state,[11] the legalization of world politics,[12] or, as in the present volume, the reconfiguration of statehood and political authority through forms of *perforated* or indeed *complex sovereignty.* Those - such as, arguably, most contributions to this volume - who fall into this camp seek to preserve a central role for inter-state relations while also acknowledging the many transgressions of the Westphalian ideal-type.

Arguably, it is only the first of these two reactions that allows an easy defence of the 'international' as a separate field of inquiry. The second reaction necessarily mandates a questioning of the analytical value of the 'international.' By situating the units constitutive of international relations among other social forms and inquiring into changes in their form, we force ourselves to ask whether 'international relations' as a specific form of social relations actually exists: Is it something so unique that it cannot be described by another heading? More radically, this second reaction begs the question of whether the 'international' is just semantic custom or – in the extreme case – merely disciplinary tradition.

The persistence of the figure of the international within the discipline of IR, as well as other disciplines and in everyday language, cannot be fully attributed to the assumption that international relations is an ontologically distinct form of social relations. Neither can this persistence be fully explained by reference to the dynamics of social semantics. It can, however, be explained by the fact that the figure as well as the practice of the 'international' (and the expression of the 'international system' in scientifically rationalized language) provides a powerful structural and semantic resolution to the central paradox of political authority at this level.

The figure of the 'international' represents sovereignty as inextricably linked to a given territory. Yet 'international relations' must not be understood as the area of politics among states, assuming that within states political authority rests on their sovereignty. Rather, seen from the vantage point of political theory, the figure of international relations is more: it does offer a powerful solution for a central problem of the political, namely the problem to provide a place in which political authority *ultimately* rests, yet *at the same time* it hides the fact that this 'ultimate' place is in reality highly contingent. It is in this sense that the figure of international relations allows to combine the political system's *inside program* of producing the legitimacy of political authority with the political system's *outside program* which insinuates that this political authority in need of permanent production and reproduction is fixed against its environment (of other loci of political authority).[13]

Thus understood, the territorial boundaries of the sovereign state – which function as structural containers of social processes and as epistemological containers for conceptualizing politics – attempt to resolve the paradox that results from the need to provide (or simulate) a firm grounding for political authority. They do so by constructing an image of the 'political' that is closely tied to the state, which consequently establishes a strong claim to the spatial dimensions of the institutions and exercise of political authority.

Alternative conceptions of such political authority are imaginable. One possibility is suggested in this volume: *complex sovereignty*. Here, the attempt is to characterize newly emerging structures of politics and governance 'beyond' the nation-state as differentiations, complications, and bifurcations of the programs allowing for the temporal resolution of the paradox of political authority. My claim here is that this resolution is not only upheld, but that with the figure of sovereignty it is also relaxed. On the one hand, that figure itself is refined by pointing out that sovereignty is a historically contingent form of political authority, by emphasizing its relative character, and by pointing to its double-edged characteristic as a form with both an internal and an external dimension. On the other hand, the primarily spatial representation of the figure of sovereignty is relaxed, particularly when newly emerging forms of political authority are read to entail not only a spatial but also a functional reconfiguration. Such emerging forms are also read as the increasing importance of functional over spatial understandings of political authority.[14] This functional reading of sovereignty allows for highly sophisticated interpretations of reconfigurations of political authority. It allows us to conceptualize a number of important developments in the figuration of political authority – from the emergence of global governance structures to emergent forms of micropolitics – *without* conceptually abandoning the Westphalian paradigm. Accordingly, despite the regularity of observed violations of the spatial dimensions of sovereignty (reflected in the territorial geography of the state), sovereignty still provides the analytical anchor for envisioning forms of political authority in and beyond the state.

It is, of course, possible to read these remarks as attempts to engage with critical theoretical approaches to the notion of political authority, or, better put, the 'political.' 'Critical theory' here is understood in a broad sense, and would include a number of deconstructive exercises that lay bare the *différence* – or alternatively, the moment of groundless 'violence'[15] – at the core of the concept of sovereignty and point out the discursive simulations necessary to uphold sovereignty as a stable concept.[16]

It is not my purpose to argue for or against the merits of the various lines of research concerned with the reconfiguration of political authority through the figure of complex sovereignty in the broad sense outlined above, nor is it to judge the various contributions of critical theory in this respect. As mentioned already, these are all primarily seen as proposals for reacting to substantial conceptual uncertainties that result from the tension between the destabilization of the Westphalian mode of thought, and the idea of the 'international' that is constituted by it, on the one hand, and the inability to entirely disengage from the semantic understandings it commands, on the other.

It is against this background that the increasing popularity of ideas of 'society beyond the nation-state' requires particular attention. Notions of a global civil society or a world society can be read as proposals to engage conceptually with the delegitimization of the Westphalian mode of thought by radically transforming the inside/outside distinction that constitutes the observed (international) realm through an internal differentiating principle within a more encompassing social realm. Such ideas, for example, an internal differentiating principle, raise the question of political authority in a new way: seeing the contemporary global social realm as a manifestation of some sort of society rather than as an 'international' realm of competing sovereign units, devoid of societal elements, moves us away from the question of the constitution of political authority. This requires us to rephrase questions of political authority in terms of its role and function in society.

A change of analytical perspective that moves us from questions of the constitution of political authority to those of its role and function remains highly unspectacular, however, if it leads to a reproduction of Westphalian-style methodological nationalism on a societal scale. Examples would be, for instance, if notions of a global or a world society were to remain wedded to the classic idea of society as a normatively integrated whole or, alternatively, signify only a change of disciplinary perspective from political theory or international relations to sociological theory. The claim put forward here is that while a re-reading of the global social realm as a form of a world society through the lens of sociological theory can serve as a new entry point into considerations of the role and function of political authority in a non-Westphalian manner, a second step to re-engage with the traditional questions of how political authority is constituted in and through an *international* system of complex sovereignty is required if *complex sovereignty* is to serve as a useful conceptual and heuristic tool. The notion of world society developed within modern systems theory demonstrates how traditional questions about political authority and sovereignty can be posed in a new manner.[17]

Debordering the 'Political'

The modern systems theory of society, whose major proponent is Niklas Luhmann, is a theory that does not see societies in the plural (except as a semantic construction) but views society as a *world society*.[18] In contrast to other concepts of world society, or for that matter, 'global (civil) society,' it does not conceive of this world society as an emerging social form. Rather, as this theory sees society as being constituted by communication, world society is understood as having come into existence with the full discovery of the globe (i.e., with the possibility, at least in principle, for all communication to connect to all other communication).[19]

This notion of world society, which was taken up by Luhmann early in his work but never occupied a central place in his writings, is also non-classical in that it refers to all communication and not to the idea of society as a normatively integrated whole moulded together by common norms and values. As society is understood to be constituted by communication alone, it is therefore not possible to see society as being integrated by some pre-existing form of *Gemeinschaft* or societal community.[20] Among other things, the idea that society does not form a normatively integrated whole is one of the markers that sets modern systems theory apart from its Parsonian forerunner. Certainly, what they share is the idea that society is functionally differentiated. However, world society is not accorded the status of a unit existing in and for itself that is subsequently differentiated; instead, its unity is achieved only through its internal differentiation.

As there is nothing social that is external to world society,[21] all social systems form internal environments. Given the primacy of functional differentiation (which is not an ahistorical given but a product of social evolution), world society is internally differentiated into functional systems, such as the political system, the economic system, and the educational system.[22] The major contribution to social theory of the theory of 'autopoietic' systems, as expressed in the natural sciences in the work of Maturana, Varela, and others, lies in the conceptualization of social systems as operatively closed systems. This means that as autopoietic systems, social systems produce all of their elements within themselves. Function systems use a specific basic code and specific forms and (symbolically generalized) media of communication. Under the condition of autopoietic self-reference and operative closure, there is no communication between a system and its environment; there is only communication within a system about its environment.[23] While there can be no communication between function systems, some function systems build relatively fixed models of their environment into themselves. These representations of an environment provide constant perturbations[24] for the system and thus affect a form of structural coupling between functional systems. In this way, a constitution can be seen as a form of structural coupling between the political and the legal systems of society. In addition, society also takes place in and through organizations. Organizations form a special case, in that they differentiate themselves from their environment on the basis of membership and are the only social systems that can communicate with their environment directly through decisions.[25]

Although this chapter cannot provide a comprehensive overview of this complex body of theory, the basic ideas already outlined can be further explored through two topics of interest: first, political authority or the political system, and second, the 'international' or politics beyond the state. Although these two themes are often closely (if not in fact constitutively) linked, it is noteworthy that only political authority and the political system have been given extended consideration in systems-theoretical writings. Issues of *international* politics have received only marginal attention.

Although the political system forms one of society's important functional systems, Luhmann deals with it at length only in his later writings.[26] The reception of Luhmann's writings has attributed his reluctance to deal with the political system to difficulties associated with applying his theoretical vocabulary to that particular functional system. I argue however, that many of the difficulties with the analysis of political system within a systems theory of world society are more the result of its neglect of any form of politics beyond the nation-state than problems of theoretical vocabulary. It might be thus possible to argue, strangely enough, that the only full-fledged theory of society that conceives of society as world society from the outset leaves little to no room for world politics! This theory does observe a political system of world society (as the *only* political system), yet when it comes to empirical observations, these almost exclusively refer to what is in common parlance described as 'domestic politics'.

Of course, this neglect has to be understood against a basic theoretical observation of modern systems theory. Whereas world society is internally functionally differentiated, the main differentiating principles within functional systems do not also have to be principles of functional differentiation. In that sense, modern systems theory observes that the political as well as the legal systems of world society remain the only functional systems of world society whose internal differentiation is primarily by segmentation. Within the political system, this internally segmented differentiation takes the form of a regional differentiation into states. Although my argument thus far has followed Luhmann's work on the political system very closely, the idea of the internal regional differentiation of the political system demonstrates a number of shortcomings in a systems-theoretical perspective. These can be overcome, I propose, by supplementing systems theory by re-embedding insights from more traditional forms of IR theorizing.

Modern systems theory is a radically non-ontological and constructivist theory. For modern systems theory, there is nothing but communication in society. Its main explanatory interest therefore is to show how communication can and does continue through the operation of social systems and the employment of basic codes of communication, through the evolution of semantic forms, and through the evolution of symbolically generalized media of communication. Given this, the concept of the state as a form often ontologized in political as well as international theory may provide a particularly apt entry point for understanding the political system of world society. The state does not form a unit, nor can it be reduced to the organizations of a political-administrative system. Moreover, it cannot be understood as an organization itself. Instead, the state is the primary form through which the political system, as a communicative system, describes itself. As such it functions as an important point of orientation and as a selection criterion for political communication, although the latter cannot be reduced to the state. In this sense, the systems theoretical idea of the state is that of a (constructed but extremely stable) semantic form. Still, it is important to remember that in such a theory it is not the state that is understood primarily through its function, but the political system that is understood in the context of society.

For society, the political system fulfils the important function of providing collectively binding decisions. Emphasis is placed here on the specific function of collectively binding decisions as that of producing decisions of whatever kind required for the continuance of communication, fulfilled by the system form 'organization.' In this view, the most important thing is not that collectively binding decisions are taken, but that the function for society is fulfilled in the main by the political system's provision of an adequate capacity for the production of such collectively binding decisions. While this capacity is the prime function of the political system, it operates through and uses power as a symbolically generalized medium of communication (in the same way the economic system utilizes the symbolically generalized medium of money and the scientific system the medium of truth). Power here is understood as the medium ensuring that communications and/or decisions achieve the characteristic of being collectively binding. This happens when Alter follows a decision taken by Ego without being forced to do so. The actual use of force is thus not political communication.[27]

Like any functional system, the political system must adapt to the complexity of society in order to fulfill its function. While the code of the political system is basically that of power/non-power, this code has undergone a number of re-codings and has been supplemented by a number of programs for the processing of political communication. In modern politics, the medium of power is usually coded in the form of government/opposition, while democracy serves as a powerful program that, on the basis of this code, allows for the absorption of conflicts without the capacity to provide for collectively binding decisions being put in question. Democratization and the institutionalization of elections in this sense can be seen as a contribution to the full differentiation of an autonomous and operatively closed political system: 'What we call "democracy" and link to the establishment of political elections is thus nothing but the completion of the differentiation of a political system. The systems bases itself on decisions which it has institutionalized itself. It thus simultaneously creates the conditions for the possibility of further decisions which need to be taken by the elected "representatives." '[28]

Without dwelling on the details of and difficulties with the systems theoretical description of the political system, its view of the foundation of political authority seems to be clear: There is none. To be fair, such considerations are irrelevant from the systems-theoretical point of view. Its main interest lies in explaining how political communication continues inside a system that is typically seen to require a collectively-binding character resting on a final or at least temporarily unquestioned illusion. In other words, the political system needs to constantly tackle and negotiate (and from time to time adapt in scale to) the fundamental paradox of providing a grounding, an authority of last resort, where there is none. Such a grounding needs to be supplied in a semantic form that allows us to perform the trick of providing a delimitation of the system calling into question its unity, or, by searching for that grounding outside the system itself, outside its autopoietic closure. The political system, in other words, requires contingency formulas 'which denote conditions for political thematizing in a way that they cannot be dissolved further by questioning the conditions of their possibility ... They thus form stylistic prescriptions for the denotative operations of the system. It is therefore necessary that they can be generalized and respecified. They need to be valid for an indeterminate number of situations but also mean something in every situation, i.e., be able to exclude something and guiding delimiting communication.'[29]

In the political system, the prevailing contingency formula within its semantic tradition is that of the common good,[30] which in turn can be defined in relation to and be applied through values and norms, or rather through procedures (which appeal less to substantive definitions of the common good but endeavour to ensure that the way it is ascertained through public discourse is fair). Put positively, such a contingency formula seems to form the operative counterpart of sovereignty, the form by which the solution to the political paradox is represented; put negatively, it masks that sovereignty presents a fictional figure of unity that masks a fundamental paradox.

It is not difficult to see that the idea of the common or public good has semantic equivalents in relation to international politics. While a global public good (or for that matter, global public goods) is of relatively recent vintage, the 'interest of the international community' is traditionally invoked when the existence of a *colère publique*[31] outside the nation-state (but within the political system!) is to be ascertained. The argument that builds on this rather simple observation is, however, a more far-reaching one: Something needs to fulfill the function of sovereignty or what is usually seen as the internal dimension of sovereignty. Yet now it must be performed within the political system but beyond the nation-state. It is at this point where a systems theoretical perspective provides an alternative reading of emerging forms of global governance, the diagnosed denationalization of politics, demands for problem-solving, or, broadly speaking, politics beyond the state. Work done on these issues in IR and related disciplines reminds those who take a systems-theoretical perspective of the amount of 'stuff' that exists beyond the segment-differentiated spaces of the political system that define the boundaries of politics. So understood, the political system of world society currently does exactly what it is supposed to do in contemporary world society: It adapts itself to provide the capacity for collectively binding decisions in the face of a growing (or at least changing) form of complexity in its environment.

It is in this sense that what is witnessed today is in fact a two-sided development. On the one hand, the political system must and does react to increasing and new forms of complexity in its environment; it also reacts to the accompanying demand for collectively binding decisions beyond the realms that can be clearly ascribed to nation-states. On the other hand, and inextricably linked to the first development, this is reflected in an ongoing modification of semantic practice.

Regarding the first point, it is important to note that this development cannot be seen independently from the evolution of other systems in society. Moreover, this development cannot be considered without acknowledging that the increasing demand for capacities for collectively binding decisions might also be met by the legal system.[32] However, there are strong reasons to assume that just as in national contexts (where the ideas of legal and political sovereignty are inextricably linked to each other) a strong relation of structural coupling exists or emerges between the political and legal systems of world society beyond the nation-state. This suspicion is nurtured by the emergence of formal or quasi-constitutional arrangements in European politics (in the form of an explicit design for a constitution for the European Union) and in global politics (in the form of the human rights regime and the International Criminal Court).[33] The main point here is that in order to provide the capacity for collectively binding decisions, it is not a logical necessity to somehow extend or transfer the semantic form of sovereignty to a global level. But given that the semantic form of sovereignty has achieved such a dominant status in the political system, its adaptation to the new situation can be expected.

Of course, much in the contemporary IR / political science debates, including this volume, do just that. They describe the emerging new complexities and the resulting increase in demand for capacities for collectively binding decisions and experiment with semantic adaptations of sovereignty (as in 'complex sovereignty'). This approach thus observes what systems theory does not observe. Nonetheless, systems theory can assist IR and political science by providing re-phrasings and new questions.

Describing Global Politics

To reiterate some of the points raised above, the modern systems theory of society does not conceive of the political system, let alone of international politics, as a world of its own. The political system is rather one of world society's functional systems – one that, in the view of systems theory, is internally differentiated into territorial states. Like any other functional system, the political system needs to devise a form, supplemented by specific programs and contingency formulas, in order to ascertain the unity of the system in spite of its paradox. In the political system, this paradox of the 'political' – that is, the necessity to effect a temporary fix of an unquestioned grounding for collectively binding decisions where there is no such naturally given grounding – is resolved through sovereignty. Sovereignty itself is two-sided, with external sovereignty playing an important role in claiming (or simulating) an atemporal characteristic of sovereignty (in its embeddedness in an anarchical international system).

So far so good, if indeed Luhmann's claim (which, strangely enough, he shares in the end with classical realism) that the political system of world society remains internally differentiated regionally is left unassailed. If doubt is cast on this claim by the existence of political dynam-ics beyond the state, such as newly emerging forms of global governance, post-Westphalian international relations, and the like, then it is high time to reassess the implications of these developments for mapping the configuration of the political system of world society in systems-theoretical terms.

The most important point is that through its description of the polit-ical system as a function-system of world society systems theory reminds us that the way sovereignty resolves the political paradox and represents this resolution in spatial terms (the sovereign territorial state) are by no means the necessary resolutions and representations. What is necessary is some kind of operative resolution of that paradox in order to enable political communication to continue (and capacities for collectively-binding decisions to be provided). Alternatives to the semantic form of sovereignty are possible, although there are some prima facie reasons to also expect an adaptation and persistence of the semantic form of sovereignty in this context, given that it has under-gone numerous changes over a long history.[34]

Both IR and modern systems theory need to be reminded that unity and homogeneity are not the exception but the rule in social systems. Systems theory requires the further reminder that although the political systems of world society might still be differentiated territorially or spa-tially, functional differentiation becomes more important within the political system (note the problem-solving orientation in the 'global governance' literature) and also that political organizations both as important loci of decisions and the forms in which the political system describes itself need not necessarily stick to the figure of the sovereign state for these purposes. On the contrary, heterogeneity of organiza-tional forms and of differentiating principles is not only possible, it is to be expected. As such, the primacy of the strict differentiation of the political system of world society into territorial states and the Westpha-lian paradigm can and should be interpreted as an historical exception. Arguably, the closest the international system has ever come to this par-adigm was the period between the two world wars. Between empires, colonies, and dominions on the one hand and the 'postmodern' polity of the European Union on the other, the organization of political space in the form of sovereign territorial states is more of an exception than sug-gested (or allowed) by methodological nationalism.[35]

From such a perspective, the emergence (or in fact existence) of dif-ferent ways of organizing and representing political space is to be expected.[36] These forms need to be depicted in their own terms and in relation to the varying forms of structural coupling to other function systems. The admittance of such heterogeneity of forms seems reason enough to fundamentally challenge any semantic of the 'international.' In the end, the problem – one that is both a practical and theoretical – remains that the political system requires something to fulfill the function of sovereignty for its operation. Something (a person, a principle, an organization, or a procedure) must be constructed or projected at the top of the political system that introduces the necessary authority to make decisions binding. In a globalized world society, such a demand cannot be met by the simultaneous presence of 200 such differentiated 'tops' (sovereigns) in the political system. Something else is required for that purpose.

The obvious candidate here would be a world state or at least an organizational equivalent. Given that the obvious candidate, the United Nations Security Council, does not, for known reasons and functional restrictions, seem to be able to provide sufficient capacity for collectively binding decisions, there are strong reasons to assume that alternatives do emerge in the political system. It is possible to read the global human rights regime, processes of quasi-constitutionalization, and the emergence of a weak global public as indicators of the emergence of functional equivalents of the form of sovereignty within the political system.[37] Taken together with the heterogeneity of forms of organizing and representing political space alluded to above, this means that the evolution of the political system in world society can be read as being characterized by *complex sovereignty*. This perspective points to more than a complication of existing sovereignties. *Complex sovereignty* highlights the emergence of a number of functional equivalents to sovereignty – whether formally recognized as such or not. Accordingly, what others have described as 'bifurcation' or 'fragmegration'[38] can in fact be read as the evolution of the political system of world society, in the sense that it adapts to the complexity of its environment in order to provide adequate capacities for collectively binding decisions. In this light, it is possible to read the persistence and transformation of the 200 or so formal sovereign entities, the process of international organization, the emergence of forms of private authority and regional integration processes – all taken together - as a modification of organizational forms and of sovereignty so as to permit the continuous resolution of the political paradox to identify and name places where political authority ultimately resides. These developments, however, also require the system's codes and programs to adapt to the new political context. How these codes and programs should adapt and whether new ones should be created could serve as guiding questions for future attempts to utilize a systems theoretical perspective to map the political system of world society.

It is important to note that the emergence of functional equivalents for sovereignty does not necessarily entail a 'diminution' of sovereignty. If sovereignty is primarily understood as a semantic form describing what is necessary to resolve the political paradox of undecidability and thus to guarantee a successful 'unity-in-diversity' of the political system, then there is no reason why this semantic form itself should not evolve further and at some point encompass the functional equivalents mentioned. Such a development could be witnessed if and when 'sovereignty talk' proliferates to contexts beyond the nation-state to a significant degree. The process of constitutionalization within the European Union is of particular interest in this respect.

Conclusion: Modern Systems Theory as a Non-traditional Vista for the Study of World Politics

The perspective outlined in this chapter does not amount to a call for a wholesale adoption of systems theory for the analysis of world politics, nor does it advocate abandoning specific inquiries into world politics by International Relations scholars. Instead, it calls on IR scholars critically to inspect the analytical framework offered by modern systems theory in order to understand the evolution of the political system of world society in a way that reflects its embeddedness in a wider social context, a context not adequately depicted as an agglomeration of national societies or through the 'international.' Underwriting the proposed dialogue between traditional international relations scholarship and a more sociologically oriented view drawing on modern systems theory is more than a mere heuristic plea to join two seemingly different theoretical perspectives. Not only does IR research into changing forms of sovereignty and the constitution of a post-Westphalian system require important modifications in the way in which modern systems theory observes the operation of the political system of world society, but also a systems theoretical reading of world politics demonstrates (by the very definition of one political system of world society) that 'international relations' and 'world politics' are an area in which the disciplinary separation of 'political theory' and 'international relations' cannot be maintained meaningfully.[39]

It is hardly illuminating – if not outright impossible – from a systems-theoretical perspective to determine the constituent 'units' of the political system of world society, one of the basic questions of IR theory, if world society and its political system are seen as communicatively constituted systems. What becomes important in such a theoretical perspective are the codes of social systems, the way communication is loosely coupled, the different media of communication (such as power), and how political systems describe themselves (for example, as states), not the units and the interactions among them.

That said, like this volume as a whole, I am not advocating a single approach to understanding the reconfiguration of political authority in the twenty-first century. My objective has been to contribute to the ongoing process of newly emerging, decidedly post-Westphalian semantics. Examining the ideas of modern systems theory helps us understand that a new conceptual map – for instance, a fully developed 'methodological cosmopolitanism,' to use Beck's term – requires a radical change in established vocabularies so that old questions can be reformulated or abandoned, new questions can be asked, and new answers can be given.

NOTES

1 Bull (1977).
2 Lipschutz (1992).
3 Beck (1999).
4 Stichweh (2000).
5 This chapter touches on a number of discourses in a number of disciplines and the extensive literatures that go with them. Most of the references are therefore meant only to point to suggestive examples.
6 Beck (1999). See also Beck (1997c) and Zürn (2000a).
7 Hollis and Smith's (1991: 10) convention of capitalizing International Relations (IR) when referring to the discipline and using lowercase letters when referring to the subject is adopted here.
8 This theme is also the one explored in Albert (2002), but with a rather different focus.
9 Adler and Barnett (1998).
10 Bigo (2001).

11 See, among others, Hewson and Sinclair (1999).

12 Goldstein et al. (2000).

13 See Walker (1993).

14 On this issue, see also the concluding chapter of this volume. Whether it is actually sensible to speak of 'functional spaces' is a point that will not be explored here. Although elsewhere I have argued in favour of 'functional spaces,' I am currently much more sceptical on this issue. See Albert (1997).

15 Derrida (1990).

16 Biersteker and Weber (1996) and Weber (1995)

17 The aim here is modest. It is not to come up with a 'better' theory or 'better' answers, but only with a way to engage with questions central to political and international theory from a different angle.

18 Luhmann (1972; 1997: 145ff), Stichweh (2000). In general on Luhmann and IR, see Albert and Hilkermeier (2004).

19 Despite the common shorthand of 'systems theory,' this body of theory is based on a combination of a systems theory, a theory of differentiation, and an evolutionary theory. It thus differs radically from other theories of society and systems theories in several respects: its notion of systems is a decidedly post-cybernetic notion of autopoietic social systems; its notion of differentiation is decidedly post-Parsons; and its notion of evolution decidedly non-Darwinian. Most importantly, however, its notion of communication is one of reflexive communication, conceived as a unity of information, message, and understanding. Luhmann (1997) is where most concepts of modern systems theory are given their most extensive treatment.

20 Parsons (1969:2)

21 Its 'external' environment is, strictly speaking, formed by psychic or physical systems only.

22 It is because of this that Luhmann talks about the political system *of* society. Society, according to Luhmann, is differentiated into function systems and achieves its unity only through this differentiation; it is not somehow 'assembled' by and through function systems.

23 This is not to say that there are no relations of causality, only that these can only be observed by systems and only unfold meaning as *attributions* of causality.

24 The relevant German word here is *Irritation*, connoting some kind of variation which is noted by the system – with or without consequences. It is thus more than a mere 'variation,' but notoriously hard to translate either into the English 'irritation' or 'perturbation' since these usually carry more negative connotations.

25 Organizations also form autopoietic systems that produce all of their ele-

ments – i.e., organizational decisions – within themselves and achieve operative closure by deciding on decisional premises (cf. in particular Luhmann 2000b). Interaction systems also form a kind of social system, but are formed only by those present.

26 In fact, Luhmann's (2000a) *The Politics of Society (Die Politik der Gesellschaft)* arguably had a somewhat strange history in that a manuscript version was circulated, read, and discussed for years in the wide community of students of modern systems theory, with the book finally published only posthumously.

27 Nassehi (2002).

28 Luhmann (2000a: 104f; translation my own).

29 Ibid., 120; translation my own.

30 Ibid., 120ff.

31 Fischer-Lescano (2002).

32 Albert (2002).

33 Brunkhorst (2002).

34 Badie (2002).

35 See Krasner (1999) for the same point argued differently.

36 At first glance, one might suspect here a basic incompatibility with the diagnosis made by sociological neoinstitutionalists. However, this is not the case so long as sociological neoinstitutionalism, and the 'world polity' approach in particular, are seen as referring to organizations alone and not to either society or to semantic forms. See Thomas (2004).

37 Brunkhorst (2002).

38 Rosenau (1997).

39 See Brown (2002) for a powerful argument in the same direction.

4 Governance: A Garbage Can Perspective

B. GUY PETERS

Governance is a very old concept, and an even older reality.[1] Societies have always required some form of collective steering and management. Variations in the political and economic order have produced different answers to the fundamental questions about how to provide that steering for society and how to cope with the range of challenges arising from the society. Some answer has been required and continues to be required. Governance is not a constant, but rather tends to change as needs and values change. The usual answer to the questions has been the 'state,' Yet, solutions that have been effective and popular with the public at one point in time may rather quickly become both ineffective and politically unpopular at another. The process of governing represents a continuing set of adaptations of political and administrative activities to changes in the environment, not least of which are changes in the ideas that define appropriate modes of developing and implementing collective goals.[2]

The introductory chapter of this book points to the need for an adaptive capacity in contemporary governance. For a variety of reasons the assumptions on which much of what may now be deemed traditional approaches to governing are subject to question. In particular, assumptions about the centrality of the nation-state and the centrality of authoritative public actors in governance are subject to question. Put differently, as the editors did in Chapter 1, the notions of a single locus of sovereignty, and of a simple hierarchical ordering within the system of governance, can no longer be accepted as reasonable descriptions of the reality of contemporary governing. As yet, however, there are no generally accepted replacements for those guiding assumptions, and as a consequence, both the academic world and the real world of governance are more problematic than they have been in the past.

This chapter will address some contemporary issues in governing and attempt to provide one means of understanding changes in governance. The answer provided here, if indeed it is an answer, may be somewhat unsatisfying because it will focus on the indeterminacy of governance in a world without the guiding assumptions of hierarchy and simple sovereignty. The approach that will be developed, however, may better reflect the reality of governance than do more deterministic models. An unstructured approach does not mean that decisions are not made. Indeed, I will be arguing that decisions are made, but not always in the open and participative ways implied in much of the literature on changes in governance. The absence of guiding assumptions about the location and use of authority in governing means that decision situations have become less unstructured, so that a variety of influences are brought to bear on both foreign and domestic policy choices.

Contemporary shifts in governance styles involve corresponding shifts in the instruments used for governing, as well as in the content of governing.[3] Shifts in the content and goals of governance are the more obvious of the transformations. This change in solutions to the basic questions of the political economy was obvious during the 1980s and 1990s as most countries of Western Europe, North America, and the Antipodes adopted neo-liberal ideas of the role of the state, and significantly reduced the role of the public sector.[4] The transformations of the goals of governing in Eastern Europe and some countries in the Third World, driven in part by international organizations and other donors, were even more dramatic. Likewise, the welfare state continues to be redefined, as neo-liberal ideas shape how governments manage social problems of inequality and providing income for people throughout the life cycle.[5]

No matter what the overall goals and content of governing may be, a range of instruments are available to achieve the goals. The instruments literature coming from public administration and public policy has concentrated to a great extent on understanding these 'tools' at the level of the individual tool.[6] For example, how does a loan guarantee differ from a voucher as a means of putting a program into effect?[7] At a more general level, however, changes in governing have tended to entail movements away from authority based instruments and to involve governments working through less intrusive means. In the terminology developed by Hood, there has been a shift away from authority-based instruments in favour of instruments based on treasure and nodality (information).[8] In particular, the 'new governance' involves using the financial resources of the public sector to leverage the involvement of significant private sector actors.

The movement away from authority-based instruments and ruling through those conventional mechanisms of social control has occurred in large part because of a variety of changes occurring within government itself, and perhaps more importantly, because of changes in public reactions to the actions of the public sector. There is by now a significant literature documenting the declining public confidence in government institutions and in the politicians who populate them.[9] This decline in public confidence in government has been most pronounced in the United States,[10] but it has been observed even in other countries with long histories of benign and effective government.[11]

With the decline in confidence in government the capacity to achieve goals through instruments that depend on authority, and therefore on legitimacy, is diminished. One strand of the instruments literature[12] has stressed the importance of less intrusive means of governing, but that point is now being forced on governments. Further, as intimated above, the declining confidence of the public has led to shifting provision of services to the private sector, whether the organizations involved are for profit or not for profit.

As well as a generalized debate about the capacity of governments to govern, there is a more specific debate over how governments can govern, and the appropriate distribution, or melding, of authority among types of government. Given that the loss of public confidence has been most pronounced for national governments, decentralization has become a frequent strategy for maintaining effective governance.[13] Both the choice of decentralization and the choice to utilize private sector organizations are conscious strategies, designed to *sauve qui peut*. The introductory chapter of this book reminds us that some, if not most, of the erosion of governance capacity has not been dealt with systematically and that the dynamics of the international political and economic systems have pervasive consequences for governance.

The Governance Debate

Changes in the reality of governance have been significant and have transformed what governments do, as well as how they do it.[14]

Changes in the academic debate concerning governance have been, however, at least as pronounced as those within government. In the first place, there is now an active discussion of governance, rather than having scholars assume that societies would and could continue to be governed as they had always been. Further, the changes in the academic discourse have paralleled the transformation of governing in the real world and have attempted to provide some interpretation of those changes. The important shift in the academic literature is represented by the very use, and now the widespread use, of the term *governance*, rather than terms such as *government*, *state*, or even *ruling*, to describe how *steering* is accomplished within society.

The concept of steering is central to this discussion of governance, with the underlying idea being that there must be some mechanism for making and implementing collective goals for society. By considering the issue of steering as a basic requirement, we can then in governance research consider how that need is fulfilled.[15] This approach to the analysis of governance is much like that taken in the implementation literature that held as basic the requirement to put law into effect and then used the extent and manner of making that happen as the basis of comparison.

Although anchored by some concept of steering, students of governance who use this approach have been somewhat like Lewis Carroll's characters, making the term mean exactly what they want it to mean. As the literature has developed, the term *governance* has taken on a wide range of meanings. At one end of a spectrum of state involvement, governance means very much what has been *government*, with the state remaining the most important actor in steering and authority the means through which the state steers society. Despite pressures from globalization, from declining public confidence, and from decentralization of policymaking, the argument of the state-centric approach is that the only actor, or set of actors, capable of setting and attaining collective goals is the central government. Indeed, globalization in this view may strengthen the need for strong, effective, and above all democratic, government provided through the nation-state.[16] In less extreme versions of the state-centric approaches, government remains an important player in governance, but government must also involve itself in partnerships and other arrangements with societal actors in order to be more effective.

At the other end of this spectrum, some have argued that the state has become, if not totally superfluous, then extremely ineffective.[17] The argument put forward by the 'governance without government' school is that society is now sufficiently well organized through self-organizing networks that any attempts on the part of government to intervene will be ineffective and perhaps counterproductive. Society is presumed to be more capable than government of understanding its own affairs and of finding remedies for any problems that are encountered in its functioning. In that context, government becomes a bureaucratic and rather clumsy structure for making decisions. Further, the autopoietic, self-organizing nature of society is taken in these approaches to mean that society will be able to avoid or deflect any attempts on the part of governments to control its affairs – government in essence becomes dispensable and expensive.[18] This view about the declining steering capacity of government is based largely on domestic factors, in contrast to other views that consider the role of the state as an international actor.

Between these two extreme views of governance, we can find approaches that recognize that societal actors have increasingly assumed greater involvement in governance activities, just as the state has been an increasingly more involved in what are presumably private activities and organizations.[19] In these more moderate versions of governance, the process of steering involves an interaction between the public and the private sectors, as well as an interaction between top-down and bottom-up conceptions of how society can be steered. While less sharply defined than the more extreme versions, these more temperate versions of governance represent somewhat more accurately the complexity that is entailed in contemporary governing. These moderate conceptions of governance are represented in part by the 'Dutch school' of governance, which considers governance to be a 'sociopolitical' process.[20] In this version of the process networks of societal actors are heavily involved in providing governance, yet they do so in cooperation with, and to some extent under the direction of, the state actors. Governance in the Dutch and similar models is cooperative rather than adversarial, with policy outcomes resulting from overcoming the decisional and coordination problems inherent in large complex policy arenas.

We should also consider that some forms of governing that function through authority sharing rather than imposition could be seen as intermediate forms of governance. For example, the well-developed discussion of corporatist and corporate-pluralist models popular during the 1970s and 1990s presented a variety of available mechanisms for linking state and society in governance.[21] The state remained an active, and in some cases essentially dominant, player in these proceedings, and yet there was bargaining and mutual accommodation in making policy. Further, societal actors have been involved in implementing policies for decades if not centuries, so that the output side of government has been linked effectively with society for some time. Any number of public policies depend on private sector or not-for-profit organizations to implement programs in the name of government, whether to save resources or to create more effective and humane service delivery.

Factors other than political change are involved in driving shifts in the prevailing styles of governance. The nature of the problems confronting governments also have changed, in several ways. The most fundamental transformation in the environment of the public sector is that change itself – technological, social, and economic – tends to be more rapid and less predictable than in the past. Whether the extreme versions of change associated with chaos theory[22] or more moderate versions of unpredictability in the environment are considered the best way to consider environmental change, governments must find ways of coping with rapidly changing problems and a socioeconomic environment that is now less predictable than in much of their previous experience. This change in governance will require enhanced flexibility, and with that flexibility come designs for governance that recognize the modification of preferences through learning[23] and the inadequacy of many technologies for achieving programmatic goals. Decisions that once might have been programmable will, under these circumstances, be more subject to circumstance and opportunities, rather than planning and formalized procedures.[24] Not all policy problems and decision situations will become so chaotic; many will remain but little changed, and the same actors and the same problem definitions will dominate.

Associated with the increasingly rapid pace of change in many policy sectors is a shift in the involvement of actors in governing. On the one hand, many traditional actors in governing are becoming weakened, perhaps most notably political parties. On the other hand, there is a wider variety of organizations that are organized sufficiently to exert some pressure on government. Further, transnational actors, whether formal organizations such as the European Union or the World Trade Organization or looser international regimes (like those discussed in the Coleman, Skogstad, and Porter chapters in this volume) can influence or even supplant national actors. This shift in the involvement of actors tends to increase the uncertainties created by socioeconomic change and to make policymaking even less determinate.

The concept of governance therefore conforms rather well with the ideas motivating this book, in particular, that there has been a shift away from an authority-based style of governing that has assumed the capacity of governments to exercise hierarchical control over society. *Governance* is one of several terms used to describe that change. Governance when taken to the extreme attaches little importance to state actors in providing collective steering for society. I am not adopting anything near such an extreme conception of governance and am retaining a stronger role for the state than in the extreme versions. Even this moderate perspective, however, does ascribe a lesser role to the state than do the state-centric assumptions that have guided a good deal of work on governing, and it also directs us to think about steering in a less deterministic manner.

The Garbage Can Model

Although there has been a good deal of thinking and writing about governance, the term remains largely descriptive rather than explanatory. This descriptive nature of a great deal of the governance literature reflects in part its attempt to capture virtually the entirety of the policy process, becoming something of a latter day systems analysis, or structural-functional analysis, of politics.[25] To the extent that the term is used less generally, the concept often relies upon network thinking and is hampered by the absence of mechanisms of conflict resolution and decision-making. Politics is about contradictory and conflicting interests, and the argument that social networks are capable of governing is contingent on their capacity to resolve those differences.

Whatever approach one may take to governance, save the most state-centric, the very use of the term *governance* represents an acceptance of some movement away from the conventional authority-based style of governing. That movement is in favour of approaches to governing that rely less on formal authority and more on the interaction of state and society actors. Further, the questioning of state authority and capacity implied in the use of the form means that some of the rationalist perspectives on the role of governments in governing may also be brought into question.[26] The 'new governance' literature stresses networks, bargaining, and interaction rather than hierarchies, as the best way to govern and the best way to understand governance. Thus, this literature contains both normative and empirical dimensions.

One way to move beyond a strictly descriptive treatment of governance is to employ the garbage can model of organizational behaviour developed by Cohen, March, and Olsen.[27] This model provides a means of exploring the ways in which governance can be supplied in a world that is less clearly governed through authority and hierarchy. Based, not surprisingly, on the management of universities,[28] the garbage can model rejected conventional linear models of organizational decision-making in favour of a less determinate and less rational (in the usual interpretation of that word) forms of making decisions. The fundamental assumption driving this model is that, rather than being programmed or predictable, decisions in many situations are more the result of the serendipitous confluence of opportunities, individuals, and ideas.

The garbage can model was developed as a means of examining the behaviour of organizations, but its authors discussed the possibility of it being applied to decisional situations as well as to organizations per se. Further, at least one of the authors of the original article has discussed the possibility of its application to the European Union as a relatively diffuse, unstructured political system.[29] Likewise, Christopher Hood has examined the relationship of this model to governing somewhat more generally, focusing on the relationship of unstructured decision-making situations to risk and regulation.[30] The model does appear to have some utility for understanding decisional situations that are broader than individual organizations, and it may well be applicable to situations in which individual organizations themselves are the principal players. Organizations that embody these broader decisional settings may be the most integrated and decisive actors in what are in many ways anarchic decisional situations, and therefore such organizations will have some advantages in producing actions that conform to their preferences or, at a minimum, in blocking their least preferred alternatives.

The garbage can model of organizational decision-making is one link in an extended chain of intellectual development in organizational theory that is described as 'bounded rationality,' and is founded on the insights of Herbert Simon and other members of the so-called Carnegie School of decision-making.[31] Simon famously argued that the demands of full-blown rationality were too great for any individual person or any organization to be able to achieve when making decisions. Therefore, organizations are best understood as acting rationally only within narrowed boundaries, with their range of rational action determined by their own routines, norms, technologies, and interests. Thus, Simon's familiar concept of 'satisficing' can be used to describe behaviour that seeks outcomes that are 'good enough' rather than ones that comprehensively maximize utility. This criterion of rationality should not be seen, however, as excessively minimalist. Finding policy solutions that are good enough can itself be extremely demanding, and is rational from the perspective of minimizing decision-making costs rather than maximizing the utility of the outcomes produced.

The garbage can model is capable of being used to understand governance in the transnational political environment explored by the contributors to this book. In particular, given that the capacity of authoritative actors to structure decisions has been diminished in such an environment, and that even many structured modes of political participation have been weakened, the garbage can model appears to be more applicable than others. With those changes both the inputs into politics and the processes by which decisions are reached are less predictable, and less likely to be effective on a regular basis. The outcomes of the policy process may represent the confluence of streams of possibilities rather than a rational search for the best option. This model of governing is itself not predictive, but it does provide a useful means for interpreting many changes in contemporary governance.

Organized Anarchies

The garbage can model grew out of the general concern with bounded rationality within organizations, and other decision-making situations, in which linear and fully rational modes of choice would be unlikely if not completely impossible.[32] Although Bendor, Moe, and Shotts find reasons to distinguish the garbage can model from the remainder of the bounded-rationality literature, there does appear to be a strong family resemblance, if not a direct parental connection, among these approaches to organizations and decisions.[33] If nothing else, the garbage can model and bounded rationality both reject fundamentally rationalist perspectives and seek alternative means of understanding how institutions are able to muddle through in complex and poorly defined decisional situations. As for the organized anarchies that are central to the garbage can model, three features characterize these organizations or situations.

Problematic Preferences

In a setting such as that assumed to exist within an organized anarchy, it is difficult to impute the consistency of preferences that are required for standard, rationalistic models of decision-making to perform well. Preferences in the model of the garbage can are inconsistent among the participants and/or ill-defined. Further, preferences may be subject to limited discussion because of the political difficulties that such inconsistency may generate within an organization or a political system. The point here is that preferences held by individual actors may well be consistent, and could be held quite passionately, but preferences within the decision-making structure as a whole are not consistent.

In an organized anarchy preferences are *discovered* through actions. Note that in this context individual actors (individual or collective) may have consistent preferences, but the policymaking system qua system is assumed to encounter substantial difficulty in reconciling those varied preferences and making them coherent. The transformations in policymaking characteristic of non-hierarchical governance make resolving any conflicts all the more difficult. Those difficulties are analogous to what political scientists have identified with 'blocked' policymaking or 'stalemate' for some time,[34] but these blockages may be more severe because of the decline of authority-based instruments for resolving blockages.

To the extent that it can move, the organized anarchy faces the danger of falling into something like a 'joint decision trap,' with decisions being made by the lowest common denominator. Scharpf's analysis is based on policymaking within the European Union, as well as at the federal government level in Germany.[35] The EU is one *locus classicus* of shared and complex sovereignty, and with that multiple and competing preferences; Sbragia refers to the EU as an 'ambiguous political space.'[36] These anarchical tendencies are all the more true given that national governments tend to have conflicting views about levels of integration, which are often based on individual policy areas in which their own economy is likely to benefit or lose from shifts in control over the sector.

If preferences are discovered for the system as whole, rather than being imposed through authority and sovereignty, then the only ones available may represent minimal movements away from the status quo – the classic incremental solution to policy problems. This behaviour is itself consistent with the logic of bounded rationality and can be seen as rational from that perspective.[37] If there are to be movements away from this minimalist form of governance through accepting only the points on which there is agreement, then intersections with at least one other stream within the garbage can – either individuals as entrepreneurs or opportunities (crises, windfalls, or whatever) may be necessary. For example, the rather lurching movements of European integration can be conceptualized as the intersection of preferences with defined opportunities for bargaining.

Unclear Technology

The processes through which organized anarchies are able to survive, and even to prosper, are often poorly understood by the members of those structures. There may be a rather simple trial-and-error process of learning, and incremental change in the system, but the structuring of the system is largely done by adaptation rather than comprehensive strategic planning from the centre. Thus, just as the goals of governing may emerge rather than being imposed from a central 'mind of government,' the means of achieving the goals are also likely to emerge and not be planned.

This absence of clear and centrally controlled technologies for governing is consistent with much contemporary discussion about governance. Whereas government might once have had well-known and accepted means of implementing policy and producing the required actions, now a less clear armamentarium is available to would-be governors. The good news is that there is a wider range of instruments available for government to use in implementing its programs, many of which involve using the private sector. Part of the wide-scale reform of government over the past several decades[38] has been to create means of achieving collective purposes through less direct, partnership methods,[39] or other means involving private and not-for-profit actors.

As well as a wider range of 'technologies' for achieving ends for the public sector, the very lack of clarity inherent in the garbage can model of governing may be an advantage for the emergent public sector. While the more traditional public sector and its limited range of responses to problems (and opportunities) may have been able to produce results, it did so at some cost, and the lack of clarity that is typical of bounded rationality and its more evolutionary and trial-and-error style of governing has the potential for political benefits, if not necessarily for enhanced effectiveness in governing.

This emergent style of more tentative governing may be an antidote to the apparent need of many governments, and many politicians, to claim that they have the answers for the problems that confront society. While claiming that solutions to policy problems are not only possible but even readily available may be politically necessary at times, it may not reflect the reality in many policy areas of the knowledge base available to governments when attempting to govern. Several decades ago the economist Richard Nelson[40] argued that governments did not have the technology to cope with most social problems.[41] Regrettably, that conclusion still stands, so that the public sector is often making decisions without a clear understanding of the process into which it is intervening. Given that weakness of the knowledge base available to many decision-makers, and the associated uncertainty about policy, recognition of the problem and a willingness to avoid premature closure of policy options may represent a more 'rational' approach to governing than does a more self-assured approach.

Fluid Participation

Members of organized anarchies vary in the amount of time and effort that they are prepared to devote to any structure or situation, and indeed, membership in such anarchy may itself be problematic. Thus, the boundaries of the organizations, or the decision situations, are fluid and uncertain, and the decision process within them tends to be poorly defined. The attempts of any actor to become involved in any particular decision may be capricious and certainly cannot be predicted readily, even from prior, analogous situations. Given the gamelike nature of this process, the potential participants never totally ignore the possibilities of involvement; they may choose the degree of involvement depending on the perceived probabilities of winning or perhaps on the basis of less utilitarian criteria.

This description of life in an organized anarchy bears some resemblance to discussions of policymaking in networked governments.[42] In the conventional state-centric conception of governing, participation in the policy process might be managed in one of several ways. Perhaps most importantly, the principal players would be governmental actors, rather than actors from civil society, and they would be mandated to participate or would find it in their political and/or organizational interest to do so. To the extent that elements of civil society are involved in the policy process, their participation tends to be organized by the state, rather than autonomous decision-making by those actors themselves. Such structuring of participation may be through pluralist selection of a limited number of quasi-official representatives of societal segments or it may be more corporatist or corporate-pluralist so that multiple interests are brought together in an official decision-making process.[43] These structures are capable of creating more integrated preferences for the society, and the segmentation that characterizes much of government can be alleviated through these participatory mechanisms.

This characteristic of erratic and uncertain participation does not necessarily mean that there will be less participation. In fact, it may mean quite the contrary. As state-imposed constraints on participation become more relaxed, more demands for involvement arise, and with that more participation in decisions. Charles Jones[44] argued some years ago that the 'iron triangles' in American politics had been transformed into 'big sloppy hexagons,' but the geometry of political participation can now be described only by even more complex structures. At the same time that societies are presumably becoming more atomistic and less organizational, the level of mobilization around particular issues remains strong or has perhaps even increased in intensity.[45] This is certainly political participation but not of the conventional kind. It may be that we are not bowling alone, but simply bowling in new leagues each week.

Shifting forms of participation lead into another issue concerning the nature of societal participation in this garbage can model of governance. The nature and structure of the groups attempting to participate in government are changing in a manner that emphasizes the fluid and uncertain nature of contemporary governance. There is a good deal of evidence that involvement in the available range of stable political organizations – both interest groups and the traditional political parties – that were deeply embedded in the political process is declining. In their place are numerous short-lived and/or single-issue organizations that have begun to attract greater participation. We may speculate about the reasons for the apparent failure of the traditional interest groups and parties as the mechanisms for political mobilization,[46] but that they are less capable of channelling participation does appear clear.

The decline in political participation through conventional means enhances the fluidity of participation in government and hence some of the predictability of the process. This fluidity affects not only the types of pressures being placed on decision-makers but also the political calculations that those decision-makers are likely to make about policies. In a less fluid process the decision-makers can calculate the likely political consequences of decisions, even if they may be uncertain about the effectiveness of the policies being adopted.[47] This aspect of fluid participation is closely related to the problematic nature of preferences in an organized anarchy. Again, individual actors have preferences and hold to them with some intensity, and perhaps with even greater intensity than in more structured situations of decision-making, but their multiplicity and the fluidity of participation make integration across the policy system more difficult than in a more structured system.[48]

A final point about the more uncertain nature of participation in contemporary governments is that more participation appears to be directed at the output side of government than at the input side. That is, rather than worrying about attempting to influence the policy decisions made by legislatures or political executives, a greater share of political activity is becoming directed at influencing the behaviour of bureaucracies. Further, this is not only aimed at the top of the bureaucracy, but also at the lowest levels of the administrative system. Members of the public as well as organized interests now find it more useful to limit attempts at exerting influence to local schools, or their own housing projects, or local environmental problems,[49] rather than acting on a national scale. This may make perfect sense in terms of the capacity to change policies and programs that have direct impacts on the individual, but it also directs the emphasis of policymaking to the particular rather than to general policies and their (possible) coherence.

Governing in the Garbage Can

The discussion above of the nature of organized anarchies at the heart of the garbage can model may well make one pessimistic about the possibilities of governing in a non-hierarchical political system. That pessimism would, of course, be based on accepting the notion that the garbage can is a reasonable approach to understanding contemporary governance. While this is not the only way in which to approach governance in this significantly altered environment, it does provide a reasonable and useful window on the process of governing. The three properties of the organized anarchy are, as noted, descriptive of many aspects of contemporary policymaking.

The next step in using this approach is to consider the way in which decisions are made in the context of an organized anarchy. The basic argument of the garbage can model, given its anarchic basis, is that decision-making is not structured, orderly, and rational in the way that might be expected from much of the decision-making literature in policy analysis and allied fields.[50] Rather, decision-making in the public sector as seen through the lens of this model reflects the serendipitous, and almost accidental, confluence of streams of problems, solutions, opportunities, and actors. In this view the rationalistic conception of problems searching for solutions and actors pursuing their interests in a purposive manner is replaced by decision-making that may be dominated by the appearance of opportunities. As John Kingdon has argued, 'policy windows' open and then policy entrepreneurs must be prepared to exploit the opportunities.[51]

This basic description of policymaking in organizational settings has parallels in decision-making in contemporary political systems. There may have been a heyday of rationalist policymaking, but the contemporary world of governance does not resemble it.[52] As faith in government has dropped, the faith in rational planning, forecasting, and other forms of rational decision-making has dropped even more. This does not mean that the quest to make 'government work better and cost less' has waned; if anything the reforms of the past several decades indicate quite the opposite. There are continuing attempts to improve government performance, but these depend more on the use of market or political power to impose greater efficiency and responsiveness, than on rational processes to produce optimal answers to policy problems.[53]

Agenda setting is a crucial aspect of policymaking in the garbage can model. That is true of all approaches to public policy, but the loose structure of the organized anarchy and the absence of dominant institutional drivers in the system mean that deciding what issues will be considered is crucial for deciding outcomes. The model of convergent streams and problematic preferences means that issues that might rationally be considered important for governing may be avoided. Avoidance is one of the more common outcomes of the computer simulations of decision-making in the garbage can, given the absence of coherent preferences and a mechanism for driving action ahead. In the context of the European Union there is a similar tendency to avoid decisions until there is adequate agreement to make the decisional process (relatively) non-conflictual.

Other studies of management taking the garbage can perspective have found that individual entrepreneurs become the crucial means of producing action and programmatic change.[54] This finding is, of course, not dissimilar to Kingdon's argument about agenda setting in governments and the role of entrepreneurs in shaping outcomes, but research in private-sector and third-sector organizations also demonstrates that individual involvement and entrepreneurship are crucial for generating collective action. The centrality of individuals is not only a consequence of their personal power and political skills. It may also be a function of the uncertainty of many decision-making situations and the desire of participants to be able to associate proposals for resolving the issue with individuals who advocate them. Further, research on crisis management points to the need for individual leaders to 'keynote,' and to define the nature of the crisis before effective organizational action can commence.

Governance beyond the Nation-State: The Garbage Can Perspective

The discussion thus far has dealt with decision-making from a garbage can perspective on policymaking in rather general terms. The utility of the approach becomes more apparent if it is applied to empirical examples of transnational governance. Some of the most obvious, and most important, examples of these dynamics can be found in the European Union. Although it is a single political entity, several different decisional processes are going on simultaneously within the EU,[55] and the informality of some emerging decisional processes represents clear movement away from simple linear and national models of governing towards styles of governing that look more like the garbage can. Within the EU two processes that best illustrate these patterns of policy making well are the open method of coordination (OMC)[56] and multi-level governance.

The OMC is a newer form of coordination and harmonization of economic policies, following the Lisbon European Council of 2000. This summit emphasized the goal of making European economies more competitive in the globalized market, but rather than using the conventional methods of harmonization, the OMC relies on more informal means such as guidelines, benchmarks, and the like. The openness of the method is, rather like the garbage can, in part one of fluid participation by the member states of the EU. Thus, rather than substituting one form of hierarchy for another, the open method is based on agreements on basic goals and then achieving those goals through uncertain technologies that are in national, regional, or even private hands.

The OMC has at once moved important elements of policymaking to the transnational level and strengthened the nation-states who are members of the European Union. On the one hand, there is an obligation to coordinate on a range of issues, including more and more social policy issues that may have an impact on employment.[57] On the other, there are a variety of means through which individual nations can elect to achieve that coordination. This method further pushes the EU in the direction of 'soft law' and a style of policy that emphasizes such garbage can features as uncertain technologies and more diffuse goals. In this mode of decision-making sovereignty is indeed complex, and therefore corresponds clearly to the complexity and indeterminacy of the process itself.

In addition to the open method of cooperation, multi-level governance (MLG) is in many ways analogous to the garbage can model. While similar to policymaking in federal political systems in that there are multiple levels of government involved in a policy area, each with some capacity for autonomous action, MLG does have some distinctive features of its own. The creation of the structural funds and other instruments for implementing regional policy has increased the prevalence of this style of decision-making, with decisions that involve all levels of government. Having no formal constitutional arrangements that specify the powers and responsibilities of the actors involved, multi-level governance establishes an indeterminate decisional situation, again with somewhat fluid participation and an unclear mechanism for establishing priorities. That indeterminate character of the decisional situations created by multi-level governance, in turn, creates situations for garbage can decision-making.

In particular, as Marks and his associates put it, multi-level governance in the European Union is described by structures in which 'political arenas are interconnected rather than nested ... Sub-national actors ... operate in both national and supranational arenas, creating transnational associations in the process. States do not monopolize links between domestic and European actors, but are one among a variety of actors contesting decisions that are made at a variety of levels ... The separation between domestic and international politics, which lies at the heart of the state-centric model [of EU governance], is rejected by the multi-level governance model.'[58]

In such a diffuse and unstructured situation, those actors who have the clearest preferences and the greatest capacities to present solutions are likely to be the most successful players, just as has been argued in the garbage can literature. For example, Smith[59] found that multi-level governance in France actually strengthened the central state, rather than diffusing its power, in large part because the state can mediate in conflicts between localities and provide the continuing contacts with Brussels that the commission needs for its own political purposes. Indeed, it is generally central state agents, the prefects, who play a major role in these negotiations and in maintaining relationships.[60]

Following from the above, as I have argued elsewhere, multi-level governance may constitute a 'Faustian bargain' for sub-national governments and also for diffuse interests in the European Union.[61] That is, while these governance arrangements appear open and conducive to the influence of less powerful actors, their very unstructured nature makes them in fact friendlier to more powerful interests, whether they be bureaucratic actors within the European Union, national governments, or organized capital interests seeking favourable regulatory treatment. The exact nature of the impact may vary by policy area and by interest, but the general pattern will be maintained.[62]

The above discussion has focused on the European Union, but some of the same logic would almost certainly apply in other international governance arrangements. Organizations such as the World Trade Organization appear to provide a locus in which clearly defined preferences backed with power will prevail, even if the model is meant, perhaps, to be more inclusive and bargaining. Likewise, international regimes that are less clearly defined will provide the locus for control by the more organized who can 'keynote' and define the issues and set an agenda, as opposed to the more diffuse and less organized who might have hoped for some opportunities for exerting greater influence.

Paradoxes in the Garbage Can

The seemingly irrational and disorderly assumptions characteristic of the garbage can model, and to some extent much of the 'new governance' literature, masks more determinate patterns of policymaking that belie the seemingly unstructured, chaotic pattern of making decisions. The 'Faustian bargain' that is implied in multi-level governance and many of the same normative and empirical questions appear to exist within models of governance more generally, and within the garbage can conception explored in this chapter. The loose structure and seemingly participatory nature of the arrangements within the garbage can hide rather effectively the exercise of power and the ability of a limited number of actors to shape outcomes.

The most fundamental paradox is that a system of governance that is assumed to be (and in the case of multi-level governance is designed to be) open, inclusive, and indeterminate may be more determined by power than may be the case in more structured systems. From an agenda-setting perspective, issues that are appropriately formulated, that is, ones that match some of the preconceptions of individuals and organizations charged with making decisions, are more likely to be successful than are less clearly defined issues and ideas. As Heimer and Stinchcombe have argued, pressing an issue that is not formulated 'appropriately' for a decisional situation may be dismissed simply as complaining, and the outcome may be quite the opposite of that which was intended.[63] Framing issues such as the European Employment Strategy in a clearly European and competition-enhancing manner has helped to legitimate the variety of actors that are involved at the national and transnational levels.

The garbage can model may place an even greater emphasis on agenda setting than do other varieties of decision-making. Given that the garbage can depends upon a confluence of streams, and the emergence of opportunities for action, one may not expect a great deal of ex ante preparation of issues by public sector actors. Much the same absence of planning of decisions can be assumed of networks that reside at the heart of a great deal of governance thinking in contemporary academia, as well as among active participants in the process of governance.[64] The absence of authority at the heart of this model makes the emergence of issues more uncertain than might be the case in more routinized and regulated structures for decision-making.

If we consider the remainder of the policy process, some of the same dominance of actors who are well integrated into that process and who can exercise some form of power within the process, also can be observed. Governance ideas, and especially the garbage can conception of governance used in this chapter, imply more loosely structured, indeterminate, and uncertain processes of steering society than is characteristic of traditional hierarchical forms of governing. However, as at the agenda-setting stage, the policy-formulation stage of the process may be dominated by actors who have clear ideas and who are able to put those ideas into operational forms. Perhaps most obviously, bureaucratic organizations are accustomed to translating their conceptions into policies and so are likely to be major players when there are fewer hierarchical constraints.

A significant source of the advantage for more powerful actors is the general absence of legal frameworks within which the garbage can functions. Formal rules, and especially constitutional rules, are mechanisms for ensuring access and protecting minority rights in the decision-making process. Part of the logic of the garbage can model is that there are few formalized rules governing the interaction of the actors, and the actors themselves make most of the decisions about their involvement. Further, the governance literature tends to de-emphasize formal rules in favour of negotiation, networking, and bargaining. Although those terms are neutral and appear benign, more powerful actors tend to be more effective in all of these processes, everything else being equal.

Having an answer to the policy problem and having clear preferences also tend to favour the more powerful actors in the decision-making process. As noted above, the advantage of having clearly defined preferences is enhanced when there are fewer rules and formalized procedures. In such a decision-making system it may not be the societal actors who might have been advantaged by a shift towards a governance model, but rather it may be bureaucracies and other formal institutions that are able to prosper in that setting. Thus, the garbage can may be a natural locus for bureaucratic politics[65] rather than the locus for more open and effective participation by societal actors – the presumed winners in governance. This is, of course, exactly the opposite of the expected outcomes of a model of decision-making that appears as loosely structured as this one does.

Although my own research experience leads me to focus on the role of bureaucracies in governance within the garbage can perspective, other formal institutions may share similar advantages in this type of process. For example, in transnational politics, organizations such as the World Bank that have clear and relatively consistent preferences are likely to be able to prevail over individual countries or non-governmental actors that have less coherent plans of action.[66] Even less clearly defined groups such the G-8, may also be able to prevail because of their capacity to develop relatively clear and unified preferences and strategies within the context of poorly structured processes of making decisions.

Another component of the advantage for bureaucracies and other institutional actors in a governance or garbage can situation is the control of information. Management scientists who have used the garbage can model to understand organizational processes have found that control of information is crucial to controlling the decisions of those organizations.[67] We should expect that bureaucracies would gain a substantial advantage here over societal actors, despite the attempt of those actors to enhance their capacity to provide alternatives to official views of policy or even the actions of governments to create paid interveners and other information alternatives.[68] Information is crucial in all decisional processes, but its power may be enhanced when the process is itself poorly defined, and the problems become defined along with the solutions. All the above having been said, however, changing information technologies gives actors who once might have been at a severe disadvantage greater capacity to participate, which to some extent strengthens the fluidity of participation in the model and thereby creates more indeterminacy.

Conclusion

This chapter has been an exploration of whether the concept of the garbage can, developed as a means of understanding behaviour in organizations, can be used to understand contemporary governance more generally. The principal reason for pursuing this concept is that the apparent decline in the authority of the state has produced conditions analogous to conditions that were presumed to exist in 'organized anarchies' within organizations. Indeed, the analogies between these two decisional situations are sufficiently striking to suggest the usefulness of the garbage can as an image for understanding contemporary governance. Particularly suggestive are the declining level of structure in the manner in which demands are being made on government and the apparently greater difficulty in making decisions within government.

By looking at the process of governing as analogous to the garbage can model of organizational decision-making we can begin to understand better the implications of changes in the capacity of governments to impose their programs through authority-based mechanisms. In particular, the uncertainty of technology and the difficulty in making preferences coherent, given the increased variety of participants in the process, may help to explain the difficulties many governments now encounter when making decisions. Governance is a game that many people and organizations get to play, and such wider participation combined with some uncertainty about the rules make outcomes less predictable. These same characteristics of policy processes may be found in international settings where multiple sovereignties exist and interact.

Perhaps the most important outcome of this analysis is that the rather benign assumptions of much of the governance literature may disguise some less open and democratic implications of the concept, a point that intersects with the one underlined in the chapters herein by Greven and Eberlein and Grande. While governance implies wider participation, the analogy with the garbage can would lead us to expect power to be as important or even more important than in state-centric conceptions of governing. The role of political and institutional power may be especially pronounced when governments are forced to think and act horizontally and to attempt to create more coherent patterns of governing. Integration across issue domains may be achievable only through the use of some form of power, whether derived from expertise or position. If governing is providing a relatively coherent set of priorities to society, then governance may find power not lessened but only redefined.

NOTES

1 This chapter draws on a larger project done in collaboration with Jon Pierre, University of Gothenberg, Sweden. As I worked through revisions, I realized that I was to a great extent returning to the dominant themes from one of my first books, *Can Government Go Bankrupt?*, which was written with Richard Rose and published in 1978. That book and this chapter both deal with the authority of governments and their capacity to govern. Dror (2001) has provided a very detailed analysis of governance capacity, but much of that analysis actually comes down to the presence of legitimacy for the governing system and the capacity to use steering instruments effectively to reach desired collective goals. The issues raised in this chapter are concentrated primarily on governance questions at the level of central governments and multi-level interactions, but much of the same logic is relevant to issues of sovereignty and authority at the international level.

2 The use of the word *appropriate* here is deliberate, representing the influence of the 'logic of appropriateness' as a basis of institutions. See March and Olsen (1989).

3 Salamon (2002b).
4 Campbell and Pedersen (2001).
5 For a rather extreme view, see Pierson (1994); for a more tempered view, see Fawcett (2002).
6 Salamon (2002a), Peters and Van Nispen (1998).
7 For a more sceptical conception of the tools approach to governance, see Ringeling (2002).
8 Hood (1986).
9 Norris (1996), Dogan (1999).
10 Bok (1997).
11 Holmberg and Weibull (1998), Ministry of Finance, Denmark (1998).
12 Phidd and Doern (1978), Woodside (1992).
13 The decline of public confidence in the United States, for example, is tracked by the American Customer Satisfaction Index Project at the University of Michigan Business School. See http://www.theacsi.org/
14 See, e.g., the European Union 'White Paper on Governance' (2001) and the wide range of responses to that paper.
15 If we do posit the need for steering, then the governance literature does have some element of functionalism. Steering becomes, in essence, a functional prerequisite for a society, with the question then becoming how to fulfil that prerequisite. See Peters (2002).
16 Hirst (1999, 2000).
17 Rhodes (1996, 2000).
18 These ideas are, of course, derived in large part from the work of sociologists such as Niklas Luhmann. See Luhmann (1995) and Mathias Albert's chapter in this volume.
19 Bozeman (1987).
20 Kooiman (1993).
21 Schmitter (1974), Olsen (1978), Wiarda (1997).
22 Morçöl (1996).
23 Sabatier (1988).
24 In Weber's terminology these simplistic problems and products of government are 'mass goods'; Mintzberg speaks of the 'machine bureaucracy.'
25 Peters (2002).
26 These rationalist assumptions are perhaps clearest in the international relations literature that has focused on the state as a unitary actor pursuing its goals – Allison's rational actor model. Even in the domestic politics literature, however, there is sometimes a tendency to anthropomorphize the state.
27 Cohen, March, and Olsen (1972).

28 March and Olsen (1976).
29 Olsen (2001). See also Richardson (2001) for a brief application of some of these ideas to the European Union, focusing on the loosely structured nature of the process through which decisions are made. That is, although there is a process that generates decisions, the multiple actors, the variety of interests, and the absence of integrating actors such as political parties make the processes within the EU less capable of management (especially by political leaders) than analogous processes within national governments.
30 Hood (2000).
31 Simon (1947), March and Simon (1958), Cyert and March (1963), Bauer and Gergen (1968).
32 Jones (2001).
33 Bendor, Moe, and Shotts (2001: 174).
34 See, e.g., Crozier (1979).
35 Scharpf (1997a).
36 Sbragia (2002).
37 Cyert and March (1963).
38 Peters (2001).
39 Pierre (1997).
40 Nelson (1968).
41 Nelson (1968) contrasted the success of government in getting a man on the moon with the lack of success in dealing with the social problems of the ghetto. The former involved using a known, if highly complex, technology, while the latter task could use no known technology and hence was a much more challenging task for government. See also Moynihan (1973).
42 Kickert, Klijn, and Koopenjan (1997).
43 Schmitter (1974), Rokkan (1976).
44 Jones (1982).
45 Tarrow (1998).
46 Dalton and Wattenberg (2000).
47 For a discussion of the differences between success from policy and political perspectives, see Bovens, Hart, and Peters (2001).
48 More continuous participation in decision-making may, it could be argued, tend to make preferences more consistent across the system. For one thing, the need to continue to participate in what is an iterative game may force actors to moderate their views and to cooperate more.
49 Sorenson (1997).
50 Nurmi (1998).
51 Kingdon (1995).

52 More accurately, there may have been a period in which reformers believed that they could transform complex and often chaotic systems of governing into more rational, planned systems. The captivation of reformers with techniques such as a planning, programming, and budgeting system (PPBS) and indicative planning were examples of the pursuit for rationality and efficiency.

53 Devices such as performance management that are central to contemporary management reforms are more akin to incremental solutions of trial and error than they are to rational planning systems. See Bouckaert (1995).

54 Padgett (1980).

55 Wallace and Wallace (2000).

56 Hodson and Maher (2001).

57 Ferrara, Matsanganis, and Sacchi (2002), de la Porte and Pochet (2004).

58 Marks, Hooghe, and Blank (1996: 346–7).

59 Smith (1997).

60 Balme and Jouve (1996).

61 Peters and Pierre (2001); Pollack (1997).

62 Scharpf (1997b).

63 Heimer and Stinchcombe (1999).

64 One obvious case is the Governance White Paper, European Union (2001).

65 I have made the similar argument that the European Union and its governance arrangements tend to become bureaucratic politics in the face of the need to steer in a complex and largely unstructured situation. See Peters (1992) and Peters and Pierre (2001).

66 Their control of financial resources is, of course, also crucial here, but we should not dismiss the importance of structure and clear preferences in gaining control of decisional situations.

67 Padgett (1980).

68 See Gormley (1983).

5 Globality and Transnational Policy-making in Agriculture: Complexity, Contradictions, and Conflict

WILLIAM D. COLEMAN

States and other collective actors are seeking to reconstitute political authority in the twenty-first century, in part to regulate an ongoing series of globalizing processes. These processes are adding to the spread of globality, a consciousness that the world is one place. Such attempts to reconstitute authority require states to cooperate with one another in ever increasing ways, a process favouring what is called in this book the transnational cooperation state. The global scope of such cooperation, its regularity, level of institutionalization, and frequency have all contributed to the growth of densely networked transnational policy spaces on an unprecedented scale.

Policies on agriculture and food may not first come to mind as candidates for transnational policymaking. The cultivation of plants and the husbandry of animals are activities firmly rooted in physical places, sculpting landscapes that themselves become central components of local and regional cultures. Similarly, the preparation and presentation of food are deeply tied to local ways of life and become cherished components of many local, regional, and national cultures. Nonetheless, basic agricultural commodities have long been traded. Advances in transportation, storage, and communications technologies, when coupled with advances in food processing and preservation, have permitted a rapid rise in the trade of prepared and processed foods over the past three decades. As a consequence, local ways of preparing foods and the foods themselves have shifted to accommodate and to indigenize foods from other places around the globe. This movement of plant and animal products has increased the likelihood of the spread of animal diseases and of unsuspected toxins and allergens in processed foods. Finally, the development of genetic engineering has permitted the transfer of basic information codes of living matter not only across physical space, but also from one species to another. Together these and other developments have pushed states to cooperate with one another on an ever increasing number of agricultural and food policies.

The emergence of a transnational policy space governing agriculture and food, however, has not led to orderly policymaking or the shared understandings necessary for regime formation at the global level. As the concluding chapter of this book emphasizes, there are serious obstacles to transnational cooperation that reduce the likelihood of effective governance. Certainly, this particular policy space features intense political conflict on an increasing number of fronts. In the absence of fixed boundaries based on territory, a ready division of internal and external sovereignty, and a state apparatus to exercise that sovereignty while controlling these boundaries, transnational policy-making may be bound to lose some of the predictable, ordered character of policymaking that can be found at the nation-state level and in some regional political arrangements like the European Union.

To develop this argument, I begin with some thoughts on the implications of globalization theory for understanding transnational policy-making. I argue that this theory highlights the likelihood of a shifting, unpredictable, and disorderly policy space. I then reflect on these theoretical points by describing the development of a transnational policy space in agriculture. I show that this space had largely taken form by the beginning of the Uruguay Round (UR) negotiations in the mid-1980s. I then demonstrate that the conclusion of these negotiations, in tandem with the entry of genetic engineering into the transnational agricultural policy space in the 1990s, not only globalized the space further, but added considerably to its complexity, its contradictions, and its conflict. I conclude the chapter with some preliminary thoughts on the problems of transnational cooperation and their implications for global governance.

Globalization Theory and Transnational Policymaking

I use the concept of a 'transnational policy space' in this chapter for several reasons. I begin by accepting that the concept of globalization and its companion term *globality* are helpful for understanding the contemporary context in which public policy is made. When the many definitions of globalization are surveyed, some common properties become evident. First, although globalization theorists differ on whether globalization marks a distinct rupture in modernity, they do agree that the separation of space from place is a basic characteristic of modernity that continues but in accentuated form under globalizing processes. Giddens writes: 'The advent of modernity increasingly tears space away from place by fostering relations between "absent" others, locationally distant from any given situation of face-to-face interaction ... What structures the locale is not simply that what is present on the scene; the "visible form" of the local conceals the distanciated relations which determine its nature.'[1] Spaces in this sense are 'products'[2]; they are created through particular kinds of 'work,' in this case, policymaking work. Spaces also contain 'locations' or 'places' where people live and work.

It is important to note that *transnational* and *global* refer to different spaces. Transnational refers to spaces that cross extant territorial boundaries but may be limited to particular regions, the EU being the foremost example. Global, by contrast, denotes a space that operates on a worldwide scale. Transnational spaces therefore can be regional or global. This chapter examines the governance of agriculture and food to illustrate an example of a global transnational space.

Second, individuals and organizations in these spaces are increasingly highly interconnected in complex ways. Some, particularly world systems theorists, see this phenomenon to be a long-standing historical development. Others, like Tomlinson, accept this position but argue that new information and communication technologies have created a kind of 'tipping point' where this connectivity takes on exceptional density and global extensity.[3] Both groups do agree, however, that these connections create a measure of interdependence in social relations that is unprecedented in history. The combination of connectivity and interdependence, with the separation of space from place, also leads scholars to emphasize the supraterritorial or transboundary character of many of these social relationships.[4] For these reasons as well, globalization scholars often use the metaphor of 'flows' of capital, ideas, cultural forms, information, and peoples to describe these social relationships.[5] The concept of a *flow* speaks to the idea of movement unconstrained by usual borders.

The state of living and experiencing globalizing processes is often described as *globality*. Robertson has emphasized that this state is one of being increasingly conscious of the world as one, as 'unicity.'[6] What happens in one part of the world is more likely over time to have an impact on other parts of the world. Appadurai elaborates on this point by suggesting that such globality creates new possibilities for the social imagination; in fact, social imagination becomes a social practice and a key component of agency under globalizing conditions.[7] All these things said, seeing the world as one place does not mean that there is less conflict. To the contrary, Robertson emphasizes that it brings 'an exacerbation of collisions between civilizational, societal and communal narratives.'[8]

Using the concepts of globalization and globality to understand transnational policymaking has important implications for epistemology. Sociologists such as Robertson, Albrow, and Beck[9] and anthropologists such as Tsing and Geertz[10] have noted that many of the core concepts we use in the social sciences – nation, state, identity, border, citizenship, society – were developed in a time when nation-state borders 'contained' most of the relevant activity in politics and policymaking. They suggest that these concepts must be questioned, and perhaps supplemented or replaced, if we wish to understand well social relationships and social actors in the contemporary era. Both Beck's call for a 'cosmopolitan methodology'[11] and Robertson's suggestion of looking at a 'global field' are helpful here. Beck notes the decoupling of space and politics and the differentiation between sovereignty and autonomy.[12] In referring to the growth of a 'transnational state,' he points to the need to act transnationally to realize relevant outputs. In this respect, states give up autonomy in order to retain and even expand sovereignty.

Robertson speaks of a global field that includes individuals or 'selves,' nation-states, the system of states, and humanity. What has developed over time, he suggests, is the gradual differentiation of each of these poles from the other, such that each has its own dynamic. For example, the individual or self comes to define an identity in reference to being a citizen of a nation-state, a world citizen of a system of states, and a human being with something in common such as rights with all other human beings. For Robertson, then, the traditional concepts of social science must be used in conscious relation to one another as part of the 'global field,' all the while recognizing that differences and consciousness of difference are multiplying apace.

The choice of the word *space* coincides with the epistemological position that borders and boundaries are variable and are being created and recreated in response to globalizing processes. This space is transnational because states have come to act more and more in coordinated ways where they yield autonomy and pool sovereignty in order to achieve policy objectives. In Chapter 1, Grande and Pauly refer to this phenomenon as the 'transnational cooperation state,' while Cox refers to the 'internationalization of the state.'[13] Cox refers to the emergence of a 'complex political structure' that is the counterpart to economic globalization. He adds that this structure 'appears to be more evolved, more definitive in some of its parts; less formed, more fluid in others; and the connections between the parts are more stable in some cases and more tenuous in others.'[14] We can anticipate as well that the states participating in the space will vary in their willingness and capacity to pool sovereignty, as Grande and Pauly argue in the concluding chapter. Finally, not only states 'act' in this transnational space, but also transnational economic actors participating in an increasingly integrated, global capitalist economy and transnational social movements and interest organizations comprising a global civil society.[15]

In choosing to use the concept of a transnational policy space, I continue to stress, however, the importance of places and specific sites of power. What is changing, perhaps, is the multiplication of these sites. Moreover, actions in one place are not necessarily coordinated or consistent with actions in another. In fact, they may contradict one another. Complex connectivity and high interdependence associated with globalization mean that, as Dirlik argues, we are in a situation 'where place-based differences ... are incorporated into the very process of globalization, abolishing the boundary between the external and the internal, bringing differences into the interior of the process of globalization, and presenting the global with all the contradictions of the local.'[16] As Tsing cautions, we must avoid making distinctions between global 'forces' and local 'places.'[17] Processes of 'place-making' and 'force-making' are both local and global.

Finally, I accept the methodological advice of many of these scholars who suggest that we come to understand globalization by beginning with specific problems. In particular, I focus on bids for power evident in the micro-level politics of agricultural trade. In the concluding chapter of this book, Grande and Pauly suggest that politics at this level provides significant scope for transnational policymaking. Efforts to agree on multilateral rules for trade in agricultural commodities and foods, particularly as they involve biotechnology, highlight growing transnational cooperation and the increasing complexity of sovereignty, on the one side, and the obstacles to reconfiguring authority, on the other.

Drawing from Held et al.,[18] we can begin to assess the degree to which globalizing processes produce new global transnational spaces by observing shifts in *extensity*, the degree to which cultural, political, and economic activities are 'stretching' across new frontiers to encompass the 'world'; *intensity*, changes in the magnitude and regularity of interconnectedness; and *velocity*, changes in the speed of global interactions and processes. Shifts along these dimensions should lead to increasing *enmeshment*, that is, the level of interdependence of the global and the local.[19] In charting the contours of such a space, we must keep in mind that nodes of power congealed in institutions give structure to flows. The contours of the space and the locations where such institutions are constructed and activated are strongly influenced by coalitions of actors, some private and some public.[20]

Towards a Global Transnational Policy Space, 1947–1986

In the immediate postwar period, there was very little transnational policy space for agriculture. Although international agreements such as the General Agreement on Tariffs and Trade (GATT) existed, they were full of exemptions for agriculture, permitting national policymakers to construct policies tailored to domestic political needs only. Relatively closed, often corporatist, policy networks provided the forum for the design and implementation of these policies. Over the course of the three decades following the signing of the GATT, more extensive and intensive contacts developed between national policymakers, providing the basis for creating a nascent transnational policy space largely limited to developed countries in the Organization for Economic Cooperation and Development (OECD). These contacts accelerated in the late 1970s and early 1980s, in particular, when the effects of crises in domestic agricultural economies spilled into the international trading system. In beginning to frame a policy response to the crisis, policymakers drew another set of actors into the space, a nascent transnational epistemic community anchored in the discipline of agricultural economics. The knowledge produced in this epistemic community facilitated the growth of ever more extensive and intense global contacts among policymakers in the sector. Accordingly, by the mid-1980s, agriculture had reached a position of thin globality, where policymakers, farm organizations and agribusiness had a deeper consciousness of transworld agriculture.

From Protectionist National Policy Communities to Crisis

Two clauses in the 1947 GATT reinforced strong boundaries associated with national autarky in agriculture. Article XI called for the elimination of quantitative restrictions on imports, but permitted such restrictions for agriculture when they were needed either to enforce governmental measures that limited quantities produced or 'remove a temporary surplus of the like domestic product.' Although this derogation was inspired, in part, by section 22 of the U.S. Agricultural Adjustment Act, it was also inconsistent with the U.S. law. Section 22 permitted the use of import quotas even when there were *no* controls on production. Concerned with this inconsistency, farmers' advocates in the U.S. Congress succeeded in securing the primacy of domestic over international rules by amending the Agricultural Adjustment Act in 1951. The revised legislation stipulated that no trade agreement or other international agreement could be applied in a manner inconsistent with section 22. The Congress went on to impose import quotas on a host of products where there were no supply controls. This violation of GATT rules precipitated a struggle with President Truman and the GATT. The Congress emerged triumphant in this dispute in 1955, when the United States secured a broad waiver, with no time limit, from its obligations under article XI.

As Josling, Tangermann, and Warley observe, the waiver had a 'chilling effect on international trade policy.'[21] They note that 'at a crucial moment in the development of the Agreement, the United States gave primacy to its national agricultural interests over its international trade obligations.'[22] The combination of this waiver and of very few tariffs being bound in agriculture left the door wide open for other states to reinforce the borders around their agricultural economies. For example, the European Economic Community (EEC) was able to set up its autarkic Common Agricultural Policy (CAP) with variable import levies.

The second important derogation from international trade discipline in agriculture came in article XVI (section B) of the GATT, which prohibited export subsidies for manufactured goods, but made an exception for agricultural and other primary products. In 1955 article XVI was amended to read that export subsidies were not to be used to gain 'more than an equitable share of world export trade.' The meaning of the term *an equitable share* was to remain very vague in the ensuing years. When prompted in 1958, the United States refused to accept a total ban on export subsidies in agriculture. Accordingly, when the Common Agricultural Policy was conceived in the 1960s, export subsidies or 'restitutions' joined variable levies as key policy instruments for protecting the common market in agriculture in the EEC.

Under these conditions, agricultural policymaking took place overwhelmingly within states. Various producer organizations also participated through corporatist arrangements in most western European countries, Japan, and Australia. Peak associations representing agricultural producers participated directly in the policy formulation process, and more specialized commodity groups usually worked with public officials in implementing policy. Relations between producers and politicians were more pluralist in the United States, but an 'iron triangle' involving informal coalitions of producers, the U.S. Department of Agriculture (USDA), and the agriculture committees of the Congress tended to control the policy process.[23] More open pluralism was characteristic of general farm policymaking in Canada, but corporatism also featured in selected sectors where production of commodities was 'managed.'[24]

These domestic policymaking boundaries, created under the legal exceptions in the GATT regime, came under increased economic and political pressure during the 1970s and early 1980s, as problems in international agricultural markets fostered expensive pathologies in implementing domestic policies. Grain prices often trigger wider economic changes in agriculture, because they are an input not only for the direct production of human food, but also for raising livestock, whether in the meat or the dairy sectors. At the beginning of the 1970s, grain prices rose as supplies became tight. This combination of economic conditions led to increased trade in agricultural commodities. Supplies rose in the middle of the decade, triggering a decline in prices, only to become short again as the decade ended. Governments increased price supports to encourage production – a step that led, in turn, to falling international prices and rising production surpluses.

This production cycle had several unfortunate consequences. The combination of a growing surplus in the European Community (EC), and an appreciating U.S. dollar, allowed the EC to use export subsidies to dislodge U.S. grain companies from some traditional markets, particularly in the developing world. Consequently, U.S. stocks rose quickly, making the cost of agricultural policies more onerous for domestic consumers and taxpayers. In addition, many economists and finance ministers began to argue that the rising fiscal outlays to the agricultural sector represented a misallocation of resources that undermined overall economic growth. Washington responded to these circumstances by introducing the Export Enhancement Program (EEP), a new set of export subsidies designed to recapture market share from the EC. The resulting trade war was not only costly to citizens in both the United States and Europe, but also to other grain-exporting countries that were caught in a low price squeeze precipitated by the export subsidies. By 1986, wheat prices had fallen to one-third of their 1974 value.[25] Farmers in Australia, Canada, and the United States were facing financial difficulties as a result of the high interest rates they were paying on the large loans they had taken out to expand production in the late 1970s and early 1980s. Politically, it gradually became clear that domestic policy problems would require some international policy coordination, if the economic situation were to be stabilized.

An Agricultural Economics Epistemic Community

In company with the increased levels of conflict over removing obstacles to the trade of agricultural commodities, flows in the production of knowledge about agricultural trade were taking on more of a transnational form. Agricultural economics provides the knowledge base for the epistemic community most relevant to agricultural policy. Historically, this discipline had existed outside mainstream economics, often housed within faculties or colleges of agriculture, themselves closely linked to agricultural producers in their particular locale. These local ties helped give the discipline a broader, more interdisciplinary character, and more applied orientation than economics per se. Gradually, in the United States and in the Anglo-American countries, however, these characteristics changed over the postwar period as agricultural economics took on the neo-classical, mathematical, and more quantitative orientation of standard economics.

This shift in research ethic provided the basis for the development of a transnational policy evaluation framework that could be shared between agricultural economists in the academic world, agricultural economists and mainstream economists in official bureaucracies, advisory councils and semi-public think-tanks, and even economists employed by some producers' interest groups. Further institutionalization of a transnational epistemic community came in June 1980 with the formation of the International Agricultural Trade Research Consortium (IATRC), an informal association of government and university economists interested in agricultural trade. The growth in discussions around this expanding body of knowledge added to the extensity, intensity, and velocity of relationships in this transnational policy space.

Accordingly, in company with the nascent globalization of a knowledge framework for policy evaluation, a framework that shared important elements with globalist, neo-liberal frameworks in other policy areas, the sites for agricultural policymaking became more transnational, albeit still largely confined to developed countries. Two distinct, but clearly linked, intergovernmental organizations provided the environment for this change in policymaking: the OECD and the GATT, with the agricultural economics epistemic community featuring prominently in the proceedings of both. Perhaps its most crucial contributions came first in the provision of mathematical models that showed the gains to be reaped by all countries, developed and developing, from trade liberalization. Second, the epistemic community endorsed and placed on the table a new measure of level of protection originally proposed by Timothy Josling at a meeting of the Food and Agriculture Organization (FAO) of the United Nations in 1973. The so-called production subsidy equivalent permitted participants in the policy community to lift policy measures out of their highly specific national contexts and place them on a common scale of 'trade-distorting' protectionism. The simple introduction and acceptance of this instrument increased globality by opening the door to seeing better the 'distortions' in world markets.

In summary, by 1986, a transnational policy space had formed, and it was increasingly extensive in its global reach. Interactions in the space had become more regularized and institutionalized, providing an element of institutional stability. The velocity of interactions had increased significantly, as meetings became more frequent, both in global and regional policy forums. The density of the networks and the flows of expert knowledge had risen dramatically, and these became more stable as they were drawn into the OECD and the GATT. Consequently, local agricultural practices and global policymaking were significantly more enmeshed than they had been a short two decades before.

New Flows and Shifting Boundaries since 1986

Transnational policy spaces functioning under conditions of increasing globalization differ from national policy spaces. There is no state exercising some control over flows within a specific territory, the increased complexity of internal and external sovereignty key to managing these flows means authority is more shared and dispersed, and boundaries are no longer necessarily fixed. As Grande reminds us, space is now defined functionally rather than territorially.[26] Of course, boundaries continue to exist, but they are porous, open to new flows as interconnections between actors and sites of power are formed and reformed. Moreover, these boundaries are impossible to control as the dialectics of globalizing processes create new social relationships, reconstruct identities, and create new sites of power – while diminishing others. Accordingly, ever increasing globality, as reflected in higher levels of extensity, intensity, and velocity in social and political relationships, may add to the instability and conflict in policymaking.

These very tentative hypotheses gain some credibility when examined in the light of developments in the transnational policy space in agriculture since 1986. In the following section, I analyse briefly two changes to the space that have stimulated these hypotheses: the institutionalization of policymaking at the World Trade Organization (WTO) and the entry of agricultural biotechnology into the space in the 1990s.

The World Trade Organization and Policymaking in Agriculture

The Agreement on Agriculture from the Uruguay Round of trade negotiations added to the extensity, intensity, and velocity of social relationships in the transnational policy space, perhaps most notably by strengthening connections with developing countries. The negotiation of the agreement was protracted, politically explosive at times, and ultimately dependent on the reform of the Common Agricultural Policy.[27] The final accord focused on three areas – market access, domestic support measures, and the use of export subsidies. Article 17 of the Agreement on Agriculture made provision for the establishment of a Committee on Agriculture at the World Trade Organization, while Article 18 laid out its responsibilities. The committee was to review the progress of member states in the implementation of commitments negotiated under the Uruguay Round reform program. Members were also enjoined to notify the committee of any new domestic support policy, or of a modification an existing policy, for which an exemption from the agreement was to be claimed. Finally, members were to be given the opportunity to raise any matter relevant to implementation of commitments under the reform program, or to bring to the attention of members any policy of another member that was thought to require committee notification.

Sanitary and phytosanitary matters are covered by a separate Agreement on the Application of Sanitary and Phytosanitary (SPS) Measures that sets out a series of core norms and principles for their development. Parallel to the agriculture agreement, there is also an SPS Committee, which has similar responsibilities for monitoring the implementation of policy. The preamble of the SPS Agreement notes the advisability of harmonized SPS measures based on international standards. Three pre-existing international organizations – the Codex Alimentarius Commission (CAC), the Office International des Epizooties (OIE), and the International Plant Protection Convention (IPPC) – were written into the agreement as recognized standard-setting bodies. The addition of these three sites of authority wove new ties into the policy space between makers of trade policy, on the one side and formerly rather autonomous groupings of food scientists, veterinarians, and plant biologists and entomologists, on the other.

The increased institutionalization of agricultural policymaking at the WTO signals a 'thickening' of globality in agriculture. The creation of active committees on agriculture and SPS increased the *extensity* of global relations. In setting up committees open to all 128 members of the WTO, the international policy forum for agricultural trade policy expanded well beyond the OECD and the more elite groupings of the GATT that had dominated the arena prior to the Uruguay Round. With the committees meeting four times per year at a minimum and with the additional interchanges taking place in preparation for the next set of negotiations, the *intensity* of political connections between states rose significantly. With the more extensive use of the Internet by many governments and at the WTO, the *velocity* of interchange has also increased sharply.

Finally, the committee's activities signal an increasing *enmeshment* of local agricultural policies with the new global arrangements. On the one side, new domestic policies and amendments to existing policies must all be designed with WTO rules and policy in mind. On the other side, what happens locally becomes of ever more interest globally. In this respect, the WTO rules have become increasingly internalized in domestic policy-making circles. The former chair of the Agriculture Committee, Nestor Osorio Londoño, captured this idea of enmeshment and the resulting globality in a speech to the IATRC in December 1997. 'As a result, implementation has generally become a more open, "hands-on" process. What goes on in your domestic backyard is increasingly a matter of legitimate interest to your fellow WTO members.'[28] Londoño added 'The basic idea was to enable WTO members to keep a "collective eye" on how commitments were being implemented and to exert peer group pressure at the multilateral level.'[29] Accordingly, global suasion was expected to discipline what happened locally. 'It was felt as long ago as the pre-Uruguay Round preparatory work, that a regular monitoring or review process would be useful in strengthening the hands of governments in dealing with pressure groups who, in many instances, would be unaccustomed to international constraints on domestic or trade policy options.'[30]

Two concrete examples illustrate this growing enmeshment and reflexivity of the global and the local. First, a person close to agricultural policymaking circles in India talked in 2001 about the impact of the actions of the agriculture and SPS committees in his own country.[31] He noted that initially India did not attend these meetings, primarily because the government of India had not fully appreciated the potential impacts of the agreements on domestic policy. 'It took two or three years for the fact to sink in that now there were certain principles in place which meant that India could not just do what it wanted to do.' He added that as the changes did become better known, political practices changed domestically. 'In the last two to three years, when it comes to major policy decisions, the agriculture ministry is now coordinating very closely with the trade ministry. It even has its own WTO staff, who works with the trade ministry. This coordination did not happen before.'

Moreover, domestic policy is now 'seen' differently, as the concepts in the Agreement on Agriculture become internalized by domestic officials. My interviewee illustrated this change with the following example. India has a long-standing policy to build up food stocks that might be deployed in case of famine. After a series of bountiful harvests, the accumulated stocks had reached such levels in the late 1990s that storage costs had become prohibitive. So the country proposed to sell off some of the stocks to other developing countries at a rather low price. When officials of the agriculture ministry reported on these actions to trade ministry officials, they were told that such common acts of the past were now constituted as 'export subsidies' under WTO rules. Moreover, the U.S. government had expressed its opposition to the sale at a meeting of the Agriculture Committee of GATT. My interviewer, however, concluded by noting the reflexivity in the process. In response to internalizing the WTO concepts and understanding their implications for Indian agriculture, India has become much more active in the Doha Round negotiations, either developing its own policy proposals or working more closely with other countries. Almost all observers of the latest trade discussions in agriculture comment on a significant increase in the activity of the developing countries when compared with the time before. Things are much more 'complex,' they will add, because agreement between the United States and the European Union, although still a necessary condition, is no longer a sufficient condition for an overall accord.

A second illustration of reflexivity through enmeshment comes in how states construct 'regions,' spaces larger than a nation-state, but not globally extensive. Appadurai argues that the capability to imagine regions and worlds is now itself a globalized phenomenon.[32] He adds, 'the principal challenge that faces the study of regions is that actors in different regions have elaborate interests and capabilities in constructing world pictures leading to new forms of interaction that affect global processes.'[33] In a transnational policy space, such regions may be 'non-territorial.' Speaking of non-territorial regions in the world economy, Ruggie introduces the idea of 'a decentered yet integrated space-of-flows, operating in real time, which exists alongside the space-of-places that we call national economies.'[34] Such a conception can be extended to policy flows as well. If Appadurai and Ruggie are correct, we might see some new imaginings of non-territorial regional spaces, as developing countries build on their deeper knowledge of the agriculture and SPS agreements gained in the respective WTO communities and propose new policies in the Doha Round.

The behaviour of two countries, Mauritius and Cuba, is suggestive of new imaginings of 'region.' Mauritius submitted its own proposal, joined in with an 'African Group' of thirty-nine states to submit a second, then partnered with Antigua and Barbuda, Barbados, Cuba Dominica, Grenada, Jamaica, Saint Kitts and Nevis, Saint Vincent and the Grenadines, and Trinidad and Tobago as part of a 'small island developing group,' and with Barbados, Cyprus, El Salvador, Fiji, Malta, Mexico, Saint Lucia, Singapore, and Trinidad and Tobago, the 'non-trade concerns' group. Cuba participated in the 'small island developing group' as well, but also in a 'developing country' grouping that included the Dominican Republic, El Salvador, Haiti, Honduras, India, Kenya, Nicaragua, Nigeria, Pakistan, Sri Lanka, Uganda, and Zimbabwe. No former Eastern bloc country is a member of either group, but three continents are spanned. At this stage of development, the status of these arrangements is unclear. They may be 'alliances,' commonly found in the first nation-state modernity, or they may be reflexive, new constructions of non-territorial 'regional' spaces in a transnational policy space in the second globalizing modernity. Given their formation in response to experience with the Agreement on Agriculture in the Uruguay Round and the consequences of not playing a strong role in these negotiations, I am inclined towards the latter interpretation.

Agricultural Biotechnology: Expanding the Range of Governance

Castells argues that the introduction of information and communication technologies has brought on a technological revolution as important and as fundamental as the industrial revolution in the eighteenth century.[35] Characteristic of such revolutions is their pervasiveness, that is, their penetration of all domains of human activity. At the core of the current transformation are technologies of information processing and communication. Unlike many analysts, however, Castells includes genetic engineering in this group of core technologies. He sees this activity as focused on the decoding, manipulation, and eventual reprogramming of the information codes of living matter. In this respect, genetic engineering is similar to the converging sets of technologies in microelectronics, computing, telecommunications, and optoelectronics commonly associated with the 'information technology revolution.'

The advances of biotechnology are inherently globalizing processes. Genetic engineering involves moving the information coded in a given gene or gene sequence from one living organism to another. Unlike past efforts of this kind, recombinant DNA techniques permit this transfer of information to occur outside the bounds of *place*, whether defined as physical location or as species. A gene can be removed from a living organism found in one physical location in the world and placed in another living organism that would never have had any physical contact with the first. Moreover, the species of the second organism may be completely different from that of the first. Under these conditions, genetic engineering unleashes information flows in a whole new translocal and trans-species space.

As a core technology in the information communications revolution, genetic engineering began to be studied in relation to plant and animal development in the late 1970s and early 1980s. Since that time, questions regarding the proper use and diffusion of agricultural biotechnology have gradually entered the transnational agricultural policy space along two paths. First, some fear that novel traits from genetically modified (GM) crops will escape to wild species, leading to the development of herbicide tolerant weeds or pesticide resistant insects and in the longer term, to a reduction in biological diversity. The unpredictable and perhaps irreparable nature of the effects of such gene interaction on biodiversity contributes to such unease. Second, an increasing number of individuals and organizations worry that foods with GM components may contain higher levels of toxins or allergens that may become a significant threat to human health over time.

Approvals were given for the commercialization of several GM plant varieties by the United States and Canadian governments in the early 1990s. The four most widely planted GM crops – soybeans, maize, canola, and cotton – are highly traded. In addition, the first three of these are basic components of a large number of processed foods. Soybeans and maize are also widely sold for animal feed. Concerns over biological diversity and food safety related to the international trade of GM agricultural commodities and processed foods became more pronounced in the policy space after the first GM modified soybeans entered the EU market from the United States in 1996.

The introduction of political, economic, knowledge production, and bioprospecting flows related to biotechnology has reconfigured, in turn, the transnational policy space for agriculture. These flows have fostered the creation of new networks between formerly more isolated sites of power and authority, bringing much more to the fore the contradictions between their core principles and norms. In their wake, these networks have also encouraged the active participation of new sets of transnational non-state actors, ranging from corporations to ecological and peasants' social movements.

The reconfigured policy space features four interlocking nodes of power and policy activity: trade, food security, intellectual property, and conservation and sustainability of biological diversity.[36] The following discussion highlights how the latter three nodes relate to that of international trade already described above.

Food Security

The Rome Declaration on World Food Security[37] provides a summary statement of the focus of a food security node in the policy space: 'Food security exists when all people, at all times, have physical and economic access to sufficient, safe and nutritious food to meet their dietary needs and food preferences for an active and healthy life.' The concept of food security includes both physical and economic access to sufficient food and ensuring the availability of food that is safe and nutritious. The FAO is the principal organizing site, having promoted the general principles of food security and their associated norms. It has also drawn a linkage between food security and biotechnology. In its Statement on Biotechnology issued in January 1999, the FAO recognized this technology to be a powerful tool for the sustainable development of agriculture. It noted the potential of genetic engineering for increasing productivity, whether through furnishing higher yields on marginal lands, providing healthier plant material, or improving food quality. Finally, the FAO acknowledged concerns about the potential risks to human health and the environment from biotechnological products intended for agricultural and food use. It advocated a rigorous system of risk assessment based on a 'science-based evaluation system that would objectively determine the benefits and risks of each individual [GM organism].'[38]

Four institutional families operating under the FAO umbrella have an actual or potential role as sites of authority in the international governance of agricultural biotechnology. As already noted, three of these are tied directly to the WTO: the International Plant Protection Convention, the Office International des Épizooties, and the Codex Alimentarius Commission. The fourth is the Commission on Plant Genetic Resources (CPGR) and its Global System for the Conservation and Utilization of Plant Genetic Resources. The latter constitutes a potential pole for opposition to the activities at sites of authority for intellectual property protection outlined below.

The CPGR was formed following agreement in 1983 on an International Undertaking on Plant Genetic Resources (IUPGR). The undertaking was conceived with the purpose of ensuring that plant genetic resources (PGRs) of economic and/or social interest for agriculture be explored, preserved, evaluated that and made available for plant breeding and scientific purposes. The premise such resources, belong to the public domain as 'a common heritage of mankind' and should be available without restriction anchored this agreement. The definition of PGRs in article 2 of the IUPGR is sufficiently broad to include new products of biotechnology as well as farmers' varieties and wild species. Annexes to the undertaking, adopted in 1989 and 1991, added the concept of *farmers' rights* and subjected the common heritage norm to the principle of the sovereign rights of nation-states to govern their PGRs. The 1996 Leipzig Declaration[39] on conservation and sustainable use of PGRs stressed that world food security would require integrated approaches that would combine the best of traditional knowledge of plant varieties and of plant breeding with new technologies.

Intellectual Property Protection

The rise in economic importance of plant and animal biotechnology also gave increased significance to policy questions related to intellectual property rights (IPRS) and to sites of authority for building agreement on a transnational intellectual property protection framework. Such a framework began to develop with the drafting of the Paris Convention for the Protection of Industrial Property in 1883. Including its seven revisions up until 1979, this formal agreement, along with the 1970 Patent Cooperation Treaty (PCT), sets out an international system to coordinate the granting of IPRs among states. These specific principles and norms became the responsibility of the U.N. World Intellectual Property Organization (WIPO), established in 1968, which has set up a Committee of Experts on Biotechnological Inventions and Industrial Property and a Working Group on Biotechnology to begin to frame policy proposals.

Intellectual property was tied in more directly with the trade regime with the Agreement on Trade-Related Aspects of Intellectual Property Rights (TRIPS) of the WTO. TRIPS is based on the norm that the measures adopted by contracting parties to enforce intellectual property rights should not themselves unnecessarily restrict trade. Article 8 makes provision for members to adopt measures to protect human health and nutrition consistent with the SPS Agreement. It also permits members to exclude from its twenty-year patent protection term those inventions that (among other things) are a threat to human, animal, or plant life or health. Article 27(3) allows members to exclude from patentability plants and animals (other than microorganisms) and essentially biological processes for the production of plants or animals (other than non-biological or microbiological processes). In these cases, members must provide for an effective sui generis system of protection for new plant varieties. The International Convention for the Protection of New Varieties of Plants (1961, 1972, 1978, and 1991) under the auspices of the International Union for the Protection of New Plant Varieties (UPOV) offers one alternative, so-called sui generis, framework. Presumably, any request for exclusion from patentability of a GM organism under article 27(3) based on a threat to life or health would be subject to submission of relevant scientific evidence. If accepted, the state's way is open for adoption of a legitimate SPS measure. Responsibility for overseeing the implementation of the policies rests with the Council on TRIPS, a standing committee of the WTO.

Conservation and Sustainable Use of Biological Diversity

The third additional node of political import in the policy space is built around the principles to conserve and sustainably use biological diversity as a means to ensure an environmentally sustainable world economy. The most important, legally binding agreements in this evolving policy framework that have become part of the agricultural policy space are the 1992 Convention on Biological Diversity (CBD) and the 2000 Cartagena Biosafety Protocol (BSP). The CBD set up five interrelated international institutions: the Conference of Parties (COP); the Subsidiary Body on Scientific, Technical, and Technological Advice; a Secretariat; a Financial Mechanism; and a Clearing House Mechanism. The protocol adds a Biosafety Clearing House to these institutions. The CBD establishes duties for states to conserve the biological components of the earth's ecosystems and to use genetic resources sustainably to meet food security, health, and other needs of a growing world population.[40] The protocol sets out procedures to protect states' environments from risks posed by the transboundary transport of living GM organisms, including GM agricultural commodities and seeds.

Several aspects of these agreements have become crucial parts of the transnational policy space and provide key sites for organizing against the rules embedded in the WTO. The CBD creates duties for states to prevent environmental harm within *and beyond* their jurisdictions,[41] and corresponding rights to regulate and control cross-border movements that could be environmentally harmful, including the diffusion of GM organisms.[42] In the area of intellectual property, in accordance with Article 1 states are enjoined to share the benefits arising out of the utilization of plant genetic resources, 'including by appropriate access to genetic resources and by appropriate transfer of relevant technologies [including biotechnology] ... and by appropriate funding.'[43] The special needs and environmental situations of developing countries, often centres of origin, are seen as key to ensuring equity and fairness in the sharing of the benefits of, access to, and transfer of biological resources available.[44] Besides compensation to state holders of biodiversity, parties are encouraged to distribute any gains arising from the use of PGRs and associated traditional knowledge to indigenous peoples and local farmers in recognition of their unique rights and contributions.[45]

In the face of scientific uncertainty about risks to the environment, the CBD and the protocol provide an additional counter-power to the WTO institutions by invoking the norm of precaution as a means to permit states to take regulatory action to avoid potential harm.[46] Specific applications of precaution, as incorporated in the BSP,[47] include duties placed on states to carry out impact and risk assessments of the potentially adverse effects of GM organisms on the environment and to follow Advanced Informed Agreement (AIA) procedures in their transboundary movement. Living GM organisms are not to be imported into a country without its AIA, which is independent of the risk assessment and authorization for release in the exporting country.

Global Conflict over Rules

When the principles and norms underlying these various international institutions and the ties between them are examined, it is clear that they are unlikely to coalesce into a single global governance regime.[48] The previous discussion suggests that the transnational policy space features two foci for policymaking. The first is centred on the international trade system and includes the WTO, food security organizations like the CAC and IPPC, and intellectual property rules found in TRIPS and the agreements overseen by WIPO and UPOV. The second clusters around the Convention on Biological Diversity, its associated biosafety protocol, an international undertaking revised in 2001, and the CPGR. Behind this competition lie power blocs led by the United States, the European Union, and by developing countries.

Conflict between these two nodes of governance is rampant, with three areas of incompatibility and dispute being particularly crucial:[49]

- The use of precaution or strict science-based risk analysis in determining food safety
- The flexibility of international property rights in accommodating claims for benefits from the use of plant genetic resources.
- The relationship between liberalized trading rules and trade measures adopted in pursuit of biodiversity objectives under relevant multilateral environmental agreements like the CBD

In summary, the emergent transnational policy space in agriculture has quickly come to feature a complex, if not chaotic, politics. The porous boundaries of the space undermine attempts to close off more focused and limited areas of policy where some of the arguing and truth-seeking preparatory for the agreement on principles, norms, rules, and procedures necessary for regime formation might be possible. The U.S. government has often acted as what Grande and Pauly call an 'autonomous state,' in giving priority to the WTO and its linked international organizations and in refusing to ratify the Convention on Biological Diversity. Even if the EU were to join with the United States in giving ultimate priority to the international trading system rules, it is unclear whether different groupings of developing countries would cooperate. What is more, the presence of alternative nodes of power and authority such as the CBD will continue to provide a focus for non-state actors seeking a counter-power.

Conclusion: Asymmetries of Power in the Policy Space

In their analysis of the barriers to transnational cooperation in the concluding chapter, Grande and Pauly note the importance of asymmetries in power. The functioning of the transnational policy space in agriculture illustrates some of the factors contributing to such asymmetries. First, the growing importance of expert technical knowledge disfavours some developing countries. They are willing to cooperate in transnational policymaking forums, but lack the capacity to do so. In this respect, many fall into the category of 'weak states' discussed in the concluding chapter. Expert knowledge can become an exclusionary device; only those who have the 'credentials,' who can 'talk the talk' are assumed to be relevant for policymaking. When dealing with the technical complexity involving tariff quotas for market access, measuring likely costs of export subsidies, or assessing and measuring the trade-distorting aspects of domestic programs, one needs considerable technical expertise in agricultural economics and international law. When assessing the potential impacts of genetically modified organisms on the health and safety of humans and animals, and on biological diversity in the wild, one requires considerable expertise from a range of disciplines in the physical and life sciences. The resources needed to engage such experts are not only much more readily available in developed countries, but also these countries already have a tradition of thinking and working this way. Key concepts like aggregate measure of support, risk assessment, and risk management are part of the systems of government in developed countries, but less familiar in the much more poorly resourced bureaucracies of developing countries.

The following example illustrates how this imbalance works. In the Committee on Agriculture, member states have the right to bring to the agenda issues related to the programs of other member states. That is, they might challenge whether a given program or programs actually fit the criteria laid out in the Agreement on Agriculture. To make such a challenge, a state needs not only the technical expertise in agricultural economics and trade rules to assess another state's program structure and its effects, but it must also have sufficient expert personnel that it can afford to devote its scarce resources to this task. In an interview, in June 2001, with a representative of a developing country, the interviewee said when questions are raised in the committee 'usually the respondent is a developing country, but on the front side you rarely see developing countries. Why? Is it because of the lack of resources? It's definitely not because of a lack of concern.'[50]

To assess this observation more systematically I examined all of the cases raised at the Committee on Agriculture where one country sought a review of another country's policy. The results are in Table 5.1. They confirm definitively the observation made by my interviewee. Developed countries initiated 130 of the 145 reviews, with the United States alone responsible for eighty-eight of them. Only developing countries in the Cairns Group initiated reviews, and these accounted for a paltry 10 per cent of the total. In the initial stages of the committee's activity, developed countries often interrogated other developed countries; by the last stage, the targets for reviews were primarily nation-states in the two categories of less-developed developing countries.

Table 5.1

Initiators and respondents of program reviews at the WTO's Committee on Agriculture, 1996–2000

	Developed countries N	(USA) (n)	Cairns Group developing[a]	Relatively self-sufficient[b]	NFIDC[c]
Year 2000					
Initiator	17	(8)	1	0	0
Respondent	1		2	9	6
Year 1999					
Initiator	17	(9)	0	0	0
Respondent	1		1	6	10
Year 1998					
Initiator	17	(10)	3	0	0
Respondent	7		1	8	4
Year 1997					
Initiator	46	(39)	6	0	0
Respondent	21		6	12	13
Year 1996					
Initiator	33	(22)	5	0	0
Respondent	15		9	9	5
Total Initiators	130	(88)	15	0	0
Total Respondents	45		19	44	38

[a]Developing countries in the Cairns Group include Argentina, Bolivia, Brazil, Chile, Colombia, Costa Rica, Fiji, Guatemala, Indonesia, Malaysia, Paraguay, Philippines, South Africa, Thailand, and Uruguay.
[b]Includes Panama, Korea, Turkey, Poland, Rumania, Slovak Republic, Hungary, El Salvador, and Ecuador.
[c]Net food-importing developing countries, a group composed of the 48 least-developed developing countries as recognized the UN Economic and Social Council plus Barbados, Côte d'Ivoire, Dominican Republic, Egypt, Honduras, Jamaica, Kenya, Mauritius, Morocco, Peru, Saint Lucia, Senegal, Sri Lanka, Trinidad and Tobago, Tunisia, and Venezuela.

This problem extends beyond the Agriculture Committee to the SPS Committee. A person at the WTO Secretariat who works with the SPS Committee spoke about developing countries and their role at the committee and at Codex: 'when you're trying to find really world class experts, in some countries they don't exist. And so it's very difficult to have the expertise needed. And this is a more serious problem than whether they are actually at a meeting. Can they constructively participate at a meeting?'[51] The interviewee added a related point: 'And the other concern with setting standards is even if they are there and setting standards, what happens when they are finished? You know, can they actually make use of these standards when they get back to the domestic level? That is much more problematic as well.' The permanent representative of a developing country who attended the SPS Committee threw up his hands during an interview and said, 'We're reactive. All we can do is react in an unprepared way. I have to cover five or six committees by myself. The Americans have ten persons doing what I am doing.'[52]

A second problem relates to selective cooperation by key developed states when it comes to implementing the 1994 Agreement on Agriculture. A representative from India noted that during the Uruguay Round, developed countries had promised that developing countries would gain some U.S. $600 billion worth of additional exports from the UR Agreement. This economic breakthrough has not occurred. What is more, there remains a huge disparity between the amount of money spent by the United States and the European Union on support for farmers and that spent by developing countries. From the point of view of developing countries, the United States and the EU countries are acting like 'autonomous' states when it comes to the spirit of the Agreement on Agriculture. As an interviewee from another developing country said, this financial support creates a 'production crisis' in many Global South countries. With the arrival of subsidized commodities or processed foods from developed countries, the 'likelihood of a farmer producing what he does now goes down and more widely the production of the broader agriculture sector goes down and thus the chances of further investment in this sector get reduced. These kinds of trade-distorting policies are impacting on domestic production systems in countries.' Speaking of India, another respondent noted that 700 million of India's 900 million people are dependent on the agricultural sector. 'If trade impacts negatively on the livelihood of this huge population dependent on the sector without providing appropriate safety nets, then it's a major threat.'

Third, both of these contributors to asymmetries of power – lack of technical expertise and the actions of 'autonomous' states endangering vulnerable domestic production systems – are compounded when it comes to agricultural biotechnology. A great deal of technical knowledge is needed, including knowledge of intellectual property law, microbiology, risk assessment for human and animal health and safety, assessment of the impacts of dispersion of GM organisms on biological diversity in the environment, and so on. Because much of the technology is controlled by a relatively small number of transnational, primarily U.S., corporations, it is largely unavailable to poorer developing countries. When it is available, they must accept the technology on terms set by these corporations. Given the emphasis in development of the technology on improving productivity and efficiency of agricultural production, it may hasten further the demise of traditional production systems. It may also have a detrimental effect on the wealth of genetic resources and biological diversity in developing countries.

In summary, the political globalization of agricultural policy-making and the development of a global transnational policy space do not appear to have lessened asymmetries of power in this sector. What appears to be happening is that these developments have made longstanding asymmetries more transparent and more open to view. Some would add that those asymmetries have deepened, reflecting a transfer of wealth from the more marginal farmers in the developing world to the 'industrial' farmers and agribusiness corporations in the developed countries.

These features of the transnational policy space in agriculture illustrate well the obstacles to transnational cooperation, even in microlevel, low politics, policy areas. The United States acts as an 'autonomous' state in its favouring of the trade node of the space, frustrating cooperation with the EU and many developing countries who wish a more equal consideration of biological diversity and food security issues. Both the United States and the European Union states have assumed 'autonomous' state roles in implementing the Agreement on Agriculture, adding to the frustration of many states in the Global South. Although some of the larger of these like Brazil, China, and India are building sufficient policy capacity to move from being 'weak' to 'cooperative' states, the vast majority remain in the weak category and are increasingly alienated from the process. And countries like Brazil, China, and India often find the EU and the United States less than cooperative. Accordingly, political order and effective global governance are not on the immediate horizon in the transnational policy space in agriculture.

NOTES

1 Giddens (1990:18).
2 Dirlik (2001: 18).
3 Tomlinson (1999: 3).
4 Scholte (2000).
5 Appadurai (1996) is a classic example.
6 Robertson (1992).
7 Appadurai (1996, 2002).
8 Robertson (1992: 141).
9 Robertson (1992), Albrow (1996), Beck (2002).
10 Tsing (2000), Geertz (2000).
11 Beck (2002).
12 Ibid.: 92.
13 Cox (1987: 255).
14 Ibid.: 258.
15 Beck (2000: 114ff).
16 Dirlik (2001: 26).
17 Tsing (2000).
18 Held et al. (1999).
19 Robertson (1992).
20 Tsing (2000: 330).
21 Josling, Tangermann, and Warley (1996: 29).
22 Ibid.
23 Hansen (1991).
24 Skogstad (1987).
25 Swinbank and Tanner (1996: 17).
26 Grande (2002).
27 Coleman and Tangermann (1999).
28 Londoño (1998: 4).
29 Ibid.: 7.
30 Ibid.: 7.
31 Confidential interview, Geneva, June 2001.
32 Appadurai (2002: 8).
33 Ibid.: 12.
34 Ruggie (1993a: 172).
35 Castells (1996: 30–32).
36 Coleman and Gabler (2002).
37 FAO and UNDP (1996a: 3).

38 FAO Statement on Biotechnology (2002: 2). Available at http://
    www.fao.org/biotech/state.htm
39 FAO and UNDP (1996b).
40 Convention on Biological Diversity (1992: Preamble).
41 Ibid.: Article 3, UNCED (1992: Principle 2).
42 Convention on Biological Diversity (1992: Article 8).
43 Ibid.: Article 1.
44 Ibid.: Article 20.5.
45 Ibid.: Article 8j.
46 Cameron (1999: 241).
47 Cartegena Protocol on Biosafety (2000: Preamble and Article 10.6).
48 Coleman and Gabler (2002).
49 These areas of dispute are described more fully in Coleman and Gabler
    (2002).
50 Confidential interview, developing country delegation, Geneva, June 2001.
51 Confidential interview, WTO Secretariat, Geneva, June 2001.
52 Confidential interview, Permanent Representative of the Islamic Republic
    of Pakistan, June 2001.

6 Financial Crises, the United Nations, and the Evolution of Transnational Authority

LOUIS W. PAULY

The opening chapter of this book hypothesizes the existence of a state rooted in transnational cooperation.[1] Such a state is ever more tightly networked into problem-solving structures that span traditional functional and territorial boundaries. As those structures become increasingly accepted as effective and legitimate, a transformation may begin to occur in the political practice, if not the formal legal doctrine, of state sovereignty. One indicator that such a process is indeed under way in our world might be predictably hostile reactions from traditional nationalists and political realists. Such reactions are clearly in evidence today. In Europe, they find expression in passionate opposition to a new constitution for Europe. In the United States, 'new sovereigntists' rekindle old debates over national prerogatives and the existence of international obligations.[2] Unilateralist impulses are obvious in hot spots all over the world.

Still, the problems now needing to be confronted on a global scale – from environmental deterioration, to the proliferation of weapons of mass destruction, to the stabilization of complex markets, to public health emergencies – demand political innovation. And moments when such innovation seems possible now present themselves with regularity. Perhaps they signify nothing, but the idea of the cooperation state, the state that cannot secure its vital interests unless it collaborates ever more intensively with others, becomes increasingly difficult to reject out of hand. The existence of broadly based collaborative institutions hints at that idea; their contemporary adaptation and reinvigoration do more than that.

In March 2002, the United Nations convened a conference on 'Financing for Development' in Monterrey, Mexico. For decades the focal points for effective governance in this policy arena had apparently been shifting away from national authorities towards private markets and the specialized international agencies closely associated with them. Eventually, however, states seeking cooperative solutions to intractable developmental problems began discussing new and more general kinds of governing structures. One prominent idea involved turning the G-8 forum into a more representative and authoritative G-20, a kind of global economic security council. The Monterrey Conference, however, represented a more immediate attempt to reinvigorate the diplomatic and coordinating machinery of the United Nations itself, the only body yet in existence with established claims to represent the whole of humanity. The potentially transformative institutional opportunity thereby presented was grasped not only by specialized agencies (always jealously protective of their own autonomy), but also by an American administration then widely viewed as sceptical of the United Nations and of the very notion of an authoritative community of cooperation states that the United Nations has come to symbolize.

The conference and its continuing aftermath reflect an ever more obvious tension between the prerogatives of sovereign power and the necessity of shared authority in the face of a problem too large to resolve in the short run but too important to ignore in the long run. The majority of the world's population simply could not be left out of an economic system resting on a promise of prosperity and peace. More immediately, recurring international financial crises and the responses they summoned suggested the intractability of a basic dilemma. Inadequate and unreliable financing for economic development cast a shadow of illegitimacy over the great post-1945 global experiment in economic interdependence. In the early years of the new millennium, it seemed clear that an ambitious and far-reaching attempt to resolve that dilemma directly would find no constituency inside leading states. But with their own financial markets regularly threatened by instability in developing countries, those states also could not turn away. Had the United Nations not existed, the case recounted below suggests, leading states would likely have tried to find a substitute. This would have been complicated, however, by a political economy no longer simply 'international,' as it was in the post–Second World War period, but also not yet truly 'global.' The United Nations, in concert with affiliated collaborative agencies provides a modicum of legitimacy for border-spanning markets and keeps alive the promise that the whole world will eventually benefit from their expansion and deepening.

Reviving the United Nations?

A straightforward empirical phenomenon calls for explanation. After years spent in obscurity, the economic and social affairs department providing secretariat support to the U.N. Economic and Social Council (ECOSOC) suddenly re-emerged in 2002 to play a central role in a new global initiative to increase the quantity and improve the quality of external financial flows to developing countries. After the post-1945 system of development finance came to depend quite clearly on private capital markets, supplemented occasionally by bilateral aid and resources from specialized multilateral agencies like the World Bank and the International Monetary Fund (IMF), the economic function of the U.N. Secretariat had been relegated to very modest roles, mainly involving research and administrative support. Over time, that research role was overshadowed by active research departments in the World Bank and the IMF, while the administrative role often appeared even to insiders as formalistic and ephemeral.[3] On substantive questions of world order, moreover, the U.N. Security Council eclipsed ECOSOC.[4]

Careful students of the subject had long predicted that the central economic functions of the United Nations would fall into desuetude. Some fifty years ago, in one of her first published articles, the late Susan Strange anticipated great difficulty for the U.N.'s economic operations and suggested a future marked by inadequate resources and excessive expectations: 'The United Nations evolved its machinery for dealing with international economic problems before it became fully aware of the magnitude or even the nature of those problems. In a way, it was as if someone were told that an all-purpose outfit for plumbing would be a useful thing to have – and were then faced with the task of using it to build an irrigation system.'[5] In the 1970s, that machinery came back briefly into public view. But with the ultimate failure of an ambitious U.N. initiative to construct a 'new international economic order,' many saw oblivion just over the horizon. As Stephen Krasner later put it 'Symbolically, the United Nations compound on the East River in New York is coming to resemble the Guantánamo Naval Base in Cuba. Both are an affront to the principles and norms of the territories that surround them and both are vestiges of past power configurations ... Increasingly, the United States has carried out policy in forums with limited membership and functionally specific tasks.[6]

During the following two decades, the organizational action shifted to the World Bank and the IMF, which possessed their own legal charters and financial resources, their sometimes distinct memberships, and their expanding linkages to private capital markets.[7] But ECOSOC and its supportive apparatus did not disappear. It could be, as public choice analysts might explain, that bureaucracies once established are intrinsically difficult to dismantle: clever bureaucrats find ways to keep their jobs.[8] Such an explanation, however, is too facile, too cynical, and too simple. Developments in the immediate aftermath of a series of financial crises that shook the post-1945 system to its core suggest more complicated reasons for the persistence of the United Nations in this arena. They also suggest that the character of broadly multilateral political instruments reflects both the necessity and the continuing fragility of public authority underneath a globalizing economy.[9]

Students of international relations now widely note the resurgence of unilateralism in the United States and elsewhere. Many also point to the apparently increasing reliance of states on market-based forms of policy coordination. In such a context, the revival and expansion of the mandate of the United Nations in the field of development finance and the linking of that mandate not only with the evolving mandates of other multilateral institutions but also with new kinds of development assistance are especially puzzling. The classic intergovernmental organizations established after the Second World War had once served as focal points for understanding relationships among states as well as between state power and the power of markets. In recent decades, as those organizations came to look sclerotic, scholars interested in such matters turned their attention to less formal international regimes, informal political clubs, and the hidden structures of global capitalism. Against such a backdrop, evidence of the revival and adaptation of the United Nations and the post-1945 vision of global governance to fit new circumstances is worthy of deeper investigation.[10]

The Politics of International Organizational Adaptation

The formal study of international organizational adaptation is peculiar. On the one hand, very little rigorously focused literature exists on the subject. On the other, almost all contemporary research on international relations is relevant to it in some way.

The late Ernst Haas provided seminal insights that first led towards disciplined micro-level analysis of the adaptive process in organizations like the UN.[11] Haas would surely not have minded anyone tracing his scholarly roots to the cosmopolitan ideals mentioned in Chapter 1 of this book. Moreover, similar to Inis Claude's pathbreaking work, Haas's approach to international organizational change put a premium on the ability of specific agencies to provide collective legitimation for larger global projects.[12]

Haas's research was decidedly empirical and his interpretation of institutional development was commonly labelled neo-functionalist. In the background was the dominant realist view of international organizations as mere reflections of the underlying power and interests of member-states, or of organizational adaptation as mainly a function of bargaining among members as their interests change. Haas, by way of contrast, laid emphasis on the possibility of institutionalizing complex processes of adaptation, and under the best circumstances, of routinizing social learning.[13] On the basis of an analytical frame organized around the concept of 'cognitive evolution' and an obviously related normative commitment to the idea of progress in international affairs, one of his seminal studies compared the economic and social agencies of the United Nations with the Bretton Woods institutions. The former, he concluded, enjoyed a brief period of 'incremental growth' in their early years, but were soon overwhelmed by a series of internal and external forces. Over time, he depicted the U.N. agencies as enduring, at best, 'turbulent non-growth' in their core authorities.[14] Simultaneously, in Haas's view, the IMF, and especially the World Bank, moved beyond incremental growth (and a brief period in the 1970s of turbulent non-growth in the IMF's case) to the successful 'management of interdependence.' The key difference between the United Nations and the Bretton Woods twins, in his view, lay in dynamic processes of organizational learning. Crucial here and in other successful cases of adaptation was the emergence of respected expert groups outside the organizations, or 'epistemic communities,' which formed intellectual alliances with innovative, reflective thinkers inside national governments.

Any institutional flowering of the seeds that Haas called consensual knowledge also depended on a powerful enough supportive coalition of states with a stake in a progressive global outcome. Such an outcome might often appear conflicted, but there was no doubting a certain underlying positive impulse in policies actually coming into force.

Anticipating the way in which what would come to be called the post-1970s market-led Washington Consensus actually spread, Haas cited the successful adaptation by the Bretton Woods twins and the sidelining of the United Nations: 'We thus arrive at a paradoxical picture in which epistemic communities encouraged by the Bank and the Fund – associated with Western thinking even though the individuals are often nationals of Third World countries – dominate policy-making and the administration of loans, while antidependency-minded delegates from the same Third World countries denounce the Bretton Woods twins as 'heartless' in the U.N. General Assembly and in UNCTAD.'[15] By resisting the notion that such a sidelining was necessarily permanent, however, Haas laid the groundwork for a later renaissance of sociological research on international organizational adaptation.

John Meyer provides a widely cited exemplar of such work. Meyer and his colleagues depict post–Second World War international organizations as the embodiment of a process of global sociocultural structuration. For them, those organizations constituted a 'framework of global organization and legitimation' that both created and assembled 'components of an active and influential world society ... The forces working to mobilize and standardize [that society] gain strength through their linkage to and support by the United Nations system and the great panoply of non-governmental organizations around it.'[16] However much that system can seem powerless, it is in fact an essential part of a larger process through which the form of the nation-state itself is reconstructed and transmitted, through which state identities are shaped, and state behaviour is deeply transformed by the universalization of an essentially dominant Western culture. The Second World War ushered in the decisive phase. Afterwards, 'rationalized definitions of progress and justice (across an ever broadening front) are rooted in universalistic scientific and professional definitions that have reached a level of deep global institutionalization'[17] Like Haas, they conclude, 'conflict is to be expected, but their authority is likely to prove quite durable. A world with so many widely discussed social problems is a world of Durkheimian and Simmelian integration, however much it may also seem driven by disintegrative tendencies.'[18] Embodying the process through which 'world society' is actually rationalized, the adaptation of international organizations would seem on this view necessarily to reflect a politically authorized mechanism for the working out of tensions, for coping with contradictions, and for sustaining the forward movement of societal construction on a global scale. Not by coincidence have such views, much like Ulrich Beck's in this book, attracted favourable attention from a new generation of international relations scholars seeking to combine the insights of institutionalism and constructivism.

Similar thinking is evident in studies of organizational adaptation undertaken in international relations by scholars like Robert Keohane, who invokes models more clearly borrowed from micro-economics than from sociology and who uses them to combine both realist and functionalist insights. He leads us essentially to expect that organizations, once created, will continually work to lower transaction costs and help directly to clarify and resolve problems of collective action. They become useful instruments for encouraging long-term thinking and exploiting new policy ideas. In such a context, they will tend to persist as long as the problems they seek to address remain in existence.[19] By their collaborative operation, moreover, they might begin subtly to alter the terrain upon which state interests are recalculated, even in the security arena.[20] On this view, the process through which actual organizations develop is therefore iterative, and it is more likely to be characterized by adaptation than by abrupt change. Not dissimilarly, scholars advocating a constructivist approach in this field have recently been trying to model just such an organic experience, one tied to underlying interests of a long-term nature.[21] Related to such an effort is the work of organizational analysts inspired in part by postmodernism. While acknowledging the reality of organizational adaptation, and strategies of 'muddling through,' they contend that avoiding festering problems calls for intensive critical examination of the core purposes of agencies like the United Nations. Some have pushed this perspective to the limit by calling for radical moves away from incremental reform towards structural redesign.[22]

The case history outlined below might discourage those seeking early indications of conditions conducive to the emergence of new grand bargains between indebted developing states and dominant creditor states. But it should also discourage those who place inordinate emphasis on the ability of impersonal, unguided markets to mediate their continuing relationship. Set against the experience of instability and inequity in those markets, leading states as well as follower states apparently find themselves repeatedly reliant on networks of cooperation, networks with formal international organizations at their core. As Haas had earlier discovered, both retain an abiding interest in 'managed interdependence,' which begs the questions of who would actually do the managing and what mutually acceptable objectives might exist.

Some three decades ago, as noted above, developing countries sought to use their collective voice in the United Nations to rebalance power at the system level, to redistribute economic resources through authoritative political action, and to steer private markets. The United Nations stood, in short, for a kind of solidaristic ideal at a time when globalizing capitalism was perceived to be stimulating a harsh competition between rich and poor countries, and among poor countries themselves.[23] Krasner observed the anti–United Nations reaction of the rich, and assessed its implications in the following terms: 'As Northern commitment to universal multifunctional organizations declines, the demand for a New International Economic Order may wane, not because the objectives of the South have changed but because they cannot be expressed. The North has the option of exit as its loyalty to U.N. agencies erodes; the South has only the option of voice.'[24]

Why, despite scandals and controversies, is there a commitment on the part of industrial countries to the United Nations? And why after decades of carefully defending their autonomy within the loose U.N. system are the World Bank and the International Monetary Fund now collaborating more intensively with the ECOSOC and the U.N. Secretariat? At first glance, such questions might be expected to interest only a handful of scholars intrigued by the continuous evolution of the central economic and financial unit of the United Nations, not just since 1945 but since the unit's beginnings in the League of Nations during the 1920s.[25] But broader issues are at stake.

The search for answers speaks to the main issue of this book. In this important arena, might we be witnessing something more than the deepening of 'governance without government' at the international level?[26] More than the issue of better coordination between bureaucratic agencies could be involved. After decades of apparent decline in the field of economic policy, the United Nations might just be making a serious comeback. In this regard, the simultaneous about-face of Republicans in the executive and legislative branches of the U.S. government on the issue of funding for the United Nations is worth more than passing interest. So too is the high-profile announcement by President George W. Bush on 12 September 2002 that the United States was rejoining UNESCO after an eighteen–year boycott.[27] Such developments, together with the rapprochement between the United Nations and the Bretton Woods institutions apparent in the wake of the Monterrey Conference, might be more than coincidental.

The Monterrey Conference

Late in 1997, the U.N. General Assembly passed a resolution relating to the continuing financial challenges facing developing countries.[28] The resolution called for the 'convening, *inter alia*, of a summit, international conference, special session of the General Assembly or other appropriate high-level international intergovernmental forum on financing for development (FfD) to further the global partnership for development, not later than the year 2001.'[29] Since analogous resolutions had been passed regularly since 1991, the casual observer may be forgiven for having ignored this one. Surely few would have expected much to come of it, especially since the principal question appeared to have been settled in the mid-1970s. The bulk of future financing for development would be delivered by private capital markets, which could increasingly be accessed by the straightforward reform of domestic policies within developing countries themselves. Sound macroeconomic fundamentals plus increased openness were expected to deliver development and prosperity.

As it happened, the 1997 FfD U.N. resolution coincided with the onset of a downward spiral in international capital markets, a spiral that would eventually reawaken memories of global depression. Both professional apocalyptic analysts and normally quite sober-minded participants in those markets soon forecast the imminent demise of global capitalism.[30] In the end, the system did not collapse, but severe payments crises did overwhelm financial policymakers as they spread rapidly from Thailand to Korea, Indonesia, Russia, and Brazil.[31] The IMF and the World Bank were quickly swept into the maelstrom, and when it ended, their very credibility was in question.

By 1996, the IMF in particular had become the principal advocate for a world without financial walls, and a serious effort was under way to amend the organization's articles to bring the capital accounts of its members under its formal purview, with the clear aim of promoting more complete liberalization. In 1999, however, the IMF and the World Bank were pressed to retreat from efforts both to curtail cronyism in developing countries and open their financial markets to external competition. They were not alone in recoiling. In September of the previous year, it seems almost embarrassing to recall, the most open and supposedly transparent exemplar of the world of financial globalization fractured the ideological foundation of the then conventionally accepted development agenda, a foundation often referred to as the Washington Consensus. Efficient markets were asserted, and both winners and losers needed to accept the inevitability of adjustment. Developing countries needed to open up their financial systems to the bracing winds of competition, and investment, it was held, would flow to where it was needed and where it was fairly rewarded. But in the United States, in a time of trouble and deepening fear, the process of adjustment would be politically managed. Instead of letting Long Term Capital Management, a speculative and highly leveraged hedge fund, fail after its bets were swamped by a financial panic just then rolling in from East Asia and Russia, the Federal Reserve unofficially organized a bailout.[32] What was good for the goose appeared not, in the end, to be good for the gander.

It is implausible to argue for simple coincidence in the fact that desultory discussions just then under way within the United Nations on the 1997 FfD resolution suddenly attracted new attention. Although it looked like the 2001 deadline for a high-level meeting might slip, momentum began to build for bringing together debates on a range of new issues spawned by two years of global crisis, issues now graced with the ambitious label 'new financial architecture.'[33] In the background too was a refocusing of the World Bank's core mandate to reduce poverty, an erosion in official development assistance commitments on the part of industrial countries, a break in the longstanding resistance of those countries to providing debt relief to the poorest developing countries, and the abrupt end of negotiations on new OECD guidelines to govern foreign direct investment.[34]

An agenda-setting process began within the United Nations, and a 'preparatory committee' suddenly attracted the active participation of the IMF, the World Bank, the International Labour Organization, the World Trade Organization, the OECD, and the new Financial Stability Forum. The process engaged U.N. ambassadors, but the ultimate goal soon came to complement ongoing discussions among officials drawn not only from foreign ministries but from trade, development, and finance ministries, and central banks as well. As its work rapidly advanced, the preparatory committee also began to receive input from a wide range of non-governmental organizations. In February 2001, a week-long dialogue opened by the president of the U.N. General Assembly and the Secretary General attracted a wide range of national officials, as well as senior managers from the IMF, the World Bank, and the WTO.[35] This, in itself, was seen by insiders as a signal accomplishment. As one participant observed, 'If FfD had ever been construed as a way for the U.N. to instruct or even give advice to other international organizations, the initiative would have died an immediate death ... The other [organizations] had to see FfD as a serious initiative that was relatively free of the usual negotiating rigidities of the U.N. ... [and] if not an advantage, then at least no danger in drawing closer to the U.N. ... Thus diplomats in New York have succeeded in involving all the major "institutional stakeholders" in the FfD process. Some have come warily and some enthusiastically, but all have been engaged one way or another.'[36] Working in parallel with officials at this level, separate discussions had commenced at the senior governmental level under the chairmanship of Ernesto Zedillo, past president of Mexico.[37]

After these discussions, it was still far from certain what the next step might be. Political transition in the United States, among other things, added a new wrinkle; a commonplace view was that the Bush administration would be decidedly less receptive to using international organizations as forums for addressing global financial matters. But such a view soon proved wrong, or at least too simplistic. Given the importance of Mexico to the Bush administration's early agenda, it likely helped that Mexico just then offered to host a high-level summit in Monterrey.[38] In this regard, insiders say that more important was direct lobbying by American business associations in Washington. Most prominently, the Business Council for the United Nations, an affiliate of the U.N. Association of the United States (UNA-USA), bolstered a campaign it had begun during the late Clinton years to build support for an International Conference on Financing for Development.[39] It should be noted that one of the assets the United Nations brings to this and other policy tables is, indeed, its NGO network, which it has officially sanctioned and nourished ever since its founding. Many NGOs have official status at the UN, are formally empowered to address ECOSOC and other bodies, actually deliver certain UN programs, and play a recognized role in many U.N. activities.[40]

On 27 January 2002, the U.N. preparatory committee completed its consultations with national delegations, with other international organizations, and with recognized NGOs. The result was an agreed draft text for a final conference communiqué. Implicitly labelled in such a way as to replace the tattered Washington Consensus, the document spoke of a 'Monterrey Consensus.' Its main headings were: 'Mobilizing

Domestic and International Financial Resources for Development';
'International Trade as an Engine for Development'; 'Increasing International Financial and Technical Cooperation for Development';
'External Debt'; and 'Addressing Systemic Issues: Enhancing the Coherence and Consistency of the International Monetary, Financial, and Trading Systems in Support of Development.' Even the aficionado would be hard-pressed to find much surprising or controversial in the paragraphs organized under these headings. But future historians may well look back and see in the following lines a summary of lessons learned during the crises of the late 1990s, and at least an opening for profound change in the way international organizations and governments actually confront debt crises.

> While recognizing that a flexible mix of instruments is needed to respond appropriately to countries' different economic circumstances and capacities, we emphasize the importance of putting in place a set of principles for the management and resolution of financial crises that provide for fair burden sharing between public and private sectors and between debtors, creditors and investors. We encourage donor countries to ensure that resources provided for debt relief should not detract from ODA [official development assistance] resources intended to be available for developing countries ... To promote fair burden-sharing and minimize moral hazard, we would welcome consideration by all relevant stakeholders of an international debt workout mechanism in the appropriate forums, that will engage debtors and creditors to come together to restructure unsustainable debts in a timely and efficient manner. Adoption of such a mechanism should not preclude emergency financing in times of crisis.[41]

In March 2002, these careful preparations culminated in the Monterrey Conference itself, which was attended by fifty heads of state or government. Those leaders were joined by finance, foreign, and development ministers, who traditionally had not been happy to meet together in collaborative forums where divergent perspectives and domestic interests were likely to become public and obvious. Behind the scenes, the conference provided a focal point for unusually intense and unusually open collaboration among officials from the U.N. Secretariat, the World Bank, and the IMF. For their part, IMF officials later explained their newfound interest in going down this path as rooted in three perceptions: (1) the process would give them a chance to affect the agenda and avoid being blindsided, (2) it would reinforce concurrent moves to encourage a broad base of member-states to 'buy-into' modified IMF policies, and (3) the 'legitimacy' associated with a well-prepared U.N. conference would enhance the possibility that borrowing states would 'take ownership' of their own adjustment programs.[42] In retrospect, it seems clear as well that the United Nations itself had changed: gone, or at least much muted, was the rhetoric of radical global redistribution associated with it in earlier decades.[43]

In the end, the conferees agreed to the text proposed for their final communiqué.[44] With a degree of hyperbole, but also with some justification, the text left the distinct impression that both rich industrial countries and poor developing ones were dissatisfied with the conventional wisdom that had dominated the international discourse on development financing during previous decades. Where the Washington Consensus basically left the challenge of development to the internal discipline of poor countries, on the understanding that this would enable them to attract adequate capital flows of a mainly private character to meet that challenge, the Monterrey Consensus reopened the space for the newly energized post-1945 machinery of intergovernmental cooperation to harness and redirect new kinds of private *and* public capital flows, especially for the poorest countries in the world. In the months following the conference, unusual joint meetings were held between IMF and World Bank executive directors and U.N. ambassadors, while staff reporting to them sought new ways to collaborate more intensively on specific country-level operations.

Perhaps most surprisingly, even the Bush administration welcomed the initiatives coming out of the Monterrey Conference. Indeed, the president himself attended the conference and personally endorsed its final report. The fact that his government considered it to have been more than a passing moment was signalled six months later in its high-profile *National Security Strategy*. In the relevant chapter, the document best known for its argument in favour of pre-emptive war in the struggle against global terrorism asserts: 'Including all of the world's poor in an expanding circle of development – and opportunity – is a moral imperative and one of the top priorities of U.S. international policy ... Decades of massive development assistance have failed to spur growth in the poorest countries ... Working with other nations, the United States is confronting this failure. We forged a new consensus at the U.N. Conference on Financing for Development in Monterrey that the objectives of assistance – and the strategies to achieve those objectives – have changed.[45] The document goes on to reaffirm a commitment first made by President Bush just before the Monterrey meeting to increase by 50 per cent the core development assistance provided by the United States. This would mainly take the form of a new 'millennium challenge account' for projects in countries that demonstrated 'real policy change' or a clear desire 'to implement reforms.'[46]

In subsequent months, the detailed proposal finally put to the Congress specified a permanent U.S. $5 billion increase in American public funding for development assistance, to be distributed through a new government-owned agency called the Millennium Challenge Corporation (MCC). The MCC would complement traditional bilateral assistance efforts coordinated by the U.S. Agency for International Development. Countries would compete for the new funding on the basis of a series of tests designed to measure equitable local governance, the quality of investment in people, and progress towards economic freedom. With relatively well-off developing countries likely to qualify in the first instance, the plan anticipated existing USAID funding being redirected to countries that needed post-conflict, transition, or humanitarian assistance. The plan also called for careful and explicit coordination among the MCC, USAID, the World Bank, the IMF, and other multilateral and regional agencies.[47]

It took eleven months for the administration formally to propose its plan to the Congress, and it took longer for it to emerge from the normal appropriations process. In the midst of mounting domestic fiscal problems and difficulties in stabilizing a war-torn Iraq, moreover, the actual first-year budget of the MCC was only U.S. $994 million.[48] Despite a repeated commitment to ramp this amount up to U.S. $5 billion by fiscal year 2006, the possibility remained that the program could turn out to be more symbolic than substantive. Even if eventually fully funded, it could also turn out mainly to benefit relatively well-off developing countries central to heightened U.S. national security interests.[49] But U.S. officials resolutely defended themselves and the basic novelty of the plan.[50] At the same time, they affirmed their continuing support for the formal declaration of the U.N. General Assembly on a broad set of 'millennium development goals,' thereafter routinely cited by multilateral and national development agencies as specific expressions of the 'Monterrey Consensus.'[51]

The consensus document unveiled in Monterrey specified a commitment to 'make fuller use' of the U.N. General Assembly and ECOSOC in following up the conference, partly by regularizing 'preliminary exchanges' on related matters with the executive boards of the World

Bank and the IMF, and with 'the appropriate intergovernmental body of the World Trade Organization,' by holding a spring meeting among ECOSOC, the Bretton Woods institutions, and the WTO, and by 'reconstituting' every two years in the General Assembly 'the current high-level dialogue on strengthening international cooperation for development through partnership.' 'To underpin these efforts, we request the Secretary General of the U.N. to provide – with collaboration from the major institutional stakeholders concerned, fully utilizing the United Nations System Chief Executives Board for Coordination mechanism – sustained follow-up within the U.N. system to the agreements and commitments reached at the Conference and to ensure effective secretariat support. This support will build on the innovative and participatory modalities and related coordination arrangements utilized in preparation of the Conference.'[52]

Interpreted in light of political practice since the 1970s, this is all potentially very significant.[53] If, as is often assumed, bureaucrats are creatures of habit, then here is an attempt to break some moulds and encourage new habits. Permanent and regular consultations were to occur among key institutional stakeholders across the board. In other words, both directly and through a revived international civil service, foreign ministries, development ministries, and finance ministries would have to consult routinely on FfD inside national governments and with their counterparts in other countries. Of all the institutional stakeholders, the United Nations would likely be the one most rejuvenated by this process. The interesting thing is that other ministries agreed that a foreign ministry–dominated United Nations could now be useful. What it offered was what it had always represented in-principle – a sense of international legitimacy, a good now apparently deemed so valuable as to be worth putting up with the 'inefficiency' of broadly based and continuing consultations stressing accountability for results. ECOSOC provided the forum, and representatives from the Bretton Woods institutions now regularly attended.[54]

In addition to interaction at the ministerial level, the Monterrey Consensus strongly suggested a renewed interest by leading states in a permanent bureaucratic apparatus for more intensive communication among the UN secretariat, the affiliated UN economic agencies (including the IMF and the World Bank), the WTO, and regional institutions, both at the level of senior management and at the level of operational staff.[55] Of course, this interest may prove ephemeral. Scepticism is a reasonable position in the field of international organization, where unbridled idealism has frequently met with disappointment. If the actual practice of intensive communication across different organizations at different levels endures, however, it might plausibly be interpreted as recognition of the ultimate need for public authority to underpin a global economy.[56]

Complex Sovereignty and Real World Policy

Would it not be reasonable to see such recognition as reflecting a reawakened impulse towards 'government'? Indeed, would it not be fair to see in it the suggestion of the term *cooperation state*? Certainly the events surrounding the Monterrey Conference cannot reasonably be construed as reviving the old liberal dream of automaticity in the process of international economic adjustment. Certainly market mechanisms were now accepted by a wider range of U.N. members than had been the case in the 1970s. But even the states dominating international markets pulled back from an insistence on unthinking liberalization. Along the same line, a conservative administration in the United States, the once and perhaps future leader of the post-Monterrey system, now signaled a willingness to work not only with the World Bank and the IMF but also with central economic organs of the United Nations in coordinating policies on the provision of financing for development, policies that certainly reopened basic issues of international monetary and financial governance. That a sense of post-crisis defensiveness was involved did not obviate the resurgence of the idea that cooperation states interacting to advance and facilitate systemic adjustments could reduce systemic instability and promote shared prosperity. Scholars have long recognized that cooperation can be associated both with the fear of mutual losses as well as the desire for mutual gains, but also that the former motivation is the more reliable. It seems clear that in the late 1990s, something had shaken the attitudes of both international agencies that had been wary of collaborating too closely in the past and policymakers who had placed too much faith in the ability of markets alone to resolve distributive questions at the system level.

Having accelerated a global movement towards deregulation of capital markets during the 1980s and 1990s, a once seemingly marginalized IMF and World Bank are now back in the centre of the continuing global dialogue on financing for development, and a once seemingly irrelevant United Nations now faces an expanding work agenda linked to that dialogue. Simplistic or cynical interpretations of the moment may miss the dynamism of the process through which financial power and political authority are now being mingled through the adaptation of established international organizations and the forums they provide. What is being sought through that adaptation seems to be the right balance among the values of systemic stability, efficient resource allocation, and distributive justice. With notable exceptions during the past half century, that balance was sought and recalibrated in international finance mainly by practical people who accepted the world as they found it and not as they wished it to be. Moreover, as much as the more market-oriented among them may have wished to avoid seeking that balance in authoritative institutional settings, they seem regularly to have been driven back to them. 'Governance without government' may not have been a theoretical impossibility[57]; it was just not possible in fact. After 1945, a broadly based multilateralism may not always have been the preferred solution for the wielders of power, but resistance to every alternative, especially in the wake of repeated crises, left no better option.[58] Contrary to expectations widely held in the mid-1980s, by the turn of the new century the leaders appear to have rediscovered that they could not exit and that the followers had to be heard.

I began this chapter by asking why international organizations established after the Second World War persist and even find their mandates expanding in an era when global market forces and U.S. unilateralism had been commonly expected to push them towards oblivion. The Monterrey Conference and its outcomes suggest that renewal and adaptation of those organizations were conditioned by severe financial crises. In fact, every severe debt crisis in the modern period required public authority to resolve the situation, and the more severe the crisis, the more the key wielders of public authority were forced to come out of the shadows.[59] Whenever possible, leading states acted through international organizations, but even when they had to act alone, they typically as quickly as possible withdrew back behind deeper and more intrusive mandates for those organizations. Over time, the fundamental roles of the most broadly based organizations became more obvious and more obviously attractive: to mediate varied interests, to provide political buffers, to ameliorate conflicting claims, to bolster the legitimacy of the system – and to hold out the promise that shared prosperity was still possible.

In conclusion, the case history examined in this chapter might prompt further reflection on the contemporary political response to financial crises at the international level in light of what Ulrich Beck and others have termed *a cosmopolitan perspective*. Are fully authorized agents of an incipient 'global community' coming into sight? Are duly constituted organizations emerging that are at least potentially capable of articulating and promoting the global common good? Is it possible that intergovernmental instruments, dominated by strong states but representing all states in some way, are providing a nascent form of government to globalizing markets? As mediators, scapegoats, and adjudicators, are international institutions beginning to undertake the political work of economic redistribution? If national capitalism required the nation-state to accomplish such tasks, is it reasonable to imagine that any system resembling 'global' capitalism could avoid creating an analogue? The undisputed economic realities of the early twenty-first century, especially the perverse fact that net financial capital flows as well as net human capital flows were actually going not from advanced industrial countries to developing ones but instead in the opposite direction, made it awkward not to begin answering such questions.

Are we, in short, beginning to see cooperation states shifting governing authority, not just tacit power, in the direction of broadly based multilateral organizations, organizations at least potentially capable of promoting both efficiency and equity? We would expect institutions capable of identifying and brokering the requisite trade-offs to be difficult to create and sustain. But that expectation should be the beginning of debate on such a question, not the end of it.

The financial crises of the late twentieth century could come to be associated with a dawning realization on the part of states and peoples that their economic destinies are now inextricably bound together and that therefore they must accept the inevitable task of constructing a global Leviathan to resolve the fundamental dilemmas implied by the existence of a global commons. If they eventually came together in a way that rendered collective power legitimate as well as effective at the global level, we could be certain that a key component of political authority in the modern world would have been reconstituted. But would this not be too hard a test of 'the cosmopolitan thesis'?

Consider the essential task confronting the founders of the United States of America. In the aftermath of the revolution, there was significant confusion about how political authority should be reconstructed. No one, however, argued that a true Leviathan was needed. Indeed, the very notion was anathema, even to proponents of a strong national government. Political authority itself would, in the end, wind up being subjected to a permanent contest. It would not, however, be rendered unnecessary. Order and efficient governance, the consensus held among America's founding fathers, needed to be balanced against fundamental expectations of liberty. Justice, moreover, would continually have to be discerned and reinterpreted in light of that ever-changing balance. In times of supreme national crisis, of course, order might trump liberty and simple justice might be deferred. The reconstitution of authority in the early days of the United States, especially as it evolved in practice, allowed for such exceptional circumstances. In 'normal' times, however, the continuous recalibration of that balance was facilitated, not frustrated, by intentionally leaving political authority divided and deliberately obscuring the borderlines between political authority and private life. As it turned out, this penchant well suited the industrial economic system that would begin to arise during the nineteenth century.

So why should we demand to see hard evidence of the emergence of a Leviathan at the global level before we concede that the notion of constructing global political authority is at least a possibility? Of course, we can rule it out by definition. If the very nature of the international system is held to be radically anarchic, only the fleeting delegation of authority by sovereign actors can occur at the global level. At best, we might be able to imagine the emergence of a kind of primitive rule in an organic society of states, which could thrive when common interests exist but, finally, survive only as long as the existence of a modicum of mutual obligation is understood by those states.[60] Such views still constitute key elements of the core disciplinary paradigm within the international relations field, and much of the research therein understandably highlights the fragile nature of international political authority. But are we not missing something important when we take that fragility to signal the end of the story?

'Global markets' remain political projects. Promoting and stabilizing those markets involves managing systemic risk and ensuring some semblance of symmetry in the adjustment burdens required to sustain the logic of interdependence, or at least to keep the coercive face of modern capitalism as veiled as possible. For just such reasons, the governments of leading states cannot walk away from the challenge of providing adequate financing for development, even in the far reaches of the world economy. In such a context, the adaptation of the economic functions of the United Nations suggests a complicated process of social learning.[61]

Multilateral economic organizations created during the Second World War are perhaps now receptive to deeper collaboration among themselves and with newer instruments for collaboration, because their own essential legitimacy was severely weakened by repeated financial crises in the developing world and by the associated concentration of the gains from globalization in rich countries. Recognizing the threat posed by that weakening, states collectively moved to abandon the pretence that a more cohesive political understructure for a global economy is not required. In short, states themselves learned, and they built with the tools at hand. The story of international organizational change, which Ernst Haas first began telling, continues.[62] It becomes more compelling after subjecting the main alternative stories to critical scrutiny: the IMF and the World Bank are only engaged in public relations operations when they involve themselves more vigorously with the United Nations and associated NGOs, national governments really believe that their citizens are willing to bear the costs of abandoning serious and deepening multilateralism, or cooperation state politics has been superseded by the automaticity of markets.

In her early article, quoted near the beginning of this chapter, Susan Strange came to the conclusion that 'if the United Nations has failed in its over-optimistic aims, the reason is not – as with the League of Nations – that interference by governments with the laws of capitalism was considered improper.' Instead,

> the responsibility assumed by sovereign governments for economic stability and progress within their own territory took precedence, in their view, in case of doubt or conflict over the wider responsibility for economic progress and stability throughout the world. And that in this, as in other older vital interests, they were unwilling to share their responsibility or to delegate power. Where the earlier axiom that the world was postally indivisible could be readily accepted, the new one that it was economically indivisible and that poverty anywhere was a threat to prosperity everywhere, could not.[63]

Fifty years later, the Monterrey Consensus held out the possibility that the situation was changing.

NOTES

1 I am grateful to Marc Kosciejew and Nisha Shah for research assistance;
   Edgar Grande, Barry Herman, John Ruggie, Pier Carlo Padoan, Emanuel
   Adler, Jacques Polak, Jim Boughton, and the staff of the archives of the IMF
   for valuable help and advice; and to the Social Sciences and Humanities
   Research Council of Canada for financial support. Events surrounding the
   Monterrey Conference discussed below are also explored in Steven Bernstein and Louis W. Pauly, eds. *Global Governance: Towards a New Grand Compromise?* (forthcoming).
2 See, e.g., Rabkin (2004). That some basic challenges to established patterns
   of governance were rising even inside the United States was certainly
   reflected in much popular literature. Bestselling biographies of Alexander
   Hamilton (Chernow, 2004) and Benjamin Franklin (Isaacson, 2004) retraced
   founding debates over the nature of American sovereignty. Other studies
   reexamined the first failed attempt to subordinate national authority to
   international organization in the aftermath of the Second World War. See,
   e.g., Chace (2004) and MacMillan (2003).
3 For example, the economic support unit of the League of Nations had pio-
   neered the annual *World Economic Surveys*, a task passed directly on to the
   U.N.'s economics department. Although still produced, as the *World Economic and Social Survey*, it is arguable that the IMF's *World Economic Outlook*,
   the World Bank's *World Development Report*, and even analogous OECD surveys, now garner more attention, as does the *Human Development Report*
   produced by the U.N. Development Program. On the history of the
   League's economic functions, which were in any case far more centralized,
   by an official who helped move them into the United Nations, see Hill
   (1946); see also, Wallace (1933).
4 Pick up any standard text on the organization and purposes of U.N. headquarters and the chances are that economics, development, and finance
   will feature only in a minor way. To some extent this reflects the fact that
   the post-1945 system was intentionally designed in a highly decentralized
   fashion, with economic functions assigned mainly to specialized agencies.
   For a particularly good, concise history, see Taylor (2000); see also, Hill
   (1978).
5 Strange (1954).
6 Krasner (1985: 299–300) argues further that 'tension between the North and
   South may also decrease because developing countries lack effective
   forums at which to present their demands. The NIEO program could not
   have developed without the United Nations system. ... However, the effec-

tiveness of universal forums has depended, in the final analysis, on the continued attention of the North. '

7 The precise nature of the relationship between the Bretton Woods institutions and the U.N. has long been problematic. Various issues arose in the early days of the IMF, e.g., including disputes over control of administrative budgets, over the distinction between 'technical' agencies like the IMF and 'political' agencies like the U.N., over duplicated efforts with regard to the collection of statistics, and over the right of U.N. delegates to intervene in lending decisions. The U.N.'s first secretary general, Trygve Lie, and the IMF's first managing director, Camille Gutt, initiated discussions on such issues. (See IMF Executive Board Document No. 46, rev. 1, dated 10 Sept. 1946, IMF Archives.) A formal inter-institutional agreement came into effect on 15 November 1947. Among other things, it recognized that the IMF has 'wide international responsibilities that ... required it to function as an independent international organization.' It granted 'full autonomy' regarding the content and form of the IMF's budget, and it allowed the U.N. and the IMF to make formal recommendation to one another 'after reasonable prior consultations' but not with regard to specific loans. (Memorandum from IMF General Counsel to Deputy Managing Director, 21 Feb. 1951, IMF Archives). On the general topic, see Jolly (1995).

8 See, for example, Vaubel and Willett (1991).

9 For timely assessments of U.N. conference machinery, see Schechter (2001) and Cooper, English, and Thakur (2002).

10 Hall and Biersteker (2002) and Cutler, Haufler, and Porter (1999).

11 See Ruggie et al. (2005).

12 Claude (1966).

13 Contrast with Waltz (1979) and also with the more subtle 'liberal intergovernmentalist' view of Moravcsik (1998).

14 For an excellent treatment of key underlying concepts, see Hurd (1999).

15 Haas (1990: 149). See also Kahler (1995).

16 Meyer et al. (1997: 163).

17 Ibid.: 174–175.

18 Ibid.

19 Keohane (1984). See also Haftendorn, Keohane, and Wallender (1999). Again, a narrower institutionalist approach under the public choice label typically emphasizes the critical role played in organizational evolution by narrow-minded and mainly self-regarding bureaucratic interests within such organizations themselves. See, esp., Vaubel (1986).

20 Also see Nye (2002).

21 See, esp., Adler and Barnett (1998). More generally, see Ruggie (1982),

Murphy (1984), Onuf (1989), Katzenstein (1996), Wendt (1999), and Adler (2002).

22 The exemplar here is Knight (2000) and Knight (2001).

23 For a timely intellectual defence, as well as for useful historical background, see Emmerij, Jolly, and Weiss (2001: Chapter 5).

24 Ibid., p. 301.

25 The files, the mission, and many of the people involved during League days made a transition, unnoticed by many, from Geneva to the U.N. in New York, but also from Geneva to the Bretton Woods institutions in Washington. I wrote about the latter transition in Pauly (1997).

26 Rosenau and Czempiel (1992).

27 *New York Times*, 28 September 2002, 3.

28 This section relies on the detailed account of an insider, the chief of the Finance and Development Branch of the U.N.'s Department of Economic and Social Affairs. See Herman (2002).

29 United Nations General.

30 Soros (1998).

31 For a fascinating and detailed account of the crisis based on extensive interviews with key participants, see Blustein (2001).

32 Ibid.: chapter 11.

33 See Pauly (2001).

34 Herman (2002).

35 Note that the IMF and the World Bank are officially designated as 'specialized agencies of the U.N.,' although they have always jealously guarded their autonomy. The WTO is not formally affiliated with the U.N.

36 Herman (2002).

37 Zedillo, with assistance from John Williamson, was commissioned by Kofi Annan to think through the issues that a U.S. Congressional initiative, the Meltzer Commission on the International Financial Institutions, had recently examined. The expectation was surely that they would come to a much less anti–institutional conclusion than the majority Meltzer report countenanced. Confidential interviews, Washington, 30 April and 3 May 2001.

38 For related background, see Herman, Pietracci, and Sharma (2001).

39 Interview, UN, New York, February 5, 2002.

40 O'Brien et al. (2000).

41 U.N. General Assembly (2002: paras. 45 and 54).

42 Interviews, IMF Headquarters, 3 February 2003. One official recalled that the World Bank had first proposed that the IMF join in preparing for the Monterrey meeting. Michel Camdessus, just then leaving his position as

managing director, was so inclined, and eventually his successor, Horst
Koehler, came to the same positive conclusion. In the wake of the East
Asian financial crisis, the IMF has been roundly criticized for aggressively
expanding the scope of its lending conditionality practices. Around the
time of the Monterrey meeting, 'streamlining' those practices had become
the new order of the day. Reinforcing their legitimacy, and therefore their
effectiveness in the long run, had become a widely acknowledged goal.

43 That a concession had been made was clear to senior U.N. officials from
that earlier era. 'Many still feel that the U.N. is missing an opportunity to
reassert itself as a significant and independent player on the field of economic and social policies. By seeking consensus with the private sector and
OECD and close working relations with the international financial institutions, the value added by the U.N. in developing an alternative paradigm
may be threatened' (Emmerij, Jolly, and Weiss, 2001: 144–5).

44 U.N. General Assembly (2002).

45 United States Government (2002).

46 Ibid.: 22.

47 See the March 2003 Congressional testimonies from the Treasury Department and the Administrator of USAID at www.usaid.gov.mca

48 To put this number in perspective, total U.S. foreign aid budgets approxi-
mated $20 billion in 2004 (in constant dollars), excluding funds for the
reconstruction of Iraq. This was up from the post-1945 low of $15 billion
budgeted in 1996. Of that total amount, actual funding managed by USAID
was $5.7 billion. At its promised FY2006 level, the millennium challenge
account would just about double this latter amount (see Tarnoff and Nowels 2004).

49 For an early assessment, see Brainard et al. (2003). Note that the sixteen
countries initially listed as eligible for MCA grants included eight from
Africa, three from Latin America, and five from Asia. They ranged from
Benin and Lesotho to Honduras and Vanuatu (see *New York Times*, 8 May
2004).

50 See U.S. State Department, 'MCA Update No. 3,' 23 July 2003. Accused by
Congressional Democrats of 'fraud' on both the MCA and HIV/AIDS initiatives, the head of the relevant appropriations subcommittee in the House
of Representatives responded: 'We are constrained by a spending cap that
required reductions ... We allocated 40 percent more to global AIDS programs than Congress appropriated last year, and the money [allocated this
year] is enough to get the AIDS program and the Millennium Challenge
Account started. A plan doesn't take off at 30,000 feet; it takes off slower
and it climbs. We do the same thing with programs, which is how you ramp

them up' (*New York Times*, 11 July 2003, A7). For views that strike a balance between scepticism and optimism, see Radelet (2003) and Brainard et al. (2003).

51 United Nations General Assembly, Resolution A/RES/55/2, 18 September 2002. Targets were set for the achievement by 2015 of a broad set of objectives related to reducing poverty and improvements in health as well as other global economic, environmental, and social conditions.

52 Ibid.: paras. 61 and 63.

53 Interview, U.N., New York, 5 February 2002.

54 See, e.g., *IMF Survey*, vol. 32, no. 8, 5 May 2003, 126–7.

55 As the noted international economist Gerry Helleiner framed the matter: 'Among the reasons why the conference is potentially so significant is that it marks the first time that the more representative procedures of the U.N. have been permitted to 'intrude upon' the procedures and practices of the international financial institutions ... Finance ministers are forced by this event to talk about financial issues with their 'more political' counterparts in ministries of foreign affairs, not only in U.N., IMF, and World Bank circles but also at home within their own national systems ... However small a step it may now appear to be, its long-run significance, as a precedent, may be profound' (Helleiner 2002). In this regard, see also Van Houtven (2002), Scholte (1998), and Woods (2001).

56 For the most sophisticated recent exploration of the notion that the emergence of 'private authority' is filling some of the political vacuum at the global level, see Cutler, Haufler, and Porter (1999).

57 Rosenau and Czempiel (1992).

58 See Ruggie (1993b). In this regard, however, the essence of what is meant by the term multilateralism remains highly contested. See Kagan (2002).

59 For more on this phenomenon, see Pauly (2004).

60 For a recent articulation of the latter position, one long associated with Martin Wight, Hedley Bull, and the 'English School,' see Jackson (2000: 408–9). '"Civilization" is not the best term to capture this international minimum,' Jackson writes. '"Civility" is a better term to avoid the erroneous conclusion that there is a global civilization' superior to particular civilizations. His 'global covenant' 'consists of the minimal standards that people from different cultures and civilizations have managed to arrange between themselves to conduct their political business with each other ... [It] ought to be understood as a constitutional arrangement that seeks to accommodate human diversity while trying to uphold common humanity. It gives institutional expression and substance to pluralism. That pluralist ethos was already evident in Europe in the Westphalian accommodation of reli-

gious differences between Protestant and Catholic rulers. The global expansion of international society from Europe to the rest of the world can be understood as the universalization of the same ethic of accommodation.'

61 It is certainly seen this way within the U.N. among some staff on the ECOSOC side. Confidential interviews, U.N. headquarters, 25 Jan. 2000 and 5 Feb. 2002.

62 Haas (1997) himself later focused on the difficulty the United States would have in adapting its own system to global needs.

63 Strange (1954: 140).

7 Reconstituting Political Authority in Europe: Transnational Regulatory Networks and the Informalization of Governance in the European Union

BURKARD EBERLEIN AND EDGAR GRANDE

Regional integration in Europe has been one of the most significant developments in the recent transformation of political authority.[1] European integration has been distinct from other forms of regional integration, such as Asia-Pacific Economic Cooperation or the North American Free Trade Agreement, not only because of its far-reaching transfer of legal competencies, functions, and activities from the national to the supranational level, but also because this process has been accompanied by the establishment of a comprehensive framework of supranational political institutions. The result is not just a larger space for (almost) unrestricted economic transactions, but a completely new system of political governance, shaped by a unique institutional architecture.

Since the very beginning of this process, the scholarly literature has keenly developed new concepts and coined new labels to grasp the peculiarities of this new, 'post-Hobbesian political order.'[2] There is widespread consensus that the European Union is distinct from both modern-day international organizations and from the established concepts of modern statehood. Although based on intergovernmental cooperation to a considerable extent, the EU is much more than a 'complex international organization,' an extended 'international regime,' or a confederation of states. And, despite its far-reaching supranational authority, the EU is still less than a state, even if we apply models of decentralized or federalist statehood to it.

Evidently, existing concepts of statehood and of political authority are only of limited use for an adequate understanding of the transformations of sovereignty and of governance in Europe.[3] Therefore, to escape the impasse of old-fashioned concepts and outdated debates, we must overcome some of the distinctions characterizing the modern state; in particular, those between national and international, between public and private, and between formal and informal institutions. For this purpose, two concepts can be utilized, both of which have gained some prominence in characterizations of the institutional structure and the policy process in the EU in recent years: *networks* and *multi-level governance approaches.*

The role of institutions in the policy process has been emphasized by various concepts of institutionalism in political science, sociology and economics in the last two decades.[4] These *institutionalist approaches* are based on the assumption that institutions are not mere shells for (individual or collective) political action. Rather, they shape rules and norms of political action, allocate resources and authoritative power, and structure opportunities for political action. Various authors have shown that it is possible to apply these institutionalist concepts to the study of European institutions and European integration.[5] In empirical research on the European policy process, these institutional aspects have been highlighted mainly by authors contributing to the literature on 'multi-level governance.'[6] These scholars emphasize how decision-making powers in the EU are dispersed across different territorial levels and integrated into complex, non-hierarchical institutions of decision-making.

Whereas institutionalist approaches focus on the peculiarities of the institutionalist framework of the EU, *network concepts* highlight the actor constellations of the European policy process, in particular the role of social actors.[7] Accordingly, the EU is often called a 'network state,'[8] a 'network type of governance,'[9] or a 'networked polity,'[10] to mention only a few of the most recent and ambitious attempts to conceptualize the unique features of the EU.[11] In a recent article, Chris Ansell summarized the basic aspects of the European networked polity in the following way:

> The networked polity is a structure of governance in which both state and societal organization is vertically and horizontally disaggregated (as in pluralism) but linked together by cooperative exchange (as in corporatism) ... The logic of governance emphasizes the bringing together of unique configurations of actors around specific projects oriented toward institutional solutions rather than dedicated programs. These project teams will crisscross organizational turf and the boundary between public and private. State actors with a high degree of centrality in the web of

interorganizational linkages will be in a position to provide facilitative leadership in constructing or steering these project teams.[12]

It is true that all these features can be observed in national policy-making as well. Modern nation-states are far from being ideal-type hierarchies, and interest groups are an indispensable factor of the polit-ical system of any modern democracy. In the EU, however, these fea-tures are so dominant and combined in such a unique way that it seems reasonable to make them central in a new concept of European governance.

Both approaches, networks and multi-level governance, although emphasizing different variables, share some assumptions about the major features of the European polity and the most relevant aspects of the European policy process. These shared assumptions can be sum-marized as follows:

- In the *political dimension*, they highlight the fact that the EU is domi-nated by a non-hierarchical style of political decision-making and that actors from lower organizational levels (i.e., national and sub-national actors) are an integral part of supranational policymaking;
- In the *social dimension*, they emphasize the fact that participation in decision-making is extended beyond the group of legitimized office holders, and that private actors (lobbyists, interest groups, and non-governmental organizations) play a prominent role in public policy-making;
- In the *institutional dimension*, they stress the importance of informal institutions and procedures in the European policy process and of the interplay between formal and informal modes of decision-making.[13]

Moreover, they have a common research agenda, and they focus on the same problems of governance in the EU. For network enthusiasts, the most interesting and important questions are those of effectiveness, power, and accountability: Does a network structure of governance actually work? Who benefits in such a differentiated policy process? And can it be made democratically accountable despite its complex-ity?[14] The multi-level governance approach, in contrast to neo-func-tionalist and (liberal) intergovernmentalist theories, has put similar problems of governance on the research agenda: the democratic legiti-macy of European policy processes, on the one hand, and the power distribution and problem-solving capacity of European policy–making on the other.[15]

The purpose of this chapter is to analyse the role of networks and of informal institutions in the European policy process in greater detail and to provide an adequate understanding of the interplay of national and supranational actors, public and private organizations, and formal and informal institutions in the European Union. Empirically, it is based on a case study of regulatory policy. Arguing against prevailing opinions, mainly academic, about the necessity and the limits of regulatory policy in the EU, we will show that the organization of regulatory authority in Europe is facing a dilemma that has significant consequences. The bulk of formal powers and the institutional focus of regulatory activities continue to be located at the national level, and the political resistance of member-states has so far not permitted any transfer of regulatory power to a supranational 'regulatory state.' And even though national regulatory regimes are embedded in a European framework of rules, the resistance to create formal regulatory institutions at the supranational level complicates the search for solutions to real problems within contemporary Europe. Our thesis is that the need for European standards and the heavy national bias in regulatory activity result in a regulatory gap that is filled partly by new types of informal institutions called *transnational regulatory networks*. These regulatory networks offer an alternative, in certain circumstances, that favours the informal Europeanization of public regulation. As Beck anticipates in his chapter in this volume, actual political authority in the EU now involves the integration of formal institutions, both at the national and supranational levels, with informal transnational policy networks.

The Rise of Europe as a Regulatory State

Despite considerable expenditures on the agricultural budget, regional funds and research and technology policy, and despite the advancing process of integration, the budgetary and financial capacities of the EU remain very small compared with its member-states. Furthermore, EU governance differs from that of its member-states in that its focus is on the creation of regulatory policy rather than distributive and redistributive policies.[16]

The growth of European regulation has been remarkable, steadily expanding over the past twenty years. This is not a consequence of some 'regulatory fervour' on the part European bureaucrats, as maintained in critical discussions of Europe. Instead, there are at least three developments that have contributed to the growth of European regulation. First, it is the expression of a characteristic asymmetry in the European integration process. As the powers of the EU have expanded in the past two decades or so, with an accompanying and steady Europeanization of wide areas of social policy, no redistributive programs at the supranational level have been established. Essentially, developments at the level of European social policy contrast with national welfare programs, as European social policy tends to occur in the form of 'social regulatory' rather than 'social [re]distributive' courses of action.[17] Additionally, in a number of risk-associated policy areas, protective norms have taken on greater importance.[18] Among these, labour and health policy and consumer and environmental protection are of particular note. Finally, with the privatization of public enterprises and the liberalization of markets, the monitoring of market power has taken on greater importance. These developments have considerably raised the need for public regulation all round – and the European Union has also profited from this.

A particularly strong push for European regulatory policy came from the privatization of public enterprises and the liberalization of markets. In the past twenty years this has undoubtedly been one of the most important new developments in the political economy of Western industrial societies. Extensive privatization and liberalization have come about in all European countries, and there seems hardly an area that has been exempted from this trend. This development has been especially noteworthy in the area of public infrastructures and utilities (including telecommunications, electricity and gas, railways, and water), where traditionally, for a number of different reasons (e.g., natural monopoly, public goods, and external effects), it was assumed that the market was not a suitable form of economic coordination. Accordingly, the provision of services by the state and the restriction of competition were regarded as indispensable.

In Europe, the liberalization of public monopolies and the privatization of public utility providers were strongly favoured by the creation of a single market. Individual member-states with neo-liberal governments, such as Great Britain, admittedly had already taken the initiative to create economic deregulation programs, but the 'negative integration'[19] of the European internal market, with its emphasis on market openness and competitive uniformity, gave these market reforms an additional impetus. In those countries where market reforms were blocked, the EU played an important role in overcoming domestic political resistance.[20]

The privatization of public enterprises and the liberalization of markets have not, however, led to a retreat by the state from its responsibilities, or to a complete 'deregulation' of the economy. Instead, these reforms frequently, and paradoxically, have resulted in an increase in governmental rules and regulatory activity.[21] This was particularly clear in Britain, where the comprehensive privatization of public enterprises was accompanied by the setting up of numerous regulatory authorities and by far-reaching regulatory activity.[22] State functions, consequently, have been changing – not simply diminishing – in response to an increase in privatization and liberalization: the 'positive state' which dominated the political economy of Europe for most of the twentieth century has been replaced by a new type of state, increasingly labelled the 'regulatory state.'[23] With its new functions, the state is no longer immediately assumed to be competent in the provision of public services. Still, however, as a regulatory state, it has been held responsible for providing them through private means.

This analysis of the regulatory state, one which has become widely accepted in the political science literature, has both a *functional* and a *territorial* aspect. In the *functional* dimension, the regulatory state thesis maintains that state supervision and control of the economy through regulation are not simply a transitional phase with the neo-liberal minimal state as the end goal. Rather, regulatory functions will remain a *necessary* and *lasting* governmental task.

This argument is supported in two ways.[24] First, it has become evident that the breaking down of barriers to market access does not alone succeed in creating competition in the infrastructure sector. Competition requires continued public involvement in market processes in order to create the conditions for effective competition and to ensure the maintenance of competitive markets. The first task for regulation thus lies in establishing and maintaining effective markets (market-creating regulation).[25] In this situation, the state's role is essentially to prevent the abuse of market power (e.g., the abuse of natural monopolies in network industries like the provision of electricity and gas). Second, regulation also has the task of correcting or compensating for the undesired outcomes or consequences of functioning markets in light of a politically defined perception of 'public interest' (market-correcting regulation). Thus, regulation should ensure that even private companies exposed to competition provide public services. This may take the form of guaranteeing the comprehensive provision of utilities.

Regulatory practice has shown that although these two functions of regulation, correction of market failure and compensation for market outcomes, can be separated analytically, they frequently come into tension with each other. This in part explains why the scope and content of public regulation cannot simply be determined from economic or technical necessities; it must be decided *politically*. The regulatory state is thus by no means lacking in political substance. Experience to date has also shown that the transition from the positive state to the regulatory state has not followed some sort of noiseless automatism, but is characterized by considerable political tension and conflict.

The focus of this chapter, however, is not on functional but instead on territorial dimensions of the regulatory state. In Europe, political conflicts over the establishment and expansion of the regulatory state were accentuated and intensified because the transition from the positive state to the regulatory state came about in a political and institutional context differing considerably from the conditions of national regulation. Unlike the positive state, the regulatory state had to be established under the conditions of a multi-level system of governance, considerably complicating the answer to the question 'who should regulate?' Hence, issues of the extent and means by which markets ought to be regulated were and *remain* politically controversial. Moreover, additional tensions and controversies arise over the appropriate territorial level at which emerging demands for political authority are to be met and how institutional arrangements for new regulatory tasks are to be organized.

The Organization of the Regulatory State in Europe

How is the regulatory state in Europe organized? What institutional form does the regulatory state in Europe actually display? At first sight, the transition from the positive state to the regulatory state seems to be clearly associated with a transfer of state powers from the national to the European level. The tasks of the regulatory state seem to be primarily handled by European institutions, a view strongly held by Majone.[26] The growth and extent of European regulation can be demonstrated by statistics on the number of legal documents. Whereas EU authorities were submitting an annual average of twenty-five directives and six hundred regulations in 1970, a total of 1,564 legal acts (directives and regulations) were enacted in 1991. This was more than the number (1,417 legal acts)[27] enacted by the French legislature in the same period. Furthermore, after 1993, a number of new, independent regulatory authorities were set up at the European level.[28] Currently, fifteen institutions belong to the group of so-called agencies, the European Food Safety Authority being the most prominent recent addition.[29] As specialized administrative bodies, they are distinctive because they were set up independently, outside the purview of both supranational institutions and the European treaty framework, by means of an EU Council regulation. These bodies exercise their specific technical and scientific tasks (e.g., observation, analysis, and dissemination of information) and administrative duties under the leadership of a supervisory body made up essentially of representatives of EU member-states and the EU Commission, and they are supported by scientific and technical committees. Moreover, the director of any given agency is appointed either by the EU Council or by the relevant supervisory body.

The European agencies cover a wide spectrum of tasks ranging from pharmaceuticals licensing, food safety and environment protection, to translation services, vocational training, and the monitoring of racism and xenophobia. While a first group of agencies develops common standards in the internal market (e.g., the pharmaceuticals agency), the main task of a second group lies in collecting and processing information in cooperation with national partner agencies as well as acting as coordinators of transnational networks (e.g., the environment agency). A third group, in addition to information gathering and networking, primarily promotes dialogue between employers and unions (e.g., vocational training). Finally, a fourth group carries out specialized European programs (e.g., reconstruction in Kosovo and elsewhere in the former Yugoslavia).

A closer look at the organization, tasks, and powers of these agencies shows that the EU suffers from several weaknesses in regulatory policy. First, it is striking that the European agencies, insofar as they at all carry out regulatory tasks, do not have the powers (rule setting, implementation, and dispute settlement) typical of independent regulatory agencies. The European Environment Agency (EEA), for example, is limited by its statutes to collecting and disseminating information. Even the European Agency for the Evaluation of Medicinal Products (EMEA), which comes closest to the model of a regulatory authority, takes no independent decisions on the licensing of pharmaceuticals – it merely puts forth recommendations for decisions made by the EU Commission. For this specific agency, decision-making authority lies with the regulatory committees for human and animal medicaments, comprised mainly of representatives of member-states. These modest powers and resources of European agencies further reveal that they are not intended to replace their corresponding national institutions for the goal of a larger 'European regulatory state.' Accordingly, they are effective only insofar as they supplement the activities of and cooperate with member-states' regulatory agencies. To this extent, the European agencies are a long way from forming the institutional core of a new regulatory state.

In addition, an empirical analysis of these agencies shows that institutionalizing regulation at the European level displays a peculiar asymmetry between different areas of EU regulatory activity. All of the European agencies described above are involved in social regulation. Things are quite different, though, in the sector of economic regulation. In the economic realm there has been no comparable building up of European regulatory institutions that can meet the need for regulations arising from privatization and liberalization. This is also true of the telecommunications and electricity sectors, where, ironically, the EU has played a decisive role in the liberalization of national markets. To the extent that the introduction of regulatory functions has played a role in the creation of new institutions, the institutions have been formed at national and sub-national levels. Thus, by now all EU member-states have independent regulatory authorities for the telecommunications sector; and with the pending exception of Germany, this is also the case for electricity. Institution building is particularly impressive in Britain, where numerous new regulatory authorities were set up in the wake of the Conservative privatization policy.[30]

Evidently, then, the regulatory state is far less developed at the European level than it is at the national level, much to the surprise of advocates of a European regulatory state. Furthermore, where regulatory activity has become institutionalized, it remains largely confined to social regulation, leaving the responsibility for large areas of economic regulation with national and sub-national authorities.

Empirical analyses of the organization of the regulatory state in the European context clearly show that, in all European countries, highly complex and differentiated regulatory regimes have emerged as a consequence of privatization and liberalization. By a regulatory regime we mean the full set of actors, institutions, procedures, instruments, norms, and rules relevant for the course and the outcome of public regulation in a given sector. If we consider the role of the European level from the conceptual angle of the regulatory regime, while avoiding an exclusive focus on independent regulatory authorities or agencies, we can see that the various regulatory regimes not only show marked internal differentiation within nation-states, but they also extend clearly beyond them. Regulatory powers are not more or less exclusively located at the national level. Neither, however, have they been overwhelmingly transferred to the European level. Regulation, as will further be shown, covers both levels.[31]

The territorial differentiation of regulatory institutions, regulatory levels, and their interaction and integration occurs in various ways in Europe. Alongside the establishment of the independent European agencies already mentioned, the formal powers of the EU Commission are another important aspect of the Europeanization of regulation. The commission is tied into the regulation of infrastructure sectors in two ways. The first has to do with the EU Commission's competition law powers, which have ensuing regulatory effects. It is well known that European competition law gives the commission extraordinarily far-reaching powers vis-à-vis EU member-states.[32] The Directorate-General for Competition, the European competition authority, monitors national compliance with or transposition of European competition rules. These are directed, on the one hand, against anti-competitive practices of private actors (e.g., cartel formation, or abuse of market power), but on the other, also against distortions of competition caused by member-states (e.g., state aids, or giving special rights to public enterprises).

In line with the argument in this chapter, the importance of European competition law is that it exerts significant regulatory power over the national economic sectors of EU member-states. A recent illustration is the legal proceeding brought forward by the EU Commission against French electricity provider EDF. The Commission held that the French state had failed to collect some 1.2 billion Euro in taxes and interest from the state-owned company, thus providing EDF with indirect state aids considered illegal under EU law. This Commission initiative, part of a larger drive to establish a truly level playing field for national companies, has, in turn, accelerated French legislation to convert the two state-owned energy utilities (EDF and GDF) into 'public companies,' thus removing state guarantees on their finances. Moreover, the monitoring of mergers of Community-wide importance, which is incumbent on the EU Commission, can be used as a regulatory lever to shape market systems. In the case of the merger of Veba and Viag (or more precisely, their electricity subsidiaries PreussenElektra and Bayernwerk) to form E.ON, the Director General of Competition worked closely with the German Cartel Office to develop detailed regulatory provisions for the German electricity market. Regulatory activity, however, need not be as direct as the above example; less formalized market supervisory functions, such as monitoring, can be exercised by the Commission's Directorates-General.

Regulation in Europe, whether market creating or market correcting, thus includes two levels: the nation-state and Europe. The institutional focus undoubtedly lies at the national level, but the national regulatory regimes are embedded in a comprehensive European regulatory structure. This arrangement can best be termed *state-centred multi-level governance*.[33] The relations between the national and the European levels of regulation are characterized by a division of labour in which the European level typically is responsible for framework regulations while their concretization and implementation are administered by national regulatory bodies. In this system of 'two-tier regulation,'[34] the latter deal directly with the targets of regulation, whether enterprises or citizens, whereas European agencies principally 'regulate' national regulatory authorities.

In practice this means that a European directive, supplemented or reinforced by European competition law, sets out a more or less narrowly defined framework. In the case of liberalized telecommunications markets, this can take the form of defining minimum requirements for the regulation of network access. A narrowly defined framework allows national authorities some choice between different ways of reaching objectives and advocating specific national solutions towards stakeholders operating in national markets. In turn, this leaves national institutions with some room to manoeuvre as they develop different national regulatory regimes. Allowing national discretion in the interpretation of the European regulatory framework is often a decisive factor in gaining member-states' acceptance of the European Council's regulatory decisions, particularly in situations where decisions must be made by consensus. The importance of allowing national governments some freedom to customize paths of regulation to their own domestic contexts was key, for example, to securing member-states' acceptance of the regulations surrounding the liberalization of the electricity industry.[35]

The structural pattern of the European regulatory state – a Europe-wide framework with nationally variable implementation – possesses a severe weakness that arises from a 'decentralization problem.' Allowing national differences carries the risk of asymmetrical implementation of European norms, as different national regulations and institutions diverge rather than converge on regulation goals and strategies. Ultimately, such asymmetry threatens the paramount objective of European regulation, namely, creating a level playing field for competition in the internal market by setting common standards. The obvious solution to this problem would be greater centralization of regulatory powers at the European level. This has, however, not been politically feasible, given structural limits to re-regulation at the European level. Member-states have to date strongly resisted giving up regulatory powers.[36] Such reservations have been particularly acute in the area of economic regulation, because regulation potentially infringes on highly sensitive, 'close to state' economic sectors in which the nation-state has traditionally taken on special responsibilities towards its citizens. Centralization is also resisted in the area of social regulation discussed in this chapter. Powerful, independent regulatory authorities with far-reaching regulatory powers at the European level are not to be found here; and even the EU Commission has neither far-reaching nor exclusive possibilities to intervene.

Regulation in the European Multi-level System of Governance: Transnational Networks as Agents of Informal Harmonization?

The European regulatory state is evidently facing a dilemma. Despite the rising need for uniform European rules, the European level lacks the formal powers and the institutional capacities necessary to generate rules and monitor and enforce their compliance and transposition in member-states. Given this, the EU's most important regulatory instrument continues to be competition policy, although this only covers a small section of the area in need of regulation. Moreover, as the most functionally obvious solution – greater centralization – to the problem has been politically resisted by member-states, a gap has emerged that threatens to considerably weaken regulatory effectiveness at the European level.

In light of the regulatory gap, alternative roads were taken to secure a substantive Europeanization of regulatory activities. It is our argument that these alternatives, mainly the creation of transnational regulatory networks, have partly closed the regulatory gap. Transnational regulatory networks have developed into an increasingly important form of European coordination and informal, soft harmonization of member-state regulatory activities. The decisive advantage of these regulatory networks is that they remove the deficits of heavy decentralization, without being dependent on formal centralization.[37]

Transnational regulatory networks are composed of experts and representatives of national regulatory bodies, who come to agreement among themselves, led or supported by European bodies. In appropriate cases they are joined by market participants or those who will be subject to regulations. On an informal basis, these networks develop common 'best practice' rules and procedures for regulation in their sector. These bodies are particularly influential when they take preliminary decisions for formally competent bodies, such as the Council of the relevant ministers. In this way, without affecting national prerogatives, de facto coordination or even harmonization of regulatory practice is achieved. The most important advocate of this kind of informal harmonization is the European Commission. Accordingly, it proactively promotes the emergence of transnational regulatory networks as a means towards realizing common regulatory concepts and best-practice solutions.

A good example of this strategy is the European Electricity Regulation Forum, set up by the Directorate-General for Transport and Energy (TREN) to accompany national implementations of the 1996 European directive on the opening of the electricity markets.[38] This informal body sits semi-annually; it brings together national regulators, the relevant ministries, and important market actors such as network operators, representatives of the electricity industry, customers, and electricity traders. For the EC, which takes the lead, representatives of the Competition Directorate also take part. Supported by the active agenda setting of the internal-market division of the Directorate-General TREN, the forum has managed to develop a common understanding of regulatory requirements, concepts, and procedures, with a consensus among all member-states on the most important issues. On the basis of this common understanding, the electricity regulation forum, aided by specialized working groups, develops operational solutions for regulatory problems in the European internal market. For TREN, the central focus is on creating rules for cross-border trade and the use of transmission networks. The crucial point is that the solutions developed by the forum are usually taken up by the Council of energy ministers, which has formal competence, as the basis for its own decisions. Transnational energy cooperation through the forum has recently been complemented by a 'European Regulators Group for Electricity and Gas,' which is composed of national regulators and serves as an advisory group to the EU Commission and is designed to promote regulatory convergence.[39]

Examples of this type of 'soft harmonization' are also found in the telecommunications sector. The Directorate-General Competition and the Directorate-General Information Society supported the creation of the Open Network Provision (ONP) Committee. This committee brings together national regulators and ministries, permanent representatives of member-states and the EU Commission to address questions of licensing and implementation at bi-monthly intervals. Over time, it has taken on an increasingly important regulatory role. As a result of the 7 March 2002 framework directive for electronic communications networks and services,[40] the Commission also set up an advisory body, the European Regulators Group, designed as an 'interface between national regulatory authorities and the Commission' and intended to contribute to 'the consistent application of the new regulatory framework.'[41] A corresponding Radio Spectrum Policy Group is to produce similar results in coordinating the exploitation of the internal market's frequency spectrum.

The most important instrument of informal coordination through networks is *information* – not law or money. Particularly where regulatory policy is concerned, which overwhelmingly involves knowledge-based and technically specialized areas of regulation, the availability and dissemination of credible information meeting professional technical criteria proves to be the most effective instrument for soft control. Making information available also strengthens the role of European agencies involved in social regulation, which are considered to be formally weak.[42]

In a certain sense the agencies make a virtue out of necessity, relying on information as a resource of power instead of 'command and control.'[43] Lacking formal powers, the European agencies do not act like decision-making bodies but as information brokers that are networking between various national agencies.[44] Embedding the activities of national representatives in European-orchestrated networks makes them more 'cosmopolitan' in outlook, as opposed to focusing primarily on 'local' concerns.[45] This has the effect of smoothing the way to a certain convergence of national regulations on more Europe-wide standards.[46] The common basis and criteria of regulatory practice are then technical expertise and relevant technical standards, the observance of which enhances the reputation and credibility of national regulators. Through the establishment of ideas and discourses – aspects of information – that guide actions, informal regulatory practice may, in the long term, facilitate the opening of new legitimate areas for further European integration.[47]

Transnational regulatory networks should not, however, be simply understood as a tool of the EU Commission. These networks are connected to larger professional 'regulatory communities,' which extend beyond Europe into the whole OECD world. This enhances their independence vis-à-vis national or supranational policy agendas. On the basis of their technocratic logic, now apparent not only in a national regime context but also vis-à-vis the EU Commission's 'soft' control efforts, national agencies may be more able to embark on a regulatory course of their own. Thus, in the telecommunications sector, an 'independent regulators' group,' derived from the meetings of presidents of the various national regulatory authorities, has formed outside the Community framework. This group, which is also internationally active, exerted its independence by rejecting the Commission's attempts to incorporate its coordination activities into the supranational EU structure. In the electricity and gas sector, the Council of European Energy Regulators (CEER) was created in March 2000. Although CEER closely cooperates with the Commission through the forum and the new European Regulators Group mentioned earlier, the association sees itself as an independent coordinating body of national regulatory authorities, disseminating best-practice proposals for European electricity and gas regulation. These intergovernmental variants of informal coordination partially escape the Commission's influence. However, from the viewpoint of European regulation they can be regarded as a second-best solution, preferable to the non-coordination of national regulations.

It seems as if both transnational regulatory networks, promoted at the European level, and intergovernmental networking among national regulatory authorities, make an important contribution towards at least alleviating, if not solving, the dilemma between needed functional harmonization and politically blocked centralization. Successful coordination of European regulation through informal regulatory networks is, to be sure, tied to a number of internal and external conditions. Internally, the most important requirement is that, among the networked regulatory bodies, there is a high degree of trust and willingness to cooperate. It is only then that information can be disclosed and exchanged. This willingness to cooperate is particularly notable when all bodies involved are aiming for similar professional standards and share a common regulatory philosophy.[48]

Externally, regulatory networks can perform their coordination functions only on the precondition that participants are allowed a certain degree of independence and room to manoeuvre in their decisions. A national regulatory authority that has no significant powers in its respective national regime will find it hard to get effectively involved in transnational networks because its ability to secure commitment in its own country will be doubted. The political willingness to leave de facto regulatory powers to informal networks presumably also depends partly on how far the object of regulation affects opposing interests among member-states. If distributive conflicts among member-states emerge, they may compromise the effectiveness of informal harmonization. Thus, the European Electricity Regulation Forum, for example, was very successful in creating common regulatory concepts and approaches to solutions requiring specialized technical knowledge. When, however, the distributive effects of the regulatory solution became clear, the conflict between transit countries and trading countries delayed agreement on appropriate rates for utilizing transmission networks.

This example of the electricity sector makes it clear that regulatory networks do not offer some sort of patent solution the to European regulatory dilemma. They remain liable to 're-politicization,' becoming victims of blocking practices when member-states' interests do not converge, something that Scharpf has already identified as a central obstacle to formal European re-regulation.[49] A thorough de-politicization and rationalization of decision-making is evidently not possible in the European regulatory state. Even at the European level, public regulation is unavoidably caught in the tensions that emerge from conflicting political interests.

Conclusion: Transnational Regulatory Networks and the Informalization of Governance in the European Union

As a specific form of state supervision and monitoring of market processes, and in response to privatization, liberalization, and internal-market integration, regulation is gaining importance in Europe. Establishing European regulation, however, has faced some unanticipated challenges and brought several unintended consequences. In the EU, the supranational level seems particularly suited to becoming the preferred level of regulation. Since much of the EU's activities are regulatory in nature, moreover, and given increasing levels of European integration in different areas, there is a need for uniform European rules. Yet, the EU's member-states have resisted a transfer of regulatory competencies to the European level, thereby limiting the chances of a 'positive' re-regulation of negative market integration.[50] As a consequence, the EU's formal regulatory powers and its institutional capacities have so far remained underdeveloped. European regulation is most pronounced in the area of social regulation (e.g., environment and consumer protection), which has essentially developed in tandem with and as a complement to the emerging internal market. By contrast, European regulation in the economic sphere, specifically where market regulation is concerned, exerts less influence, with the important exception of competition law. The bulk of regulatory activity in this area rests unambiguously at the national level.

Our analysis has nevertheless shown that informal regulatory activities at the European level play a significant role in the EU's governance structure, even in the sphere of economic regulation where positive integration is regarded as particularly difficult and unlikely. This is because the EU regulatory state has evolved and developed differently than many observers once expected. Regulatory policy has partly succeeded in evading existing political obstacles, creating an innovative and informal approach to the need for Europe-wide rules and standards. Transnational regulatory networks have been central in the development of this structure of European regulation. By bringing together experts from national regulatory agencies and European bodies, these networks use informal procedures to develop common best-practice rules and procedures for regulation in any given sector. Through information exchange and networking oriented towards generating professional standards, de facto coordination or even harmonization of regulatory practice is achieved without infringing on national prerogatives. These transnational regulatory networks are responsible for the relatively high degree of substantive Europeanization, even in areas where obstacles to European re-regulation particularly abound. In this way, transnational regulatory networks provide a solution to the European regulatory dilemma. To be sure, transnational regulatory networks are not always available or feasible for soft harmonization. In the particular instance of politically controversial distributive debates, efforts of informal regulation, even through networks, can be undermined by the diverging interests of EU member-states.

The area of regulatory policy thus contradicts the view that an essential feature of European political authority requires formal institutions. In fact, as our discussion points out, attempts to regulate through formal institutions may be counterproductive because they are resisted by EU member-states. Informal structures, as reflected through networks, demand a shift in how European political authority is understood and studied: informal structures must be seen as fundamental aspects of supranational governance.[51] Indeed, the formal institutions of the EU have retained their formal powers. But they have not proven to be a necessary requirement for European regulation; on the contrary, regulation seems most effective when it is not formalized.

Informalization is by no means a unique characteristic of the European Union, as chapters in this book by Coleman, Porter, and Börzel and Risse indicate. Indeed, even inside modern constitutional states, informal tools of governance are generally regarded to be indispensable.[52] Some analysts even argue that they are becoming more important in democratic systems that assign a high priority to consensus-based decision-making.[53] In the EU, informal institutions and procedures take on an added significance. In a system best understood as a forum of negotiation between actors with divergent interests, each of which has veto power, the EU must rely on having available alternatives that can overcome the weaknesses of its formal procedures in order to avoid the costs of getting stuck in political stalemates resulting from conflicts of interest.[54] Moreover, the obstacles that stand in the way of formalizing regulation make evident the need for informal strategies for the development of Europe-wide regulations.

It is no coincidence that the EU is particularly fertile ground for the growth of policy networks of the most varied types.[55] And, due to the complicated, though dynamic, relationships among the EU Council, Commission, and Parliament, it is hardly surprising that the legislative process has been conducive to the emergence of informal institutions.[56] It is possible that informalization may simply be a step towards formalization, in turn strengthening the powers and support for formal institutions; however, given the current structural features of the EU multi-level system of governance, informal governance will undoubtedly gain significance, regardless of the outcome.

In the end, what should be made of the informalization of the European political process? Informal forms of governance must be assessed in two categories: their functionality and their legitimacy. Their *functionality* is generally assessed positively in the political-science literature: 'the informality of the decision-making processes guarantees an outcome that really solves the problems, or at least prevents complete blockage.'[57] This appears to hold true for the area of regulatory policy we have studied. In the area of economic regulation, informal governance makes an essential contribution to closing the regulatory gap at the European level, despite underdeveloped supranational competencies. This finding is confirmed by further case studies on the EU's problem-solving capacity, which have shown that small-scale informal arrangements, in particular, frequently enable the European multi-level system to function.[58]

Concern for the effectiveness of European governance should not, however, overshadow questions about the democratic *legitimacy* of informal decision-making processes. Greven makes this point forcefully in his contribution to this volume, and it is a solid one. Informalization privileges those interests relevant for decision-making and is therefore inherently exclusionary. Access to informal decision-making bodies, like the transnational regulatory networks we have studied in this chapter, is necessarily selective and not subject to any classical democratic control. Even more, the effectiveness of informal decision-making bodies often depends on the confidentiality and non-transparency of decisions, or influences. From the perspective of democratic legitimacy, therefore, informal forms of governance must be seen with some scepticism.[59] Accordingly, legitimating political authority in the European 'regulatory state' remains a significant challenge – and this challenge will likely become greater as informalization advances and proliferates. The editors of this volume rightly take up this theme in the concluding chapter, for it is not out of the question that the back road of informal governance may end up in a cul-de-sac – not only in Europe but also more generally, as transnational authority structures continue to evolve.

NOTES

1 This chapter is based on findings from a research project entitled ' The Regulatory State and Infrastructure,' supported by the Deutsche Forschungsgemeinschaft in connection with its program on 'Governance in Europe.' We

would like particularly to thank David Coen, Ute Hartenberger, Markus Jachtenfuchs, and Olivia van Riesen for information, suggestions, and comments. In addition, we would like to thank Iain L. Fraser, who translated large parts of the manuscript.

2 Schmitter (1991).

3 See Beck and Grande (2004).

4 See March and Olsen (1989), Steinmo et al. (1992) Weaver and Rockman (1993), Mayntz and Scharpf (1995), Hall and Taylor (1996).

5 Bulmer (1994), Kerremans (1996), Pierson (1996), Pollack (1996).

6 See Marks (1993), Marks et al. (1996), Scharpf (1999a), Leibfried and Pierson (1995), Hooghe (1996), Hooghe and Marks (2001, 2003), Grande (1996, 2000), Grande and Jachtenfuchs (2000), Héritier (1999b), Jachtenfuchs and Kohler-Koch (1996), Benz and Eberlein (1999).

7 See Börzel (1997).

8 Castells (1998).

9 Kohler-Koch (1999), Kohler-Koch and Eising (1999).

10 Ansell (2000).

11 The 'network concept,' as it is used here should be clearly separated from the concept of a 'policy network,' as employed in policy analysis. Both approaches are currently used in European studies (Richardson 2000a, 2001). However, they are related to different aspects of the EU and its decision-making processes. Whereas the former is related to basic structures of the European polity in general (as opposed, e.g., to majoritarian, parliamentary government), the latter describes a specific type of interest intermediation within a democratic political system (distinct, e.g., from 'policy communities' or 'corporatist' arrangements).

12 Ansell (2000: 311).

13 These features of the European polity have been widely neglected in comparative analyses that distinguish the 'old' – institutionally based – type of regional integration in Europe from a 'new' – network based – type of regional integration in Asia (see, e.g., Katzenstein 1996). It is certainly true that regional integration in Asia and in North America lacks the institutional capacities of the EU, but this is not to say that formal and informal networks are less important in the European policy process.

14 Ansell (2000: 323).

15 See Scharpf (1999a).

16 This statement still holds if regulation is understood to mean only one *specific* form of government action, namely, supervision and control of private enterprises and market behaviour (Baldwin and Cave, 1999; Noll, 1985) and not the whole spectrum of state activities, as is often the case in British

scholarship on the topic (e.g., among others, Dyson, 1992). Regulation in this narrower sense differs both from governmental ring-holding and from ad hoc interventions. In general, it can be described as external, permanent, and case-related supervision of markets by public actors laying down and applying rules in the 'public interest' in a formal procedure (Selznick 1985).

17 Majone (1996).

18 Beck (1992).

19 Scharpf (1999a).

20 See Schmidt (1998), Eising (2000), Cowles, Caporaso and Risse (2001), Héritier et al. (2001).

21 Majone (1990), Majone (1994b), Majone (1999), Grande (1993), Grande (1994), Grande (1997), Vogel (1996).

22 See, e.g., Thatcher (1998).

23 The distinction between the 'positive' and the 'regulatory' state was introduced by Harold Seidman and Robert Gilmour (1986). In their view, the rise of the regulatory state is the very essence of a fundamental change in the way the state conducts its business by 'providing services without producing them' (1986: 119). See Majone (1994b, 1996, 1999, 2000), Grande (1994, 1997), Grande and Eberlein (2000), Scott (2000), Moran (2002).

24 See Grande (1997); Schuppert (1997).

25 This should not be confused with 'negative integration,' as outlined by Scharpf's (1999a) regulatory-state thesis; even the creation of effective competition requires 'positive' rule setting.

26 Majone (1990, 1994b, 1996).

27 Majone (1996: 57).

28 For a recent summary of the creation and development of European regulatory agencies, see Keleman, who posits that the 'establishment of agencies at the European level is one of the most notable developments in EU regulatory policy' (2002: 93). See also, Kreher (1997), Chiti (2000), Vos (2000), Yataganas (2001: 22–6).

29 For an updated survey of these European agencies see: http://europa.eu.int/agencies/index_en.htm

30 The role of the nation-state takes on a greater significance when the focus of analysis is extended beyond the new European regulatory agencies, e.g. to national ministries and general competition authorities. See Eberlein (2000b).

31 See Begg (1996).

32 Schmidt (1998: 56).

33 Levi-Faur (1999: 201).

34 McGowan and Wallace (1996).

35 Eberlein (2000a), Eising (2000).
36 This, e.g., has prevented the long-discussed creation of an independent European regulatory agency for telecommunications.
37 See Dehousse (1997), Coen and Doyle (2000), Eberlein and Grande (2000), Majone (2000), Eberlein (2003).
38 Directive 96/92/EC; for a detailed analysis of the electricity forum as an informal, transnational regulatory network see Eberlein (2003, 2005).
39 Commission Decision 2003/796/EC of 11.11. 2003. This is part of the new legislative framework under directive 2003/54/EC for electricity and directive 2003/55/EC for gas, which prescribe further energy market opening and integration.
40 Directive 2002/19/EC
41 Commission Decision 2002/2874/EC of 29.7.2002
42 See Majone (2000).
43 Majone (1997).
44 Dehousse (1997: 257).
45 Gouldner (1957, 1958).
46 See Majone (2000: 295f.).
47 See Kohler-Koch and Edler (1998).
48 See Majone (2000: 297).
49 Scharpf (1999a).
50 See Scharpf (1999a).
51 Kohler-Koch (1999), Ansell (2000).
52 See Schulze-Fielitz (1998: 48).
53 See Mayntz (1998a).
54 See Héritier (1999b).
55 See Ansell (2000).
56 Farrell and Héritier (2003).
57 Mayntz (1998a: 56). The position of constitutional lawyers, who describe the informal rules as ambivalent, is more differentiated (see Schulze-Fielitz, 1998).
58 See Grande (2000: 24).
59 See Greven's chapter in this volume.

8 The Primitive Realities of North America's Transnational Governance

STEPHEN CLARKSON, WITH SARAH DAVIDSON
LADLY, MEGAN MERWART, AND CARLTON THORNE

Europe's astonishing development of a unique form of regional political authority, in which transnational governance combined member-state governments with players from the marketplace and the citizenry presents those trying to understand other regions with a conceptual conundrum.[1] Does the evolution of the European Union towards some kind of constitutionalized federation of states with its strong commission, its ambitious parliament, its asymmetry-reducing voting, and its effective judiciary provide the heuristic model for understanding changes, even if embryonic, in the political underpinnings of other regions?

During the past decade, such a question has informed much analysis of developments in the western hemisphere. With Mercosur bringing Brazil, Argentina, Uruguay, and Paraguay into a common market, and with the Canada–U.S. Free Trade Agreement (CUFTA, 1989) eventually pulling Mexico into a North American Free Trade Agreement (NAFTA, 1994), many see the New World following in the footsteps of the Old, albeit with a few decades' delay.

While agreeing that North America in the past ten years has developed new forms of transnational decision-making and while accepting that NAFTA coordinates significant political-economy functions among its three member-states, this chapter argues that a putatively 'free trade' agreement masks the enhancement of the United States' hegemonic relationship with its periphery. In other words, while NAFTA opened up a more integrated economic space and while it constitutes a codified legal system which formally reconstituted political authority for its three members, it did this with a very different valence for each. By causing Canada, and then Mexico to accept some of its norms, the hegemon extended its sovereignty beyond its borders. By ingesting in their own legal orders rules designed to further U.S. corporate interests, the two peripheral states curtailed their own sovereignty.

To address the general complexities involved in assessing the significance of the United States' evolving relationship with Mexico and Canada, this chapter will develop the case that, behind its façade of trinational equality, NAFTA's reconstitution of political authority in North America undermines its peripheral states while strengthening its centre. We will start by looking at the continental system created by NAFTA as if it were a traditional government, analysing it in the way that the European Union often is understood, that is, in terms of:

1 Its *constitution*, which defines the system's norms and establishes its institutions and is to be found in the various treaties signed during the community's first half-century of existence
2 An *executive* that makes decisions and policies to sustain its operation and is located partly in the European Commission and partly in the Council of Ministers in Brussels
3 A *legislature* whose prime electoral function is to represent member-states' publics in the EU's policy-making process and is located in the European Parliament which sits both in Brussels and Strasbourg
4 A *judiciary*, which resolves conflicts among constituents by interpreting the constitution's norms and is located in the European Court of Justice, also in Strasbourg
5 A *bureaucracy*, located in the European Commission in Brussels, where an elaborate system of directorates and committees makes the whole system actually function
6 An ability to *enforce* public law, administrative regulations, and judicial rulings, which is assumed by the member-states' coercive agencies.

To talk of an emerging European *government* in terms of these six criteria is not to negate the importance of the *governance* that takes place on the edges of the formal political system as public-private entities, civil-society organizations, and market players struggle less visibly over public policies, create norms, and exercise power within their own subsystems. In contrast to the nuanced analysis in the contributions to this book by Eberlein and Grande, Greven, and Beck, this chapter uses the notion of European government as a heuristic device. We are interested less in comparing the fuzzier configuration of governance in the two systems and more in establishing the remarkable extent to which the political manifestation of transnational integration has *not* been formally institutionalized in North America – because this 'reluctant trinity'[2] of states did its best not to create any kind of new political authority.

Examining this region's government under the same six rubrics should allow us to determine whether North America is undergoing a transformation as a region analogous to the European case examined by other contributors to this volume. Because the two continental regimes are so startlingly similar in economic system and demographic size and because their dominant cultures share common Judaeo-Christian roots, looking at one in terms of the qualities of the other has an inherent fascination.[3] But we note at the outset that there are important differences complicating any effort at comparison. Ethnically, North America has an indigenous population whose political salience ranges from high in Mexico to medium in Canada to low in the United States. Developmentally, the discrepancy between the wealth and technological capacity of the American and Canadian societies, on the one hand, and Mexico, on the other, as well as the crushing power asymmetry between the central state and its two neighbours stand in sharp contrast to the greater homogeneity among the fifteen members of the European Union, which are nevertheless more divided linguistically and historically than their North American counterparts.

Constitution

If a polity's constitution is the rulebook that defines its institutions and establishes the norms by which they are run, then the complex transnational jigsaw puzzle in North America has various constitutionalizing elements. For instance, sixty years of binational defence cooperation between the United States and Canada generated an elaborate structure of reciprocal defence obligations that were in effect constitutionalized by over eighty treaty-level defence agreements such as the North American Air Defense Command (NORAD), 250 memoranda of understanding, and 145 bilateral defence discussion forums. CUFTA created a more general constitutional framework for the U.S–Canada relationship with strong rules but weak administration. Though much more conflictual, even antagonistic, the U.S.–Mexico relationship also developed constitutionalizing elements, particularly in the form of treaties defining modalities for managing flows of all kinds across the common border.

NAFTA was the first North American accord with trinational scope. But, compared with the elaborate system created by the European community's various treaties, it contains a thin, even unidimensional set of economic norms – national treatment being of prime importance – which have supralegislative weight in the sense that they can trump acts of the member-states' legislatures. The agreement also contains hundreds of pages of rules directing member-states' legislative and regulatory actions, whether negative, 'thou shalt not' injunctions (Canada was forbidden to set different prices for exported and domestically consumed petroleum products) or positive, 'thou shalt' commandments (Mexico had to create a new trade law system). These measures applied to a wide range of policy fields such as telecommunications and agriculture, government procurement and energy, cultural development and industrial promotion.

Beyond these norms and rules, the constitution that NAFTA created for North America comprises a weak executive, a non-existent legislature, an uneven set of adjudicatory mechanisms, an ineffectual bureaucracy, and almost no coercive capacity – institutions to whose analysis we now turn.

Legislature

Constitutions cannot be the only source of a polity's norms, as no single document can anticipate future conditions that will require existing rules to be adapted or new ones to be created. In liberal democratic societies, it is the legislature that is the most visible and publicly legitimate source of rule making. At the transnational level, legislators may confer in interparliamentary associations, but they do not get together to legislate. In obvious contrast to the World Trade Organization, whose Doha Round of ministerial negotiations will create still more global trade rules, NAFTA has no institution through which its rulebook can be adapted to changing circumstances.

NAFTA's legislative incapacity leaves the evolution of new, continentally applicable economic rules to other negotiating forums. For instance, the rule stipulating that, when tariffs on a good have fallen to zero, its cross-border commerce may not be subjected to anti-dumping or countervailing duties, resulted from the bilateral negotiations between Canada and Chile. New trade norms were expected to emerge in the western hemisphere through the negotiation of a Free Trade Area of the Americas, which, had it not been blocked in 2003 by Brazil's opposition, would presumably have trumped those of NAFTA.

Executive

The North American Free Trade Commission is defined in Article 2001 as supervising the implementation of NAFTA, overseeing its further elaboration, resolving disputes that arise from interpretations of the agreement, and supervising the work of the committees and working groups it established.[4] As outlined in NAFTA, the commission's powers are to: establish and delegate responsibilities to ad hoc or standing committees, working groups, or expert groups; seek the advice of non-governmental persons or groups; and take such other action in the exercise of its functions as the parties may agree.[5]

This substantial mandate notwithstanding, the North American Free Trade Commission turned out to be no institution at all. It has neither headquarters nor address. Nor does it have a secretariat to call its own. 'Trade Commission' is just a label for meetings of the signatory states' three trade ministers, which, according to the U.S. Trade Representative, are 'intended to assess the implementation of the agreement, resolve any new disputes, and oversee the work of numerous committees established to address specific issues described in each chapter in the agreement.'[6] It convenes quite infrequently: 'only as required, or for annual meetings,'[7] at which it typically:

- Receives and adopts reports regarding the work of the agreement's several dozen committees, working groups, and subsidiary bodies
- Instructs officials on how to address a broad range of NAFTA implementation issues
- Approves agreements on unresolved issues
- Discusses pending issues that require ministerial-level attention
- Implements trade-facilitating technical modifications to the NAFTA rules for determining which products receive the favourable tariff treatment afforded by NAFTA.[8]

This last role suggests that, as an executive institution, NAFTA's Free Trade Commission potentially has some legislative capacity because, in principle, the three ministers could make determinations that substantially transform the North American rulebook. In practice they have shown no taste for such leadership.

Judiciary

No constitution is effective unless it has some means by which to resolve disputes that inevitably surface when opposing interests take differing positions on the meanings of its norms. Although NAFTA was established without an actual court and judges, it does have provisions for resolving general disputes about the agreement's implementation (Chapter 20), for mitigating disputes over trade harassment (Chapter 19), for empowering aggrieved companies to sue member governments (Chapter 11), settling conflicts concerning financial institutions (Chapter 14) and energy, (Chapter 6), and for addressing certain environmental law and labour law issues, using the complex procedures established in the two supplementary North American Agreements on Environmental and Labour Cooperation.

Chapter 20: General Disputes

Continental dispute settlement was meant to de-fang intergovernmental conflicts through having them resolved by neutral arbitrators who would apply common rules. In this spirit, NAFTA's Chapter 20 provides for binational panels to be struck when member-states are unable to resolve their differences over issues generated by the agreement. Although Chapter 20 dispute settlement was considered expeditious at first,[9] later decisions have not been able to settle conflicts without resort to power politics. For example, when it lost a panel decision to Canada in a wheat case,[10] Washington responded by threatening to launch a separate investigation into Canadian wheat exports. Closure was achieved only when Ottawa gave way to U.S. pressure and agreed to limit Canada's wheat exports.[11] With Chapter 20 rulings failing to constrain the hegemon, so that it became futile for the peripheral governments to submit general issues to NAFTA arbitration, continental government proved unable to deliver rights that its weaker members had 'paid' for when negotiating the original compact. In this example NAFTA's rule-based judicial trappings disguised a continuing power-based authority system on the continent.

Chapter 19: Trade Remedy Disputes

Had NAFTA created a true free trade area, its members would have abandoned their right to impose anti-dumping (AD) or countervailing duties (CVD) on imports coming from their partners' economies. Refusing to give up its sovereignty over trade remedy actions and so allow a real levelling of national trade barriers, which would have created a single continental market, the United States simply agreed to cede appeals of its protectionist rulings to ad hoc binational panels that were restricted to investigating whether the defendant's AD or CVD determinations properly applied its own *domestic* trade law.

Chapter 19's putatively binding judicial expedient turned out to be less binding than originally billed. When the U.S. countervailing duty against Canadian softwood lumber exports was remanded for incorrectly applying the notion of subsidy as defined in U.S. law, Congress simply changed its definition of subsidy to apply to the Canadian situation. Beyond softwood lumber's long-lasting evidence – the United States was, in 2005, still pursuing Canada on the grounds of its exports being subsidized – Canada has not had a satisfactory experience in using Chapter 19 to appeal other U.S. trade determinations. In 1993, for instance, there were multiple remands in five cases, which led the panels to surpass their deadlines significantly. Further problems have arisen over the inconsistency among Chapter 19 panel decisions, which have shown significantly different degrees of deference to agency determinations.

Although AD and CVD jurisprudence may have been ineffective in helping the peripheral states constrain their hegemon, the opposite is not true. Canadian trade agencies have had to adjust the standards that they apply in AD or CVD determinations to U.S. interpretations out of a concern for what the binational panels, which necessarily include American jurists, may later decide on appeal.

In striking contrast to this minor modification of its trade remedy interpretations that Chapter 19 panels imposed on Canada's protective administrative procedures, NAFTA caused Mexico to import holus bolus into its legal system a complete trade remedy system. This was the more extraordinary because, despite its civil law tradition, Mexico had to create from scratch judicial procedures to satisfy its interlocutors that their companies would be treated the same way in challenging Mexico's protectionist rulings as they would in the United States or Canada's common law systems.[12]

Thus Chapter 19 confirms the experience of Chapter 20: NAFTA's judicial function is asymmetrical in its impact. It does not constrain the behaviour of the hegemon on politically sensitive issues, but this does not stop the hegemon using Chapter 19 to enforce NAFTA rules to its advantage in the periphery. Moreover, when these processes do not satisfy Washington, it can still exercise its raw power to achieve its objectives. But if Chapters 19 and 20 are surprisingly weak as institutions of continental governance, Chapter 11 is surprisingly strong.

Chapter 11: Investor-State Disputes

NAFTA's Article 1110 stipulates that no government may 'directly or indirectly expropriate or nationalize' or take 'a measure tantamount to expropriation or nationalization' except for a 'public purpose,' on a 'non-discriminatory basis,' in accordance with 'due process of law and minimum standards of treatment' *and* on 'payment of compensation.'[13] What is remarkable about this article is not the wording, which is identical to that found in CUFTA, but rather its empowerment by a judicial process that gives corporations from other NAFTA parties the power to overturn democratically generated legislative or regulatory decisions deemed necessary to secure the health and safety of a particular jurisdiction's citizenry. Under these investor-state tribunals, an American or Mexican corporation with interests in Canada, for instance, can initiate arbitration proceedings against a municipal, provincial, or federal 'measure' that harms their interests on the grounds that it has been the victim of expropriation. These disputes are taken for arbitration before an international panel operating by rules established under the aegis of the World Bank's International Convention on the Settlement of Investment Disputes between States and Nationals of other States (ICSID) or the U.N. Commission on International Trade Law (UNCITRAL) for settling international disputes between corporations.[14] Since these forums operate according to the norms of international corporate law, Chapter 11 disputes actually transfer the adjudication of disputes over member-state policies from the realm of public law to private law and from the domestic to the global level.

Article 1110 gives transnational corporations important rights without balancing them with obligations. There are no continental institutions with the clout to regulate, tax, or monitor the newly created continental market that has proceeded to emerge.[15] In other words, NAFTA supported a regime of continental governance less by creating a new institutional structure for it than by reducing member-states' capacities to exercise sovereignty over their own political space. Corporations with continental scope were given both greater freedom from state regulation and a privatized, transnational legal device to discipline governments that stood in their way.

Although NAFTA has no legislative competence, its Chapter 11 tribunals have proven their ability to create new norms. More accurately, the cases launched by Ethyl, S.D. Myers, and Metalclad corporations resulted in *un*making legislation that had already been passed:

- In the first instance, when Ethyl of Virginia initiated an investor-state dispute process, Ottawa settled privately by withdrawing the law that forbade the trade of MMT, a gasoline additive alleged to be a neurotoxin.
- In the second Chapter 11 affair, the tribunal ruled that a federal law banning the export of PCBs both expropriated the waste disposal company's property and denied it national treatment, even though only a phantom company operated in Canada to generate business for its processing plant in the United States. In supporting the notion that S.D. Myers had suffered action 'tantamount to expropriation,' the tribunal was both invalidating a federal law and amending the notion of expropriation employed in the Canadian legal order.
- In the third case, the tribunal deemed illegal the action taken by a Mexican municipality to close an industrial waste site.

The Chapter 11 investor-state dispute settlement mechanism is powerful in good part because UNCITRAL and ICSID arbitrations have direct effect in domestic courts. This means that the coercive power of the defendant member-states themselves ensures their compliance with this part of NAFTA's de-territorialized adjudicatory system.

The direct effect of Chapter 11 decisions points out the limitations of NAFTA's legislative capacity. Because the Free Trade Commission has the authority to make 'interpretations' that investor-state tribunals are bound to accept, the Canadian government lobbied its NAFTA counterparts from 1998 to amend the investor-state dispute feature of Chapter 11. Mexico opposed this – on the grounds that its attractiveness to foreign capital lay in offering ironclad guarantees of investor rights – and so resisted the necessary trinational consensus. Finally, on 31 July 2001, the three trade ministers were able to agree on an interpretation of 'international law' in Article 1105 – declaring that it means international customary law – for use by Chapter 11 arbitrators. The clarification is thought unlikely to have much consequence.[16]

Bureaucracy

Just as constitutions establish a judicial system to interpret them, they also set up administrative institutions which need civil servants to staff them. The NAFTA text established a 'NAFTA Secretariat [which] administers the NAFTA dispute resolution processes under Chapters 14, 19 and 20 of the NAFTA, and has certain responsibilities related to Chapter 11 dispute settlement provisions.'[17] In their anti-institutional wisdom, the signatories never created this secretariats, contenting themselves with opening their own national NAFTA secretariats, which in each case has turned out to be a small office within the member-state's trade department with only minor record-keeping responsibilities such as maintaining a courtlike registry relating to panel, committee, and tribunal proceedings.

NAFTA established some twenty committees and working groups (CWGs) to monitor and direct the implementation of each chapter of the agreement.[18] Since these groups had the potential to become instruments for a genuine, coordinated, and transnational decision-making authority within the new continental structure created by NAFTA, we will devote considerable attention to comparing their official purposes with their actual performance.

Official Purposes

The CWGs were officially set up to be not supranational, but rather intergovernmental and explicitly *professional*. They were to be forums in which civil servants from the three countries' various ministries could exchange relevant information, resolve minor disputes, and discuss further liberalization. Their structure and composition were intended to favour objective analysis and the pre-emptive resolution of conflicts through the formation of small networks of experts.[19] It was hoped that the resulting epistemic communities would be inclined to treat issues impartially and focus on long-term benefits of increased economic activity that would be mutually rewarding, rather than on the short-term costs of immediate dislocations that might be politically contentious.[20]

Indeed, the implicit connotation of professional was *apolitical*. The thinking behind the CWGs was grounded in a desire to create forums where all three member-states could voice and transmit their interests in a de-politicized arena. Although 'political direction for the NAFTA work program [was to be] provided by ministers through the Free Trade Commission,'[21] the groups were to be insulated from direct political pressures in their day-to-day activities. The basis for having specialized groups staffed by civil servants who were drawn from various agencies and ministries and were selected for their detailed knowledge of the issue at hand – whether pesticides, trucking standards, or customs issues[22] – was the belief that NAFTA was more likely to operate by its rules if their operation was at least partly removed from the sphere of domestic politics and placed in new, problem-solving transnational institutions. [23]

Central to the working groups' professional make-up was their *trilateral* nature. In the spirit of the new continentalism, the CWGs were created with a view to trilateralizing relations by evaluating and even helping direct trade-related public policy-making within all three member-states. The groups were mandated to meet from one to four times a year, or as issues arose, and to produce reports for the Free Trade Commission. Meetings were to take place in Canada, the United States, and Mexico in rotation.[24] Trilateral forums were expected to be more likely to defuse bilateral conflicts and so provide a means to transcend the traditional bilateralism of North American trade politics.

Trilateralism had its own implicit corollary – *symmetry* – a step in the direction of a new continental relationship founded on the legal equality of its constituents. There was to be approximately equal representation of the three countries on each group, which was to be co-chaired by an official from each member-state. The mere existence of such trilateral institutions could be expected to offset the asymmetry in power that existed between the United States and its neighbour-partners, ensuring that all three states were given 'voice opportunities' with which to make their views known and possibly give them effect. [25]

The CWGs' trilateral, professional, and symmetrical nature marked a significant innovation for North American relations. Whether this novelty had any substance was another matter entirely.

Activities and Processes of the Committees and Working Groups

Just as the CWGs' mandates vary, so do their actual processes and functions. Most committees and working groups are engaged in a combination of activities that fall into the following five categories.

1. *Implementing or Overseeing the Implementation of the Agreement.* The majority of the CWGs are involved in the oversight of NAFTA's implementation. The group most directly and successfully involved in this implementation of NAFTA was the Committee on Trade in Goods. Having completed all four rounds of its tariff acceleration mandate, this committee no longer meets regularly.[26]

2. *Exchange of Information.* All groups act as forums for sharing information, including tracking each country's administration or implementation of the agreement, formulating understandings around various problems, laying the groundwork necessary for generating further integration, and more generally, understanding the needs and concerns of each member-state. This information exchange sometimes results in the production of trilateral statements or reports and has become the groups' primary function.[27]

3. *Resolution of Conflicts.* The groups have resolved or worked on low-level disputes concerning, for example, the appropriate classification of goods (Customs Subgroup of the Working Group on Rules of Origin[28]), the increased Mexican duties on the importation of frozen Canadian geese and United States ducks (Committee on Trade in Goods), and the application of a merchandise-processing fee by the U.S. on imports of some Canadian textile products (Committee on Trade in Goods).[29]

4. *Harmonization of Regulations.* Some CWGs had explicit mandates to harmonize, or to generate new regulations that would directly affect how NAFTA was implemented and administered. For example, the Working Group on Rules of Origin was one of the most active in 2002, particularly when it reconfigured and realigned seven NAFTA rules of origin in order to ensure their conformity with changes in the World-wide Harmonized System announced by the WTO in January 2002.[30]

5. *Forums for the Relay of Information between the Governments and Interested Parties.* The final function of the committees and working groups is to facilitate the exchange of ideas between any interested non-governmental players in the private sector. In this respect, the CWGs encourage a high level of private sector participation and appear to create new and more explicit access points for these interests. For instance, the key responsibility of the Telecommunications Standards Sub-Committee (TSSC) is the coordination of efforts and exchange of information with the Consultative Committee for Telecommunications (CCT), an organization that represents the interests of the telecommunications industry in North America. The TSSC's membership consists of two to three government officials from each of the NAFTA member-

states. But since 1999, the chair and the vice-chairs of the CCT have additionally been invited to all of the committee's meetings with the intention of enhancing the degree of feedback coming from the pertinent business communities of the three countries.[31]

While most CWGs operate as forums for relaying private sector concerns and ideas to government officials charged with interpreting and implementing NAFTA, the degree of private sector participation and consultation varies from group to group.[32] Although the involvement of private sector interests is appropriate in the context of a free trade agreement, CWGs blur the lines between consultant and consulted in some cases. Despite the fact that the level of consultation is 'nothing beyond the usual day-to-day interaction' for an administrative entity such as the U.S. Department of Commerce,[33] the democratic legitimacy of these groups is questionable. Their almost total lack of transparency prevents individual citizens or civil-society organizations from countervailing private sector access.

Actual Performance

Rather than become new agents of continental government, the CWGs have proven largely inconsequential in terms of governance. After six years, by 2002, approximately 60 per cent of them were inactive. In the case of the Committee on Trade in Goods (CTG), inactivity signified success, as its final round of tariff acceleration, completed ahead of schedule, left it without an agenda. However, the CTG stands out as the only example of a group that has completed, to the satisfaction of all three member-states, NAFTA's mission, which specified the items requiring further tariff reduction.[34]

If a CWG's mandate is too politically sensitive to be dealt with in such a forum, the CWG becomes deadlocked and thereby inactive. Some groups such as the Committee on Trade in Worn Clothing and the Working Group on Emergency Action, were born out of the inability to reach consensus on certain controversial issues during the NAFTA negotiations. To forestall delay in signing the agreement, some unresolved but contentious issues were assigned to working groups as a way to 'soften the failure of a lack of resolution.'[35] In these cases, establishing working groups was simply a 'graceful way of pretending there would be more discussion' about a failed negotiation.[36] These CWGs encountered considerable difficulties operating, as issues that were too contentious prior to 1994 did not become any easier to navigate subsequently.

For instance, the Chapter 19 Working Group on Trade Remedies was established in 1993 as a face-saving device for Ottawa, for which eliminating the application of U.S. anti-dumping and countervailing duties to Canadian exports had been the prime objective when soliciting a trade agreement with Washington. The group was mandated 'to seek solutions that reduce the possibility of disputes concerning the issues of subsidies, dumping, and the operation of trade remedy laws regarding such practices.'[37] The exceptionally controversial nature of these issues ensured that the group would be unable even to approach them. Not surprisingly, the working group is completely inactive.[38]

Two particularly instructive cases of contentious bilateral issues that defied resolution through NAFTA's bureaucratic and judicial frameworks are trucking and energy.

THE MEXICO–U.S. TRUCKING DISPUTE

In the NAFTA negotiations, the United States agreed to end long-standing restrictions against Mexican trucking companies and to gradually allow them to operate in the United States in a process that was to have been completed by 1 January 2000.[39] Although the Canadian and Mexican ministers of transportation signed memoranda of understanding permitting Canadian and Mexican truckers equal access within both countries, the restrictions were maintained by the Clinton administration because of strong domestic pressure from interest groups benefiting from the status quo.[40] Financial stakes were substantial: The cross-border trucking industry carried U.S. $250 billion in Mexican–U.S. trade. If American truckers were to be transporting fewer goods, the U.S. insurance companies' market share and profits would decrease.[41] For their part, American trucking unions argued that Mexican trucks would not sufficiently adhere to American safety standards.

In 1995, the Mexican government requested that a dispute resolution process be activated under the aegis of NAFTA's Chapter 20. American manoeuvring managed to drag out the adjudicatory process, but finally, in February 2001, the panel ruled that the U.S. moratorium violated NAFTA and ordered the U.S. Department of Transportation (USDOT) to begin processing all Mexican applications.[42]

Beyond confirming the impoverished justice offered by Chapter 20, this long, unhappy episode illustrated the failure of NAFTA's working group system. The Land Transportation Sub-Committee (LTSC) had been established under NAFTA's Chapter 9 specifically 'to address developments of more compatible standards related to truck, bus, and rail operations and the transport of hazardous materials among the United States, Mexico and Canada.'[43] Within this general mandate, the LTSC established a Cross-Border Operations and Facilitation Consultative Working Group (TCG 1) to deal with the Mexican–U.S. border issue. Since its inception, however, TCG 1's most significant activity has been to arrange for 'a meeting of the trilateral *ad hoc* government-industry insurance group formed by TCG 1.'[44] Thus, the LTSC has primarily functioned to exchange information and study national regulatory systems, despite Annex 913.5.a1 explicitly directing that 'the Subcommittee shall implement the following work program for making compatible the Parties' relevant standards-related measures. No later than three years after the date of entry into force of the Agreement, [it shall determine] standards-related measures respecting vehicles, including measures relating to weights and dimensions, tires, brakes, parts and accessories, securement of cargo, maintenance and repair, inspections, and emissions and environmental pollution levels.'[45]

This list contained many of the safety concerns subsequently expressed by the United States as its rationale for non-compliance. The task of harmonizing weight standards for bus and truck operations fell within the mandate of the LTSC, and as such, it was an issue that was meant to be resolved in a trilateral, professional fashion by a group of experts. The bilateral nature of the dispute is one reason TCG1 did not function well in the trilateral framework. Canada remained involved in this issue only to the extent that it desired to be kept informed of developments and that it wanted to see the dispute resolved. Despite being formally a NAFTA issue, it remained primarily a bilateral dispute.[46]

Politics played a contradictory, but illuminating role both in provoking and resolving this dispute. On the one hand, it was the highly politicized nature of the dispute that prevented the LTSC from dealing with the issue in any meaningful way. On the other, the transnationalizing of the southern border of the United States gave Mexico more clout than it had before NAFTA. The increasing importance of Mexican-Americans in U.S. presidential and congressional politics built up pressures for a negotiated solution. As the issue was the U.S. government's refusal to act in the face of powerful domestic interests that were opposed to granting national treatment to Mexican trucks, a solution was required that would allow Mexican trucks into the United States while also taking into account the domestic political sensitivities. This issue was only resolved in 2001 by high-level negotiations between presidents Bush and Fox.[47]

The Land Transportation Subcommittee was reinvigorated as a result of the Bush administration's decision to honour the panel's decision. The procedures for implementing the dispute panel's ruling were defined when the U.S. Congress set specific guidelines that the USDOT was to follow. In November 2002, President Bush modified the moratorium on granting operating authority to Mexican motor carriers and enabled the USDOT to review the 130 applications already received from Mexico-domiciled truck and bus companies.[48] Ultimately, the LTSC had little to do with the resolution of this dispute. Washington's conformity with its obligation was primarily determined by executive will and other political considerations such as a continuing obstruction through the U.S. trucking interests' use of the courts.

THE U.S.–MEXICO ENERGY RELATIONSHIP

Energy has long been a contentious issue central to the United States' political agenda with Mexico. Public ownership of oil and electricity was written into the Mexican constitution,[49] deliberately and effectively excluding foreign capital from developing the country's energy resources.

Mexico has the second largest proven crude oil reserves in the western hemisphere, after Venezuela,[50] and in 2000 Petroleos Mexicanos (Pemex) exported 1.4 million barrels of oil a day, making it the fourth largest foreign source of crude oil for United States.[51] Facing ever-increasing domestic demand for natural gas, Washington viewed Mexico as a critical source of new supplies,[52] and it was also anxious to increase U.S.–Mexico electricity integration, linking Mexican electricity generation capacity to the power grid and market in the U.S. southwest.[53] The Bush administration envisioned a North American energy market characterized by the free flow of oil, natural gas, and electricity across U.S. borders both to the north and south,[54] but its determination to build a continental market for energy was more than matched by Mexico's resistance to such an arrangement.[55]

Energy generates 3 per cent of Mexico's gross national product, and 8 per cent of all its exports, as well as providing the government with more than one-third of its tax income.[56] Since Mexicans view their energy resources as part of their national heritage, the maintenance of a national oil industry is a symbol of Mexican sovereignty,[57] and strong political forces in Mexico oppose increasing foreign corporations' control.[58] Wary of job losses if foreign companies move back, Mexico's electricity sector labour unions, with a combined membership over 100,000, oppose privatization of energy,[59] as does Pemex, whose labour unions control 40 per cent of its board of directors. Within this context, the United States, anxious to bring Mexico into the same kind of energy interdependence as it had achieved with Canada, pushed for a continental approach to energy policy development.

On 22 April 2001 in Quebec City, a North American Energy Working Group (NAEWG) was set up by the three countries' energy ministers to build a deeper continental understanding regarding energy[60] and to help 'foster communication and co-operation among the governments and energy sectors of the three countries on energy-related matters of common interest, and to enhance North American energy trade and interconnections consistent with the goal of sustainable development, for the benefit of all.'[61] Since its creation, the NAEWG has been quite successful in accomplishing meaningful, but politically unrisky tasks.[62] As with the NAFTA CWGs, the NAEWG operates informally and by consensus. Most of Canada's members come from its Ministry of Natural Resources, although a small number work for its Departments of Foreign Affairs and International Trade or serve on its National Energy Board.[63] In the same spirit as that of the CWGs, the NAEWG's mandate is to be a trilateral forum and perform a range of low-key functions such as the exchange of information and the harmonization of statistical methodology among the three member-states. The NAEWG has served as an effective tool through which Canada can promote its goal to have Alberta's oil sands reclassified as part of North America's petroleum reserves.[64]

The question arises why a trilateral group of energy officials, who are chiefly exploring issues around continental energy supply and the harmonization of the energy practices, was not set up under NAFTA. The answer lies in energy's controversial yet central status in each of the three member-states. NAFTA's Chapter 6 established rules governing trade in energy and basic petrochemical goods among the parties, but it was not meant to facilitate the same degree of open and secure access as other chapters of the agreement. Although it added to existing GATT norms prohibiting export taxes, 'national security' justifications for import or export restrictions, and proportional access requirements (which forbid Canada from reducing its export of energy to the United States unless it cuts back its own consumption by the same proportion), Mexico was not bound by either the national security or the proportional access provisions.[65] More than a third of Chapter 6 consists of extensive reservations qualifying those provisions under which Mexico is obligated.[66] The first guiding principle – 'the Parties confirm their full respect for their Constitutions'[67] – was an indirect confirmation that Mexico did not share its partners' enthusiasm for opening up this area of the economy.

The fact that the NAEWG was created on an ad hoc basis supports our contention that highly politicized issues involving powerful interests, long-term national security concerns, and billions of dollars do not get channelled through transnational institutions that might exert a political authority which reduces the member-states' sovereignty.

The Resurgence of CWGs

The CWG story is not only about decline. It is also partly about revival. Certain groups have been revitalized as a result of a particular working group incorporating the continued bilateralism of North American relations. Some of the more active trilateral committees are those that deal with bilateral issues, such as the Committee on Standards Related Measures, the Temporary Entry Working Group, the Committee on Sanitary and Phytosanitary Measures, as well as the technical working groups set up in this area to deal, for example, with pesticides and animal health. That these groups maintain fruitful information exchanges and meet more regularly than some of their more exclusively trilateral counterparts is consistent with the view that bilateral realities continue to drive the North American relationship.

A further factor contributing to higher levels of working group activity can involve political leaders redirecting activity from related areas of government policy. Since the negotiation and implementation of 'smart border' initiatives between the United States and Canada and Mexico following 11 September 2001, the Customs Subgroup of the Working Group on Rules of Origin has been largely concerned with issues of border security.[68] That extraneous political motivations recharged this CWG's mandate suggests that the existence of a latent structure has the potential to generate an active function.

In sum, due to the incongruity between the CWGs' trilateral, professional, and symmetrical nature and the bilateral, political, and asymmetrical reality which continues to characterize the power relations of Canada and Mexico with their common behemoth, the committees and working groups set up under NAFTA have turned out to be largely insignificant. In practice, purportedly continental issues play out bilaterally, and therefore are of little interest to the uninvolved government, thus rendering the CWGs an inappropriate mechanism for the resolution of disputes or the discussion of emerging issues. Furthermore, the stakes in these relations are generally too high for discussions and disputes to be channelled through technocratic institutions built on the principle of formal legal equality. It appears that NAFTA-style CWGs can only deal with low-level and low-interest disputes. More politically sensitive controversies require a political arena with more appropriate representation of the interests involved and more flexible processes that provide room for compromise and trade-offs between one issue area and another. Such bilateral political realities constitute a serious impediment to the formation of active and effective transnational institutions in partnership with the continental hegemon.

Enforcement

No executive, no bureaucracy, and no judiciary has clout without having some means by which the decisions of those in command, the rulings of the judges, and the determinations of the bureaucrats can be given effect. Not having coercive power at their disposal is generally the Achilles' heel of regimes established by intergovernmental agreements, but many a system operates effectively nonetheless, because its members find it in their interest to play by its rules and participate in its institutions. In these cases, even when they suffer some losses along the way, the members feel they gain in the long run.

In a transnational institution as unbalanced as NAFTA, the problem of compliance is constantly on the agenda. 'Trucking' and 'softwood lumber' are phrases that evoke for Mexicans and Canadians the problem of U.S. non-compliance. If Washington uses its muscle with threats of direct coercion to enforce rules or rulings that serve its purpose, it may get its way in the short term, but, in the long term, this does not increase the legitimacy of a system of which it may be the prime beneficiary. Asymmetrical compliance produces asymmetrical justice. With the United States so obviously able and willing to flout both NAFTA's letter and spirit, its peripheral member-states have ample reason to look elsewhere to defend their interests.

Connecting the Continental to the Global

NAFTA's patent failure to generate the transnational government that was predicted by its more optimistic defenders generated a search for solutions in both theory and practice.

In an interesting example of transnational epistemic cooperation, the American political scientist Robert Pastor developed a strong theoretical case for reforming NAFTA's institutions by moving them along the trail blazed by the European Union.[69] His thesis persuaded his Mexican colleague Jorge Castañeda who, as policy adviser to Vicente Fox, induced the presidential candidate in 2000 to adopt these ideas for his campaign platform. Following his victory, Fox made Castañeda his foreign minister and promptly proposed these reforms to his NAFTA partners. Ottawa proved sceptical and, as soon as Fox fell from grace with the White House following 11 September 2001, these proposals to bolster NAFTA's institutions disappeared from Mexico's agenda as well.

In practice, the three governments have voted with their feet. For resolving bilateral conflicts, they have increasingly gone to Geneva to use the World Trade Organization's dispute settlement mechanism. When trying to generate new transnational economic norms and rules, they have ignored NAFTA's castrated Trade Commission and spent their efforts negotiating hemispherically in the attempt to develop a Free Trade Area of the Americas and globally in the WTO's Doha Round.

Inserting the global level of governance into our analysis of North America's regional transnationalism is necessary because the efforts of both the hegemon and its neighbours to develop a continental form of political authority have always had a multilateral context. Already in the mid-1980s, the United States had a two-level strategy. Tactically, it had a genuine interest at the regional level in resolving its specific trade and investment irritants with its periphery and extending its market power there in order to guarantee better access to Canada's abundant resources and Mexico's cheap labour, as well as to expand its consumer market in both economies.

Restraining the interventionist capacities of the Canadian and Mexican states, however, was secondary to the broader strategic objective, of the United States, namely, to use breakthroughs achieved in bilateral negotiations – such as including services in CUFTA – as a lever to having these new norms accepted globally in the GATT's Uruguay Round

negotiations. The strategy has succeeded brilliantly. Not only by sign-
ing NAFTA and negotiating Asia-Pacific Economic Cooperation did
Washington manage to bring the European Union to serious bargain-
ing. The United States also used norms for services such as intellectual
property rights in these lesser agreements to make the World Trade
Organization include the document entitled Trade-Related Aspects of
Intellectual Property Rights (TRIPS) in its path-breaking General
Agreement on Trade in Services.

For their part, the peripheral member-states played on the global
stage with a reverse strategy. Whereas in their intimate relations with
the United States they were necessarily in a subordinate position, both
Mexico and Canada could use their transnational cooperation with
like-minded states in international institutions as an instrument
through which to exert countervailing pressure on Uncle Sam. The
autonomy demonstrated by both peripheral member-states on an issue
of the highest importance to Washington, namely, its war against Iraq
in spring 2003 clearly demonstrated that, while Ottawa and Mexico
City were subservient to the United States on domestic political-economy issues (whether inside or outside NAFTA's formal institutions),
they could assert genuine autonomy in multilateral forums – provided
that other states in these forums shared their views.

NAFTA under Anti-terrorism

North America's transnational authority structure was put to a telling
test following the catastrophe of 11 September 2001, when NAFTA's
institutions played no role in resolving either the economic or political
problems created by the tragedy. When the United States closed down
its borders in panic – and so brought continental trade to a standstill –
no special meeting of NAFTA's executive, the Free Trade Commission,
was convened. Even though Washington's next response was to
toughen U.S. national security, with substantial implications for the
management of Mexico's and Canada's airports, seaports, and borders,
the heads of government of the three North American member-states
did not call a special trinational summit or even set up a working
group.

North America continued to be managed as two separate, U.S.-
directed relationships. While the national leaders in both peripheral
states made appropriate gestures of support, initially it appeared that

their governments would not be crafting the responses to the crisis – these were to be made in the USA. The Bush administration made it clear that the United States would decide what counted as adequate security. Canada and Mexico were left the role of deciding how to conform to Washington's concerns and criteria.

The continental economic integration induced by NAFTA and the business relationships it had engendered dominated the three governments' actions. In this sense, *government* in North America was supplemented by considerable *governance*. Business associations with an interest in the unhindered flow of goods, services, investment, and specialized personnel across North America's borders hurriedly met and desperately called on the three governments to guarantee free, but more secure, flows across the two U.S. boundaries. Because the voices of business were heard loudly and clearly, the Bush administration ultimately responded to its northern and southern border security problems more with economic than military means. The same was true in Ottawa and Mexico City, where business virtually dictated the governments' proposals for action. In a situation where the hegemon depended on cooperation from the peripheries, Ottawa became proactively involved in working out the nature and scope of the enhanced security measures, which became known as the thirty–point Canada–U.S. border security plan. With this program as a template, Mexico City's involvement in drafting the Mexico–U.S. border security plan was somewhat less proactive.

Considerable confusion continued in North America as the United States restructured its machinery of government around its new Department of Homeland Security – a massive reorganization that involved bringing twenty-two agencies with more than 170,000 officials under one institutional roof and would take years to complete. Meanwhile, the governments of Mexico and Canada struggled hard to be included within the U.S. anti-terrorist defence zone rather than be condemned to exclusion outside its perimeter. That NAFTA itself had nothing to offer by way of institutions or processes that might generate continental decision-making on the many issues involved suggests that the politics of post-catastrophe North America will see a reprise of the double dialogue of Canada–U.S. and Mexico–U.S. relations, perpetuating a double bilateralism that keeps the United States comfortably in control.

Conclusion

This study has three main implications for conceptualizing the state in the context of growing transnational connections.

First, the various patterns of global transformation that are occurring have different effects on sovereignty in the region where the global hegemon is situated than in regions where more symmetrical power relations prevail. NAFTA not only allowed the United States to resist giving up any of its sovereignty, but on the contrary, extended its sovereignty over its peripheral neighbours by inducing them to accept a legal regime that it defined in a number of sectors such as intellectual property rights.

Second, in the fallout from 11 September 2001, a reterritorialization took place, whereby Washington extended its security border to North America's perimeter by pressuring its two neighbours to adopt immigration and counter-terrorism measures that were the functional equivalent of its own. While the dominant reality of Washington as *rulemaker* for North America was to strengthen the sovereignty of the United States, there were limits to this process. Ultimately, Washington was constrained in some cases by its own values, and eventually the United States had to comply with NAFTA's Chapter 20 ruling on Mexican trucks, if not its Chapter 19 ruling on Canadian softwood lumber. Although its control of various aspects of the peripheral political economies increased, the United States was not, however, able to impose its will on a purely political issue: waging war on Iraq.

For the peripheries as *rule-takers*, the dominant reality was to have their sovereignty reduced by accepting constraints on their policymaking powers. For Ottawa, this represented less a loss of its monopoly over decision-making – a condition Canada had never achieved in its evolution from a British colony to an American dependency – than a change in the form and degree of its relative autonomy. Having never enjoyed a sovereignty defined as freedom from external interference, Canada, as did Mexico, saw its territory become further de-nationalized as U.S.-dictated norms prevailed in Canada's political space. It was not so much a question of transcending the separation of domestic and foreign policies as intensifying the porosity of NAFTA's peripheral member-states.

These cooperative member-states were not just able and willing: They were forced by pressure from the outside and by their own elites on the inside to intensify their continental integration under U.S. terms.

Nevertheless, Canada and Mexico continued to enjoy considerable internal policy autonomy. Ongoing pressures to privatize their public services continued to be met with strong internal resistance. Moreover, U.S. pressure in another domain actually served to increase their sovereignty. The demands from Washington that Canada and Mexico strengthen their border security compelled the two countries to strengthen their own security apparatus.

Mexico, which had made a titanic effort throughout most of the twentieth century to forge its own identity independent of its neighbour to the north, made an abrupt change in ideological direction and opted for a radical, neo-conservative solution to its own problems. Whereas NAFTA intensified and formalized Ottawa's relationship of dependency with the United States, it did not radically transform it. By contrast, for Mexico City NAFTA was the central agent in its attempt to transform the country's whole system. Making a bold leap of faith based on dubious political-economy assumptions, Mexico abandoned substantial aspects of a national sovereignty that previous governments had zealously defended.

Third, in contrast to the highly integrated, relatively symmetrical, and member-controlled European Union, NAFTA has not created a more balanced framework for North American governance – let alone continental government. But despite its institutional ineffectiveness, NAFTA's legitimacy is precarious. As the 2004 U.S. presidential election campaigns showed, the connotations that NAFTA had acquired were entirely negative in the United States, where it was associated with outsourcing and the growth of unemployment. In Mexico, where the elites had forced NAFTA down the country's collective throat, hostility to it was rife in the countryside, where the corn economy has been devastated by massive imports of subsidized U.S. product. Only in Canada, where the triumphalist discourse of trade liberalization has not been effectively challenged, has there been high approval for what is still seen as a trade-generating deal.

Unlike the case with the European Union, NAFTA's lack of institutional content leaves North American governance without an overarching structure. Nation-states still provide most of the continent's government, and North American politics remain constituted by two separate, asymmetrical, U.S.-dominated relationships. Studying the

192 Stephen Clarkson et al.

actual transborder governance of the new North America, however, is no longer a simple matter. Much more work needs to be done on transnational governance that is largely generated by corporations and their business associations in the marketplace.

NOTES

1 The original research in this paper was conducted primarily through a series of interviews in early 2002: Toronto in January, Mexico City in February, and Washington, DC, in April. The trips to Mexico City and Washington were made possible by the generous support of Carl Amrhein, then dean of the Faculty of Arts and Science at the University of Toronto, and by a standard research grant from the Social Sciences and Humanities Research Council of Canada. We are grateful to David Biette, director of the Canada Institute at the Woodrow Wilson International Center for Scholars, for his support and his institution's hospitality.
2 De Palma (2002).
3 Clarkson (1998).
4 NAFTA, Article 2001, 2.a–e.
5 Ibid., 3.a–c.
6 Pastor (2001: 73–4).
7 Available at http://www.ustr.gov/regions/whemisphere/organizations.shtml#trade
8 Ibid.
9 Davey (1996: 65).
10 CDA-92–1807–01, Interpretation of Canada's Compliance with Article 701.3 with respect to Durum wheat sales.
11 Davey (1996: 56).
12 Clarkson (2002).
13 NAFTA, Article 1110.
14 Horlick and DeBusk (1993: 52).
15 Blank, Krajewski, and Yu (1995).
16 Todd Weiler. See http://www.cyberus.ca/~tweiler/naftaclaims.html
17 See http://www.ustr.gov/regions/whemisphere/organizations.shtml#trade
18 Although NAFTA's Annex 2001.2 lists twenty CWGs, it is virtually impossible to establish a precise number for these entities because some have the authority to generate ad hoc working groups as needed.
19 McKinney (2000: 17).

20 Ibid., 22.
21 Interview with Claude Carrière, director general, Trade Policy Bureau, Department of Foreign Affairs and International Trade, 10 April 2002.
22 Ibid.
23 McKinney (2000: 22).
24 Carrière interview.
25 McKinney (2000: 14).
26 Interview with Kent Shigetomi, director for Mexico and NAFTA affairs, Office of the U.S. Trade Representative, Washington, 10 April 2002.
27 Organization of American States' (OAS) Foreign Trade Information System (FTIS) [SICE] 'NAFTA Reports' [Online]. Available at http:// www.sice.oas.org/trade/nafta/reports/goods_e.asp
28 Ibid.
29 Ibid., http://www.sice.oas.org/trade/nafta/reports/remed_e.asp
30 Shigetomi interview.
31 Response from a Canadian civil servant via questionnaire.
32 Interview with Jeffrey Dutton, Office of NAFTA and Inter-American Affairs, U.S. Department of Commerce, Washington, 10 April 2002.
33 Ibid.
34 Shigetomi interview.
35 Ibid.
36 Interview with Charles Doran, of Johns Hopkins University, Washington, 11 April 2002.
37 OAS FTIS [SICE] 'NAFTA Reports.' Available at http://www.sice.oas.org/trade/nafta/reports/remed_e.asp
38 Shigetomi interview.
39 Condon and Sinha (2001: 238).
40 Ibid., 237.
41 Ibid., 235–6 and 240.
42 Ibid., 238.
43 Meeting of the NAFTA Land Transportation Standards Subcommittee, Baltimore, 25–8 Oct., 1999. Available at http://www.dfait-maeci.gc.ca/nafta-alena/report13–e.asp
44 Ibid.
45 NAFTA, Chapter 9; Annex 913.5.a1, 2(a)iii.
46 Interview with David Decarme, chief of the Surface, Maritime and Facilitation Division, USDOT, Washington, 11 April 2002.
47 Dutton interview.
48 USDOT (27 Nov. 2002) Press Releases [Online]. Available at http:// www.dot.gov/affairs/dot10702.htm

49 David Bacon, 'Mexican Workers Fight Electricity Privatization,' *Global Exchange*, 6 Jan. 2002 [Online]. Available at http://www.globalexchange.org/campaigns/mexico/energy/bacon010602 .html

50 Elisabeth Malkin, 'Mexico's Energy Crunch,' *Business Week* (int'l ed.), 7 Aug. 2000 [Online]. Available at http://clinicalfreedom.org/Mexico02.htm

51 H. Josef Hebert, 'Bush Expected to Push Energy-Market Idea,' *Associated Press – North County Times Net*, 16 Feb. 2000. Available at http://www.nctimes.com/news/2001/20010216/q.html

52 Ibid.

53 Bacon, 'Mexican Workers.'

54 Hebert, 'Bush Expected.'

55 Ibid.

56 David Lindquist, 'Energy Reforms in Mexico Being Held up by Politics,' *Union-Tribune* 30 Oct. 2002 [Online]. Available at http://www.signonsandiego.com/news/mexico/20021030–9999_1b30mexen .html

57 Malkin, 'Mexico's Energy Crunch.'

58 Hebert, 'Bush Expected.'

59 Lindquist, 'Energy Reforms.'

60 Interview with Carl Hartill, Economic and Trade Policy Division, Canadian Embassy to the USA, Washington, 12 April 2002.

61 The North American Energy Working Group, 'North America – The Energy Picture' [Online]. Available at http://www.nrcan-rncan.gc.ca/es/energypicture/index.html

62 Hartill, interview.

63 Ibid.; equivalent data for the U.S. and Mexico not given.

64 Ibid.

65 OAS FTIS [SICE] 'NAFTA Chapter Six Summary' [Online]. Available at http://www.sice.oas.org/summary/nafta/nafta6.asp

66 NAFTA, Annexes 602.3, 603.6, 605, 607, and 608.2.

67 Ibid. Article 601.1.

68 Shigetomi interview.

69 Pastor (2001).

9 Public-Private Partnerships: Effective and Legitimate Tools of Transnational Governance?

TANJA A. BÖRZEL AND THOMAS RISSE

Public-private partnerships (PPPs) as governance tools have a long-standing presence in the domestic affairs of highly industrialized states.[1] Corporatist arrangements, for instance, constitute one such form. It is only within the past few years, however, that the development and activities of PPPs beyond the nation-state, in the international context, have become interesting subjects for research. For decades, the study of international institutions has concentrated on interstate regimes aimed at solving collective action problems and providing common goods.[2] To the extent that non-state actors have been taken into consideration at all, they generally appeared either as actors shaping state interests through domestic politics[3] or as transnational actors such as multinational corporations or international non-governmental organizations (INGOs) lobbying international negotiations and/or international organizations (IOs).[4] Only recently have non-state actors emerged in the international relations literature as direct partners of national governments and IOs in evolving structures of international governance.[5] Many authors celebrate public-private partnerships as a significant solution to a whole variety of problems of governance beyond the nation-state.[6] PPPs are said to increase both the effectiveness (problem-solving capacity) and the legitimacy (democratic accountability) of international governance in terms of democratic participation and accountability.

An analysis of the current state of our knowledge on PPPs speaks directly to the core themes explored in this volume. In this chapter, accordingly, we first present an overview of types, forms, and functions of existing transnational relationships between public and private actors and then identify PPPs as a particular subset of these interactions. Second, we argue that conceptualizing the issue as 'private actors on the rise' and as 'the demise of the nation-state' is empirically questionable. We contend that PPPs should not be seen as zero-sum games between states and private actors and question to what extent PPPs actually exist beyond the nation-state. Third, we tackle questions of sovereignty, effectiveness, and legitimacy. On the issue of sovereignty, we claim that discussing PPPs in terms of either formal–legal sovereignty or material sovereignty, understood as the autonomous action capacities of states, misinterprets their significance. Traditional and even contemporary international relations scholarship has been far too focused on the impact that private actors have on state authority. Instead of focusing on state sovereignty, we argue that PPPs should be evaluated in terms of their capacity to increase the effectiveness and legitimacy of actual processes of transational governance. Nevertheless, little empirical evidence is available on PPPs and their influence on such processes, and the evidence that is available is often selective and compiled in such a way as to limit its analytical value. As we seek to demonstrate in this chapter, the role of PPPs in increasing the effectiveness and legitimacy of governance beyond the nation-state is likely to vary and is worthy of further study.

Types, Forms, and Functions of Public-Private Partnerships in International Governance: What's New?

Public-private partnerships have become a part of the new governance problematic beyond the nation-state.[7] *Governance* is a contested term, one that has become a catchword in the social sciences. Governance is often interpreted so broadly that its content is said to describe, steer, and produce for a whole variety of social order activities ranging from states (governments) to markets and networks.[8] In this chapter, we are not concerned with governance in the general sense of steering, but with new modes of governance that are distinct from the hierarchical control model characterizing the interventionist state. Governance is the type of regulation typical of the cooperation state, where state and non-state actors participate in mixed public-private policy networks.'[9] Concerning such new modes of governance, we need to further distinguish between actors involved in governance (public and private), on the one hand, and modes of steering, (hierarchical versus non-hierarchical), on the other. Hierarchical modes of steering are usually typical of states and public actors who allocate values authoritatively and

Figure 9.1 New modes of governance

Steering modes	Public actors only	Public and private actors	Private actors only

Hierarchical

| Top-down

Threat of sanctions | Traditional nation-state

Supranational institutions (EU, partly WTO) | | Corporate hierarchies |

Non-hierarchical

| Positive incentives

Bargaining

Non-manipulative persuasion (learning, arguing, etc.) | Intergovernmental bargaining

Institutional problem-solving | Delegation of public functions to private actors

Corporatism

Public-private networks and partnerships

Bench-marking | Private interest government / private regimes

Private-private partnerships (NGOs-companies) |

Key:

☐ New modes of government

■ Public-private partnerships

enforce rules. Non-hierarchical modes of steering are typical of the activities of non-state actors and are distinctive of new modes of governance (see the lightly shaded area in Figure 9.1). Concerning types of non-state actors, we can further distinguish between the for-profit sector, i.e. firms and private interest groups, and the not-for-profit sector, i.e. the world of domestic and international non-governmental organizations.

Of course, the distinction between hierarchical and non-hierarchical forms of steering is primarily an analytical one. Many non-hierarchical forms of steering take place in the shadow of hierarchy, and it may well be that some more or less implicit form of authoritative decision-making by states and governments is a crucial condition for successful interactions between private and public actors.

Public-private partnerships can be identified as a form of governance (the darkly shaded area in Figure 9.1). From a public management perspective, Linder and Rosenau have defined public-private partnerships to be 'the formation of cooperative relationships between government, profit-making firms, and non-profit private organizations to fulfill a policy function.'[10] Transnational PPPs would then be institutionalized cooperative relationships between public actors (both governments and international organizations) and private actors beyond the nation-state for governance purposes. By *governance purposes*, we mean the making and implementation of norms and rules for the provision of goods and services that are considered to be binding by members. In the case of transnational PPPs this would be members of the international community. Such processes could involve international regimes with explicit norms, rules, and decision-making procedures, but informal governance arrangements pertaining to specific-issue areas of international life, as well. Non-state actors (both domestic and transnational) can be for-profit organizations (including corporations), interest groups (business, trade unions), and the non-profit sector such as public interest groups and INGOs, including voluntary organizations and advocacy networks.[11] Thus, to use international relations language, PPPs constitute a specific subset of transnational relations in world politics.[12]

This understanding of PPPs covers a broad range of potential cooperative arrangements. However, certain forms of public-private interaction are also excluded (see the shaded area on the right-hand side of Figure 9.1). We exclude the lobbying and mere advocacy activities of non-state actors aimed at governments and IOs for the provision of some goods or services. Transnational actors who are not active participants in governance arrangements or negotiating systems pose few challenges to existing concepts and theories in political science and international relations. Of particular note are the literatures on 'two-level games,' transnational politics, epistemic communities, and advocacy networks where such a challenge would be expected.[13] Also excluded are those arrangements among private transnational actors that are based on self-coordination (markets), constitute self-regulation among private actors (private regimes),[14] produce public goods and services as unintended consequences (e.g., rating agencies), or provide public 'bads,' such as a transnational mafia, international drug cartels, or transnational terrorism (see Figure 9.2). Our understanding includes at least four distinct types of PPPs, each with one of the following characteristics co-optation, delegation, co-regulation, self-regulation in the shadow of hierarchy. PPPs can further be classified according to their purposes and functions into one of three categories:

1 Rule and standard setting, with the direct participation of non-state actors in negotiating systems engaged in international rule making
2 Rule implementation according to the degree to which public and non-state actors are engaged in various activities geared towards ensuring compliance with international rules
3 Service provision, with the participation of private actors in the delivery of goods and services, be it for their own members or for other groups in transnational society.[15]

We develop these classifications in the following section.

Types of Public-Private Partnerships

Co-optation

This type of PPP engages in regular consultation and co-optation of private actors in international negotiation systems. This is probably the most common, 'weakest,' and also least problematic type of PPP. Given the complexity of most international negotiating systems – from those concerned with nuclear non-proliferation to international trade to international climate change – most governments and international organizations increasingly incorporate non-state actors as official members of their delegations in setting and implementating rules. Such stable co-operative arrangements between private actors – both firms and INGOs – are particularly pervasive in the issue areas of international human rights and the international environment. Non-state actors provide consensual knowledge and expertise, but also moral authority and legitimacy. In many cases, co-optation has resulted in striking influence by non-state actors in the making of international treaties. In exchange, they receive closer information about the details of the negotiations and gain better access. Since the 1980s, for example, Amnesty International has established itself as a legitimate source of knowledge and moral authority in the human rights

Figure 9.2 The realm of public-private partnerships

Private self-regulation (purely private regimes) no public involvement	Private self-regulation in the shadow of hierarchy (e.g., voluntary agreements) involvement of public actors	Delegation to private actors (e.g., standard setting) participation of public actors	Public adoption of private regulation output control by public actors	Co-regulation of public and private actors (e.g., private actors as negotiation partners) joint decision-making of public and private actors	Consultation and co-optation of private actors (e.g., private actors as members of state delegation) participation of private actors in negotiating systems	Lobbying of public actors by private actors	Public regulation no involvement of private actors

increasing autonomy of private actors

increasing autonomy of public actors

area – a position that no other human rights INGO has been able to match. As a result, Amnesty has helped to shape most international human rights agreements in crucial ways, from the Convention against Torture to the recent establishment of the International Criminal Court.[16] Similar developments can be observed in international environmental politics.[17]

As noted especially in the Pauly, Porter, and Coleman chapters in this volume, the regular consultation of private actors has extended beyond the issues of human rights and the international environment into the international economy and even international security. Multinational corporations (MNCs) and INGOs have gained formal and legitimate access to international economic negotiations and organizations, such as the International Monetary Fund, the World Bank, and the World Trade Organization.[18] The movement to ban anti-personnel landmines is a telling example of similar developments in the area of international security. During the Ottawa negotiations, the International Campaign to Ban Landmines had formal observer status, which included the right to make statements and to table treaty language.[19] Despite the ability of the non-state actors to influence international governance, it is important to note that, in some instances, as examples from the U.N. system make clear, official consultative status also provides a powerful tool for states and IOs to control non-state actors and to sanction 'non-cooperative behaviour.'

Delegation

International regimes, states, and IOs have increasingly begun to delegate certain functions to non-state actors. This is particularly common practice in technical standardization and in the 'contracting out' of public services previously provided by states to private actors. Although most common in these areas, delegation actually covers a wide array of PPPs – from rather weak forms, such as 'outsourcing' and 'contracting out,' in which private actors are held accountable by states in a rather tight way, to cases in which delegation amounts to and resembles private self-regulation in the shadow of hierarchy. The International Organization for Standardization (ISO) and the European Committee for Standardization (CEN) are high-profile examples of the latter where public authority to set technical standards is delegated to private actors who are active in standardization.[20] Private expertise increases the efficiency and the acceptance of standardization outcomes and is thus a major reason for international organizations to contract out certain functions to private actors. In both development aid and the humanitarian sector dealing with complex emergencies, the United Nations and the European Union increasingly contract out the provision of humanitarian aid, health services, and other functions to private organizations, charities, churches, and INGOs. In some cases, oversight functions are delegated to private actors, and no longer supplied by international agencies (this partly has to do with the lack of resources of U.N. agencies, like the U.N. High Commissioner for Refugees, to carry out these functions).

In rare circumstances, core state functions, such as the monopoly on the legitimate use of force, are delegated to private actors. Many weak Third World governments are no longer able to provide national security for their citizens and have started to contract out military security to private firms such as Executive Outcomes, a modern-day mercenary group.[21] The privatization of security and defence policy, however, appears to be rare and is usually closely scrutinized by other states, including Western powers.

Co-regulation

True joint decision-making, where private actors hold veto power, is rare in international politics. But non-state actors can be increasingly found as equal partners in the making and implementation of international rules. While nation-states remain the primary signatories and ratifiers of internationally negotiated agreements, business associations and trade unions are increasingly seen as negotiating partners with equal status, particularly at the International Labour Organization. Examples of this type of PPP abound. The World Commission on Dams (WCD) is an example of a negotiating mechanism between national governments, international organizations (in this case the World Bank), firms, and INGOs in which the construction of big dams has been reconciled with principles of sustainable development.[22] The Transatlantic Business Dialogue (TABD) represents a forum in which firms negotiate trade and investment regulations for the transatlantic area under the auspices of the U.S. government and the European Union Commission.[23] In the EU, the 'open method of coordination' represents an instrument of co-regulation between public authorities and (business) interest groups. It is important to note, however, as

Héritier shows, that true co-regulation accounts for only a tiny fraction of EU policymaking.[24]

The main difference between co-regulatory governance mechanisms and the co-optation model is that co-regulatory PPPs raise the status of non-state actors to equal and legitimate partners at the negotiating table. Some of these PPPs have operated rather smoothly for decades, (like the ILO), while others like the WCD have been far more conflict-ridden. In most cases, however, negotiating dynamics do not pitch the 'society world' of non-state actors against the 'state world' of governments and IOs.[25] Rather, the more the different stakeholders in an issue area are represented at the bargaining table, the more we observe cross-cutting coalitions among private and public actors.

Private Self-Regulation in the Shadow of Hierarchy

International organizations and state governments have occasionally induced the self-regulation of private actors at the international level by threatening formal legislation. For example, in response to the WTO's code of ethical and scientific standards, the International Federation of Pharmaceutical Manufacturers and Associations voluntarily adopted a Code of Pharmaceutical Marketing Practices to avoid further regulation.[26] Another example is the U.S.–European Union 'Safe Harbour' agreement pertaining to the European Data Protection Directive. As the Directive's rules protecting the privacy of consumers are more stringent than U.S. legislation, the United States initially failed to qualify as a country to which data could be exported from the EU.

Subsequent negotiations resulted in an agreement between the EU and the United States stipulating that if U.S. companies voluntarily signed on to a set of privacy principles, previously formulated by the U.S. administration and interested companies, the EU would not take action against them.[27] Thus, the U.S.–EU agreement reflects the 'shadow of hierarchy' under which business actors have opted to accept more stringent privacy standards than those delineated by U.S. law.

State Adoption of Privately Negotiated Regimes: A Case of Public-Private Partnership?

Self-regulation by private actors is often triggered by the lack of effective international norms and rules. In the absence of an international legal system for dealing with transborder interactions between private individuals and organizations, economic actors have negotiated trade codes such as the lex mercatoria moderna. Such private regimes may then become 'publicly sanctioned.'[28] They are enforced by national courts or, as in the case of the rating agencies, even adopted in legal statutes.[29] Another example of a state-adopted private regime is Internet domain name regulation. In this particular case, private regulation and an IO-sponsored system of domain names initially competed. Private regulation won, and was then adopted by national governments.

Does adoption by the state of privately negotiated regimes really qualify as a public-private partnership? Unlike co-optation or co-regulation PPPs, where public actors initiate dialogue and negotiation, the involvement of public actors in privately negotiated regimes is purely ex post. Public actors have certain control over output since international organizations and states cannot be forced to adopt private regulations. However, they do not cooperate with private actors in the rule-making process. Nor can they set any framework guiding the process and outcome of the private negotiations.

Evidently, both the frequency and the significance of PPP arrangements vary enormously according to both type and purpose. While valid data on the number and importance of PPPs do not exist, it is probably safe to say that PPPs most frequently serve the function of service provision. Service-providing PPPs of all types are particularly widespread in the areas of development and humanitarian aid. This might be related to the fact that states and international organizations drastically reduced their resources for development programs during the 1990s. Consequently, they have increasingly come to seek and rely on the financial resources and expertise of private actors of various types, ranging from firms to agencies in the voluntary NGO sector. Moreover, PPPs also result from the recent emphasis on 'good governance,' 'sustainable development,' and 'strengthening civil society' in the development policies of Western donors and international organizations.

PPPs appear to be far less frequent in the areas of international rule setting and implementation. Where rule setting is concerned, states are still reluctant to delegate authority to private actors or to include them in their negotiating systems. This is particularly true for questions of international security, where co-optation is the best mechanism of participation that private actors can currently hope for (see the above discussion about the negotiations to ban landmines). Private regimes appear to be particularly confined to one issue area of international relations: international political economy.[30] This can probably be best explained by the fact that the rule targets in international markets are mainly private actors. However, it might also be a consequence of neo-liberal ideas, which assert that market regulation should be left to those acting in the markets. Yet, even still, most private regimes in international trade and financial markets seem to operate in the shadow of hierarchy.

Recent trends towards incorporating private actors into rule setting through voluntary agreements with or without the shadow of hierarchy have also been observed in the areas of human rights and environmental protection. There are several reasons for this. First, the failure of national governments to agree on internationally binding and effective rules often leads to voluntary agreements by private actors as second-best solutions. Examples are the social rights and the climate change regimes. Second, learning may play a role. States and international organizations increasingly understand that incorporating rule targets – 'stakeholders' - into rule making not only enhances the legitimacy of global governance, but also makes international norms more effective in terms of problem-solving. The World Commission on Dams is a case in point.

Cases like these also indicate PPPs whose purpose is rule implementation. States and international organizations such as the EU increasingly realize that ensuring rule compliance through threats of sanctions does not necessarily produce the desired results. In some cases, sanctioning mechanisms are simply lacking. In other words, the more a 'managed compliance' perspective carries the day,[31] the more we are likely to see the expansion of PPPs in rule implementation (see below).

All in all, however, and despite recent excitement about 'global public policy,'[32] states seem reluctant to provide private actors with governance authority. Moreover, PPPs in international life are not completely new, in the sense that they were previously unknown in either domestic affairs or the history of international relations. Indeed, much of the contemporary discussion on PPPs was foreshadowed in the literature on policy networks.[33] PPPs as co-optation mechanisms are quite normal in the domestic politics of most highly industrialized states. PPPs with co-regulation activities characterize most corporatist arrangements. The delegation of state functions to private actors has become quite common in the OECD world, a result of the move towards deregulation and privatization in the 1980s and the restriction of state roles in many public service sectors to oversight and regulatory functions. Self-regulation by private actors in the shadow of hierarchy, finally, is not new to domestic politics, either. In environmental politics, for instance, business associations often prefer voluntary agreements with state actors, where they voluntarily commit themselves to comply with some negotiated policy goals instead of traditional command-and-control regulation that leaves little flexibility in implementation.[34]

Last, but not least, it should be noted that the state system as the defining feature of international order is, historically speaking, probably a transitory phenomenon in international life. The pre-Westphalian system was one of overlapping public, private, and religious authorities. The linchpin of state sovereignty, the monopoly over the legitimate use of force, only emerged after extended struggles with private armies, pirates, and mercenaries during the seventeenth century.[35] Perhaps, then, the current transformation of the Westphalian order towards a more complex system of transnational or global governance including PPPs represents a 'return to normal.'

State Sovereignty, Autonomy, and PPPs: Is There a Problem?

The question of sovereignty preoccupies international relations scholars and international lawyers. For our purpose, Stephen Krasner's distinctions serve as a useful starting point here.[36] PPPs do little to affect the meaning of *international legal sovereignty*, understood as the mutual recognition of states as actors in the international system. This is also true for Krasner's notion of 'interdependence sovereignty,' which he defines as the ability of governments to control transborder movements. It is highly questionable whether states – even the most powerful ones – ever possessed the ability to control their borders. PPPs affect this only at the margins.

Complications arise when considering Krasner's definition of 'Westphalian sovereignty,' which means the exclusion of external actors from configurations of domestic authority. PPPs as the co-optation of non-state actors by state actors and as public-private negotiating arrangements do not seem to pose problems here, as the activities of non-state actors in such settings take place in the shadow of hierarchy. However, the delegation of public authority to private actors and private regimes by states does infringe on Westphalian sovereignty as understood by Krasner. For example, if weak states hire (foreign) private companies to take care of threats to national security such as insurgencies by rebel groups or guerrilla movements,[37] the constitutive functions of the Westphalian state are eroded. Moreover, whether such delegation and contracting out is consistent with Westphalian sovereignty crucially depends on the ability of states 'to take it back,' in the sense of having the capability to compensate for failures of self-regulated private actors by direct intervention. This capability might be a given in a strict legal sense (as the very term delegation implies), but how realistic is this politically? What does it mean for Westphalian sovereignty when a legal right increasingly becomes an empty possibility? Such a question is especially apt for private regimes that provide public goods and services. Here, non-state actors perform public functions previously confined to state authority. Of course, one could argue that the shadow of hierarchy still exists, even for private regimes. But, if states refuse to adopt or approve of the norms or rules inherent in such regimes, what happens? Can the regimes be sustained? In short, is state regulation capable of compensating for failures of private self-regulation?

The question of Westphalian sovereignty is not, however, that relevant for determining the implications of PPPs for global governance. With respect to questions about global governance, what becomes more significant is assessment of the resilience of understandings of sovereignty as the effective control exercised by public authorities and sovereignty as the autonomous action capacity of states.[38] There is no doubt that state autonomy and state control over policy decisions and outcomes decreases drastically as one moves from co-optation PPPs to the self-regulation of private actors. Caution, however, must be taken not to overstate the impact of PPPs on sovereignty. PPPs at the international level may only be the latest development in a transformation of the state from within. Modern democratic welfare states have long been characterized by non-hierarchical modes of governance, including formal and informal networks of public and private actors (domestic PPPs).[39] If the modern welfare state is no longer autonomous vis-à-vis its own society, why should this be different beyond the nation-state? Furthermore, the degree of state autonomy and the ability of states to formulate and attain their own goals internally and externally have always varied tremendously in the international system. Apart from the great powers, very few states have ever enjoyed the privilege of attaining complete control and autonomy over their internal and external environments.

We suggest that posing the issue of PPPs in terms of either sovereignty or loss of state control and autonomy over policies and outcomes misdirects scholarly attention away from more relevant questions. Diminished state autonomy resulting from international PPPs may be the cost of an increase in the problem-solving capacity and legitimacy of international public policy. Rather than discussing in abstract terms whether nation-states and national governments have lost control because of an increase in public-private governance networks, one should ask what PPPs can do in terms of increasing the capacity of international governance to solve global problems and to enhance the democratic participation and legitimacy of international institutions.

Are PPPs Effective and Legitimate Tools of Transnational Governance?

Proponents have long argued that private-public partnerships arrangements increase both the problem-solving capacity and the legitimacy of international governance structures.[40] On the one hand, the neo-liberal argument favours PPPs and private regimes, claiming that 'state failure' to provide public goods and services is at least as relevant as 'market failure' in international life; private actors, in short, are better suited to regulate their own affairs and coordinate their activities. Moreover, PPPs are favoured because states and IOs alike lack the knowledge and expertise to solve increasingly complex problems in international governance. Hence, PPPs satisfy the plea for an increased role of 'epistemic' or 'knowledge' communities. On the other hand, proponents of cosmopolitan democracy and transnational civil society claim that the involvement of INGOs and transnational social movements in international governance increases the democratic accountability of international institutions.[41] Transnational civil society is widely seen as the beacon of hope in the global community, representing the international common good, in contrast to narrow-minded states and for-profit firms and interest organizations.

Despite the argument in favour of PPPs, the evidence pointing to their ability to increase the problem-solving capacity and the democratic nature of international governance remains inconclusive. One difficulty is that most studies in this area suffer from a selection bias. There are many more studies of successful NGO–public partnerships than there are of failures. For instance, is the world a better place because an INGO coalition killed the prospects for a Multilateral Agreement on Investment (MAI), or would an MAI that included human rights and environmental concerns have been preferable? In addition, no empirical studies comparing interstate regimes focused on problem-solving in international life with PPPs organized for similar purposes have been undertaken.

With regard to problem-solving effectiveness, the core idea supporting PPPs concerns the mutual resource dependency of public and private actors. In areas where public actors control only limited material and ideational resources, non-state actors are said to be able to come to the rescue. The pooling of resources and burden sharing among public and private actors is said to increase the problem-solving capacity of governance arrangements.[42] In the issue areas of international development and humanitarian aid, PPPs between U.N. organizations and the private sector (mainly NGOs) were simply a necessity, given the lack of material resources of the international organizations.

Similarly, non-state actors often serve as knowledge providers for public actors. Private actors – both firms and the not-for-profit sector – are said to increase the knowledge base (scientific and other) of public actors in various governance arrangements, as evidenced by the role of knowledge-based epistemic communities in various international environmental regimes.[43] In the human rights area, we can observe that the regular provision of information by the INGO community to various U.N. human rights committees and national governments has not only greatly improved our knowledge about human rights violations, but also increased compliance with international human rights norms.[44]

It remains unclear, however, whether the mutual resource dependency of public and private actors actually leads to a net increase in the problem-solving capacity of transnational governance arrangements. If the international community strips international organizations such as the United Nations of material resources, the delegation of authority to non-state actors can easily result in problem shifting rather than problem solving, as international organization come to rely on INGOs. In many cases, PPPs are simply neo-liberal solutions in disguise; that is, they amount to the privatization and de-regulation of formerly public services. This seems to be very much the case concerning PPPs involved in the humanitarian aid and development sectors. Moreover, international organizations do not have the ability to re-assume responsibility for delegated tasks in cases of private failures, as functions were delegated because international organizations were incapable of delivering them in the first place.

A second argument favouring the increased problem-solving capacity of transnational governance through the participation of PPPs concerns compliance. The 'management perspective' posits that the more rule targets are included in the process of rule making, the greater the likelihood of compliance with international norms and rules.[45] Since many rules and regulations in international life actually involve private actors such as firms as primary rule targets, including them in PPPs is said to increase compliance. The EU's new 'open method of coordination' is an example of such a mechanism.

Yet, including private rule targets in the making of international treaties and other governance arrangements may simply lead to 'lowest common denominator' solutions. If those who have to bear the costs of compliance are involved in the negotiating process, they may attempt to weaken international rules and regulations. Ultimately, then, the purported 'good news' about private actor compliance may not tell us very much about the successful solution to problems of cooperation and compliance.[46] We might end up with international treaties that do very little to address problem-solving challenges. Furthermore, including rule targets in the treaty-making process might lead to the exclusion of the actual stakeholders. This is clearly illustrated in international environmental agreements in which rule targets such as firms are allowed to set their own standards for compliance with international norms. This has the potential effect of making the interests of ordinary citizens and of consumers in a cleaner environment irrelevant, especially if their preferences are not included in the negotiating systems.

Advocates of deliberative democracy, who focus on learning communities, provide the third argument supporting the claim that PPPs enhance the problem-solving capacities of transnational governance mechanisms.[47] The literature often contends that the involvement of stakeholders and rule targets in a deliberative process of rule making could lead to better governance, as agreements would result from a reasoned consensus rather than a bargained compromise.[48] By bringing in additional information and (authoritative) knowledge, the involvement of private actors can help to identify possible ways of handling problems. At the same time, public actors become open to deliberation since they expect private actors to bring in their knowledge and expertise.[49] Arguing and giving reasons in a transnational arena that includes public and private actors would thereby not only enhance the democratic legitimacy of the governance process at the input side (input legitimacy), but also lead to better problem solving by enabling mutual learning processes.

So, is it really the case that deliberation leads to better problem solving in a transnational context? What about the risk that arguing instead of bargaining leads to agreed-on dissent rather than reasoned consensus?[50] What about the risk of stalemate in such settings? Little is known about the scope conditions under which PPPs as learning communities actually deliver the goods on improved problem-solving capacities of transnational governance. Accordingly, some scepticism is required about the ability of deliberative democratic models to improve transnational problem solving.

This leads to questions of input legitimacy as a means of reducing the democratic deficit, improving accountability, and increasing transparency at levels of governance beyond the nation-state. Including non-state actors – 'civil society actors' such as firms and not-for-profit organizations – is said to increase the legitimacy of international negotiating systems. In turn, the presence of representatives from transnational civil society in PPPs and other governance arrangements is purported to enhance the participatory and democratic nature of these institutions,[51] by helping to improve the correspondence between the 'rulers' and the 'ruled'[52] through the creation of a transnational demos.[53] Moreover, many INGOs, epistemic communities, and other transnational advocacy networks command undisputed moral authority in a given issue area, as demonstrated by Amnesty International and Transparency International in the areas of human rights and corruption, respectively.[54] Including these moral authorities in mechanisms of governance is said to increase the legitimacy of governance.

It has to be asked, however, whether such hopes can be satisfied. Some have even argued that the inclusion of private actors, both those for-profit and those not-for-profit, augments rather than alleviates the problems of democratic legitimacy in international institutions because private actors contribute to the 'de-governmentalization' and 'commercialization' of world politics.[55] Participation of non-state actors does not make international governance more democratic, particularly if this participation is selective and lacks transparency. More than thirty years ago, Karl Kaiser raised precisely the issue of the democratic accountability of transnational actors.[56] Why is the Transatlantic Business Dialogue, as a PPP including multinational corporations and

EU and U.S. officials, more democratic than direct negotiations between the democratically elected U.S. government and the EU Commission representing equally democratic member-states? The situation is even more complicated where the participation of the non-profit sector in international governance is concerned. While the representatives of non-profit organizations are not generally elected, these actors can legitimately claim to represent the public interest from which they draw their moral authority.[57] Moreover, many NGOs have the seal of government approval through the legal recognition extended to such organizations.[58] However, there is an increasing gap (and subsequently growing conflict) between those representatives of transnational civil society who are allowed inside the governance mechanisms and those who remain outside. Although most transnational civil society groups claim to represent the public interest, some NGOs tend to be self-selected and elite-driven.[59] To some degree, the 'participatory gap'[60] is unavoidable, and the resulting conflict within civil society might actually be helpful, as it keeps both sides honest. But PPPs involving INGOs also raise concerns about transparency and exclusivity: Which INGOs are to be allowed to sit at the bargaining table and how much information about international negotiations can they disclose to the public if they wish to maximize their influence on bargaining outcomes? Moreover, the global cleavage between the rich and powerful in the North, on the one hand, and the poor and powerless in the South, on the other, is reproduced in transnational civil society. The INGO world overwhelmingly represents civil society of the OECD world, including their cultural values.[61] Southern NGOs have only limited resources to push their concerns in the INGO community. In fact, one could even argue that this is part of a broader pattern of Western global hegemony in the international system. Thus, including selected non-state sectors in PPPs does not resolve the democratic deficit of international governance.

Whether PPPs decrease or exacerbate the legitimacy deficit of transnational governance seems to depend on several conditions. The initial question is how inclusive or exclusive the governance arrangements are. The more exclusive the networks are, the less accountable and the less transparent they become. However, 'all–inclusive' governance arrangements might lead to a serious lack of efficiency and reduced problem-solving capacity. In other words, there appears to be a trade-off between (input) legitimacy and effectiveness. Multi-stakeholder networks, for example, tend to increase the participatory quality of transnational governance, since they try to include as many parties as possible that are potentially affected by the norms and policies in question. Often, however, they fail to 'get the job done' because of irreconcilable differences and strongly diverging interests. To alleviate this problem, it is often suggested that those networks should be shielded from outside interference so as to improve the deliberative quality of the negotiations. This, of course, might well result in a lack of transparency and accountability to the outside world.[62]

Conclusion

This chapter tried to map the terrain of public private partnerships as an emerging tool of transnational governance. The perceived deficits in problem-solving capacity as well as legitimacy of international regimes and organizations as governance mechanisms have given rise to numerous PPPs in the realms of international norms and standard setting, rule implementation, and service provision. Yet, as the discussion above demonstrates, it is not at all clear whether PPPs as such are indeed likely to increase the legitimacy and effectiveness of transnational governance.

We still lack the empirical knowledge to answer the question of whether PPPs make transnational governance more democratic and thus more legitimate. The answer probably depends on the scope conditions pertaining to the actors involved, the issue area and problem structure in question, and the particular institutional arrangements. We need to know a lot more about the inter- as well as the intraorganizational dynamics of transnational PPPs. Are the interaction dynamics within PPPs characterized by mutual resource dependency and the exchange of material as well as ideational resources? To what extent do successful PPPs require changes in the organizational structures and management styles of the actors involved? Do enhanced problem-solving capacities of PPPs correlate with strong commitments of actors to the respective norms, combined with strong enforcement and sanctioning mechanisms?

In any case, it is unlikely that PPPs per se will solve most of the world's problems and make governance beyond the nation-state more democratic. It is equally unlikely, however, that governance arrangements involving non-state actors can be easily discarded as not delivering the goods. In particular, one has to be clear about the yardsticks against which to measure the democratic quality and problem-solving capacity of multi-stakeholder PPPs. Are we comparing them to some ideals of cosmopolitan and deliberative democracy on a global scale, or do existing international (interstate) regimes constitute the standards of comparison? For example, many people criticize the U.N.'s Global Compact as merely committing firms voluntarily to global human rights and social and environmental norms, while lacking any mechanisms for enforcement. Yet, it is very unclear whether firms underwriting the Global Compact score worse with regard to, say, child labour in their production facilities than states that ratified the various ILO conventions banning child labour but failed to enforce the provisions in their domestic environments. More research about the various public-private arrangements in transnational governance is required to reach firm conclusions regarding their effectiveness and legitimacy.

NOTES

1 This is a further revised version of a paper presented at the workshop on 'Global Governance,' at the European University Institute, Florence, 2001, April 6–7 and at the Conference on 'The Reconstitution of Political Authority in the 21st Century,' at the University of Toronto, 15–16 March 2002, as well as at the Technical University of Munich, 18–19 October 2002. We thank the participants, in particular Edgar Grande, Dieter Kerwer, Renate Mayntz, and Louis Pauly, for their helpful comments. Moreover, we thank the students in Thomas Risse's seminar on 'Public-Private Partnerships in International Relations' for their critical input.
2 Hasenclever, Mayer, and Rittberger (1997).
3 See the literature on 'two level games,' such as Putnam (1988) and Evans, Jacobson, and Putnam (1993).
4 For an overview, see Risse (2002).
5 For example, Reinicke (1998), Cutler, Haufler, and Porter (1999), O'Brien et al. (2000).
6 Reinicke and Deng (2000).
7 For excellent reviews, see Mayntz (1998b and 2002).
8 See Peters's chapter in this volume.
9 Mayntz (2002: 21).
10 Linder and Rosenau (2000: 5).
11 Keck and Sikkink (1998).
12 Transnational relations are defined as 'regular interactions across national

boundaries when at least one actor is a non-state agent' (Keohane and Nye, 1971: xii–xiii). See also, Risse (2002). Note that we conceptualize PPPs in much broader terms than do most international organizations and development agencies, which restrict the term to what we call 'service providing' PPPs (see below).

13 Putnam (1988), Evans, Jacobson, and Putnam (1993), Keck and Sikkink (1998), Haas (1992), Risse-Kappen (1995).

14 Cutler, Haufler, and Porter (1999).

15 Once again, the distinctions are not as clear-cut as they look. There is a lot of overlap in these functions.

16 Korey (1998).

17 Arts (1998).

18 O'Brien et al. (2000).

19 Mekata (2000).

20 Ronit and Schneider (1999).

21 Lock (2001), Singer (2001/2002).

22 Khagram (2000).

23 Cowles (2000).

24 Héritier (2002); see also, Kohler-Koch (2002).

25 See Czempiel (1991) on these notions.

26 Ronit and Schneider (1999).

27 Farrell (2002).

28 Lehmkuhl (2000).

29 Kerwer (2002).

30 Cutler, Haufler, and Porter (1999).

31 Chayes and Chayes (1991); Chayes, Chayes, and Mitchell (1998).

32 Reinicke and Deng (2000).

33 Börzel (1998b).

34 Bohne (1981).

35 Thomson (1994).

36 Krasner (1999: 9–25). See also Reinicke's discussion of legal and operational sovereignty (1998: Chapter 2).

37 Lock (2001), Singer (2001/2002).

38 For the following, see Grande and Risse (2000: 253–7).

39 Rosenau (2000), Voigt (1995).

40 In the following, we use the term *legitimacy* exclusively as 'input legitimacy,' since output legitimacy equals problem-solving effectiveness. Input legitimacy requires that those who are affected by collectively binding decisions should have a say in the decision-making process. Output legitimacy, by contrast, refers to the effectiveness of policies in the sense that they serve

the common good and conform to criteria of distributive justice (see Scharpf 1999b).

41 Wapner (1997), Held (1995).
42 Wolf (2000).
43 Haas (1992).
44 Risse, Ropp, and Sikkink (1999).
45 Chayes and Chayes (1993); Chayes, Chayes, and Mitchell (1998).
46 As similar argument is made by Downs, Rocke, and Barsoom (1996) with respect to interstate relations.
47 Bohman and Regh (1997).
48 Scharpf (1997a). For an overview, see Risse (2000).
49 Brühl et al. (2001).
50 On this point, see Müller (1996).
51 Florini (2000b).
52 Reinicke and Deng (2000).
53 Brühl (2001). This is not to say that governance beyond the nation-state needs a 'transnational demos' to be legitimate. See Brock (1998), Zürn (2000b).
54 Keck and Sikkink (1998), Galtung (2000).
55 Brühl et al. (2001).
56 Kaiser (1971).
57 Wolf (2001).
58 Florini (2000a).
59 Keohane (2001).
60 Reinicke and Deng (2000: viii).
61 Boli and Thomas (1999).
62 See Risse (2004) for details.

10   The Private Production of Public Goods: Private and Public Norms in Global Governance

TONY PORTER

One of the most widely recognized aspects of the contemporary reconstitution of political authority is the changing role of the private sector in governance, a theme that is prominent in this volume. The widespread belief that the private sector is playing a greater role in governance is evident in popular discussions about deregulation, in which functions formerly carried out by the state are transferred to actors in the private sector. It is evident in discussions about global markets, in which the competitive pressures imposed by private sector actors, such as threats to flee to more lightly regulated jurisdictions, are seen as severely constraining the policy choices of states. Finally, it is evident in fears that multinational corporations are using their enormous technical and economic resources to exercise undue direct influence over policy processes at the expense of the average citizen.

In international affairs these changes have challenged conventional theories of international relations, which have traditionally seen private sector actors as playing a negligible role in international governance. Realism, the dominant theoretical approach, has long argued that states are the only significant actors, a belief reinforced by the persistence of war, an activity in which states have specialized, and by international law which, until recently, only states could create and use. Attempts to reconcile this traditional approach with the new prominence of private sector actors have spawned vast debates, as well as a whole new academic subfield, international political economy, which is often defined as the study of the relationship between states and markets.

Unfortunately, these perspectives on the role of private sector actors in governance are usually deficient because they fail to recognize the role of *private sector norms*. *Norms* are 'standards of behaviour defined in terms of rights and obligations.'[1] Even those who stress the importance of private sector actors often overlook private sector norms because they see private sector influence as being exercised either by anonymous fluid market forces or by the deployment of material resources by self-interested multinational corporations to whom norms are irrelevant. Those who stress the pre-eminence of states also often overlook the role of private sector norms, either because they focus on the primacy of powerful self-interested states, for which norms are irrelevant, or because the only norms that they recognize are those created among states, as is the case with the traditional notions of absolute sovereignty discussed in Chapter 1.

In contrast to these views, this chapter argues that private sector norms are very important in the reconstitution of political authority in the twenty-first century. They are significant not just because the relationship between the private sector and political authority is changing, but also because this changing public-private relationship is entangled with another key theme of this volume, the spatial reconfiguration of territorially based authority. In this chapter I focus especially on the role of private sector norms in global governance, although many of the changes that are occurring at the global level parallel or are linked to changes at the domestic level. I begin with a conceptual discussion in which the ways in which private sector norms may be expected to contribute to global governance are outlined. I then turn to an issue area that is often taken to be emblematic of the contemporary reconstitution of political authority – the regulation of global finance – to provide some evidence against which to assess these conceptual themes. As Beck points out in his contribution to this volume, global finance is a key source of the risks that are a constitutive feature of 'world risk society,' and thus an examination of mechanisms designed to manage these risks is especially useful. This chapter aims, then, to clarify the changing relationship between private sector actors and political authority in a globalizing world, and in doing so to enhance our understanding of the contribution of norms in general and private sector norms in particular to global governance.

Analysing Private Sector Norms

In understanding norms it is useful to start with a sense of the many dimensions on which they vary other than the dimension that is the focus of this essay – the relative influence of private sector versus public sector characteristics. Norms can vary, for instance, along the following five dimensions[2]:

1 By issue area or industry (e.g., human rights norms and semiconductor technical standards)
2 By degree of specificity (e.g., broad principles and detailed methodologies)
3 By degree of hardness (e.g., written obligatory norms, 'soft law,' and voluntary standards)
4 By degree of acceptance (e.g., accepted in all jurisdictions and new 'contested' norms)
5 By which aspect of the actor they influence (e.g., constitutive, regulatory, and declarative)

Together with others I have distinguished the following seven types of private sector institutions in which norms are important: (1) informal industry norms and practices; (2) coordination services firms (e.g., accountancy, law firms, insurance, and sellers of standards and ratings); (3) production alliances, subcontractor relationships, and complementary activities; (4) cartels; (5) self-regulatory business associations; (6) representative business associations; and (7) private regimes.[3] Public-private partnerships, extensively analysed by Börzel and Risse in this volume, may be considered another type. Analysing the institution in which a norm is embedded will tell us a lot about the purpose of that norm, how it was developed, and how compliance is fostered. For instance, norms promoted by accountancy firms are likely to be technically oriented, apolitical, and detailed, whereas the norms promoted by representative business associations are likely to be broader and more political.

Taken as a whole, private institutions differ from states in a number of key respects.[4] First, they are smaller and cannot mobilize as many or as large a variety of resources, even though some of them, such as a production alliance involving General Motors and Toyota, involve impressively large organizations. Second, the range of actors that they involve and the range of activities that they seek to regulate is far narrower than is the case for states. Third, they differ from states in their capacity to use law and legitimacy in the promotion of norms. Nevertheless, as we shall see, private sector norms can have a significant effect.

How Private Sector Norms May Achieve Their Effect

Contrary to the views of those who assume that private sector norms are irrelevant, there are two important ways in which these norms can have a significant impact on global governance. I label these *private sector interdependencies and embeddedness* and *public-private leverage*, each of which I now discuss in turn.

Private Sector Interdependencies and Embeddedness

Private sector norms can alter the conduct of private sector actors, which, because of the importance of these actors in global affairs, can in turn have an impact on global governance. The normative effect, in this case, primarily occurs within the private sector.

Norms reduce uncertainty, and in a global private sector environment characterized by escalating and frequently incalculable risks,[5] norms can, therefore, be very important in numerous ways. They can provide benchmarks against which volatility can be measured better, thereby enhancing risk management models. A record of compliance with norms can signal reliable and predictable conduct to those who might not otherwise be familiar with the risks of interactions with an actor. Jointly formulated norms can facilitate coordinated action among the authors of the norms, reducing uncertainty among them and allowing them to jointly manage external risks. Norms can facilitate collective enforcement of reliable behaviour, both by defining clearly what is unacceptable and by helping mobilize the actors and institutions needed to discipline non-compliant actors. Norms reduce transaction costs by providing a focal point around which bargaining positions can more quickly converge. These types of useful functions all suggest that private sector actors may choose to develop and use norms because doing so allows them to better manage the risks associated with their interdependencies. This could be understood as a process of strategic rational choice, but the norms thus created can have a degree of autonomy and are more than simply a fluctuating summation of the underlying changing interests of individual self-interested actors.

Once norms become well established they can begin to appear to actors as part of their external environment over which they have no control, a phenomenon that can be called *embeddedness*. Norms may be written into standard operating procedures, model contracts, technical manuals, electronic protocols, and machine systems. It is easy to forget, in looking at a production system, how integrated its discursive and physical properties are. As Callon has commented, 'a technical object may be treated as *a program of action coordinating a network of roles*. These roles are played by non-humans (the machine itself and other objects such as accessories and power supplies) and "peripheral" humans (such as salespersons, consumers, repair people).'[6] Standards and other norms are central to this process. Even in production processes in which the physical component is relatively less important, such as white collar work, standard operating procedures and routines can become so embedded in dispersed local contexts that they can be very difficult for individual actors to change.[7] Like machine systems, they can be taken for granted and be seen as an unquestioned precondition for carrying out the work. This is the case, for instance, with accounting practices or risk assessment models.

How can norms developed among private sector actors have an impact on global governance? These days the private sector itself has a sufficiently significant direct impact on the daily lives of citizens that once it begins to operate globally one can say that the organization of the private sector is itself an aspect of global governance. Shared norms within or among firms, such as those involved in corporate governance or strategic alliances between firms, can facilitate the expansion of multinational firms across borders, having major consequences for those who work for these firms. Concentration ratios that show that the top five firms control about 70 per cent of world sales of consumer durables and more than half of world sales of cars and trucks, airlines, aerospace, and electronic components[8] further reinforce this point. Private sector norms allow vast new international markets to be created that in turn can govern the conduct of other actors. For instance, the Eurobond market, in which money can be raised by selling bonds in foreign currencies, relied at its beginnings in the 1960s on a set of informal shared norms among a few leading securities firms, and the trust that this created helped launch what today is a massive global market, often thought to sharply constrain the options of governments eager not to upset their foreign bond-holders.

Shared norms among private sector actors can also strengthen their capacity to lobby public sector actors. For instance, the types of arbitration rules that the International Chamber of Commerce[9] provides for resolving international commercial disputes helps builds its reputation, which in turn helps it influence international negotiations. Similarly, the Intellectual Property Committee (a multinational grouping of the largest pharmaceutical companies) developed a set of shared normative understandings that gave it remarkable influence in the adoption of intellectual property provisions in the Uruguay Round of international trade negotiations.[10]

Public-Private Leverage

Private sector norms can also have an impact on global governance through their more direct integration with the work of globally relevant public sector actors and institutions.[11] There are numerous examples of a recent upswing in public sector enthusiasm for drawing on private sector norms for regulatory purposes. In particular jurisdictions governments have commissioned studies on self-regulation. For instance, the European Union commissioned a very lengthy study by Lex Fori, a group of lawyers, on the role of 'soft law' in which private norms are extensively analysed, and in 2001 it issued a *Better Regulation* report that focused on 'co-regulation.'[12] The Canadian government has seen itself as a leader internationally in the creation and promotion of voluntary standards and codes and has sponsored reports on this issue. The Australian government devoted a major task force to the issue of self-regulation in 1999. At the international level, the Organization for Economic Cooperation and Development (OECD) has been actively promoting a more creative use of self-regulation through its Public Management and Governance program.[13] The World Bank has displayed a similar interest, as evident in its 2002 *World Development Report*, entitled *Building Institutions for Markets*, which includes subsections such as 'Private Governance Institutions for Firms' and, under 'Society,' 'Norms and Networks.'

There are a number of reasons that states are increasingly relying on private sector norms, aside from responding to the enthusiasm of private sector actors for them. First, they can be more flexible and more easily established than statutory regulation. They can be cost effective at a time when governments are short of financial and technical resources. They can have more legitimacy among private sector actors, and this can improve compliance with the norms and enhance the government's reputation.

There are numerous ways in which public sector actors can draw on, and in turn help foster, private sector norms, especially those norms formulated as standards. These include: (a) financial and other support for standards research, (b) financing of the negotiation and administration of voluntary standards, (c) coordination across related bodies of non-governmental voluntary standards, (d) the use of references to voluntary standards in mandatory government standards, (e) licensing, for instance, professional licensing of accountants and others involved in the monitoring of firms or the inclusion of compliance with voluntary standards in the granting of licenses to those firms, and (f) the use of state power as a back-up in cases in which voluntary standards fail or to ensure that private standards are followed. For example, the self-regulatory functions of stock exchanges have generally been backed up by official regulation and supervision. Laws can be used by private actors to obtain legal remedies against other private actors. Similarly, uses by firms of private codes, such as human rights codes, can be considered by regulators and courts when assessing their behaviour.[14]

Given the reach of large firms and chains of market activities across borders, along with the interest of governments in private sector norms, we can expect an increase in the regulatory role of private sector norms at the global level. Current examples include the International Organization for Standardization (ISO); the private Internet Corporation for Assigned Names and Numbers (ICANN), which plays a key role in the governance of the Internet;[15] and the Forest Steward-ship Council, a non-governmental regulatory body.[16] Elsewhere in this volume, Börzel and Risse consider these types of arrangements under their category 'self-regulation in the shadow of hierarchy.' These involve a variety of relationships between the private sector standards and the public sector. We shall see below that there are many more such examples in global finance, as well.

Increased reliance by public sector actors on private sector norms can be potentially very significant for global governance. Institutional capacity is an even more severe problem at the global level than at the domestic level, and if reliance on private sector norms can help public sector actors extend their own regulatory capacity, then this could strengthen global governance. On the other hand, this blurring of the distinction between the public and private sectors can raise serious questions about the accountability and legitimacy of the international public policy processes that they affect, compounding problems of 'democratic deficits' connected with the migration of decision-making to international institutions seen as excessively remote from the average citizen. These problems are addressed in the chapters by Greven and Skogstad, elsewhere in this volume.

The Case of International Financial Standards and Codes

I turn now to a particular case – the development of international financial standards and codes – as a way to explore the contention that private sector norms are significant in global governance. Global finance is a good hard case with which to test this contention because it is frequently seen as the quintessential example of highly fluid, competitive, aggressive markets in which norms are unlikely to play a significant part. Those scholars who have argued that global finance can be regulated have usually emphasized the role of powerful states rather than private sector norms. Throughout the 1990s global finance was characterized by one systemic crisis after another. A key response was to create and strengthen financial standards and codes.[17] An examination of this effort will help in assessing whether norms in general and private sector norms specifically can play any significant role in global governance.

There can be little doubt today that successful global financial regulation would qualify as an aspect of global governance. Although in the past some more traditional international relations scholars would have been quick to dismiss such heavily technical matters as marginal to the real substance of international politics – war and peace – there are now numerous reasons to dismiss this traditional view. The global systemic risks associated with finance are very much the type of risks Beck talks about in connection with the new emerging forms of governance associated with the cosmopolitan character of world risk society. Certainly, international financial standards and codes received sustained high-level attention in institutions typically seen as central to global governance, including the G-7 which, in 1999, created the Financial Stability Forum (FSF) as a way to address international financial crises in large part through monitoring and reporting on work on international standards and codes, on subjects ranging from money laundering to corporate governance. Similarly, the International Monetary Fund has become heavily involved in financial standards and codes through its new and remarkably intense process of Reports on Observance of Standards and Codes in which an ever-increasing number of countries have agreed to a thorough audit of their national procedures by a team of regulators from abroad. International standards and codes generally build on efforts that go back many years or even decades, but they have received a great deal of renewed attention from policymakers in response to the global financial crises of the 1990s.

Indeed the IMF has said that standards and codes are a 'central element' in the effort to strengthen the international financial architecture.[18] Using the language of Coleman's chapter, global financial regulation is a 'transnational policy space' within which financial standards and codes are a key priority.

The Financial Stability Forum has highlighted twelve sets of standards 'as key for sound financial systems and deserving of priority implementation, depending on country circumstances.' The FSF summary of these appears in Table 10.1. In addition the FSF has produced a 'Compendium of Standards' that it has described as a 'one-stop reference' for economic and financial standards relevant to a sound financial system.[19] The number of sets of standards in the compendium had grown to ninety-four by July 2004. Table 10.2 displays the standards, differentiated by year of creation and subject area. Considering that only one standard predates the 1990s, it is clear that the 1990s were distinctive in the level of interest in creating standards. The FSF website allows users of the compendium to sort by date, subject, or sponsoring organization and to use hyperlinks to get more detailed information at the sponsoring organizations' websites.

As interesting as the quantity and range of standards is the process that the FSF has pursued in promoting them. The March 2001 'Issues Paper of the Task Force on Implementation of Standards' set out a five-stage strategy: (1) development of consensus on key standards, (2) prioritization of standards, (3) creation of an effective standards implementation plan, (4) ongoing assessments of progress in standards observance, and (5) dissemination of information on observance. It identifies three key issues: the importance of 'ownership,' including widespread involvement in the formulation and implementation of standards; the role of official and private incentives; and the question of resources.

Compliance with standards is brought about by the mobilization of private sector actors and public sector actors. The former is examined in more detail below. Official incentives include the incorporation of the observance of standards into IMF conditionality processes, such as making observance a precondition for eligibility for the IMF's Contingent Credit Line; making observance a condition of membership in international organizations; peer pressure exerted through regional and international groupings; stepped up external official assessment of compliance; stepped up information dissemination; technical assistance; reducing the capital requirements on loans to complying juris-

TABLE 10.1
The FSF's key standards for sound financial systems

Subject area	Key standard	Issuing body
Macroeconomic policy and data transparency		
Monetary and financial policy transparency	Code of Good Practices on Transparency in Monetary and Financial Practices	IMF
Fiscal policy transparency	Code of Good Practices in Fiscal Transparency	IMF
Data dissemination	Special Data Dissemination Standard General Data Dissemination System	IMF
Institutional and market infrastructure		
Insolvency	In the process of being developed	World Bank
Corporate governance	Principles of Corporate Governance	OECD
Accounting	International Accounting Standards	IASB
Auditing	International Standards on Auditing	IFAC
Payment and settlement	Core Principles for Systematically Important Payment Systems	CPSS
	Recommendations for Securities Settlement Systems	CPSS and IOSCO
Market integrity	The Forty Recommendations of the Financial Action Task Force on Money Laundering	FATF
	Eight Special Recommendations Against Terrorist Financing	
Financial regulation and supervision		
Banking supervision	Core Principles for Effective Banking Supervision	BCBS
Securities regulation	Objectives and Principles of Securities Regulation	IOSCO
Insurance supervision	Insurance Supervisory Principles	IAIS

Source: FSF (27 July 2004). See also, hyperlinks at www.fsforum.org
*BCBS = Basel Committee on Banking Supervision; CPSS = Committee on Payment and Settlement Systems; FATF = Financial Action Task Force; IAIS = International Association of Insurance Supervisors; IASB = International Accounting Standards Board; IMF = International Monetary Fund; IOSCO = International Organization of Securities Commissions.

Table 10.2
Sets of standards and codes (*n*) included in the FSF Compendium of Standards, by subject area and year of their creation, 1983–2003

Subject area	83	90	91	92	93	94	95	96	97	98	99	00	01	02	03	All
Macroeconomic policy, data transparency				2				1	1	1	1	2				8
Institutional and market infrastructure		1		1				3	2		2		3	3		15
Banking supervision	1			1		1		2	2	7	2	1	1			18
Securities regulation			1	1		2		1	2	8	2					17
Insurance supervision									2	3	3	3		5	2	18
Cross-sector supervision and conglomerates											4					18
Total	1	1	1	3	2	3	0	7	9	19	14	6	4	8	2	94

Note: Based on listing at www.fsforum.org, as accessed on 27 July 2004. Where a set of standards covers more than one subject area, it is recorded as belonging to the subject area for which it is most relevant.

dictions and thereby reducing financing costs to them; and tighter regulation of or restrictions on access for foreign offices of firms from non-complying jurisdictions.

Precisely measuring progress on the standards overall, including the degree of compliance with them, is complicated by their number and variety, and goes beyond the scope of this chapter. Reports from the FSF, such as its periodic 'Ongoing and Recent Work Relevant to Sound Financial Systems,' and from the IMF and World Bank, such as their 2001 'Assessing the Implementation of Standards: A Review of Experience and Next Steps,' summarize developments, but these include the completion of reports and the progress of agreement with the idea of standards and do not seek to review compliance in detail. The FSF issues paper of 15 March 2001 noted that 'the standard-setting bodies are in various stages of developing detailed methodologies that could be used for self-assessments or external assessments' and for those areas for which methodologies have not yet been developed an assessment of compliance would be premature.[20]

Two IMF and World Bank programs have been especially important: the Financial Sector Assessment Program (FSAP) and the Reports on the Observance of Standards and Codes (ROSCs). The former is an audit of national standards carried out by a team of external regulatory officials (from international institutions such as the IMF or from governments) in particular countries, and the ROSCs are reports on those standards. As of 27 July 2004, 429 ROSC modules involving ninety-nine countries had been published on the IMF's external website.[21] The annual numbers of modules have steadily increased, from twenty-seven in 1999 to 107 in 2002 and 122 in 2003. This willingness on the part of a very disparate set of countries to submit to this process is a significant sign of the growing acceptance of the importance of standards, given that just a few years earlier, in the 1998 G-22 reports on the international financial architecture, this type of peer review was regarded with scepticism. The IMF itself has, perhaps not surprisingly, been positive about its work on standards: 'Directors welcomed the broad based participation of member countries in the initiative, together with closer contact with standard setters and growing interest in the private sector as a sign of the increasing momentum for the work on standards.'[22]

The account above demonstrates that there has been considerable forward movement on the strengthening of international financial standards. This, combined with the high-level attention the issue has received among leaders of the world's most powerful states, shows that in this issue area norms *do* matter. Leaders and high-level officials would not expend this amount of valuable policymaking time on standards if they were irrelevant. Already the above discussion has provided indications that private sector norms play important roles in the governance of global finance, but it is useful to focus on these roles more directly, and it is to this task that I now turn.

Assessing the Role of Private Sector Norms in International Financial Standards and Codes

I identified two ways in which private sector norms contribute to global governance: 'private sector interdependencies and embeddedness' and 'public/private leverage.' I look in turn at the relevance of each of these for international financial standards and codes.

Private Sector Interdependencies and Embeddedness

Three examples will illustrate the direct effect of private sector norms on the international conduct of private sector actors, conduct that in turn is relevant to global governance: the International Accounting Standards Board (IASB), the Counterparty Risk Management Policy Group (CRMPG), and the Clearing House Interbank Payments System (CHIPS).

The IASB was formed in 1973 as the International Accounting Standards Committee (IASC). It consists of a membership of 152 professional accountancy bodies, representing more than a hundred countries. Since its inception, the IASB has been working to develop international accounting standards (IAS). Most of its funding comes from the private sector, and all of its rules are made by private sector actors. For many years the IAS lagged behind the U.S.-based Generally Accepted Accounting Principles (GAAP) in their influence but they have been gaining rapidly in importance, especially with the intention of the European Union and Australia to adopt them by 2005. Clear and precise accounting standards are crucial for the functioning of global financial markets. The IAS are enforced by public sector authorities in those jurisdictions that recognize them, by private sector bodies, such as stock exchanges, and by market pressures.

The CRMPG is an interesting example of an ad hoc private sector standard-setting body: The CRMPG played a key role in the development of regulatory policy towards hedge funds. It was formed after risky speculation caused the huge Long Term Capital Management hedge fund to collapse, which in turn came close to bringing about a disastrous system-threatening collapse of leading banks exposed to it. There were many calls to regulate hedge funds in the wake of the East Asian financial crisis of the late 1990s, as well. The CRMPG brought together senior executives from about ten of the world's top banks. It was chaired by E. Gerald Corrigan of Goldman Sachs, former head of the main international bank regulatory body (the Basel Committee on Banking Supervision) and the New York Federal Reserve Bank. By setting out detailed voluntary best practices for banks lending to hedge funds, the CRMPG played a key role in heading off stricter regulation by the public sector.

The CHIPS is owned by banks. It manages the clearance and settlement of transactions in U.S. dollars in the United States and elsewhere, transferring an average of $1.2 trillion daily, or 95 per cent of all U.S.

dollar payments. CHIPS is an excellent example of embeddedness, since its computerized system has a real-time enforcement capacity in being able to halt a participant's payment messages if that participant becomes too exposed in its bilateral commitments to other participants. This set of private sector rules is backed up by CHIPS rules that expose participants to the regulatory capacity of the U.S. state. Participants must have an office and a primary computer connection in the United States, they agree to be bound by New York law, and they must pre-fund transactions by holding funds at the U.S. Federal Reserve. CHIPS contributes to global governance by stabilizing the international clearance and settlement of dollars – a potential source of great systemic risk. It is emblematic of the very large number of cross-border financial transactions that are carried out routinely thanks to systems of private norms, thereby allowing public sector bodies such as the Financial Stability Forum to focus on less routine issues of governance.

All three of these examples illustrate the way in which private sector norms contribute to global governance through their capacity to shape the conduct of private sector actors. This capacity is built on both the interdependence of private sector actors (e.g., with CHIPS, where the system develops regulatory leverage through the need for its participants to interact with one another in the system, or with the interdependence of banks and hedge funds) and embeddedness (e.g., the way in which accounting standards and CHIPS rules become part of unquestioned routine practices).

Public-Private Leverage

There are innumerable ways in which public sector and private sector norms can work together to reinforce one another. Even in the previous section there were examples of this, for instance, in the reference to New York law in the CHIPS rules or the impact of the threat of public sector regulation on the incentive for the CRMPG to develop private sector standards. However, these examples are ones in which the rule-making initiative remains with the private sector actors. Private sector norms also play a crucial role in international rule making by the public sector. In this section I provide three illustrations of this. The first, involving private sector implementation of public sector rules, is corporate governance standards. The second, involving the incorporation of private sector norms within public sector regulatory regimes, is the reliance on private sector risk models in the ongoing revisions of the

Basel Accord on the adequacy of bank capital. The third, involving the use of market pressures to enforce public sector regulations, is the FSF's efforts to revise the way in which public sector data are disseminated in order be more easily usable by market actors.

Corporate governance refers to the rules that regulate the relationships between the actors involved in and with the corporation. In the Anglo-American tradition, corporate governance has been concerned almost exclusively with safeguarding the capacity of shareholders to hold managers accountable, for instance, through corporate boards of directors. Corporate governance can also include other stakeholder relations, such as the relationship of the firm to employees, customers, suppliers, or a local community. It was put prominently on the international agenda when deficiencies in corporate governance were seen to have contributed to the East Asian and Russian financial crises of the late 1990s and as a key development issue to be addressed by emerging market and transitional economies more generally. Enron and other U.S.-based scandals further strengthened international interest in corporate governance standards. A focal point of the international initiatives has been the public sector OECD, including the Global Forum on Corporate Governance that the OECD set up in 1999 with the World Bank. In general, corporate governance develops through states setting out a legal framework, which is then implemented by individual firms establishing organizational rules and procedures. Global harmonization of corporate governance is being pursued by creating agreed-upon guidelines at the OECD, with the hope that these will influence national governments and corporations.

An example of the use of private sector norms within a public sector regulatory regime is the ongoing development of rules on the adequacy of bank capital at the public sector Basel Committee on Banking Supervision (BCBS). This committee's 1988 accord on bank capital adequacy is the strongest international agreement on the regulation of international banks. However, while it is widely agreed that the accord was important in alleviating risk to the system from excessively risky bank behaviour, in recent years it has been seen as too inflexible to cope with current market conditions. In the 1988 agreement, the official regulators categorized all bank activities by crude estimates of the activities' riskiness, and then required banks to hold more capital against activities that fell into the categories deemed to be riskier, thereby restraining the growth of risk. In contrast, the current revisions to the accord allow banks to use their own models in calculating risks and determining the amount of capital they need. These models involve highly complex sets of rules for estimating the riskiness of particular activities, as well as the capacity of one type of risk to offset another. These sets of rules, then, are a type of private sector norm that will be integrated into the regime constructed by the public sector regulators.

The use of market pressures to enforce public sector rules is relevant to both corporate governance and bank regulation, since investors will punish firms that are seen to be deviating from public sector standards. The more general relevance of these market pressures for financial standards and codes, including standards aimed at shaping the conduct of governments, is evident in the systematic efforts of the FSF to devise standards that will be incorporated into the decision-making of market actors. The FSF, both in its March 2000 task force report, and then in a subsequent August 2000 follow-up report on the implementation of standards provided information on consultations it had done with the market participants on standards. The FSF found that awareness of standards was low and information about observance of standards was not widely used. Obstacles to further use included: the lack of an adequate track record of standards which could reduce market participants' capacity to assess their significance; qualitative or yes/no indicators were not easily integrated into existing quantitative risk models; issues not covered by standards, such as legal and political risks, were thought to be more important than existing standards; private sources of information, including commercial services and direct acquisition of confidential information were thought to be more useful; and, finally, lack of benchmarks and clear methods for comparison across countries and lack of confidence in the information being released on observance of standards. To improve the effectiveness of market incentives, the FSF proposed various mechanisms to market them, such as seminars and publications, and in these to provide analysis of the connection between observance of standards and the specific risk assessments in which market participants are interested. This represents, then, an example of public sector regulators very deliberately shaping the relationship between public and private sector norms, and as such it is yet another example of the importance of private sector norms in the governance of global finance.

These examples of public-private leverage illustrate the widespread and growing use of private sector norms in conjunction with public sector regulatory arrangements at the international level. In this type of arrangement there is room for dispute about whether this represents a surrender by public sector authorities of their responsibility to regulate or, instead, a wise use by regulators of private norms to make more effective and efficient use of their own limited regulatory capacities. In either case, it is clear that private sector norms are a crucial component of the regulation of global finance.

Conclusion

An examination of the efforts to strengthen international financial standards and codes shows the importance of private sector norms in this important arena of global governance. In some cases, private sector norms are developed and administered by private sector actors, while in others they are integrated with regulatory arrangements constructed by public sector actors. The more autonomous private sector arrangements, such as the Clearing House Interbank Payments System (CHIPS), obtain their capacity to enforce compliance through the interdependence of their participants and through embedding the norms in routine practices and machine systems. In cases in which private sector norms are more integrated into public sector arrangements, these sources of compliance can still be important; nevertheless, the coercive capacity of the state is also important. It is clear that, overall, the regulation of global finance is managed by states. The FSF, a public sector body, is responsible for monitoring the development of international financial standards as a whole and for providing leadership in drawing connections among standards. The FSF was created by and is dominated by the world's most powerful states organized in the G-7. Most of the standard-setting bodies that the FSF seeks to coordinate, like the OECD, are public sector bodies. Nevertheless, it is clear that private sector norms are important both for public sector standard setters, and for private sector standard setters such as the International Accounting Standards Board.

The remarkably small size of the FSF is an indication that compliance with financial standards and codes will not be brought about by threats and inducements involving a centralized mobilization of resources. Certainly, the FSF's sponsors – the G-7 – are very powerful, and their efforts have been important in raising the profile of financial standards and codes. However, the enormous complexity of the standards and codes involved makes it impossible for either the FSF or the G-7 to do more than encourage and endorse the work of the other standard-setting bodies. A partial exception is the IMF processes of conditionality, which come closest to the traditional realist model of compliance. If members of the G-7 work in concert, the G-7 can exercise decisive control in the IMF, and IMF lending in turn can provide formidable leverage over small borrowing countries. Even here, though, it is impossible for the G-7 to bring about compliance with standards in any systematic way, because of the number of borrowing countries, the number of criteria involved in the assessments of conditionality, and the variations in contextual factors across borrowing countries.

Rather than relying on the deliberate use of threats and inducements through the mobilization of resources, compliance with international financial standards and codes relies on the embedding of these standards and codes in legal and commercial practices that become so routine that they become part of the 'reality' that actors simply accept when they engage in market interactions. The power that mobilizes international standards setters in their varied and dispersed international venues is more discursive than material – standards evolve through a deliberative process of practical reasoning, in which the particular experiences of participants in markets are brought together with general principles that in turn have been developed from prior deliberative processes. *Codes of conduct*, *best practices*, and *core principles* are the terms used in this issue area, and they capture the way in which norms are both summations of past practices and guides to future practices.

Could it be that the lack of resources put into the Financial Stability Forum, and the absence of centralized mobilization of resources to create threats and inducements in the implementation of standards, are indications that powerful states have deliberately decided on a minimalist approach – because it is in their interest, and in the interest of powerful firms headquartered in their jurisdictions, to let the financial market run free? The suggestion that international financial standards and codes are simply useless rhetoric designed to legitimize a decision not to act is not credible. There have been far too many resources expended by both private and public actors in developing extraordinarily technical and specific arguments regarding these standards and codes. One cannot argue they do not matter. In the case of the proposed new bank standards for capital adequacy, for instance, thousands of pages of detailed industry commentary have been generated.[23]

While it is clear that private sector norms matter a great deal in the governance of global finance, it is important to ask how significant this case is relative to the reconstitution of political authority more generally. Three points can be made in answer to this question.

First, while the distinctive characteristics of the issue area of global finance – including its pace of change, its degree of globalization, the intangibility of its products, and its vulnerability to crisis – should lead us to be cautious about transferring the above lessons to other issue areas. Nevertheless, there are many ways in which these characteristics are present, or are becoming more evident, in other issue areas. For instance, in industry even more traditional 'tangible' products increasingly involve high levels of knowledge, aesthetics, and symbolic values in their production, distribution, and regulation.[24] As Beck has noted, other industries, such as chemicals or fisheries, can experience catastrophes, addressing which requires the use of abstract models and norms. In social policy areas these intangibles are even more important.

Second, an element of the distinctiveness of global finance is its centrality to the functioning of the economy and society more generally, and thus innovations in finance often have a direct practical significance in other issue areas. Corporate governance, for instance, shapes the social relations in corporations – the predominant form of economic production in contemporary society. Similarly, notions of risk and risk management that are characteristic of finance have been widely applied elsewhere as well.[25]

Third, the relationship between states and private sector norms that was evident in this issue area is, in large part, a response to developments that are characteristic of the challenge of contemporary governance more generally. In other issue areas, states will also experience shortages of resources and need to rely on private systems of norms. Certainly, the interest of governments in self-regulation and voluntary standards that was discussed above is not restricted to the financial sector. The knowledgeability of citizens, the intensity of knowledge in daily life, the 'secularization' of law, the increased tendency to frame issues in terms of rights and obligations, and the intensity of communications linkages facilitate reliance by states on non-state standards and norms in all issue areas.[26]

Often, strong norms are seen as inherently good, either because they express shared community values or because they contribute to social order. Talk of *private sector norms*, however, is a reminder that norms can be used to consolidate loyalties among participants in a particular social grouping in order to improve the capacity of that grouping to better dominate or exploit others. In contrast with coercion, however, norms rely on voluntary compliance, which in turn is enhanced by the degree to which the norms are specified in universally applicable terms and are linked to broader systems of shared norms that are not specific to particular communities. This is a feature of norms that can be termed their *universalizing predilection*. The mediating role played by states among private sub-systems of norms that was illustrated in this chapter further reinforces this point. States cannot successfully legitimize themselves with appeals to particularistic systems of norms, and thus systems of private norms – in their reliance on states – are vulnerable to challenges from other normative claims that are more successful at framing their rights and obligations in more universalistic terms.

What can we conclude about the relevance of this case and of private sector norms in general for the issues framing this volume? This case indicates that a complex form of political authority is emerging at the global level in global finance, one in which private sector norms play a key role. The reconstitution of political authority is an ongoing process in which the distribution of influence across actors and institutional processes is shaped as much by the varying capacities and character of the type of actors and processes discussed in this chapter as by enduring relations of control. While the prominence of private sector norms may seem to reinforce the power of private sector actors, their universalizing predilection and their entanglement with public sector norms and institutions suggest that this is not necessarily so. This tension has important implications for issues of democratic legitimacy, a theme taken up elsewhere in this volume, and one that can be better understood when the role of private sector norms is taken into account.

NOTES

1 Krasner (1983: 2). While Krasner seeks to differentiate norms from three other similar types of behavioural guidelines – 'principles,' 'rules,' and 'decision-making procedures' – there is no evidence, even more than twenty years later, that these distinctions have been analytically useful, and the present chapter accordingly uses *norm* as a general term to cover all standards of behaviour.

2 For discussions that were useful in constructing this list, see the FSF's work, discussed further below, and Kratochwil (2000).

3 Cutler, Haufler, and Porter (1999: 9–15).

4 Ibid., 341.

5 Beck (this volume).

6 Callon (1991: 136). See also Beck (1999: 25 and 43).

7 Porter (1999).

8 *Economist* (27 March 1993, S17).

9 Schneider (2000).

10 Sell (1998: 137).

11 This discussion is complementary to that of Börzel and Risse (this volume). Their chapter focuses on organized private-public partnerships, while this chapter focuses on public and private sector norms.

12 Lex Fori (n.d.)

13 OECD (2000).

14 Canada (1998). This list is used as well in Coleman and Porter (2002).

15 Franda (2001).

16 Lipschutz (2000/2001).

17 The first part of this chapter's discussion of the FSF draws heavily on a paper presented to the International Studies Association. See Porter (2001).

18 IMF (2001a). There are numerous other aspects of the governance of global finance than standards and codes that could be integrated into this analysis but doing so would go beyond the scope of this chapter.

19 FSF (2001b).

20 Ibid., 8.

21 www.imf.org/external/np/rosc/rosc.asp

22 Ibid.

23 Large numbers of such pages can be viewed on the committee's website at www.bis.org . These were just the non-confidential submissions. Additional large volumes of commentary can be found in industry journals such as *ABA Banking Journal* or the *Journal of Financial Regulation and Compliance*.

24 Lash and Urry (1994).

25 Beck (1992, 1999, and this volume).

26 Porter (1999), Haufler (2001).

11 Contested Political Authority, Risk Society, and the Transatlantic Divide in the Regulation of Genetic Engineering

GRACE SKOGSTAD

Legitimate regulatory governance rests on a consensus regarding authoritative rule-making principles and institutions. Such a consensus is being challenged in the early twenty-first century by what Ulrich Beck describes, in this book and elsewhere, as the emergence of a risk society: a society as a whole, in which the risks of scientific and technological innovations to individuals, society, and the environment are perceived to have escaped the control of society, its institutions, and national boundaries.[1] From the perspective of a risk society, the industrial and technological developments that mark modernity are no longer equated with progress, as they once were. To the contrary, science and the technology it develops, industry, and even government are singled out as the main producers of risk and the 'bads' that we perceive to be threatening.[2] This risk society, argues Beck, questions whether the traditional concepts of authority based on hierarchy and neutral expertise are appropriate for today's world. The science that has created the new products and technologies that are the source of manufactured and unforeseen dangers cannot be relied on to protect us from these dangers. Competing claims have arisen 'about the legitimacy of particular forms of expertise and knowledge.'[3] Faced with this contestation, and seeking answers to questions about 'who is to define the riskiness of a product, a technology, and on what grounds,'[4] governments have turned to new forms of regulatory governing that rely less on expert authority and more on other bases of legitimation. Often private actors and citizens are drawn into collectively binding decision-making, as governments seek legitimacy for their policies for regulating risk.

The debate around authoritative rule making in contemporary risk society can occasion conflicts across societies regarding legitimate regulatory governance. Although Beck speaks of a world risk society, societies are likely to vary in terms of how much they conform to that characterization. Because 'risks are at the same time "real" *and* constituted by social perception and construction,'[5] societies may diverge in the degree to which they perceive the dangers of industrial and technological innovations and mobilize politically around them. To the degree that it is possible to talk about risk and non-risk societies, divergence will also occur across societies regarding their conceptions of legitimate political authority and legitimate regulatory governance. Non-risk societies that continue to equate industrial and technological developments with progress are unlikely to experience this challenge to traditional authoritative principles of rule making; instead, rule making by scientific experts, neutral bureaucrats, or even private authority is likely to continue to be acceptable.

These differences across risk and non-risk societies in their beliefs regarding who has the right to exercise regulatory authority – and on what grounds – can lead to international conflict. Societies are likely to be in conflict with one another when the disparate regulatory regimes and ensuing outcomes have an impact on international trade. Harmonization of such regulatory divergences, informally in an international regime or more formally in an international agreement, requires states to agree on the constitutive principles of risk regulation beyond the territorial state; that is, they agree on who should make binding decisions to deal with the dangers that are the by-products of late modernity. States need to agree, for example, on whether these decision-makers should be those (experts) knowledgeable about the technology, elected politicians accountable to citizens to protect them from the technology's potential hazards, or the private companies who produce the technology and whose profitability rests on the safety of its use. One can also expect clashes between risk and non-risk societies regarding the goals of regulation, as the former seek to mitigate the risks of a technology, for example, while the latter emphasize capturing its benefits.

The implications of a risk society temperament for reconstituting political authority and sustaining legitimate regulatory governance are explored in this chapter, in an empirical study of the regulation of the novel technology of genetic engineering. The argument is that there exists a transatlantic divide in risk society with regard to genetic engineering; the European Union is preoccupied with its the risks of genetic engineering, while the United States and Canada, are much less preoccupied. The regulation of the technology in the EU has been marked by disputes over who and what comprise legitimate actors and procedures. By the late 1990s, the authority of scientific experts and 'impartial' bureaucrats to regulate genetically modified organisms (GMOs) and their products had been undermined. EU decision-makers have since struggled to reconstitute their political authority through a governance model that incorporates elements of popular authority alongside traditional/state and expert authority.

Although there are critics of the American regulatory model – in particular, of its reliance on private authority in regulating genetically modified (GM) foods – there is nothing approaching a similar risk society mentality towards biotechnology in North America. Deference to the 'neutral' authority of science, and in the United States, belief in the efficacy of market mechanisms to yield policies that are in the public interest, combine with positive evaluations of the overall benefits of the technology of genetic engineering to provide legitimacy to the different frameworks for regulating GM products. The different principles of political authority and of legitimate governance that underlie the North American and EU GMO regulatory regimes yield, as might be expected, different substantive policy outcomes. Trade tensions have ensued, with North American governments and biotechnology developers criticizing the EU GMO regulations as being trade distorting and discriminatory. Access of the North American–dominant biotechnology industry to the EU market has been blocked, and its ambitions of a global market in GM products thwarted. These transatlantic cleavages have spilled into the international arena, with developing countries becoming the battleground for supremacy of the EU or U.S. model. Tensions between the EU and U.S. regulatory models have crippled efforts in global forums to reach a consensus on international guidelines and standards for the regulation of GM products. Rooted in divergent beliefs about what and who are legitimate rule-making processes and actors, conflicts over how to regulate one of the novel technologies that epitomizes scientific innovation in our time, highlight both the necessity and the difficulty of reconstituting political authority in a global political economy.

This chapter explores the reality and significance of divergent principles of authoritative rule making and standards of legitimation for regulatory governance in this policy area. It proceeds as follows. The first section presents a typology of political authority, distinguishing between the legitimation standards and governance mechanisms that derive from four distinctive principles of political authority: state-centred, expert, private, and popular. This typology is used to characterize the European and North American GMO regulatory frameworks. The discussion of the EU case in the second section summarizes the developments that have precipitated a change in the conceptions of political authority around the regulation of GMO food products. It outlines EU efforts to reconstitute political authority and restore regulatory legitimacy through new governance mechanisms and substantive policy reforms. The third section describes the American GMO regulatory framework, contrasting its reliance on private and expert authority with the combination of popular and expert authority in the EU model. The final section probes the implications of transatlantic GM regulatory divergence for inter-regional regulatory governance.

Conceptions of Political Authority and Standards of Legitimation

There is an inextricable link between legitimacy and authority – 'political authority is frequently defined as the legitimate exercise of political power'[6] – and between political authority and the territorial state. Weber defined political authority as 'the probability that specific commands (or all commands) will be obeyed by a given group of people,' and he considered the defining feature of the state to be its monopoly to use physical force to enforce such commands within a given territory.[7] Weber's is the traditional, state-centred conception of political authority, rooted in the electoral process in representative democracies. Citizens obey the regulatory decisions made by elected and appointed officials, as long as these decisions are established in conformity with the rules and norms of democratic decision-making and accountability.

As Table 11.1 demonstrates, other models of authoritative decision-making, predicated on different standards of legitimation and entailing different governance mechanisms, have emerged alongside state-centred political authority. Because standards of legitimacy – 'a generalized perception or assumption that the actions of an entity are desirable, proper, or appropriate' – are a 'socially constructed system of norms, values, and beliefs,'[8] models of political authority that are deemed proper in one society may not be seen so in another. Nonetheless, across democracies, the norm of politically accountable decision-making is sufficiently strong that authoritative rule making by bodies that are not directly accountable to voters must be legitimated on other

TABLE 11.1
Types of political authority

Type	Source of authority	Legitimation standards	Governance mechanism
Traditional state-centred: Representative democracy	Electoral majority	Input: adherence to formal democratic decision-making rules and accountability procedures Output: consistent with majoritarian preferences	Hierarchy: state bodies of elected and appointed officials
Techno-expert	Credentialled knowledge (legal, scientific, technical)	Output: effective problem-solving	Independent bodies of experts
Private	Market Mechanism	Output: Responsive to consumer preferences; economic benefits	Private Interest Government Industry self-regulation
Popular: Participatory Democracy	Democratic Consensus	Input: procedures of consensus-building through citizen dialogue and participation Output: conformity to citizen preferences	Deliberative Democracy Network Governance Referenda

grounds. As Majone observes, 'democratically accountable principals can transfer policy-making powers to non-majoritarian institutions but they cannot transfer their own legitimacy.'[9] Denied the 'input-oriented legitimacy' of representative state-centred governing, non-majoritarian decision-making bodies must derive their authority from elsewhere.

Techno-expert or credentialled authority, stemming from the possession of valued and relevant knowledge, is one alternative. A techno-expert authoritative model prevails where good policy outcomes depend on expertise, as they do in consumer safety and environmental protection. In these domains, actors or agencies with a technical knowledge of the subject – and operating at arm's length from governments – have traditionally been delegated the regulatory function. Their performance – the effectiveness of their 'output' decisions in addressing collective problems – is key to their legitimacy. That trust and legitimacy can diminish rapidly when their performance fails to ensure publicly valued goods. In the nation-state context, such a techno-expert model of regulatory governance is buttressed by procedural controls, for example, the requirements of public reporting and transparency, which, at least in theory, ensure that regulators are ultimately accountably to directly elected officials. This chain of accountability enhances the likelihood that regulatory decisions will be consistent with the preferences of a democratically elected legislature.[10]

A credentialled or expert model of political authority can underpin governance beyond the territorial state, which occurs when states delegate their authority to set and enforce rules to institutions over which they have no direct control. Scholars argue that 'output-oriented legitimation' via non-politically accountable regulators until fairly recently sustained the momentum for European economic integration. Satisfaction with the tangible material benefits of economic integration overrode concerns about the loss of sovereignty (and political accountability) that accompanied supranational regulation at the EU level.[11] Consensus around goals of economic efficiency was joined with the belief that regulation to correct market failures was largely a technical exercise best left to knowledgeable and impartial regulators in non-majoritarian institutions.[12] For reasons to be elaborated more fully below, this model of political authority is no longer, on its own, sufficient to legitimize regulatory policymaking beyond the nation-state. But expert authority can be one – and probably a necessary – principle of regulatory governance, providing that it can be made more transparent and accountable. Accountability and transparency require that regulatory governance by independent experts provides opportunities for public participation, that regulators give reasons for their decisions, and that there are measures in place to prevent abuse of technical or administrative discretion.[13]

Private authority is another alternative, resorted to when (competitive) markets for goods and services are perceived as reliable mechanisms to achieve optimal policy outcomes, including responding to consumer preferences and maximizing material benefits. Private interest government is a modified form of private authority, one relied on when self-regulation cannot be counted on to produce desirable collective goods. In private interest arrangements of governing, private associations or firms acquire public responsibilities, but exercise them subject to the oversight, albeit often remote, of public authorities.[14] The legitimacy of private interest governance depends on the continuing perception that the outcomes of industry self-regulation serve the public interest and are responsive to consumer preferences. As elaborated below, private interest governance and output legitimacy describe the model used in the United States to regulate the risks of GM organisms, particularly GM foods and plants.

In a risk society, none of expert/credentialled, private (market) or state-centred authority is likely to be a sufficient basis for legitimiating regulatory governance. On what authoritative principles can regulatory governance be made acceptable? Beck proposes 'forms and forums of consensus-building' that transcend scientific experts and government officials, de-monopolize expertise, and open up participation to the populace 'according to *social* standards of relevance.' What is necessary, says Beck, is to transform decision-making into 'a *public dialogue* between the broadest variety of agents' to meet the challenge of building a consensus around how the technology should be regulated to minimize its risks.[15]

Beck's prescription is models of popular authority that incorporate 'the people,' or representative constituencies of the public, into policy-making (see Table 11.1). Models of popular authority or participatory democracy provide input legitimacy through public participation in decision-making; they provide output legitimacy via policy outcomes that conform to the consensus preferences of public and private policy-makers. The governance mechanisms congruent with the principles of popular authority include policy networks[16] and the mechanisms of deliberative democracy.[17] Some, but not all scholars,[18] suggest that policy networks, in which public officials share decision-making authority with representatives of the public in a non-hierarchical and informal way, can provide both input and output legitimacy. Input legitimacy is yielded by opportunities for consultation of non-state actors, even including co–decision-making,[19] while output legitimacy comes from policy outcomes that benefit the participating parties.[20] Policies that result from the mechanisms of deliberative democracy acquire legitimacy from open debate in which all contending positions enjoy the same opportunity to present themselves aired and because they can be justified publicly to be the result of public discourse.[21]

In summary, regulatory governance can rest on different principles of authority. One would expect to find a combination of these bases of authority, rather than exclusive reliance on any one model. The particular combination that is incorporated into the regulatory governance of GM products can be expected to vary across societies, depending on the presence or absence of a risk society mentality. The next section elaborates the historical developments that conspired to create a risk society mentality and a demand for incorporation of elements of popular authority into GMO regulatory decision-making in the European Union with regard to GM products.

The European Union

Risk Society and Discredited Authority

Since the late 1990s, evidence has been mounting to show that a risk society mentality characterizes the European reaction to the technology of genetic engineering.[22] Recall that a risk society is one in which the products of scientific developments are not equated with progress but, rather, are identified with hazards, with a concomitant loss of faith in scientists and scientific evidence to provide answers on how to cope with such hazards. Survey data indicate that a clear majority of Europeans believe 'genetically modified food is dangerous' and 'could have negative effects on the environment.'[23] Europeans' faith in science to produce benefits has deteriorated over time, the preponderant view now being that science and technology are not 'a panacea' and should be subject to 'social control.'[24] Public behaviour in Europe provides further evidence of a risk society mentality around genetic engineering. Strong public opposition to the licensing and marketing of GM organisms and their products in several member-states – most notably, Italy, France, Luxembourg, and Austria – led these governments to risk legal action before the European Court of Justice by refusing to comply with EU-level regulations approving the release of new GM crops.

The development of a risk society mentality around genetic engineering is linked to scares about food safety and health,[25] for example, the bovine spongiform encephalopathy (BSE) crisis. These crises have discredited government regulators and the scientific experts on whom they relied to protect public health. The BSE crisis undermined the idea of scientists as 'objective' and 'independent.'[26] The widespread perception was that the EU committees of scientific (veterinarian) experts responsible for advising the EU Commission on BSE had jeopardized human health by underplaying the nature and severity of the crisis[27] and that governments had been party to this duplicity. The link established, in early 1996, between the human variant of Creutzfeldt-Jakob disease and BSE led to a critique of practices of modern industrialized agriculture. In this climate of public scepticism and distrust, the campaign by environmental groups' against the first shipments into Europe, in summer 1996, of U.S. GM soya and maize – another risky product of industrialized agriculture – proved highly successful.

The discrediting of expert and state-centred authority in the regulation of food safety generally carried over to the regulation of GM organisms and their products. The regulatory framework established in 1990 for the licensing and commercialization of GMOs throughout the European Community was a combination of state-centred and expert and credentialled authority (see Table 11.2). Scientific risk assessments to appraise the risks of a GMO's to the environment and to human health were required at the member-state level prior to release of the GMO for development and commercial marketing. National authorities had considerable discretion as to how they carried out the risk assessment, and they exercised 'considerable flexibility' as they accommodated not only scientific but also public concerns.[28] At the European Community level, officials and politicians alike shared responsibility for the decision to license a specific GM product for release throughout the common European market.[29] At the European Community level, expert and credentialled authority played a secondary role to state-centred bureaucratic authority. The European Commission had some discretion on whether to consult scientific advisers and it exercised that discretion.[30] Moreover, there was no independent scientific body at the Europe-wide level to conduct risk assessments on GM foods.

By the late 1990s, this regulatory governance model of state-centred and expert authority had lost legitimacy. The procedures by which GM products were approved – or not – for licensing were chastised as being undemocratic. The deliberations of the EU Commission and national officials over whether to authorize the marketing of a GMO or a GMO-derived product were confidential, officials gave 'only perfunctory explanations' for their decisions, and interest groups were denied the possibility of judicial review of the officials' in camera decisions.[31] The system was accused of being opaque and poor in terms of

TABLE 11.2
EU GMO regulatory framework, 2002

Regulatory provisions	Legitimation standards
Creation of a European Food Authority of independent scientists responsible for risk assessment and risk communication	Expert authority. Output: effective problem-solving
Precautionary scientific approach	Expert authority constrained. Output: effective problem-solving
Mandatory and comprehensive labelling of GM products	Expert authority. Input: transparency. Output: conformity to citizen preferences
Compulsory traceability systems 'from farm to fork'	Popular and expert authority. Input: transparency. Output: conformity to citizen preferences
Harmonization and rationalization of authorization procedures	Output: economic benefits
Long-term monitoring of GM products	Expert authority. Output: effective problem-solving
Politicians responsible for approval of GM products for licensing (risk management)	State-centred authority. Input: conformity to citizen preferences. Output: public accountability
Publication of details of trials and risk assessments of GM crops	Popular authority. Input: transparency
Public consultation regarding experimental and commercial release of GM products	Popular authority. Input: transparency

accountability.[32] Proponents and opponents alike of GMOs criticized the commission's outputs. Proponents blamed its cumbersome approval process and the lack of harmonization of member-states' procedures of risk assessment for impeding the licensing of GM products and, thus, for making the EU biotechnology sector uncompetitive vis-à-vis its North American counterpart.[33] These biotechnology supporters argued for more efficient and scientifically based regulatory procedures that would not stigmatize and discriminate against genetic engineering. Biotechnology sceptics, or opponents of GMOs, were represented by consumer and environmental organizations. They sought a more comprehensive and rigorous set of rules to protect the environment and citizens from the risks posed by genetically engineered products. In 1996, non-accountable officials in the EU Commission attempted to invoke the authority of scientific experts to approve a variety of GM maize – on which there was no accord among elected officials in the Council of Ministers. Their action was met with indignation,[34] and the commission was accused 'of bringing the Community's GMO authorization procedure, and its own role in this regard, into disrepute.'[35] The regulatory model was sufficiently discredited to be suspended in June 1999, when a de facto moratorium was invoked on all new approvals of GM crops for commercial marketing throughout the European Union.

Reconstituting Authority and Restoring Legitimacy

Restoration of the legitimacy of the GMO regulatory framework in the European Union has entailed incorporating elements of popular authority and participatory democracy into both the formulation of a new regulatory regime and its substantive provisions. Policy reforms to 'provide for a high level of protection for human health and the environment based on sound science and [that] at the same time ... allow society to profit from the benefit of these new technologies'[36] have been agreed to in a policy network of state and non-state actors.[37] Representatives of transnational environmental and consumer organizations, biotechnology developers, and others have deliberated and bargained in regular and non-hierarchical interactions to determine the substance of EU GMO regulatory policy. The new policy regime combines state-centred, expert and credentialled, and popular authority. The objective is to strengthen the input and output legitimacy of the regulatory regime by fortifying its democratic and scientific authority. Table 11.2 summarizes these reforms, which began to be implemented in spring 2004, and their expected contribution to procedural or input and substantive or output legitimacy.

Several regulatory provisions rely on the authority of (scientific) expertise. A permanent and independent scientific body, the European Food Safety Authority, is now responsible for making compulsory risk assessments, including those for GM products. At the same time, however, the endorsement of the precautionary approach[38] suggests that there are limits to the knowledge of scientists, and shifts the burden and its standard of proof to developers of GM products to demonstrate that these products pose an acceptable risk or no risk.[39] Risk management – the final decision whether to authorize a GMO or GM product – is left to political authorities, who are to use the scientific advice provided by the European Food Safety Authority not as 'an absolute truth,' but as 'knowledge with a confidence interval'[40] on which to make decisions concerning risk management. The rationale is that risk management is 'a political decision' that 'involves judgments not only based on science but on a wider appreciation of the wishes and needs of society.'[41] Accordingly, 'all interested parties should be involved to the fullest extent possible.'[42] State-centred and popular authorities, thereby, provide a check to expert authority, and in the EU, they may even supersede it.

Several substantive provisions are consistent with a popular model of authority that bases public policies closely on citizen preferences. These provisions include comprehensive and mandatory labelling to identify products containing or derived from GMOs;[43] consultation with the public regarding both experimental and commercial release, and publication of the details of GMO trials as well as the risk assessments made by the EU Scientific Committee.[44] In their transparency and direct accountability, these provisions bestow input or procedural legitimacy. Output or performance legitimacy comes from mandatory consultation with scientific committees prior to authorization of GM crops and products, mandatory monitoring of the long-term effects of GMOs and GM products, compulsory traceability systems 'from farm to fork,' and measures to promote harmonization of risk assessment across member-states. It is anticipated that the clearer and more stringent rules, and the more timely and efficient approval of the release of GMOs and GM products, will build consumer confidence in GMOs and to yield economic benefits by promoting the sector's future competitiveness. Such outcomes would confer greater legitimacy on the regulatory framework. A response to a public wary of genetic engineering and exhibiting characteristics of a risk society, this new regulatory framework diverges in both its substantive features and authoritative premises from that in North America.

Political Authority and Legitimate Regulatory Governance in North America

Compared with Europe, in North America there is little evidence of a risk society mentality regarding genetic engineering. Although polling data are somewhat inconsistent, survey results do show that Americans are more positive than negative in their evaluations of GMOs and a good majority believe that genetic engineering improves their lives.[45] The apprehensiveness about genetic engineering that there is in Europe, and that caused European food retailers to take GM products off their shelves, knows no counterpart in North America. Certainly, there are vocal critics of the GMO regulatory process, most notably in public interest organizations representing consumers and environmentalists.[46] Their quarrel with existing U.S. GMO regulations does not, however, extend to questioning the benefits of the technology, which is generally equated with economic growth and competitiveness. Nor do critics question the capacity of scientific knowledge to provide answers to the risks of the technology. Rather, the critics' efforts centre on strengthening the scientific underpinnings of the U.S. regulatory regime and providing greater transparency (for example, through the labelling of GM foods).[47]

In contrast to the EU GMO regulatory framework, in which public authorities are left with the responsibility for the approval of the release of GM crops and foods, the U.S. framework relies predominantly on private authority, buttressed by the oversight of government administrators with scientific credentials (see Table 11.3). The developers of GM products have been delegated considerable powers of self-regulation, subject to oversight by public authorities.[48] Self-regulation has been seen to be the best governance mechanism to achieve the explicit goal of the U.S. GMO regulatory framework: 'To minimize uncertainties and inefficiencies that can stifle innovation and impair the competitiveness of the U.S. industry.'[49] The private biotechnology companies are assumed to have strong incentives to minimize any risks to the environment and human health that a GM organism or GM product may pose. Legal liability provisions in American law, which make manufacturers responsible for the safety of their products, are a fundamental part of this private authority system. U.S. manufacturers of GM products are expected to internalize food safety and environmental safety risks 'because a safety risk quickly becomes a commercial crisis.'[50]

Scientific authority is also a component of the US GMO regulatory framework in the United States. Government regulators who review private developers' applications for field tests and commercial shipments of GM plants are required by law to develop regulations based on the scientific evidence submitted by the applicant. Government reg-

TABLE 11.3
GMO regulation in the United States

	GM crop trials and commercial marketing	GM foods
Private authority/ Scientific authority	Developer notifies government regulator and presents risk assessment data	Voluntary government-developer consultationre risk assessment studies
Weak public accountability	Government review of data; government approval required in limited cases	Neither government notification nor approval required for marketing
Weak-to-absent popular authority	Public notice and comment prior to the release of some GM products, not for others	Public notification of industry-government consultations
		No public comment during consultation period
		No GM-specific labelling

ulators turn to professional scientific bodies, like the National Research Council of the National Academy of Sciences, to provide independent scientific advice. Regulatory decisions to approve (or not) GMOs are thus justified by 'appeals to objective knowledge,'[51] with science being perceived to be capable of yielding facts that are universal and that lead to certainty.[52] Such an approach contrasts with the regulatory approach, of Europeans, which disavows the value-free character of 'facts'[53] and holds that there is 'a degree of uncertainty attached to the evaluation of available scientific information.'[54]

The private interest governance of GM plants and foods in the United States, as noted, leaves the private developers of these products with much of the responsibility for ensuring their products' safety. Government regulators, lacking sufficient scientific resources of their own, are dependent on industry cooperation to provide them with risk assessment data to demonstrate product safety.[55] Industry is required to notify regulatory authorities when they release new GM plants into the environment and to obtain a permit for field trials of pesticide-resistant plants. However, neither a permit nor notification is required prior to the release of GM foods to the market; industry is only encouraged to consult regulatory authorities and provide them with the scientific data on the safety and nutritional assessment of the food. This 'non-regulation'[56] of GM foods results from the premise that GM food is 'substantially equivalent' to a conventionally produced food that is 'generally recognized as safe.' The company that produces the GM food judges whether the product meets this 'generally recognized as safe' test on the basis of its own data.

The U.S. framework does not rely to any great extent on popular authority for its legitimacy. The public has a chance to comment on the pending release of GM crops into the environment and for commercial sale, and since March 2001, the Internet site of the Food and Drug Administration posts the results of the voluntary consultations with the biotechnology food developers that precede the release of GM foods to the market. However, in the United States provision for public participation in decisions to release GM foods to the market is minimal. Transparency is further limited by the fact that GM products are not labelled as such.[57] Unlike with the EU regulations, which pay heed to the consumer's 'right to know' how food has been produced (particularly through the use of genetic engineering), U.S. law currently contains no explicit labelling requirements based on the consumers 'right to know.' The absence of labelling is intended to avoid discrimination directed at GM products. This lack of transparency in the U.S. system is a source of criticism, but one that has not yet de-legitimized the regulatory framework of private interest governance. Its legitimacy rests on the continuing perceived adequacy of its outputs, as these are defined within a model of private and expert authority. Industry self-regulation is credited with having promoted and captured the economic benefits of the technology and with ensuring the international competitiveness of American biotechnology and the agricultural sectors in the United States.

The Transatlantic Divide

The different policy outcomes that result from the divergent principles of authority in the U.S. and EU frameworks for regulating GMOs and GM products have created transatlantic tensions. These tensions derive from the actual and projected loss of markets for GM foods and feed produced in North America, initially as a result of the EU licensing moratorium, and subsequently as a result of the regulations put into effect in April 2004 that ended the moratorium and provided for the authorization, traceability, and labelling of GM foods and feed.[58]

This transatlantic conflict has been extraordinarily difficult to resolve. Informal efforts to broker a transatlantic consensus on genetic engineering in the Transatlantic Committee struck by EU President Prodi and U.S. President Clinton failed when the committee's December 2000 report was ignored by Clinton.[59] Global rules are in this policy domain underdeveloped. For example, there is no international agreement specific to plant biotechnology.[60] Nor are there international standards with respect to the labelling of GM foods. The international body mandated to build a consensus on such standards – the Codex Alimentarius Commission – has been unable to agree on labelling standards, despite some ten years of work on the issue. The European Union and the United States are at a stalemate in the CAC's Food Labelling Committee, with each party attempting to write its domestic law into international guidelines and standards.

The existing global governing body is the World Trade Organization. The objective of the General Agreement on Tariffs and Trade (GATT) – WTO regime is to minimize the impact on trade of social regulations, such as food safety and environmental laws. The WTO Sanitary and Phytosanitary (SPS) Agreement makes science the authoritative basis for discriminating among barriers erected for safety reasons and barriers implemented for non-safety and protectionist reasons. The SPS Agreement requires health and safety measures, such as those for GM products, to be based on scientific assessments of risk. Along with the WTO Technical Barriers to Trade Agreement, the SPS Agreement also requires food and feed safety measures to be based on international standards, where they exist, to be non-discriminatory, and to be no more restrictive of trade than necessary to fulfil the legitimate health and safety objective.

In August 2003, after having repeatedly threatened to do so, the United States and Canada requested the WTO to strike a panel to investigate the legality of the EU's suspension of GM food and feed authorizations which was then still in effect.[61] The decision to launch the WTO case was propelled by the desire to curb the potential contagion effect of the EU model. A successful WTO ruling would deter other countries that want to maintain access to EU markets from aligning their regulatory framework with the EU model.[62] The basis of the complaint made by Canada and the United States is that the moratorium violated WTO obligations, as defined by the Agreement on Agriculture, the SPS Agreement, the Agreement on Technical Barriers to Trade, and the GATT. Their argument is that the EU's ban on GM products contravenes these agreements because it lacks scientific justification, unduly restricts trade, and is discriminatory. The panel to adjudicate this case was struck in early 2004.

The provisions for labelling and traceability in the current regulatory framework are also viewed to be restrictive and unjustified trade barriers. The expanded labelling requirements are expected to deter, rather than mollify, the risk-averse EU purchaser. The traceability requirements impose significant segregation costs on Canadian and American farmers and food processors. North American food exporters charge that far from restoring Europeans' confidence in GMOs, the new regulatory framework will have the opposite effect and impede GM food and feed products' entry into the EU market. As a net result, the efficiency and competitiveness of the North American agri-food industry will have been undermined. Furthermore, Canada and the United States have threatened to challenge these regulations, as well at the WTO for being in breach of the Technical Barriers to Trade and the SPS agreements.[63]

The North American invocation of the WTO's legal authority to resolve the conflict over the regulation of GM products is of questionable efficacy. As an effective forum for settling trade disputes over social regulatory differences, the WTO has limitations.[64] The experience of the transatlantic beef hormone dispute is instructive. Although the WTO found in favour of the United States and Canada in this dispute, the strength of public opposition to hormone-fed beef in the EU was sufficiently strong to leave EU decision-makers with no option but to maintain the import ban and, by way of compensation, to accept duties on EU products that enter the North American market. The possibility of a repeat of the beef hormone experience, and a backlash from European consumers against genetically engineered products, cannot be discounted.

Conclusion and Implications

As others in this volume have emphasized, regulatory governance is riddled with debates and conflicts over who has the right to make binding rules and the criteria by which their actions will be judged to be acceptable. Managing these conflicts over the constitutive principles and instruments of regulation, in a manner that is consistent with a liberal economic order, has emerged as a significant problem of contemporary multi-level governance. In the European Union, the task of conflict management has been rendered more difficult by a risk society mentality and the contested legitimacy of supranational political institutions. This climate of public apprehensiveness concerning GMOs and the low regulatory credibility of institutions of the EU level limited the incentive and latitude for cooperative behaviour among EU member-states.[65] A reconstitution of political authority was necessary to secure a new and legitimate GMO regulatory regime. Elements of popular authority and participatory democracy had to be embraced to give non-state actors, both those speaking for consumer and environmental interests as well as those representing self-interests, more influential roles in the formulation and implementation of regulatory policies.

Even while the institutional form of political authority was reconstituted with this altered mode of policymaking, the scope of public regulatory authority was not. The EU's public policies with respect to the authorization, labelling, and traceability of GMOs and GM products, reveal an increased regulatory role for state authorities – not a reduced one. This example is consistent with one of the themes of this volume: to wit, the reconstitution of political authority does not necessarily translate into a narrower definition of public functions and a reduced domain of state activity.

In reconstituting the authoritative bases of its public policies for genetically engineered food and feed products in order to render them legitimate, EU decision-makers have created tensions in the global arena. Two standards of legitimate governance resting on different authoritative principles vie with one another: the EU standard of striking a balance among expert, state, and popular authority versus the American standard which is heavily tipped towards private and expert authority. To produce similar public goods of consumer health and safety, environmental protection, and economic growth and competitiveness, the EU relies overwhelmingly on public actors, while the United States relies heavily on private actors.

The differences of policy outcomes of these two models of regulatory governance may erode over time. If the logic of EU decision-makers proves well founded, the more systematic scientific bases to GMO regulation in the EU should result in similar outcomes with regard to the approval or not of specific GMOs and GM products. The strengthened scientific bases for decision-making, the greater transparency of these decisions and the products themselves, and the heightened monitoring of the safety of GM products – all these measures may well cause attitudes towards the technology to shift. The intent of the reforms may be realized: Europeans may become more open to GM products that enter their continent under a more publicly accountable regime.

Even so, there is a clear need for a third, global, tier of multi-level governance, whether in the form of formal, binding rules or informal norms and guidelines. There is now a global debate that encompasses Asia Pacific, the Middle East, Latin America, and Africa with regard to the appropriate regulatory principles that are to govern biotechnology. Despite the widely recognized need for countries to cooperate in the creation of a transnational GMO policy regime, this chapter has noted the limited success to date of existing international institutions, such as the Codex Alimentarius Commission, to persuade countries to do so. In this sense, genetic engineering defies the conventional wisdom that transnational cooperation and transnational policy regimes are likely to be more forthcoming in policy domains where technical expertise is a requisite to effective public policy-making.

Genetic engineering reveals two important constraints to transnational cooperation. As this chapter has made clear, one is the constraint of domestic preferences and cultural values. Emphasizing the role of culture in creating regulatory divergence, across the North Atlantic on genetic engineering, for example, is not meant to discount the role of vested and powerful domestic constituents in determining states' incentives for cooperation.[66] It is simply to draw attention to the role that beliefs about the authority of science, markets, and democracy as foundations of regulatory policymaking play in creating what Robert Kagan describes as 'a broad ideological gap' across the Atlantic. While Kagan perceives this gap in the area of foreign policy,[67] this chapter argues it also characterizes an important area of social regulatory policy.

A second constraint is the incentive of the world's most powerful nations to use global institutions for instrumental purposes. As Pauly points out in his chapter, organizations like the WTO and the Codex Alimentarius Commission not only promise powerful countries legitimacy, as they defend their longer term interests in the world; they also provide a practical means for them to disseminate their internal regulatory regimes around the globe. In the instance of genetic engineering, the United States is banking on international law, as a potent companion to economic power, to export its technological hegemony worldwide. It is, of course, too early to tell whether the United States will succeed in this endeavour. But at least part of its success may depend on the extent to which the current of authoritative principles flows with beliefs of popular authority and participatory democracy, rather than with private and expert authority.

NOTES

1 Beck (1999).
2 Beck (1992), Beck et al. (1994).
3 Adam and van Loon (2000: 4).
4 Beck (1999: 4).
5 Beck (2000: 219).
6 Bernstein (2002).
7 Weber (1995: 28).
8 Suchman (1995: 574).
9 Majone (1994a: 4).
10 Majone (1999), Shapiro (1997).
11 Scharpf (1999a).
12 Majone (1999), Offe (2000).
13 Majone (1999), Lord and Beetham (2001: 450).
14 Streeck and Schmitter (1985).
15 Beck (1997a: 122).
16 Börzel (1998b), Jachtenfuchs (1997), Kohler-Koch (1996).
17 Lord (2001), Joerges and Neyer (1997), Pellizzoni (2001). Referenda are another mechanism (Abromeit 1998).
18 For an alternative point of view, see Greven in this volume.
19 Héritier (1999a), Joerges and Neyer (1997), Kohler-Koch (1996), Lord and Beetham (2001), Lord (2001: 649).
20 Héritier (1999a: 273).
21 Bellamy and Jones (2000: 207), Ericksen (2000), Lord (2001).
22 Genetic engineering entails transferring specific genetic traits from one organism to another in order to modify the recipient organism's DNA. Aside from the celebrated case of Dolly the sheep, most genetic engineering occurs with plants to make them resistant to insects or tolerant of herbicides.
23 Eurobarometer (2001: 26).
24 Ibid., 30, and 37.
25 The Belgian crisis of poultry feed contaminated with dioxins and the

French tainted blood scandal are two other oft-cited examples of regulatory failure.

26 Joerges and Neyer (1997: 612).

27 Chambers (1999).

28 Levidow et al. (1996: 152).

29 If they were in agreement, member-state officials on the appropriate EU Commission regulatory committee could approve a GMO application. If they were not, a qualified majority of elected politicians in the Council of Ministers could adopt or reject the application. If the council did not take action on an application within three months, the commission was legally obliged to adopt a decision in favour of the application if the regulatory committee had approved it.

30 Joerges and Neyer (1997).

31 Hunter (1999: 225).

32 Majone (2000: 290).

33 European Commission President Romano Prodi has stated that Europe's biotech industry is worth 'roughly one-third as much as its U.S. counterpart' and lags 'four or five years' behind it, as quoted in Juca (2002).

34 The European Parliament condemned the commission's action, three countries (Austria, Italy, and Luxembourg) invoked the safeguard clause to prohibit the import and use of maize in their countries, and France banned the cultivation of maize for a while (Barling 1997).

35 Bradley (1998: 221).

36 Joint Statement of Environment Commissioner Margot Wallstrom and Commissioner for Health and Consumer Protection David Byrne. Press Release, Feb. 2001, Brussels.

37 Skogstad (2003)

38 Commission of the European Communities (CEC) (2000b).

39 CEC (2000b), Schlacke (1997).

40 Haniotis (2000).

41 CEC (2000a).

42 Ibid., (2000b: 15).

43 Eurobarometer (2001: 40) data show that 94.6 per cent of Europeans want the right to choose GM foods and demand more information about them.

44 CEC (2001).

45 Foreman (2001). Other data show Americans have limited knowledge of genetic engineering, so that their views are malleable. See Pew Initiative on Food and Biotechnology. Available at http://pewagbiotech.org/research/gmfood/

46 Among the most prominent are the Consumer Federation of America, Centre for Science in the Public Interest, and the Union of Concerned Scientists.

47 The Center for Science in the Public Interest, e.g., claims that government regulators do not always obtain requested data to evaluate GM foods from biotechnology firms. See Fabi (2003). The U.S. General Accounting Office (US GAO, 2002) recommended random verification of industry-submitted data and greater transparency of Food and Drug Administration GM-food safety evaluations.

48 Isaac (2002), Moore (2000).

49 U.S. (1984: 50857).

50 Isaac (2002: 190).

51 Jasanoff (1995: 32).

52 Isaac (2002).

53 Ibid.

54 Richardson (2000b).

55 Mellon (1994).

56 Foreman (2001: 6).

57 Like other novel foods, GM foods must be labelled to indicate substantial differences from their traditional counterparts in nutrient levels and potential safety concerns like allergenicity.

58 The EU is the America's most important export market for corn by-products, such as the corn gluten used in animal feed, and it accounts for more than a quarter of U.S. soybean exports. About one-quarter of the corn produced in the United States is genetically modified, while over two-thirds of soybeans are. The one GM soybean in general production in the United States has been approved in the EU, but the U.S. produces GM corn varieties that are not licensed for sale in the EU.

59 One of the prominent American committee members denounced the report and U.S. industry and government agencies disliked its conclusion that genetic engineering raised unforeseen threats and negative consequences and that food products containing novel genetic material should be labelled.

60 Canada and the United States jointly proposed a World Trade Biotechnology Initiative under the auspices of the WTO at the 1999 Ministerial Meeting of the WTO in Seattle, but the EU rejected the request to deal with biotechnology exclusively on trade grounds.

61 Argentina is also a party to the dispute. It is the second largest producer of GM crops, accounting for 21 per cent of global acreage, behind the United States at 63 per cent, and ahead of Canada with 6 per cent.

62 See King (2002). In 2003, the governments of Zambia and Zimbabwe refused to accept U.S. food aid with GM content.
63 Canadian officials say the regulations, because they do not cover all GMO products, also contravene section 5.5 of the Sanitary and Phytosanitary Agreement, which requires that measures be consistent in their application.
64 See Isaac (2002, Part IV) for an extended discussion of the limitations of trade diplomacy and the WTO for settling disputes over divergent social regulation measures.
65 The problem of weak regulatory credibility also extends to some national regulatory bodies (the U.K., for example).
66 The importance of cultural attitudes towards food is recognized by Echols (1998).
67 Kagan (2002).

12 The Informalization of Transnational Governance: A Threat to Democratic Government

MICHAEL TH. GREVEN

The modern nation-state, which first emerged in Western Europe in the seventeenth century, is currently undergoing change that is of epic significance.[1] Despite this change, political theory and public opinion remain rooted in seventeenth-century assumptions. The change under way challenges the 'container model' of state politics, which is at the core of mainstream political theory, both in Western Europe and other parts of the world. This model of modern statehood defines the state as a hierarchically organized system of authority that is geographically circumscribed by clearly defined territorial borders. It further assumes that the 'inside' of the modern state is marked by a common culture of belonging and history, which is called the 'nation,' where legitimate authority may reside and that more or less friendly neighbours comprise the space 'outside' the state, where no formal structure of authority exists.

In the introductory chapter, the editors of this volume convincingly argue that the statist model, and the international order associated with it, has recently undergone a 'complex and partly contradictory transformation.' The results of this period of change and transition are as yet undetermined, with observable only to speculate about whether a fundamentally new political organization will replace the state and its structures of authority. Generalizations are true only in retrospect, when the full breadth of change can be measured and appreciated. That said, it is possible to engage in a debate that attempts to map the direction, speed, and character of change. Although any conclusions may be speculative, they can reflect empirical observations of the past and the present. Dialogue and debate about contemporary political change are necessary to help us ascertain what may in fact be changing and what will likely remain relatively stable and fixed. This chapter is offered in that spirit.

Most contributions to this volume centre on observations concerning the development of the nation-state and its capacities to enforce and control policies in certain domains, both inside and outside. My contribution is focused on a derivative of this model, specifically liberal representative democracy. Up to now, no working model of this type of democracy has been practised outside of the state context, and in many ways, the development of liberal democracy itself has been tied to the evolution of the modern state.[2] If the fundamental challenge to the state today comes from transnational processes and supranational political structures, which impinge upon states' traditional governing capacities, then democracy will be affected. Even without a concerted attempt to abandon democratic principles, the way that democratic regimes react to the new challenges of political problem-solving both inside and beyond their territory may result in an eventual erosion of democratic principles and structures.

This chapter traces one possible element of a presumably multi-factor complex transformation of democracy known as *informalization*. What some see as a means of increasing the effectiveness and perhaps even the participatory character of policy-making in settings beyond the formal structures of states and democratic regimes, I see as a threat to existing structures of authority and thus of responsibility and legitimacy. Although informalization is an unavoidable factor of politics, in both the domestic and international spheres, transnational and supranational political regimes provide the ideal circumstances for informal policy-making and problem-solving. Given the emergence of transnational policy forums in various issues areas, such as the environment, finance, and agriculture, to name a few, it is imperative to examine not only the dynamics of their political processes but also the ways in which they satisfy or, as I will argue, circumvent the requirements for responsible and legitimate governance.

In developing my argument for the possible anti-democratic effects of recent political transformations, which correspond to the deepening consequences of global interconnectedness, I accept as given the empirical evidence examined in most of the chapters of this book. In my analysis here of the underlying dilemmas in the emergence of transnational decision-making, I concentrate on the most obviously relevant normative project, that of the European Union.

The New Trend of Integration and the New Problem of Legitimacy in European Politics

Examining changes in the development and coordination of EU governance in the areas of justice and home affairs, a common foreign and security policy, and policy coordination in the new economy, Helen Wallace[3] has argued that a new trend of 'informal', 'soft,' and 'open' methods of coordination between member-states is emerging, distinct from or even opposed to the traditional treaty-based arrangements between central governments, as was the case in the development of market integration policies. To be sure, the EU Commission still employs traditional mechanisms of governance, most notably through the European Court and the European Parliament, which apply 'hard' instruments of program implementation through the distribution of resources and penalties for rule breakers. Emerging alongside these conventional methods, however, the new style of governance is said to be based on common recommendations, declarations, and communications by the member governments or their respective representatives, using benchmarking, targets and score cards, policy audits, and other indirect methods of coordination.

Networking, negotiations, and informal coordination of action among participants seems to be essential for this new policy style. The Commission recently issued a White Paper entitled 'European Governance,'[4] announcing a programmatic turn towards 'a less top-down approach ... complementing its policy tools more effectively with non-legislative instruments.'[5] The instruments or strategies strengthening this new trend are such things as 'target-based, tripartite contracts,'[6] 'ad hoc consultation bodies,' already running at 'nearly 700,'[7] 'co-regulation,' which according to the White Paper 'often achieve[s] better compliance [than] rules [applied] in an uniform way in every Member State,'[8] and the 'open method of co-ordination.'[9]

These features, taken together with Wallace's observations, indicate that the new trend of European governance, especially in the process of EU enlargement, basically rests on two, at minimum, implicit developments:

1 A *decentralization* of important policy formation and policymaking processes away from the commission through more contingent bargaining and coordinating processes of member governments within

or even outside councils and especially through various public-private partnerships, or what I prefer to call public-private policy networks (PPPNs). It is important to note that both the informal coordinating processes among governments and PPPNs has set the pace and the direction of 'integration.'

2 An increasing *informalization* of European governance in all phases of the policy cycle, the result of various types of cooperation and coordination among formal actors, either of national governments or the EU administration (or both), and various interest or voluntary associations.

Although informalization is intended to and may at times enhance the problem-solving capacity and effectiveness of transnational and supranational governments, it concomitantly decreases the degree of transparency, accountability, and thus legitimacy of European politics and serves as an example of similar erosions in any kind of transnational or supranational government built on the EU model.[10] These shortcomings are often observed. However, the endorsement of nongovernmental organizations and the compliance with rules has been interpreted as a new form of democratic legitimation. But such substitutes for the formal granting of mandates violate the political equality of citizens, which is the fundamental principle of democratic government.

As *political legitimacy* is a frequently used term in academic, policy, and popular discourses, it is important to clarify how the term is defined in this chapter. Although in any given society, different sources of legitimacy exist, with legality and legitimacy often coinciding, the specific character of political legitimacy in democratic politics must not be confused with broader, especially sociological, concepts of 'legitimacy,' on the one hand, and the narrower concept of 'legality,' on the other. Whereas *legitimacy* refers only to situations or relationships in which people factually accept the authority of an office, institution, or person, on the basis of various kinds of beliefs or internalized common norms in democratic constitutionalized regimes, *political legitimacy* derives from legalized formal procedures that reflect the sovereignty of the people. Only those who have the legitimate mandate to act as representatives on behalf of the citizenry can impose political restraints on individual behaviour through laws and government action. Other offices, namely, the judiciary, may also impose restraints on the citizenry. They do so, however, on the basis of a legal authorization derived from the primary principle of popular sovereignty. These distinctions at first glance may appear to be quite abstract. But they gain enormous practical relevance as soon as the specific authorities and institutions of the European Union or forms of 'private interest' and also associative government are contemplated.[11]

The 'community method' of European integration was highly centralized, following patterns of implementation clearly legalized by its corresponding treaties. Fritz Scharpf recently characterized it as having the 'shared goal that by and large could be realized through Europe-wide and uniform rules of negative integration, liberalization and harmonization. Many of these policies could be imposed unilaterally by the Commission and the Court in their roles as "guardians of the Treaty."'[12] Such a supranational and centralistic institutional and procedural approach of European government opened, at least in principle, the way for alleviating the democratic deficit through the further empowerment of the European Parliament relative to the Commission and the Council. The formal character of these decision and co-decision procedures remains an essential prerequisite for alleviating the democratic deficit, while any informalization of intergovernmental policy coordination inside or bypassing the Council weakens the already rudimentary legal entitlements and parliamentary co-decision-making that characterizes the EU. Furthermore, informalization also diminishes the chances of rule enforcement by the European Court.

Informalization acts against the democratic integrity of the EU in a number of ways. First, informalization of European policy formation supports and strengthens the existing tendency of intergovernmentalism inherent in the original EU treaties, thus working against a pattern of integration and moving towards a supranational sui generis future regime of European governance that would open the way for more parliamentarization. If, as some presume, parliamentarization is the most promising way to reduce or even overcome the democratic deficit, then decentralization and the increase of intergovernmentalism only deepen the democratic deficit by obstructing the EU's further parliamentarization. Second, informalization influences the real power relations among the member governments, making the strong governments even stronger and turning the representatives of small member-states into second-order members. Third, informalization strengthens the 'executivism' of the EU polity, which is mainly associated with the Commission. Fourth, at the national level, informalization decouples the decision-making powers of national authorities from their respective representative bodies, which only exacerbates local democratic deficits and transforms them into a new Europe-wide democratic deficit.

The new trend of informal policy coordination among member governments and/or between the Commission and collective actors of various groups leaves both the European and national parliaments at the wayside of real policy formation. Some argue that the democratic deficit at the European level is more or less outbalanced by the various new possibilities provided for collective actors of all kinds to participate in the policy process.[13] Some claim that the emergence of a European civil society that is apparent in the lobbying channels of the commission and her directorates reflects 'new forms of representation [through] informal policy-making channels,'[14] which could potentially be expanded globally.[15] But, as I will argue, only specific forms of participation constitute and contribute to democratic or at least legitimate government.

It is important to keep in mind that the kind of decentralization of European policy formation usually called intergovernmentalism must not be confounded with a supposed disintegration of the EU. It is, or at least can lead to, a specific pathway to integration and unification of the member-states and their politics. If informalization – not exclusive to but especially prominent in intergovernmentalism – remains an essential quality of European policy-making, the well-known discourse on the EU's democratic deficit would gain an additional and substantially new dimension.

Considering Informalization

Much of the existing literature on EU informalization highlights the effectiveness of policy-making. My approach, by contrast, emphasizes the issue of democratic integrity, probing specifically into whether informalization, aimed at increasing efficiency, diminishes certain features and qualities of democratic legitimacy. A trend towards the informalization of governance is not a unique characteristic of transnational, supranational, and intergovernmental authority structures but it is especially prominent in their activities. This trend can be observed against the analytical as well as normative background of the claim that democratic politics has to rest on transparent rules of accountability, formal mandating, political equality among participating members, and rule application.

Informalization is a contested term. There is no agreement on what the term means and how it should be employed in political science. That said, most commonly the term is used to signify a contrast to legal or otherwise established formal political procedures. Along these lines, and for the purposes of this chapter, 'informalization' refers to the non-transparent institutionalized quality of the political process. It is thus characterized by:

1 Practices such as negotiations and networking that are not, or are less, rule- or law-based and mostly oriented towards outcomes on an ad hoc basis
2 Contingent roles or mandates that are not constitutionalized for the specific processes under concern
3 Programs or goals that are not necessarily laid down in laws or other binding documents
4 The lack of institutionalized structures and procedures of democratic participation, particularly voting, mandating, and representation under the principle of political equality.

It is worth drawing attention to some similarities between the informalization and the privatization of authority. In practice, many of the examples of informalization already mentioned in this chapter also include aspects of the partial or even complete privatization of government functions. The two processes of privatization and informalization thus may often be related, with privatization usually corresponding to an increase in informalization. However, in conceptual terms informalization is broader and has a different analytical focus than privatization. Informalization's breadth includes phenomena that usually appear in the sphere of formal government, particularly in practices of intergovernmentalism or interactions among different government departments and agencies. Analytically, informalization examines the disparity between formal and informal practices, which may apply to both private and public processes. Privatization, by contrast, examines only non-governmental agencies, with an analytical focus on the legal differentiation between public and private agencies.

Informalization has several consequences for democratic governance,[16] including the following:

• The distinction between a democratic mandate to govern and other sources of acceptable participation in governance erodes. Subsequently, equality no longer serves as the dominant principle of legitimate participation in the process of government.

- (Good) governance is no longer the outcome of democratically legitimized action by governments. Instead, governance occurs through the activities of various public-private policy networks (PPPNs) or ad hoc coalitions of public collective actors.
- Given the above consequences, it becomes more difficult for the public, that is, citizens, to address issues of responsibility and accountability.
- Democratic control from outside the various PPPNs, for instance, by parliaments, is weakened.
- Procedures for these informalized parts of governance are often not constitutionalized. Rather, they are the product of negotiations (arguing and bargaining) within PPPNs.
- The 'logic of collective action' relies (more or less) on chance to become a member or even successful member of PPPNs.
- Although governments, in particular the activities of executives, have never been completely controlled by law, the informalization of governance only further expands the number and type of activities not governed by any legal mechanisms. Consequently, the capacity of courts to effectively influence executive action is also reduced.
- Informalization of governance decreases the transparency of governance.
- There is no systematic evidence that connects an increase in informalization with an increase in the general effectiveness of governance.
- As transnational, supranational, or intergovernmental governance authorities become able to gain more autonomy or independence from the responsive democratic structures of parliaments, elections, and the public sphere, informalization raises greater concerns about the integrity of democracy beyond the nation-state.

Most of these features are present even in instances of good governance. My discussion of the informalization in the EU is not intended to suggest that informalization is a peculiar development only in EU politics. To a certain degree political procedures, whether at the local, national, regional or supranational level, unavoidably rest on informal communications. Yet these political communications and exchanges, although often informal, occur within a world structured and to some extent constitutionalized[17] by routines, procedures, organizations, and institutions that may, but do not necessarily, promote the legitimization of politics and policy outputs.

The degree of formalization relative to informalization can be compared diachronically and synchronically among regimes, arenas, and levels of politics. In the history of nation-states as well as in the (longer) history of individual rights and liberties, politics was formalized through a process of constitutionalization.[18] This process established not only individual rights and liberties in relation to governing authorities but also reinforced the rule-based character of governance, for instance, by restricting government spending through legalized budgets.[19] In principle, a truly constitutional state not only limits government action through formal legal rules, it also ensures that governing activities are 'visible' and thus open to juridical examination. This visibility rests on the formal structure of rules, offices, and a certain bureaucratic process of handling problems in a manner that ensures the personal accountability and responsibility of governing officials.

In most cases, the constitutionalization of states preceded their democratization.[20] It is thus critical to note that constitutionalization and democratization – the two essential components of any modern constitutionally democratic state – are not one and the same. The two, however, are related, with a certain degree of legal formalization being a necessary prerequisite for democracy. Constitutions thus are necessary but not sufficient conditions of democratic regimes. With specific reference to the EU and the current attempt to agree on an EU Covenant, it is important to keep the difference between constitutionalism and democracy in mind.

Traditionally, international politics has been seen as an area with relatively few formal procedures and institutions. The lack of a central authority at the international level is, indeed, what often distinguishes international politics from domestic politics. With the development of modern constitutional democratic states in Europe, the degree of formalization at the domestic level increased, further highlighting the difference between domestic and international politics. When considering international politics, it is important to distinguish between the degree of formalization and constitutionalization found in various national regimes and the transnational and supranational constitutionalization of politics in the form of the U.N. system and comparable supranational regimes and institutions.

I do not presume that the informalization of intergovernmentalism is a phenomenon unique to transnational and supranational organizations such as the EU. On the contrary, it can be observed in domestic politics as well.[21] Moreover, the 'denationalization,' or globalization,[22] of politics and political regimes seems to support the trend to informalization beyond the special case of the European Union. The common justification by proponents of informalization, both at the national and supranational levels, is that informal practices lead to more effective problem-solving. This justification raises problems for normative democratic theory because it corresponds only to the output orientation of large sections of populations in democratic regimes and various interests groups, rather than to governments. Those who support informalization argue that the relatively time-consuming and inflexible character of institutionalized procedures increases transaction costs and often forms barriers to goal attainment. Defenders of classical institutions of representative democracy face an additional challenge from deliberative and discursive theories of democracy, which argue that classical democracy has serious shortcomings with respect to rationality and inclusiveness and that these could and should be enhanced through an alternative model of democratic deliberation.

Recently, Rainer Schmalz-Bruns, in a very informative and sophisticated contribution, asked the question: 'What is wrong with problem-solving?'[23] in order to provide a defence of a Habermasian version of deliberative democracy against a 'voluntaristic' version of direct democracy. (There is nothing wrong with problem-solving by democratic governments as such. However, in pluralistic societies a consensus about what the 'problem' to be 'solved' is or what constitutes a solution to any given problem is rarely reached.) The real opposite of deliberative democracy is not the 'voluntaristic' approach of direct democracy but deep scepticism about the proclaimed rationality of any political approach. In the rare cases when participants and observers do agree on the nature of a problem and its 'rational' solution, the question of how the problem is framed as a problem cannot be ignored. Issues of perspective and subjectivity force critical reflection on whose interests are being served with any given set of problems and their corresponding solutions. Problem-solving, in short, is not interest-free; put differently, there is a significant element of power at work that makes problem-solving practices contentious.[24] In an important study of Germany, Gerhard Lehmbruch observed that informalization, originally intended as a means of problem-solving, resulted in the exclusive 'bargaining' of interests.[25] What is particularly crucial, in the normative dimension, is whether informalized problem-solving approaches compromise the political equality of participants, namely, by acting as substitutes for democratic legitimacy through rational solutions, rather than through the regulated activity of elected officials. The problem with arguments that support informalization on the basis of rational problem-solving is that they fail to discriminate between democracy and often inherent versions of expert- or technocracy.

The recent trend to informalize governance at the national level has resulted in an intensive debate and corresponding literature[26] that examines the changing relationship between the state (taken as a synonym for government) and society. In many cases, these reflections lack, or are only mildly sensitive to, critical normative dimensions. The primary focus of this literature is on the effectiveness of political problem-solving between different levels or branches of government or within public-private cooperatives of various kinds. If questions of legitimacy are raised at all, they are considered only in the context of 'output legitimacy' or variations of it. Most notable in this camp are Fritz Scharpf and Renate Mayntz, who developed their theoretical approach of 'actor-centered institutionalism' in an analytical as well as prescriptive (political) perspective of a 'dehierarchization.' Others developed (neo-)corporatist approaches or made reference to specific trends in public administration that lead towards the idea of a 'cooperative state.' More radical approaches – both from a neo-liberal as well as from leftist anarchist perspectives – perceived the trend of privatization of former public policies as the end of statist societies or at least as the 'minimalization of statehood.' On the issue of transnational governance, Klaus Dieter Wolf, in a recent contribution on private international authority, called 'inter-governmental political governance' anachronistic and advocated a 'problem-solving perspective' as a 'way out of the dilemma of international governance.'[27]

Although critical of such a problem-solving approach in the literature on informalization, I consider it only tangentially and focus more exclusively on the relationship between informalization and democratic governance. As already noted, there is an increasing trend towards the informalization of governance, broadly defined, particularly at the transnational and supranational levels. Although some argue that informalization creates opportunities for more inclusive participation at the transnational and supranational levels, particularly of 'civic' groups, and thus enhances democracy, I contend that the participation of such groups actually contravenes the democratic process because such groups lack formal legitimacy. Suppose for a moment that the purported positive effects of rational problem–solving by public-private policy networks could be validly demonstrated also at the international level[28] *and* that my argument about the decreasing democratic character of these policy regimes and networks also proves plausible, then democratic societies would have to choose between the 'efficiency' of problem-solving and its trade-offs for democratic legitimacy or democracy and its drawbacks for efficiency.[29]

The political culture of Western democracies seems to value output efficiency, and as a consequence favours a problem-solving approach to policymaking regardless of the concerns that this raises about democratic legitimacy. Together with other problematic changes, the once 'civic' political culture[30] of Western democracies would seem to be replaced by a kind of political consumer culture. This trend reinforces what has been called 'democratic elitism,'[31] which today often disguises itself under labels like 'deliberative' or 'associative' democracy.

More Participation Does Not Necessarily Lead to More Legitimacy

In the normative republican as well as in the deliberative approach to democracy, levels of participation are seen as measures of the legitimacy of the policy output. These approaches assume that those who are subject to policies should influence how governors are selected. This, by extension, also constitutes the citizenry's participation in the policy process. The concept of participation itself covers a wide range of possible activities, each of which affect the political process in different ways. It is obvious that the type of impact depends on the various social resources available to individuals and groups in pursuing their respective interests. One might assume that the range of resources an individual or a group is able to invest correlates directly with potential influence, with social and economic differences being indicators of potential political influence. Certainly, this assumption simplifies the complex relationship between social resources and political influence. However, it was exactly this assumption that once formed the normative core of the democratic idea of political equality.[32]

The equality of citizens, institutionalized in various ways in modern democracies, rests on a very superficial abstraction of social realities. The aim was and still is to neutralize or at least minimize the direct impact of social differences – with respect to wealth, age, education, ethnicity, or gender – in political participation. The dominant expression of political equality is free and equal voting in elections of representatives or in referenda, where each vote is equally weighted. By presenting this view, I do not express a normative preference for 'direct' democracy as a method of democratic self-government. Rather, I am referring to the fundamental principle of *political* equality. If non-elected individuals or collective actors are able to access governmental offices and functions in a context of an elected representative institutionalism, then the principle of political equality is compromised. Indeed, to make an obvious point, many social and economic variables interfere with this abstract normative institutionalization of equality. Yet this should not downplay the importance of political equality because it is equality that legitimizes democratic regimes. With political equality as the foundation of democratic legitimacy, all practices that influence the political process in a way that involves the differential mobilization of social resources or occurs 'behind closed doors' diminish the legitimacy of a democratic regime.

Today, what Hannah Arendt called the artificial distinction between the pluralistic and heterogeneous 'private' – resting on the principle of differentiation and inequality – and the 'public' political realm of citizenship – founded on principles of equality – is changing, both in theory and in practice. This is especially true in the emerging field of transnational or supranational regulation. One very significant indicator of this change is the surprising semantic and normative shift that the term *lobbying* has undergone in recent years. Until very recently the practice of lobbying was perceived to be an illegitimate political practice that introduced clandestine private measures into the public democratic process. In the EU today, lobbying is primarily understood to be a legitimate form of participation by social actors or their professional representatives in public-private policy networks.[33] Within the European Union such networking between the EU Commission – itself a central governance institution without genuine democratic legitimacy[34] – and various kinds of non-governmental actors and associations has transmuted into a new style of supranational governance. Moreover, in some fields, private actors have successfully claimed authority that traditionally would have been part of the public domain and consequently, they act with some kind of delegated semi-public authority. This normative and conceptual shift has to be seen in the context of changing practices of governments and bureaucracies within and beyond nation-states. Nation-states are no longer the passive targets of external influences by lobbyists and other private actors; states are now beginning to make strategic use of these social actors in various ways.[35] The problem for democracy is that these social actors strategically pursue their own interests, rather than those of the public at large.

The strategic use of social actors by governments is not a new practice. What is striking about it in the context of my argument, however, is the normative emphasis that various political theorists have put on these more or less visible, more or less formal, more or less institutionalized practices of cooperation and coordination as means by which civil society can directly participate in the political process. This emphasis is surprising, as the influence of these collective actors and lobbyists is not rooted in the principle of political citizenship and equality, but rather in a logic of collective action in societies where the social and economic potential for mobilizing influence is unequal. Furthermore, this kind of participation rests on professionalism and expertise. Based on them, these actors become 'agents' without 'principles.' Considered critically, their activities go far beyond the romanticism of immediate citizenship or grassroots participation.

Most normative political theory that addresses the activity of private actors points to the participation of agencies such as Amnesty International, Greenpeace, Friends of the Earth, and the World Wildlife Fund as poignant examples of how the democratic process can be enhanced. To be sure, these agencies by and large do play a positive role in the reinforcement of normative standards in their particular areas of interest.[36] However, the positive influence of NGOs is easily counterbalanced by the activities of various other NGOs that lobby for very specific and partial interests and in the process neglect the principles of democracy.[37] Normative political theory that favours NGO involvement in the political process cannot only consider the activities of humanitarian organizations as representatives of civil society.[38] Civil society is very complex, composed of both humanitarian as well as more private and partial interest groups. Civil society, as conceptualized by Adam Ferguson, consists primarily of economic and industrial firms and of egoistic individuals and their associations and representatives.[39] Today, these are by far the dominant and most powerful actors in the policy networks and other structures of cooperation and coordination in transnational policy formation, governance, and institution building. Furthermore, even those NGOs that indisputably contribute to 'common interests' or 'public goods' have a 'technocratic ... management-oriented understanding of civil society.'[40] Accordingly, national and supranational political agencies, especially of governments or the

EU bureaucracies, are inclined to establish informal public-private structures such as 'task forces' for the handling of certain programs and funds because they may at times lead to better and more effective attainment of goals.

Nevertheless, the participation of private actors in otherwise politically legitimate institutions has a price. Those who argue for informalization, such as Klaus Deiter Wolf, cannot escape the fact that there is a distinction between private actors who act for the 'common good,' such as Greenpeace and Amnesty International, and those who pursue selective private interests. Amnesty International is an example of a small number of private actors who act with a greater public focus. The vast majority of NGOs found at the European and the transnational levels have more partial lobby interests, often veiled within the discourse of 'common interest' or 'public good.' This 'veiling' raises questions about how the 'public good' is defined and highlights the degree to which transnational authority constantly remains open to political judgment and disagreement. As a result, non-governmental actors become tools for the strategic action of governments at the transnational level.

Finally, NGO participation does not stem from the democratic ideal of citizen equality. This becomes an especially acute problem in informal networks of policy coordination, where the power of those participating varies and the equalizing structural aspects of democratic recruitment do not prevail. Consequently, outputs are not determined only by 'arguing,' as postulated by models of deliberative democracy, but also by 'bargaining' among actors who have different power capabilities.[41]

To summarize, the normative principles and the logics of action of voluntary associations in civil societies are different from those in the legally institutionalized sphere of democratic government. What is appropriate in one sphere may be detrimental in the other. Combining the loose and informal structure of civil society with the more formal and legal institutions may result in an institutional loss of democratic legitimacy.

Those who want to find an equivalent form of citizen participation based on political equality at the transnational level need to counterbalance or even restrict the sources of unequal transnational social impact of organized interest groups and lobbies, even at the expense of effectiveness. The fundamental question is whether individual equality, the basic norm of citizen participation as the basis of legitimacy in a democratic society, can play a role in a transnational political regime dominated by the public-private interaction of national governments, voluntary associations, private collectives, and corporate actors. Currently, only the democratic governments in this hybrid structure can claim to be democratically legitimate for taking authoritative action and making binding decisions.

How Democratic Is Authority?

Authority, generally defined, does not necessarily have a legal foundation and will not always entail an exit option for those affected by its consequences. Usually, however, authority refers to a process or situation of recognition by those who are subject to its consequences. Authority, in other words, is an ascribed dimension of institutions, offices, organizations, or persons, none being authoritative without being *recognized* as such. Not every authority is public. As authority is based on different and contingent social and cultural preconditions, no one single institution, office, organization, or person can claim to be authoritative across time and space over all people. In most cases, authority is based on the recognition of its jurisdiction in a certain field of activity. In rare cases, this sectoral authority, for example, of a Nobel Prize-winning scientist or an outstanding athlete, becomes generalized so that the person is also seen as an authority in other fields, for instance, politics. Moral authority, based on whatever achievements and perceptions, is the most generalizable kind of authority in social relations. However, as a fact of recognition and ascription, authority is always precarious, and it can be lost as easily as it is gained.

The authority of offices, institutions, and sometimes also of individuals in democracies plays an important role, particularly in establishing the legitimacy and effectiveness of government. Authority is a useful resource for those in public office because it usually results in widespread compliance with the policies that governing officials formulate and implement.

Authority should not be confused with legitimacy, nor should it become a substitute for it. It is only legitimacy – not authority or compliance – that serves as the basis for democratic government. An essential distinction between authority and legitimacy is made in modern democracies. Legitimacy in modern democratic societies rests solely on legal foundations and is called into question only if legal duties, rights, or procedures are compromised. Only democratic legitimacy deserves and requires the compliance of those governed, even if they do not accept the legal output of governance and/or do not respect the people holding democratic offices.[42]

While authority and acceptance are helpful and desirable in democratic government, only legitimacy is necessary and can demand obedience by citizens.[43] In certain situations the authority of those in office may be questioned and their performance may not be accepted. However, this should not, at least in principle, undermine the legitimacy of democratic governments. The strict distinction between authority and legitimacy enables democratic governments to pursue – at least in some instances – unpopular policies. As much as acceptability and popularity may influence governmental action and the performance of those in office, from a normative theoretical point of view, democratic government can never rest on authority, acceptance, and popularity alone.

If all this is true, one must ask whether and how non-elected and non-governmental actors could ever play a legitimate role in transnational government.[44] In nation-states – and here I refer only to those where government is constitutionally and legally restrained – governments are legitimately entitled to prescribe behaviour and expect obedience. In severe cases of deviant behaviour, democratic governments have the legitimate right to enforce the rule of law by the use of violence or alternative means of punishment.

The normative ideals of democratic government face a serious challenge if there is a trend towards 'private interest government'[45] or the 'privatization of world politics.'[46] Such a trend entails the increased involvement of non-governmental organizations in governance structures that have the ability to enforce quasi-legal rules that can assume immediate validity in national democratic regimes.[47] On the one hand, it is not quite clear how, according to which criteria, private actors participating in public-private governance are selected. Even if this selection were transparent, the ability to transfer the formal legitimacy of democratic regimes to non-elected actors must be questioned. 'Selection' is not election, and democratic legitimacy is not a currency that can be freely converted. Legitimacy rests on a process of deliberation, itself an aspect of democratic legitimacy, whereby citizens entitle certain individuals or groups to act as public representatives.[48] In this respect, Wolf correctly observes that no 'two-step delegation of competence' from national governments to non-governmental actors on a transnational level is normatively acceptable. Yet, despite this argument, Wolf also asserts that the moral authority of private actors such as Amnesty International or Greenpeace can, under certain circumstances, substitute for the lack of formal input legitimacy.[49] This argument, however, does not sufficiently differentiate between legitimacy and authority. Although non-governmental actors may lobby, counsel, and communicate effectively at international meetings or indirectly affect international proceedings by mobilizing public opinion in favour of their initiatives,[50] these abilities alone do not make their participation in the governance process legitimate.

Wolf himself acknowledges that his understanding of different sources of authority, lending support to informal input legitimacy in transnational governance, 'does ... not coincide with the liberal understanding of *democratic* legitimacy.'[51] In fact, the participation of private actors of any kind effectively violates the legitimacy of democratic government. That the participation of private actors at both the national and transnational levels of governance is widespread is beyond dispute. The controversial issue is the normative basis for their participation. While many, in a vein similar to Wolf, see the participation of private actors as the coming future of the 'self-regulation of civil society' that is eo ipso democratic, my own view is that these developments do not register with the liberal democratic principle of citizens' equal rights of participation. Even if today's citizens, in their role as 'political consumers,' tacitly accept the involvement of private actors, democracy in the traditional sense would not be restored; diffuse support and compliance do not satisfy the requirements of democratic legitimacy.

Is Compliance a Source of Legitimacy?

As the empirical chapters in this book demonstrate, authorities that establish rules, such as governments or transnational authorities like the EU Commission, strive to attain specified goals. Their intention is to implement programmatic aims. In the case of the EU, an example would be the implementation of European environmental standards in industrial production. Norm-setting and norm implementation are thus central aspects of transnational or supranational governance. This discussion distinguishes between different strategies of norm implementation, enforcement, management, and more recently, adjudication,[52] each of which separately or in combination may lead to a certain degree of norm implementation. Since the implementation of norms is never fully successful, an additional procedure is required to evaluate its success. Usually, this comes in the form of an institution that places sanctions on rule violators. In the European Union, the European Court has the authority to make decisions on purported violations of EU rules.[53] In accordance with the normative standards of liberal democratic regimes within nation-states, one would have to expect that in this situation procedural guarantees support the equality of all those subject to established rules, especially in the case of violators. These procedural guarantees are functional equivalents to the *Rechtsstaat*, which rests on the application of laws based on equality. They cannot be substituted by 'transnational discourse-networks and publics' without violating fundamental democratic norms, contrary to the arguments made by Michael Zürn and Wolf with reference to Jürgen Habermas's legal philosophy. Zürn and Wolf suppose 'that the completed development of a transnational democratic law would already exist, if a complete, i.e. legal, political and societal internalization of (these) legal norms would have taken place.'[54] In their view, 'internalization' – compliance or acceptance – of norms counts as a source of legitimacy.

Compliance, which is widespread in regard to European norms, does not provide a valid argument for the democratic legitimacy of those norms, just as compliance in the legal system of the former German Democratic Republic could not establish the GDR's democratic legitimacy. Input legitimacy, in normative terms, has no democratic equivalent at the output side of political regimes.

Today, the EU is marked by what appears to be an unavoidable move towards informalization regarding governance, particularly in legal procedures. The recent White Paper reported that out of the '[eighty-three] internal market directives which should have been transposed in 2000, only five of them had been transposed in all Member States,' with ensuing complaints about the 'lack of flexibility [and] damaging effectiveness'[55] of EU legislation. Recent research at the European University Institute in Florence shows that more then 15,000 registered violations of the EU Commission's rules have occurred within the past thirty years. Similar formal and legal procedures, however, were rarely applied to these violations. A small minority of these cases finally came to the European Court; in most cases – more than 60 per cent – violations were 'successfully' settled in informal negotiations.[56]

Given that the tendency to circumvent formal legal procedures exists also at national levels (e.g., at tax offices) and at local levels (as clients and bureaucrats implement legal rules), what is wrong with a similar development at the transnational level? If informalization makes for better problem-solving, then is it not better for the larger community? The answers to these questions depend on the assumed normative perspective. When considering these questions, a further question arises about the 'successful' settlement of cases; in short, how is 'success' determined? With little empirical study on informalization in the EU, one must assume that 'success' is determined over a wide spectrum, from the immediate strict implementation of policy to settled bargains reached between the EU Commission and its counterparts, usually national governments or their bureaucratic counterparts. Clearly, this bargaining process is not transparent. In addition, it does not guarantee that the Commission employs the same negotiation tactics with all of its counterparts. In other words, such an informal situation is open to all kinds of strategic and opportunistic action by both sides, but especially by the Commission. In light of the recent experience of a non-sent letter to Germany referring to the 'Stability Pact,' it is also reasonable to assume that the power of a given member government will influence the outcome of informal rule enforcement. This type of 'managed compliance'[57] is typical of EU governance. By extension, one can surmise that 'managed compliance' is likely to be characteristic of transnational or supranational governance in general. Managed compliance is a strategy focused on an optimal rate of compliance based on a situational and contingent process of rule implementation, the success of which is determined by gradual or relative rule enforcements, as evaluated by the governors themselves. This is typically how international law is developed. But, as Kratochwil has asked, 'Is international law "proper law"?'[58] Anthony Aust has argued that the very nature of law is its formal character[59] because it is only through formal means that the law can be applied equally to those subject to all its jurisdiction. Accordingly, any 'laws' developed informally, as is the case with more international and transnational legal codes, contravene the fundamental principle of equal and universal application, which lies at the core of legal philosophy. As this chapter has consistently reiterated, in the final analysis, the legitimacy of any democratic regime rests on its ability to ensure the equality of its citizens, both with respect to equal chances of participation and equal treatment before the law.

To conclude, recent scholarship in political science investigating reasons for compliance with rules established outside the democratic nation-state reflects a normative shift. By focusing the research agenda on questions of successful and effective implementation of transnational and supranational norms, the questions of how democracy is challenged by transnationalism and how its integrity can be ensured and enhanced have fallen by the wayside. In the area of human rights and environmental protection, such a shift in focus may be relatively benign and will probably be applauded, despite the impediments to democratic process that this creates. But what happens when security norms such as those geared towards protection from international terrorism begin to interfere with basic human rights? Will the discipline of political science continue down its current path or return to an examination of the classical questions of democratic experience?

NOTES

1 I am very grateful to Anna Geis and Katrin Töns for corrections and to Beate Kohler-Koch and the editors for helpful advice.
2 Held (1995: Chapter 3), McGrew (1997).
3 Wallace (2001).
4 Commission of the European Communities (2001: 428).
5 Ibid., 4.
6 Ibid., 13.
7 Ibid., 17.
8 Ibid., 21.
9 Ibid., 21.
10 Since the publication of Rosenau's and Czempiel (1992) influential work, *Governance without Government*, it has become fashionable in political science circles to use the word *governance*. The precise meaning of the term, however, has never been clearly specified. Therefore, I prefer to use the term *government*.
11 For an early and influential contribution on this subject, see Streeck and Schmitter (1985).
12 Scharpf (2002: 274).
13 Joerges and Neyer (1997), Neyer (2000).
14 Banchoff and Smith (1999: 11).
15 See the title of Wapner (1997).
16 At least one public government with its policy program must be involved in a public-private policy network. Whether 'private government' without

this minimal condition should be called 'government' at all is left open. See Rosenau (1995).

17 Not yet in a legalistic perspective, but more fundamentally, as in Giddens (1986).

18 Constitutionalization as a 'strategy of partial transformation' (Carl Schmitt) does not always support democratic rights, cf. Lietzmann (1998).

19 Although subject to legalized spending restrictions, many of these governments were not yet democratic.

20 Reinhard (2000: 406–40).

21 See Lehmbruch (2000: 55–9, and 158–72), Greven (2000a).

22 See Zürn (1998: n65) for good reasons to use the concept *denationalization* instead of the vague and rarely operationalized notion *globalization*.

23 Schmalz-Bruns (2002: 275).

24 See Benford and Snow (2000).

25 Lehmbruch (2000: 162).

26 In Germany, this literature is mostly concerned with the 'horizontal policy coordination' between the *Länder* (Lehmbruch 2000). For a brilliant analytical account that only implicitly focuses on informalization, see Benz, Scharpf, and Zintl (1992). An explicit examination of the internal coordination of governing coalitions is provided in Manow (1996). For a more general account of the German case, see Schulze-Fielitz (1984).

27 Wolf (2002: 188) asks the following questions: Who is the 'self' in 'self-government' and what is the empirical reference for 'civil society'?

28 Zimmer (2001: 338), in a recent research overview of NGOs, observes as a 'primary deficit the striking lack of empirical research' to answer this question, especially on the international level of governance.

29 Over thirty years ago in Germany, Naschold (1969) prescribed a convincing complex approach with positive trade-offs (at least for formal organizations).

30 Greven (1999: 143–232).

31 See Bachrach (1967).

32 According to Sartori (1992: 23, my translation), 'It is true that democracy is more complex than any other political regime, but paradoxically it cannot persist, if its principles and mechanisms surpass the intellectual horizon of its average citizens.' I call this the 'Sartori criterion' of democratic theory, which many discussions and evaluations, particularly of transnational democracy, fail to apply.

33 See Greenwood (1997).

34 One has to assume that the founders of the European Union, in choosing to refer to the organization as a 'union,' were quite aware of the undemocratic

connotations of a 'commissionary government.' For a specific understanding of this awareness in the historical context of 'European constitutionalism,' see Lietzmann (2002).

35 Haufler (1993).

36 See Keck and Sikkink (1998).

37 For a rare example of a critical approach, see Brandt et al. (2000).

38 Some contributions in this discourse always seem to confuse the historical concept of 'civil society' (as articulated by Ferguson, Smith, and Hegel) with the Habermasian (Husserlian) normative concept of 'life-world,' a (presumed) reservoir of moral and ethical principles. The recent EU White Paper (2001) on 'European Governance' is guilty of this confusion. By evading the definition of *civil society* with a problematic enumeration of organizations (2001: 14 fn9) described as 'organisations which make up civil society [and] mobilize people and support, for instance, [from] those suffering from exclusion and discrimination.' If the White Paper demands such minimum criteria for the representativeness of civil society, then the concept of *representativeness* becomes senseless.

39 Ferguson.

40 Brandt et al. (2000: 135).

41 Steinberg (1990).

42 I have already mentioned the fundamental dilemma which arises if citizens acclaim undemocratic government or illegitimate activities. Carl Schmitt (1963) became notorious for his statement that democracy does not need 'liberal' elections, but can rest on *acclamatio* of true leadership.

43 Such acceptance or 'diffuse support' is interpreted along the lines of Easton (1965: 124ff).

44 Beisheim (1997) also provides some sceptical arguments.

45 Streeck and Schmitter (1985).

46 Brühl et al. (2001).

47 Eichner and Voelzkow (1994) provide examples in the EU.

48 Similarly, Majone (1999: 4) argued that 'democratically accountable principals ... cannot transfer their own legitimacy.'

49 Wolf (2002). Wolf also refers to similar positions held by Cutler, Haufler, and Porter (1999).

50 How could this international 'authority' ever be measured, or at least evaluated, in more problematic cases than those mentioned? Thus, how are they to be used as an uncontested manner of authorization for performing 'public' functions?

51 Ibid., 199.

52 For a comparative case study making the argument that adjudication, as

practised in the EU, would be the most effective strategy, see Zangel (1999).

53 I do not mean to imply that an effective system of sanctioning, as in the case of the nation-state's monopoly of the legitimate use of force, is a necessary definition of legal systems. However, ultimately, it may determine both the effectiveness and the fairness of any given legal system (Fearon, 1998). The EU White Paper on 'European Governance' (2001: 25) in this respect makes an interesting statement: 'as far as individual complaints are concerned, a lengthy legal action against a Member State is not always the most practical solution. The main aim of an infringement action it to oblige the offending Member State to remedy its breach of Community law.' Evidently, in some ways the EU is more concerned with efficiency than legality.

54 Zürn and Wolf (1999: 23, my translation).

55 White Paper (EU 2001): 18.

56 Börzel (2001). More information about this project can be found at http://www.iue.it/rsc/rsc_tools

57 Chayes and Chayes (1991).

58 Kratochwil (1983).

59 Aust (1986).

13 Complex Sovereignty and the Emergence of Transnational Authority

EDGAR GRANDE AND LOUIS W. PAULY

New Forms of Governance

Whether contemplating their own research or making comparisons across the chapters of this book, none of the contributors makes the claim that state sovereignty has been superseded by contemporary changes in global order. None of the authors is predicting that integrative or disintegrative economic or social pressures will anytime soon render the nation-state form of governance obsolete. Nevertheless, together they have highlighted the problems with governance that are no longer readily soluble within the confines of a systemic architecture based exclusively on the nation-state. The protection of public welfare and of individual health, the preservation of the natural environment and of agriculturally productive land, the containment of terrorism and of conventional security threats, the development of regulatory structures capable of delivering reliable growth in poor countries and more balanced prosperity in rich countries – none of these any longer seem capable of being guaranteed by individual states, however large. Transformations in each of the policy arenas surveyed in this book reveal lacunae in the traditional forms of effective, fair, and stable governance that are not easily closed.

In light of those lacunae, the authors have concluded that we are living through a remarkable period of experimentation aimed at creating collective problem-solving capacity that is beyond and below the conventional territorial and functional boundaries of the nation-state. Supranationalism and more intense forms of international cooperation coexist with tendencies towards practicable regional and local institutions of governance. This institution building has not been sparked simply by forces now commonly lumped together under the term *globalization*. The founding and adaptation of international organizations and regional institutions has accompanied the process of nation-state building itself, and certainly they reach back well into the nineteenth century. Yet, as suggested in the various chapters, there are good reasons to assume that the practical relevance of governance beyond the nation-state has expanded considerably in the past twenty years. At the same time, it is becoming clear that underlying forms of political authority are changing under the cumulative weight of proliferating experiments in policymaking.

- *Quantitatively,* the number of governmental organizations at the international level has increased significantly, as has the number of non-governmental organizations that operate globally.
- *Qualitatively,* the rule-making powers of international organizations and supranational institutions, as well as their ability to encourage compliance with these rules vis-à-vis nation-states and their citizens, have increased. Important examples here are U.N. human rights standards, expanding freer-trade arrangements, and the wide-ranging expansion of policy competences in the European Union.

In brief, governance in the sense of the authoritative setting and enforcement of collective norms is now increasingly transcending the nation-state, and in the process, a multiplicity of highly varied new organizations and institutions have been established. The outcomes of these developments include complex new architectures of political rule making, the formative principles of which are beginning to differ in principle from analogous structures in the nation-state. These new forms of governance are typified by at least the following three distinguishing features:

1 *Transnational scope.* In one way or another, new policy regimes integrate differing territorial levels of policy action above and below the nation-state and various types of public and private actors. Most importantly, they are beginning to transcend the traditional separations of domestic and international politics, inside-outside and public-private, by integrating different types of actors and organizations. In addition to nation-states, transnational policy regimes may be composed of different international organizations (e.g., the IMF, WTO, and OECD), supranational forms of regional integration (e.g., the EU, NAFTA, and APEC) and of a variety of national and transnational interest groups and social movements. Correspondingly, the

territorial scope of such policy regimes varies considerably.[1]

2 *Functional policy orientation.* Transnational forms of governance are dominated by a strong orientation to functional problems, both within individual policy arenas and embracing several policy arenas. Correspondingly, transnational policy regimes are delimited not by territorial boundaries, but by the functional scope of policy problems – however, they may be split up geographically.

3 *Complex and partial systemic character.* The sphere of transnational policymaking is, despite all its institutional complexity, typified by a high degree of what Peters calls organizational anarchy. Participation is open and variable, and the interactions are only partly directed by formal rules and legal frameworks. Instead, informal arrangements and the use of power play an important role.

This last aspect is of particular importance. There are good theoretical reasons to assume that modern societies have been mutating into 'world society,' as Albert, following Luhmann, suggests in his chapter or, to use Beck's term, we are seeing the emergence of a *world risk society.* Nevertheless, the internal structures of modern societies are highly controversial. The tightly integrated imperial forms, as outlined by Hardt and Negri, appear too simple, and thus the debate about governance remains open. The explanatory concepts suggested in this book to be more empirically supportable range from Peters's loosely organized, anarchical garbage can models to Coleman's more stable, institutionalized and integrated forms of policy spaces to Grande and Eberlein's policy networks and policy regimes to Pauly's adapted, more open, but still hierarchically organized intergovernmental forms.

Associated controversies can largely be settled with reference to empirical variation. While as yet there is little evidence of the emergence of a fully integrated global political system, we are able to observe a rich variety of different institutional architectures of transnational political deliberation, rule making and rule, enforcement, over time and across policy areas. Coleman, Pauly, and Eberlein and Grande in their chapters describe the emergence and transformation of international organizations, the intensification of their external interactions, and various forms of internal differentiation. Such developments bring to light remarkable features of actual attempts to govern.

The internal complexities of transnational policy spaces or regimes have increased significantly, as has the degree of their internal integration. What Giddens calls the 'systemness' of transnational politics has

been on the rise in recent decades.[2] However, the institutional configurations that result from these developments remain remarkably different from the organization of domestic politics and, most importantly,
they do not possess the properties of modern political systems – whatever type of systems theory we may apply. If one uses the theoretical
lens of Luhmannian systems theory, as Albert proposes, the political
system of world society described in this book is different from a
national political system and its pre-modern form: it is primarily differentiated through segmentation, rather than through basic functional
requirements, and its internal aspect takes the form of a regional differentiation into more complex forms of state.

The evidence before our eyes indicates that the term *non-system*
would be inappropriate to describe this outcome. The hints of underlying organization are too obvious. A system of complex governance is
evolving. Backsliding is of course possible. After all, this is human history that we are analysing, not some kind of mechanical machinery.
Nevertheless, it does appear to be a system, with expanding boundaries.

The mode of collective problem-solving in such a system differs
from its analogue in the nation-state. Indeed, the *national* level is losing
its monopoly in the production of collective solutions to collective
problems. The nation-state is caught up in a new architecture of statehood in which different levels of governance are institutionally differentiated and yet integrated. In this new architecture, the nation-state
continues to play an important and indispensable part, but it is no
longer sovereign in the common understanding of the term. The *classical state* form itself is losing its monopoly position in the production of
public goods. Collectively binding decisions are increasingly not being
taken by the state alone or by the state in simple concert with other
states. The growing involvement of various types of societal actors is
now quite evident and cannot be ignored. Sometimes, as suggestive
evidence in the Porter and Börzel and Risse chapters indicates, these
actors are taking decisions that meaningfully affect social life 'without
governments.'[3] In other cases, like those discussed by Coleman,
Grande and Eberlein, Skogstad, and Clarkson, states cannot ignore
practices tantamount to governance that are generated outside of traditional, official channels. The term we proposed in Chapter 1, *complex
sovereignty*, captures this dynamism.

In some parts of the world, the nation-state seems far along in its
deep engagement in a new form of governance. Less important than

agreement on a label for this outcome – that Beck proposes to call the 'transnational cooperation state' and to be understood within a paradigm of 'cosmopolitan realism' – is that we see those parts of the world as being not necessarily limited to Europe. For some years now, it has been quite clear that the member-states of the European Union have embarked on an historic venture to create a new and workable system of regional governance. The temptation for scholars interested in the international implications of this development has long been simply to place this case in an analytical box labelled 'federalism' or 'the new European state.' This has the advantage of protecting inherited intellectual categories and economizing on intellectual energy. It has the distinct disadvantage, however, of missing the actual complexity of the situation and foreclosing the possibility of meaningful analogies.

The U.S. response to the terrorist attacks of 11 September 2001 and the war in Iraq have commonly been interpreted to be fundamental reversals of any tendency towards transnational governance – and complex sovereignty – that might have been suggested by the global developments of the 1990s. Certainly, it is true that since that fateful date issues of national security have regained top priority on the political agenda, and not only in the United States. Unquestionably, different national priorities and values have nourished unilateralist and even uncooperative strategies in many places. Nevertheless, even the National Security Strategy released by the White House in 2002 concedes that transnational cooperation is indispensable if the new security threats facing the world are to be met:

> There is little of lasting consequence that the United States can accomplish in the world without the sustained cooperation of its allies and friends in Canada and Europe ... The events of September 11, 2001, fundamentally changed the context for relations between the United States and other main centers of global power, and opened vast, new opportunities. With our long-standing allies in Europe and Asia, and with leaders in Russia, India, and China, we must develop active agendas of cooperation lest these relationships become routine and unproductive. Every agency of the United States Government shares the challenge. We can build fruitful habits of consultation, quiet argument, sober analysis, and common action. In the long term, these are the practices that will sustain the supremacy of our common principles and keep open the path of progress.[4]

The difficulties of postwar consolidation and democratization in Afghanistan and Iraq have already underlined the point quite boldly. Tie into this difficulty the fact that the economic resources required to address such fundamental security challenges are now being generated in a system that depends on a remarkable degree of market openness and integration, and the point becomes impossible to miss. The need for transnational cooperation has become much more obvious, not less, and authoritative structures for effective decision-making continue to evolve responsively to this reality. The process of reconstituting political authority has not come to a halt, but its preconditions, problems, and contradictions have become manifest.

Surely the men who ratified the U.S. Articles of Confederation in 1781, with which to govern what had been thirteen colonies on the Atlantic coast, would have been surprised had they come back a hundred years later to find their confederal system replaced by a complex system that combines unitary and federal principles in the governance of a now-continental society. Moreover, as any standard American government textbook will explain, the capacity of the U.S. Constitution, which replaced the Articles, to adapt to changing circumstances has been crucial to its endurance and success. A similar story could be told in many other places in the world today, where sovereignty remains an important principle, but where its application is now enmeshed in increasingly complex sets of claims, obligations, duties, and interests. Why, then, would anyone be surprised by the idea that political authority in our world today can be and is being reconstituted by human beings in their struggle to cope with the new realities of their common existence?[5]

Varieties of Transnational Governance

From an institutional perspective, the case studies examined in this volume allow us to identify at least three paths towards transnational governance.

First, and most obvious, is the possibility of establishing new international organizations and institutions at the regional and global levels. The most prominent recent examples include the emergence of numerous international regimes for environmental policy, the establishment of international organizations such as the World Trade Organization, and the creation of various and distinctive structures of regional integration in Europe (EU), North America (NAFTA), Asia

(APEC), as well as in other parts of the world.[6] A comparison of the Eberlein and Grande and Clarkson chapters, of course, reveals striking differences in the specific modalities and short-term implications of such new institutions. Authoritative governance, however, certainly describes what all such institutional forms seek to accomplish.

This path is not entirely separated from a second one, which has centred on changes within existing institutions and practices. As a response to external demands and pressures, the missions, internal structures, and external strategies of long-established organizations have been adapting to their changing environments. This holds, among others, for most of the organizations established after the Second World War under the umbrella of the United Nations. Particularly striking examples are international financial institutions, such as the World Bank and the International Monetary Fund, which have at least partly redefined their functions and established themselves as important intermediaries in a world of globalizing finance. Nevertheless, as discussed in Pauly's chapter, even the United Nations itself is being pulled back from the brink of irrelevance in this arena. The Skogstad and Coleman chapters also suggest analogous important changes.

The third path has been the intensification of private transnational activity. By creating new private organizations, by mobilizing transnational social movements, and by establishing new forms of public-private partnerships at the international level, private transnational interactions are becoming indispensable parts of the new institutional frameworks of transnational governance. As the Porter and Börzel and Risse chapters indicate, something more than pluralist politics seems to be at work here. Whether traditionally constituted political authority is being delegated or usurped, these emerging frameworks seem to be creating a new architecture within which authoritative decisions are taken and public goods are created.

Our empirical case studies show that transnational cooperation is developing along all these paths simultaneously. They do not suggest, however, the transcendence of political conflict or power asymmetries or the sudden emergence of harmony. To the contrary, Skogstad, Coleman, and Clarkson demonstrate, in compelling terms, the enduring fact that cooperation takes enormous effort and sometimes yields unanticipated consequences. None of the authors, however, describe any fundamental, long-term backsliding away from efforts to build institutions of governance that are capable of generating authoritative decisions. Moreover, it appears that movement down the three paths of

TABLE 13.1
The scope of transnationalism

	Agenda-setting	Decision-making	Policy implementation
Macro level: High politics (foreign and security policies)	Medium	Very low	Medium
Meso level: Welfare policies	Medium	Low	Medium
Micro level: Low politics (environmental policies, technical standardization)	High	Medium	High

institutional development involves interactive and reinforcing processes. This has an important implication for future research. It could
well be the case that the isolated treatment of any one of these processes misses the dynamics inherent in the actual transformation of
governance in the contemporary setting. The transnational cooperation state, complex sovereignty, and the reconstitution of authority in
our world may only be visible if we examine those processes simultaneously.

The Limited Scope of Transnational Governance

That we may be able to glimpse a variety of emerging forms of authoritative transnational governance beyond the traditional nation-state
does not necessarily imply the inexorable or inevitable evolution of a
world government, nor does it imply that the scope for such governance in the short-term is unlimited. Together, the case studies in this
volume are evidence of both the existence and the significance of transnational authority – they also provide indications of its current limitations. To analyse the scope of transnational authority, one might
imagine a heuristic device (see Table 13.1) that would distinguish three
different levels of policies – macro, meso, and micro – and three different stages and functions of the political decision-making process.[7]

What becomes visible here is a U-shaped curve, suggestive of a hypothetical pattern in any assessment of the scope for transnationalism today. Arguably, that scope would be significantly lower at the macro- and the meso-levels than at the micro-level, and it would be considerably higher at the pre– and post–decision-making stages. Something similar may hold for the role of private actors and the functions of public-private partnerships that are involved in processes of policy-making. The chapters by Porter and Börzel and Risse clearly show that the role of private actors is far more limited than has been suggested by those who depict the dramatic emergence of 'governing without government,' 'global policy networks,' or 'global corporatism.'[8]

In short, a hard core of national power and authority remains in place, and is especially visible with regard to the main issues of foreign policy, security policy, and welfare policies. Moreover, there is no evidence that, in advanced industrial societies, the state is retreating from these functions. Even in sectors where we can observe a far-reaching privatization of public properties and a liberalization of markets, such as in telecommunications, railways, and electricity, the state retains substantial regulatory powers. In Europe as elsewhere, as the Eberlein and Grande chapter shows, states remain reluctant to transfer these powers to a supranational level. Nevertheless, the U-shaped pattern apparent in Table 13.1, and suggested strongly in the various chapters of this book, cannot be ignored. Still, the global transformation of political authority is burdened with at least two types of problems: first, problems of cooperation and effectiveness and, second, problems of legitimacy and accountability. By way of conclusion to this book, but also to specify directions for serious follow-up research, let us treat each in turn.

Problems of Cooperation and Effectiveness in Transnational Governance

Because of the absence of a global Leviathan, transnational authority must necessarily be based on *cooperation*. The cooperation and compliance of a critical mass of states and of private organizations is indispensable for the enforcement of transnational rules. Most important in this respect is the cooperation of states. The state does not disappear with the reconstitution and reconfiguration of transnational political authority. The new architecture of governance does not necessarily even signify a 'retreat of the state.'[9] The transformation of political authority may even be said to depend on the state continuing to play large and indispensable roles, because:

1 The tax monopoly of the state, however weakened by the transnational mobility of capital, enables it to continue to have privileged access to financial resources.
2 The state still has at its disposal a unique institutional apparatus for implementing collectively binding decisions.
3 The institutions of the state continue to have much greater legitimacy than international organizations and policy networks.

Consequently, successful governance *beyond* the state depends essentially on the state *itself.* The *willingness* and *ability* of a state to cooperate with other states remains the decisive preconditions for the emergence and ultimate effectiveness of transnational policy regimes. Neither the willingness nor the ability of states to cooperate can simply be presumed.

In this context, we can distinguish four types of state:

1 The *cooperation state,* which is both willing to cooperate and able to do so; in short, the type of state on which political and economic integration in Europe has been based.
2 The *egoistic state,* which would 'in principle' be able to cooperate, but would not be willing to compromise on important interests, for example, the United States as depicted in Clarkson's chapter, hegemonic states that have appeared throughout history, but also states that deliberately flout international norms, for example, small states that opportunistically exploit lacunae in transnational arrangements governing, say, money laundering.
3 The *weak state,* which although willing to cooperate, nonetheless lacks the internal (institutional, personal, and financial) requisites for actually giving effect to transnational agreements.
4 The *rogue state,* which is neither able nor willing to cooperate because, for example, it has been captured by criminal or terrorist organizations.

Although such a conceptualization does not exhaust all hypothetical possibilities, it does allow us to systematically array plausible prerequisites for the reconstitution of political authority at the transnational level (see Table 13.2).

TABLE 13.2
Types of states in transnational politics

	Able to cooperate	Unable to cooperate
Willing to cooperate	Cooperation states	Weak states
Unwilling to cooperate	Egoistic states	Rogue states

This heuristic device suggests the absence of universality in today's world, a universality on which ambitious concepts such as 'global governance' and 'global public policy' are often implicitly based. Indeed, the cooperation state compared in this fashion hardly seems an inevitable historical destination for much of humanity. Once one moves outside the fully industrialized regions, and sometimes even within them, the cooperation state can quickly become the exception.[10] In other words, contrary to much of the conventional rhetoric that surrounds the term *globalization*, we should expect actual transnational policy regimes, and actual tendencies towards transnational governance, often to be quite limited. Where the state is weak or failing, moreover, we should not expect to find much evidence of transnational authority; at most, we might expect to find external power simply imposed.[11]

The case studies in this book demonstrate that transnational cooperation and the emergence of associated authoritative forms of governance have been limited empirically mainly by these factors:

1 Asymmetries of power
2 Insufficient domestic capacities
3 Conflicting political ideas, preferences, and cultural values.

Asymmetries of power have been most important in two of the case studies in this book: the halting emergence of a transnational policy space in agriculture and regional integration in North America. Clarkson's NAFTA case demonstrates that the asymmetrical distribution of power among states can easily lead to an uneven distribution of the costs and benefits of cooperation, thereby reducing incentives to cooperate. In contrast to the European Union, with its subtle balance of power both among the large member-states and between the larger and the smaller member-states, power asymmetries have discouraged the parties to NAFTA from transferring ultimate political authority to supranational institutions. In the case of international trade agreements in agricultural policy, Coleman, too, explains that asymmetries of power between industrialized countries with their highly subsidized agricultural sectors and the less developed countries remain important impediments to a transformation of authority in this sector.

But asymmetries of power themselves result partly from *insufficient domestic capacities*. The domestic capacities of a state are crucial in various respects for its ability to cooperate with other states. As Coleman shows, lack of expertise is one of the most serious problems facing developing countries that seek to participate effectively in the process of transnational institutionalization. This problem has been aggravated by the difficulties that civil society in those states faces in organizing itself for fuller participation in transnational policy processes. Domestic administrative, and ultimately coercive, capacities are also indispensable if any arrangements reached through such processes are to be implemented. In this regard, fundamental weaknesses apparent in much of the developing world remind us that, in the end, the problem of transnational cooperation and the associated reconstitution of political authority remain highly abstract for most of humanity. To the extent that they are not isolated from the rest of the world, most developing societies with weak internal capacities face an external environment that must often appear coercive. To the extent that this complicates transnational initiatives, and it certainly does across a range of policy arenas, this can create *zones of ungovernability* that complicate transformative processes even for states that are inclined to cooperate. Here is a topic ripe for future research.

Finally, *conflicting political ideas, preferences, and cultural values* are impediments to international cooperation and enduring sources of conflict. Recently, such impediments have been evident in relations between Middle Eastern and Western societies, and even in relations between the United States and Europe.[12] Our case studies show that deep-seated differences remain obvious even among close allies. In particular, Skogstad's analysis shows that transatlantic economic conflicts are rooted not only in divergent material interests. If we follow Beck's analysis, such conflicts seem, instead, still to be rooted in substantial part in the different risk cultures, mentalities, and approaches to modernity.

Taken together, these factors highlight the serious obstacles to any form of governance that has to rely on cooperation in the first place.

For this reason, we should not overestimate the effectiveness of new forms of political authority when they nonetheless begin to appear.

Problems of Legitimacy and Accountability

Reconstituting political authority at the transnational level is not impeded only by straightforward problems of cooperation. It also faces deep problems of legitimacy, accountability, and responsibility. The 'democratic dilemma' confronting decision-making beyond the nation-state is well known and well explored in the scholarly literature.[13] The problem awaits an unequivocal solution. In principle, we can imagine three different channels to establishing transnational authority that has the requisite democratic legitimacy:

1 Directly, by popular consent
2 Indirectly, by the inclusion of transnational organizations and epistemic communities that are widely accepted themselves to be legitimate within defined spheres of activity
3 Indirectly, by delegation of state authority.

To date, transnational authority has been rendered legitimate mainly through the delegation of authority by nation-states to international or supranational organizations. In the last resort, executive and legislative branches of the state may be held responsible for the decisions made by international bodies, even when their actual influence on such bodies is attenuated. Partly because of that attenuation and partly because of a lack of transparency in their decision-making processes, but mainly because they actually have been exerting an increasing influence on people's lives in a widening range of societies, the weak legitimacy of many international organizations has recently become a more pressing problem. Indeed, this has helped bring the very notion of transnational authority to the forefront of political debate and scholarly concern. Rarely, however, have serious political actors responded with calls for disintegrating the social, economic, and political systems that increasingly seem to require transnational authority or for completely extricating a people from Peters's ever-larger decision-making 'garbage can.' The alternatives are all highly contested, and they must be faced.

Delegating authority to private actors operating transnationally, for example, in epistemic or expert communities or in non-governmental organizations capable of decision-making, may contribute to rational policy deliberation and design.[14] On the contrary, as Greven convincingly argues in his chapter, such participatory strategies suffer from serious shortcomings of representation and responsibility. Indeed, they might well be weakening the democratic legitimacy of transnational decision-making, rather than strengthening it. Certainly they violate the basic principles of formal equality, which are indispensable to any model of modern democracy. Formal equality and direct accountability are, among other features, fundamental elements of any democratic legitimation based on popular consent. Modern democracies have institutionalized various ways of harnessing such consent, most importantly through the election of representative bodies or though such direct measures as referenda. So far, virtually no attempts have been made to transfer such mechanisms to the realm of transnational authority. Even in the case of the European Union, which has the world's most powerful and secure parliamentary body beyond the nation-state, the institutionalization of democratic legitimacy based on popular consent has thus far been half-hearted. As the Eberlein and Grande and Greven chapters point out, formal decision-making bodies like the European Parliament seem to be perennially in danger of being bypassed by informal mechanisms of transnational governance.

Responding to basic problems of effectiveness and of legitimacy is, in any case, of basic importance to the continuing process of reconstituting political authority. One should keep in mind, however, that although they might require different kinds of solutions, particular responses might well interact, thus complicating any solution that is ultimately developed. Skogstad, in her comparative case study on the regulation of genetically modified food, offers an excellent example of this difficulty. A reduction of the legitimacy problem within the EU has resulted in a significant increase in U.S.–EU trade conflict, thereby reducing the effectiveness of an evolving international trade regime and making its expansion more difficult. A solution that is both effective and legitimate for all the actors involved is not easy to imagine. But so, too, is it difficult to imagine a reversion to fully separated national regimes in this policy arena or in others like it. From trade and finance to the environment and the full panoply of policies implied by the term *human security*, an opting out from the complexities of transnational authority is not entirely impossible to conceive. It is merely becoming ever more improbable.

Complex sovereignty has emerged in a world that is not bound by elegant legal theories that were developed in a simpler time and by images of territoriality that were constructed in days long past. The consequences of realistically facing the problems confronting humanity and of pragmatically reconstituting political authority transnationally cannot simply be wished away.

NOTES

1   Following Mayntz (2000), this use of the term transnational has been deliberately couched broadly, going beyond its usual use in international relations research. See, e.g., Risse-Kappen (1995).
2   Giddens (1986).
3   See Cutler et al. (1999), O'Brien et al. (2000), and Rosenau (2003).
4   U.S. Government, White House (2002), Chapter 8.
5   This theme has been well articulated in many contexts, both secular and sacred. In the latter regard, one of the most famous expressions came in 1963 from Pope John XXIII: 'If one considers carefully the inner significance of the common good on the one hand, and the nature and function of public authority on the other, one cannot fail to see that there is an intrinsic connection between them ... Today the universal common good poses problems world-wide in their dimensions; problems, therefore, which cannot be solved except by a public authority with power, organization and means co-extensive with these problems, and with a world-wide sphere of activity' John XXIII (1963): Chapter 4, paras. 136–8.
6   Young (1998), Mitchell (2002), Katzenstein (1996a and 2005), Eberlein and Grande and Clarkson, in this volume.
7   On the three policy levels, see Peterson (1995). On types of decision-making, see the Börzel and Risse chapter in this volume.
8   See, respectively, Reinicke (1998), Reinecke and Deng (2000), and Kaul et al. (1999).
9   Strange (1996). On the continuing centrality of states in cooperative processes, see Kahler and Lake (2003).
10 See van Crefeld (1999).
11 Von Trotha (2000), Schlichte and Wilke (2000), Herbst (2000), Grande (2001), Cohen and Rogers (1995).
12 Huntington (1996), Kagan (2003), Rabkin (2004).
13 Dahl (1994), Held (1995), Habermas (1998), Scharpf (1999a, 1999b), Greven and Pauly (2000).
14 Joerges and Gerstenberg (1998), Joerges and Vos (1999).

References

Abromeit, Heidrun (1998) *Democracy in Europe: Legitimising Politics in a Non-state Polity*. Oxford and New York: Berghahn.

Adam, Barbara, and Joost van Loon (2000) 'Introduction: Repositioning Risk – The Challenge for Social Theory.' In Adam, Beck, and van Loon, eds., *The Risk Society and Beyond*, 1–31.

Adam, Barbara, Ulrich Beck, and Joost van Loon, eds., *The Risk Society and Beyond: Critical Issues for Social Theory*. London: Sage.

Adams, J. (1994) *Risk*. London: VCL Press.

Adler, Emanuel (2002) 'Constructivism and International Relations.' In Carlsnaes, Risse, and Simmons, eds., *Handbook of International Relations*, 95–118.

Adler, Emanuel, and Michael Barnett, eds. (1998) *Security Communities*. Cambridge: Cambridge University Press.

Albert, Mathias (1997) 'South of Norden or Norden's South? Germany and Baltic Political Space.' In Pertti Joenniemi, ed., *Neo-Nationalism or Regionalism? The Restructuring of Political Space around the Baltic Rim*. Copenhagen: NordREFO, 85–118.

– (2002) *Zur Politik der Weltgesellschaft: Identität und Recht im Kontext internationaler Vergesellschaftung*. Weilerswist: Velbrück.

Albert, Mathias, and Lena Hilkermeier, eds. (2004) *Observing International Relations: Niklas Luhmann and World Politics*. London: Routledge.

Albrow, Martin (1996) *The Global Age: State and Society beyond Modernity*. Cambridge: Polity.

Ansell, Chris (2000) 'The Networked Polity: Regional Development in Western Europe.' *Governance* 13: 303–33.

Appadurai, Arjun (1996) *Modernity at Large: Cultural Dimensions of Globalization*. Minneapolis: University of Minnesota Press.

– (2002) 'Grassroots Globalization and the Research Imagination.' In Arjun Appadurai, ed., *Globalization*. Durham: Duke University Press, 1–22.

Arts, Bas (1998) *The Political Influence of Global NGOs: Case Studies on the Climate and Biodiversity Conventions*. Utrecht: International Books.

Asmus, R.D. (2003) 'Rebuilding the Atlantic Alliance.' *Foreign Affairs* Sept./Oct.: 20–31.

Aust, Anthony (1986) 'The Theory and Practice of Informal International Instruments.' *International and Comparative Law Quarterly* 35: 787–812.

Bachrach, Peter (1967) *The Theory of Democratic Elitism: A Critique*. Boston: Little, Brown.

Badie, Bertrand (2002) *Souveränität und Verantwortung: Politische Prinzipien zwischen Fiktion und Wirklichkeit*. Hamburg: Hamburger Edition.

Baker, T. (2003) *Insurance, Law and Policy*. New York: Aspen.

Baldwin, Robert, and Marin Cave (1999) *Understanding Regulation: Theory, Strategy, and Practice*. Oxford: Oxford University Press.

Balme, R., and B. Jouve (1996) 'Building the Regional State: Europe and Territorial Organization in France,' in Hooghe, ed., *Cohesion Policy and European Integration*, 189–202.

Banchoff, T., and M.P. Smith (1999) *Legitimacy and the European Union: The Contested Polity*. London: Routledge.

Barling, David (1997) 'Regulatory Conflict and Marketing of Agricultural Biotechnology in the European Community,' in J. Stanyer and G. Stoker, eds., *Contemporary Political Studies*. Nottingham: Political Studies Association of the U.K., 1040–8.

Bartelson, Jens (1995) *A Genealogy of Sovereignty*. Cambridge: Cambridge University Press.

Bauer, R.A., and H. Gergen (1968) *The Study of Policy Formation*. New York: Free Press.

Beck, Ulrich (1988) *Gegengifte*. Frankfurt: Suhrkamp.

– (1992) *Risk Society: Towards a New Modernity*. London: Sage.

– (1997a) *The Reinvention of Politics*. Cambridge: Polity.

– (1997b) *Was ist Globalisierung?* Frankfurt: Suhrkamp.

– (1997c) *Weltrisikogesellschaft, Weltöffentlichkeit und globale Subpolitik*. Vienna: Picus.

– (1999) *World Risk Society*. Cambridge: Polity.

– (2000) 'Risk Society Revisited: Theory, Politics and Research Programmes.' In Adam, Beck, and van Loon, eds., *The Risk Society and Beyond*, 211–29.

– (2002) *Macht und Gegenmacht im globalen Zeitalter*. Frankfurt: Suhrkamp.

– (2004) *Kosmopolitischer Blick oder Krieg ist Frieden*. Frankfurt: Suhrkamp.

– (2005) *Power in the Global Age*. Cambridge: Polity.

- ed. (1998) *Perspektiven der Weltgesellschaft*. Frankfurt: Suhrkamp.

Beck, Ulrich, and W. Bonß, eds. (2001) *Die Modernisierung der Moderne*. Frankfurt: Suhrkamp.

Beck, Ulrich, W. Bonß, and C. Lau (2001) 'Theorie reflexiver Modernisierung – Fragestellungen, Hypothesen, Forschungsprogramme,' in Beck and Bonß, eds., *Die Modernisierung der Moderne*, 11–59.

- (2004) *Entgrenzung und Entscheidung*. Frankfurt: Suhrkamp.

Beck, Ulrich, and C. Lau (2005) 'Second Modernity as a Research Agenda.' *British Journal of Sociology*.

Beck, Ulrich, Anthony Giddens, and Scott Lash (1994) *Reflexive Modernization*. Stanford: Stanford University Press.

Beck, Ulrich, and Edgar Grande (2004) *Das kosmopolitische Europa*. Frankfurt: Suhrkamp.

Begg, Ian (1996) 'Introduction: Regulation in the European Union.' *Journal of European Public Policy* 3: 525–35.

Beisheim, Mariannne (1997) 'Nichtregierungsorganisationen und ihre Legitimität.' *Aus Politik und Zeitgeschichte* 43: 21–9.

Bellamy, Richard, and R.J. Barry Jones. (2000) 'Globalization and Democracy: An Afterword.' In Holden, ed. *Global Democracy: Key Debates*, 202–16.

Bendor, J., T. M. Moe, and K.W. Shotts (2001) 'Recycling the Garbage Can.' *American Political Science Review* 95: 169–90.

Benford, R.D., and D. Snow (2000) 'Framing Processes and Social Movements: An Overview and Assessment.' *Annual Review of Sociology* 26: 611–39.

Benz, Arthur, and Burkard Eberlein (1999) 'The Europeanisation of Regional Policies: Patterns of Multi–level Governance.' *Journal of European Public Policy* 6: 329–48.

Benz, A., F.W. Scharpf, and R. Zintl (1992) *Horizontale Politikverflechtung*. Frankfurt and New York: Campus.

Bernstein, P.L. (1996) *Against the Gods: The Remarkable Story of Risk*. New York: Wiley.

Bernstein, Steven (2002) 'The Elusive Basis of Legitimacy in Global Governance.' Paper presented at the Munk Centre, University of Toronto, 15 March.

Bernstein, Steven, and Louis W. Pauly, eds. (forthcoming) *Global Governance: Towards a New Grand Compromise?* Albany, NY: SUNY Press.

Biersteker, Thomas J. (2002) 'State, Sovereignty and Territory.' In Carlsnaes, Risse, and Simmons, eds., *Handbook of International Relations*. 157–76.

Biersteker, Thomas J., and Cynthia Weber, eds. (1996) *State Sovereignty as Social Construct*. Cambridge: Cambridge University Press.

Bigo, Didier (2001) 'The Möbius Ribbon of Internal and External Security(ies).'

In Mathias Albert, David Jacobson, and Yosef Lapid, eds., *Identities, Borders, Orders: Rethinking International Relations Theory*. Minneapolis: University of Minnesota Press, 91–116.

Blank, Stephen, Stephen Krajewski, and Henry S. Yu. (1995) 'U.S. Firms in North America: Redefining Structure and Strategy.' *North American Outlook* 5 (February): 9–72.

Blustein, Paul (2001) *The Chastening*. New York: Public Affairs.

Bodin, Jean (1992) *On Sovereignty*. Cambridge: Cambridge University Press.

Bohman, James, and William Regh (1997) *Deliberative Democracy: Essays on Reason and Politics*. Cambridge, MA: MIT Press.

Bohne, Eberhard (1981) *Der informelle Rechtsstaat*. Berlin: Duncker and Humblot.

Bok, D. (1997) 'Measuring the Performance of Government.' In Nye, Zelikow, and King, eds., *Why People Don't Trust Government*, 55–76.

Boli, John, and George M. Thomas, eds. (1999) *Constructing World Culture: International Nongovernmental Organizations since 1875*. Stanford: Stanford University Press.

Börzel, Tanja (1997) 'Policy Networks: A New Paradigm for European Governance?' *EUI Working Papers RSC* no. 97(19). San Domenico: European University Institute.

– (1998a) 'Organizing Babylon: On the Different Conceptions of Policy Networks.' *Public Administration* 76 (2): 253–73.

– (1998b) 'Rediscovering Policy Networks as a Form of Modern Governance.' *Journal of European Public Policy* 5: 354–9.

– (2001) 'Non-Compliance in the European Union: Pathology or Statistical Artifact?' *Journal of European Public Policy* 8: 803–24.

Bouckaert, G. (1995) 'Improving Performance Measurement.' In A. Halachmi and G. Bouckaert, eds., *The Enduring Challenges in Public Management: Surviving and Excelling in a Changing World*. San Francisco: Jossey-Bass, 17–28.

Bougen, P. (2003) 'Catastrophe Risk.' *Economy and Society* 31: 253–74.

Bovens, M.A.H., P. 't Hart, and B.G. Peters (2001) *Success and Failure in Public Governance*. Cheltenham, UK: Edward Elgar.

Bozeman, B. (1987) *All Organizations Are Public*. San Francisco: Jossey-Bass.

Bradley, Kieran St C. (1998) 'The GMO-Committee on Transgenic Maize: Alien Corn, or the Transgenic Procedural Maze,' in M.P.C.M. van Schendelen, ed., *EU Committees as Influential Policy Makers*. Aldershot, UK: Ashgate, 207–22.

Brainard, Lael (2003) 'Compassionate Conservatism Confronts Global Poverty.' *Washington Quarterly* 2: 149–69.

Brainard, Lael, et al. (2003) *The Other War: Global Poverty and the Millennium Challenge Account*. Washington: Brookings Institution.

Brandt, Ulrich, et al. (2000) *Global Governance: Alternative zur neoliberalen Globalisierung?* Münster: Westfälisches Dampfboot.

Brock, Lothar (1998) 'Die Grenzen der Demokratie: Selbstbestimmung im Kontext des globalen Strukturwandels und des sich wandelnden Verhältnisses von Staat und Markt.' *Politische Vierteljahresschrift* 39 (PVS Sonderheft 29): 271–92.

Brown, Chris (2002) *Sovereignty, Rights and Justice.* Oxford: Polity.

Brühl, Tanja (2001) The Privatization of Governance Systems: On the Legitimacy of Environmental Policy. Paper presented at the Conference on the Global Environment and the Nation State. Berlin, 7–8 Dec.

Brühl, Tanja, Tobias Debiel, Brigitte Hamm, Hartwig Hummel, and Jens Martens, eds. (2001) *Die Privatisierung der Weltpolitik. Entstaatlichung und Kommerzialisierung im Globalisierungsprozess.* Bonn: Dietz.

Brunkhorst, Hauke (2002) *Solidarität. Von der Bürgerfreundschaft zur globalen Rechtsgenossenschaft.* Frankfurt: Suhrkamp.

Bull, Hedley (1977) *The Anarchical Society.* London: Macmillan.

Bulmer, Simon J. (1994) 'The Governance of the European Union: A New Institutionalist Approach.' *Journal of Public Policy* 13: 351–80.

Callon, Michel (1991) 'Techno-economic Networks and Irreversibility.' In John Law, ed., *A Sociology of Monsters: Essays on Power, Technology and Domination.* London and New York: Routledge, 132–64.

Cameron, J. (1999) 'The Precautionary Principle.,' In G.P. Sampson and W.B. Chambers, eds., *Trade, Environment, and the Millennium.* New York: U.N University Press, 239–69.

Camilleri, Joseph A., and Jim Falk (1992) *The End of Sovereignty? The Politics of a Shrinking and Fragmenting World.* Aldershot, UK: Edward Elgar.

Campbell, J.L., and O.K. Pedersen (2001) *The Rise of Neoliberalism and Institutional Analysis.* Princeton: Princeton University Press.

Canada. Department of External Affairs and International Trade (1993) *NAFTA: What's it all about?* Ottawa: Government of Canada.

Canada. (1998) 'Voluntary Codes: A Guide for Their Development and Use.' Joint Initiative of the Office of Consumer Affairs, Industry Canada, and the Regulatory Affairs Division, Treasury Board Secretariat (March). [Online]. Available at www.strategis.ic.gc.ca/SSG/ca00863e.html

Carlsnaes, Walter, Thomas Risse, and Beth Simmons, eds. (2002). *Handbook of International Relations.* Thousand Oaks, CA: Sage.

Castells, Manuel (1996) *The Rise of the Network Society.* Oxford: Blackwell.

– (1998) *End of the Millennium.* Oxford: Blackwell.

Chace, James (2004) *1912.* New York: Simon and Schuster.

Chambers, Graham R. (1999) 'The BSE Crisis and the European Parliament.' In Joerges and Vos, eds., *EU Committees,* 95–106.

Chayes, Abram (1995) *The New Sovereignty: Compliance with International Regulatory Agreements.* Cambridge: Harvard University Press.

Chayes, Abram, and Antonia Handler Chayes (1991) 'Compliance without Enforcement: State Behaviour under Regulatory Treaties.' *Negotiation Journal* 7: 311–30.

– (1993) 'On Compliance.' *International Organization* 47: 175–205.

Chayes, Abram, Antonia Handler Chayes, and Ronald B. Mitchell (1998) 'Managing Compliance: A Comparative Perspective.' In Edith Brown Weiss and Harold K. Jacobsen, eds., *Engaging Countries: Strengthening Compliance with International Environmental Accords.* Cambridge, MA: MIT Press, 39–62.

Chernow, Ron (2004) *Alexander Hamilton.* New York: Penguin.

Chiti, Eduardo (2000) 'The Emergence of a Community Administration: The Case of European Agencies.' *Common Market Law Review* 37, 309–43.

Clarkson, Stephen (1998) 'Fearful Asymmetries: The Challenge of Analysing Continental Systems in a Globalizing World.' *Canadian-American Public Policy* 35: 1–66.

– (2002) 'Reform from Without versus Reform from Within: NAFTA and the WTO's Role in Transforming Mexico's Economic System.' In Joseph S. Tulchin and Andrew D. Selée, eds., *Mexico's Politics and Society in Transition.* Boulder, CO: Lynne Rienner, 215–53.

Claude, Inis L., Jr. (1966) 'Collective Legitimization as a Political Function of the United Nations.' *International Organization* 20: 367–79.

Coen, David, and Chris Doyle (2000) 'Designing Economic Regulatory Institutions for European Network Industries,' *Current Politics and Economics of Europe* 9: 455–76.

Coen, David, and Mark Thatcher, eds. (2001) *Utilities Reform in Europe.* Huntington, NY: Nova Science.

Cohen, Joshua, and Joel Rogers (1995) *Associations and Democracy.* London: Verso.

Cohen, M., J.G. March, and J.P. Olsen (1972) 'A Garbage Can Model of Decision-making,' *Administrative Science Quarterly* 17: 1–25.

Coleman, William D., and Melissa Gabler (2002) 'Agricultural Biotechnology and Regime Formation: A Constructivist Assessment of the Prospects.' *International Studies Quarterly* 46: 481–506.

Coleman, William D., and Tony Porter (2002) 'Transformations in the Private Governance of Global Finance.' Paper presented at the annual meeting of the International Studies Association, New Orleans, 25 March.

Coleman, William D., and Stefan Tangermann (1999) 'The 1992 CAP Reform, the Uruguay Round and the Commission: Conceptualizing Linked Policy Games.' *Journal of Common Market Studies* 37: 385–406.

Commission of the European Communities (2000a) *White Paper on Food Safety.* COM(1999) 719, Brussels, 12 Jan.

- (2000b) *Communication from the Commission on the Precautionary Principle.* COM(2000), Brussels, 2 Feb.
- (2001) 'Directive 2001/18/EEC of the European Parliament and of the Council of Ministers of 12 March 2001 on the deliberate release into the environment of genetically modified organisms and repealing Council Directive 90/220/EEC,' *Official Journal* L 106, 17/04/2001: 1–39.

Condon, Bradly, and T. Sinha (2001) 'An Analysis of an Alliance: NAFTA Trucking and the U.S. Insurance Industry.' *Estey Centre Journal of International Law and Trade Policy* 2(2): 235–45.

Cooper, Andrew F., John English, and Ramesh Thakur, eds. (2002) *Enhancing Global Governance.* Tokyo: U.N. University Press.

Cooper, R.N. (1968) *Economic Policy in an Interdependent World: Essays in World Economics.* Cambridge, MA: MIT Press.

Cowles, Maria Green (2000) 'The Transatlantic Business Dialogue: Transforming the New Transatlantic Dialogue.' In Mark A. Pollack and Gregory C. Shaffer, eds., *Transatlantic Governance in the Global Economy.* Lanham, MD: Rowman and Littlefield, 213–33.

Cowles, Maria Green, James Caporaso, and Thomas Risse, eds. (2001) *Transforming Europe: Europeanization and Domestic Change.* Ithaca: Cornell University Press.

Cox, Robert (1987) *Production, Power and World Order.* New York: Columbia University Press.

Crozier, M. (1979) *On ne change pas la société par décret.* Paris: B. Grasset.

Cutler, A. Claire (2003) *Private Power and Global Authority.* Cambridge: Cambridge University Press.

Cutler, A. Claire, Virginia Haufler, and Tony Porter, eds. (1999) *Private Authority and International Affairs.* Albany, NY: SUNY Press.

Cyert, R., and J.G. March (1963) *A Behavioral Theory of the Firm.* Englewood Cliffs, NJ: Prentice-Hall.

Czempiel, Ernst-Otto (1991) *Weltpolitik im Umbruch: Das internationale System nach dem Ende des Ost-West-Konflikts.* Munich: Beck.

Daase, C. (2002) 'Internationale Risikopolitik – ein Forschungsprogramm für den sicherheitspolitischen Paradigmenwechsel.' In Daase, Feske, and Peters, eds., *Internationale Risikopolitik,* 3–35.

- S. Feske, and I. Peters, eds. (2002) *Internationale Risikopolitik: der Umgang mit den neuen Gefahren in den internationalen Beziehungen.* Baden-Baden: Nomos.

Dahl, Robert A. (1994) 'A Democratic Dilemma: System Effectiveness versus Citizen Participation,' *Political Science Quarterly* 1: 23–34.

Dalton, R., and B. Wattenberg (2000) *Politics without Partisans.* Oxford: Oxford University Press.

Davey, William J. (1996) *Pine and Swine*. Ottawa: Centre for Trade Policy and Law.

De Jonquières, Guy (2003) 'Zoellick Raises the Legal Stakes over GM Crops.' *Financial Times*, (4 Jan.), 6.

de la Porte, C., and P. Pochet (2004) 'The European Employment Strategy: Existing Research and Remaining Questions.' *Journal of European Social Policy* 14: 71–9.

De Palma, Anthony (2002) 'The Reluctant Trinity: Canada, Mexico and the United States.' Lecture at Carleton University, Centre on North American Politics and Society, Ottawa, Canada, 24 Jan.

Dehousse, Renaud (1997) 'Regulation by Networks in the European Community: The Role of European Agencies.' *Journal of European Public Policy* 4: 246–61.

Denmark. Ministry of Finance (1998) *Borgerne og den offentlige sector*. Copenhagen: Finansministeriet.

Derrida, Jacques (1990) 'Force of Law: The "Mystical Foundation of Authority."' *Cardozo Law Review* 11: 920–1045.

Dewey, J. (1966) *Die Öffentlichkeit und ihre Probleme*. Bodenheim: Philo.

Dirlik, Arif (2001) 'Place-Based Imagination: Globalism and the Politics of Place.' In Roxann Prazniak and Arif Dirlik, eds., *Places and Politics in an Age of Globalization*. Lanham, MD: Rowman and Littlefield, 15–52.

Dogan, M. (1999) 'Déficit de confiance dans les démocraties avancées.' *Revue internationale de politique comparé* 6: 510–47.

Douglas, M., and A. Wildavsky (1982) *Risk and Culture: An Essay on the Selection of Technical and Environmental Dangers*. Berkeley: University of California Press.

Downs, George W., David M. Rocke, and Peter N. Barsoom (1996) 'Is the Good News about Compliance Good News about Cooperation?' *International Organization* 50: 379–406.

Dror, Y. (2001) *The Capacity to Govern*. London: Frank Cass.

Dyson, Kenneth (1992) 'Theories of Regulation and the Case of Germany: A Model of Regulatory Change.' In Kenneth Dyson, ed., *The Politics of German Regulation*. Aldershot, UK: Gower, 1–28.

Easton, David (1965) *A Framework for Political Analysis*. Englewood Cliffs, NJ: Prentice-Hall.

Eberlein, Burkard (2000a) 'Configurations of Economic Regulation in the European Union: The Case of Electricity in Comparative Perspective.' *Current Politics and Economics of Europe* 9: 407–25.

– (2000b) 'Institutional Change and Continuity in German Infrastructure Management: The Case of Electricity Reform.' *German Politics* 9: 81–104.

- (2003) 'Formal and Informal Governance in Single Market Regulation.' In Thomas Christiansen and Simona Piattoni, eds., *Informal Governance in the EU*. Cheltenham, UK: Edward Elgar, 150–72.
- (2005) 'Regulation by Co-operation: The Third Way in Making Rules for the Internal Energy Market.' In Peter D. Cameron, ed., *Legal Aspects of EU Energy Regulation*. Oxford: Oxford University Press.

Eberlein, Burkard, and Edgar Grande (2000) 'Regulation and Infrastructure Management: German Regulatory Regimes and the EU Framework.' *German Policy Studies / Politikfeldanalyse* 1: 39–66.

Echols, Marsha A. (1998) 'Food Safety Regulation in the European Union and the United States: Different Cultures, Different Laws.' *Columbia Journal of European Law* 3: 525–43.

Egeberg, M., and P. Laegreid, eds. (1999) *Organizing Political Institutions: Essays in Honor of Johan P. Olsen*. Oslo: Universteitsforlaget.

Eichener, Volker (1996) 'Die Rückwirkungen der europäischen Integration auf nationale Politikmuster.' In Jachtenfuchs and Kohler-Koch, eds., *Europäische Integration*, 249–80.

Eichner, V. and H. Voelzkow (1994) 'Ko-Evolution politisch administrativer und verbandlicher Strukturen: Am Beispiel der technischen Harmonisierung des europäischen Arbeits-, Verbraucher-und Umweltschutzes.' *Politische Vierteljahresschrift* 25 (special issue), 256–90.

Eising, Rainer (2000) *Liberalisierung und Europäisierung: Die regulative Reform der Elektrizitätsversorgung in Großbritannien, der Europäischen Gemeinschaft und der Bundesrepublik Deutschland*. Opladen: Leske and Budrich.

Emmerij, Louis, Richard Jolly, and Thomas G. Weiss (2001) *Ahead of the Curve? U.N. Ideas and Global Challenges*. Bloomington: Indiana University Press.

Eriksen, Erik Oddvar (2000) 'Deliberative supranationalism in the EU.' In Erik Oddvar Eriksen and John Erik Fossum, eds., *Democracy in the European Union: Integration Through Deliberation?* New York: Routledge, 2–64.

Ericson, R., and A. Doyle, eds. (2003) *Risk and Morality*. Toronto and London: University of Toronto Press.

Eurobarometer (2001) *European Science and Technology*. Brussels: Directorate-General for Research, 55.

European Union (2001) 'Better Regulation.' *Report of Working Group 2c. White Paper on European Governance* (May).

Evans, Gareth, and Mohamed Sahnoun (2002) *The Responsibility to Protect: Report of the International Commission on Intervention and State Sovereignty*. Ottawa: International Development Research Centre.

Evans, Peter B., Harold K. Jacobson, and Robert D. Putnam, eds. (1993) *Double-*

Edged Diplomacy: International Bargaining and Domestic Politics. Berkeley: University of California Press.

Ewald, F. (1993) *Der Vorsorgestaat*. Frankfurt: Suhrkamp.

Fabi, Randy (2003) 'FDA Cannot Ensure Safety of Biotech Foods – U.S. group.' *Reuters English News Service*, 7 Jan. Available at www.reuters.com

Falk, Richard (1993) 'Sovereignty.' In *The Oxford Companion to Politics of the World*. Oxford: Oxford University Press, 841–53.

FAO and UNDP (1996a) *Rome Declaration on World Food Security and World Food Summit Plan of Action*. Rome: author.

– (1996b) *Leipzig Declaration on Conservation and Sustainable Utilization of Plant Genetic Resources for Food and Agriculture*. Rome: author.

Farrell, Henry (2002) 'Negotiating Privacy in the Age of the Internet: Analyzing the EU-U.S. "Safe Harbor" Negotiations.' In Heritier, ed., *Common Goods*, 105–26.

Farrell, Henry, and Adrienne Héritier (2003) 'Formal and Informal Institutions under Codecision: Continuous Constitution Building in Europe.' *Governance* 16: 577–600.

Fearon, James D. (1998) 'Bargaining, Enforcement, and International Cooperation.' *International Organization* 52: 269–305.

Ferrara, M., M. Matsaganis, and S. Sacchi (2002) 'Open Coordination against Poverty: The New EU "Social Inclusion Process."' *Journal of European Social Policy* 12: 227–39.

Financial Stability Forum. (2000) 'Report of the Follow-Up Group on Incentives to Foster Implementation of Standards' (31 Aug.) [Online]. Available at www.fsforum.org

– (2001a) 'Ongoing and Recent Work Relevant to Sound Financial Systems' (2 March) [Online]. Available at www.fsforum.org

– (2001b) 'Issue Paper of the Task Force on Implementation of Standards' (15 March) [Online] at Available: www.fsforum.org

Finnemore, Martha (2003) *The Purpose of Intervention: Changing Beliefs about the Use of Force*. Ithaca: Cornell University Press.

Fischer-Lescano, Andreas (2002) 'Globalverfassung: Los desaparecidos und das Paradox der Menschenrechte.' *Zeitschrift für Rechtssoziologie* 23: 217–49.

Florini, Ann (2000a) 'Lessons Learned.' In Florini, ed., *The Third Force*, 211–40.

– ed. (2000b) *The Third Force: The Rise of Transnational Civil Society*. Tokyo: Japan Center for International Exchange; Washington: Carnegie Endowment for International Peace.

Foreman, Carol Tucker (2001). Remarks before the Second Joint CSL/JIFSAN Symposium: Food Safety and Nutrition – Current Issues in Food Biotechnology [Online]. Available at http://www.consumerfed.org/biotechcomments.pdf

Franda, Marcus (2001) *Governing the Internet: The Emergence of an International Regime*. Boulder, CO: Lynne Rienner.

Galtung, Fredrik (2000) 'A Global Network to Curb Corruption: The Experience of Transparency International.' In Florini, ed., *The Third Force*, 17–47.

Geertz, Clifford (2000) 'The World in Pieces: Culture and Politics at the End of the Century.' In Geertz, ed., *Available Light: Anthropological Reflections on Philosophical Topics*. Princeton: Princeton University Press.

Giddens, Anthony (1986) *The Constitution of Society*. Oxford: Polity.

– (1990) *The Consequences of Modernity*. Stanford: Stanford University Press.

– (1994) *Beyond Left and Right*. Cambridge: Polity.

Goldstein, Judith L., et al., eds. (2000) *Legalization in World Politics. International Organization* 54 Special Issue.

Görlitz, Axd, and Peter Burth,, eds. *Informale Verfassurg*. Baden-Baden: Nomos.

Gormley, W.T. (1983) *The Politics of Public Utility Regulation*. Pittsburgh: University of Pittsburgh Press.

Gouldner, Alvin W. (1957) 'Cosmopolitans and Locals: Toward an Analysis of Latent Social Roles – I.' *Administrative Science Quarterly* 2: 281–306.

– (1958) 'Cosmopolitans and Locals: Toward an Analysis of Latent Social Roles – II.' *Administrative Science Quarterly* 3: 444–79.

Grande, Edgar (1993) 'Entlastung des Staates durch Liberalisierung und Privatisierung? Zum Funktionswandel des Staates im Telekommunikationssektor.' In Rüdiger Voigt, ed., *Abschied vom Staat - Rückkehr zum Staat?* Baden-Baden: Nomos, 371–92.

– (1994) 'The New Role of the State in Telecommunications: An International Comparison.' *West European Politics* 17: 138–57.

– (1996) 'The State and Interest Groups in a Framework of Multi–level Decision-making: The Case of the European Union.' *Journal of European Public Policy-Making* 3: 318–38.

– (1997) 'Vom produzierenden zum regulierenden Staat: Möglichkeiten und Grenzen von Regulierung bei Privatisierung.' In König and Benz, eds., *Privatisierung und staatliche Regulierung*, 576–91.

– (2000) 'Multi-level Governance: Institutionelle Besonderheiten und Funktionsbedingungen des europäischen Mehrebenensystems.' In Grande and Jachtenfuchs, eds., *Wie problemlösungsfähig ist die EU?* 11–30.

– (2001) 'Die neue Unregierbarkeit: Globalisierung und die Grenzen des Regierens jenseits des Nationalstaats.' In Werner Fricke, ed., *Jahrbuch Arbeit und Technik 2001/ 2002*. Bonn: Dietz, 95–110.

Grande, Edgar, and Burkard Eberlein (2000) 'Der Aufstieg des Regulierungsstaates im Infrastrukturbereich: zur Transformation der politis-chen Ökonomie der Bundesrepublik Deutschland.' In Roland Czada and Helmut Wollmann, eds., *Von der Bonner zur Berliner Republik (Leviathan-Sonderheft 19)*. Opladen: Westdeutscher Verlag, 631–50.

Grande, Edgar, and Markus Jachtenfuchs, eds. (2000) *Wie problemlösungsfähig ist die EU? Regieren im europäischen Mehrebenensystem*. Baden-Baden: Nomos.

Grande, Edgar, and Thomas Risse (2000) 'Bridging the Gap: Konzeptionelle Anforderungen an die politikwissenschaftliche Analyse von Globalisierung-sprozessen.' *Zeitschrift für Internationale Beziehungen* 7: 235–66.

Greenwood, Justin (1997) *Representing Interests in the European Union*. London: Macmillan.

Greven, Michael Th. (1999) *Die politische Gesellschaft*. Opladen: Leske and Budrich.

– (2000a) 'NROs und die Informalisierung des Regierens.' *Vorgänge* 3: 3–12.

– (2000b) 'Der Zweck heiligt die Mittel in der Demokratie nicht.' In Michael Th. Greven, ed., *Kontingenz und Dezision*. Opladen: Leske and Budrich, 191–202.

Greven, Michael Th., and Louis W. Pauly, eds. (2000) *Democracy beyond the State? The European Dilemma and the Emerging Global Order*. Toronto: University of Toronto Press; Lanham, MD: Rowman and Littlefield.

Haas, Ernst B. (1990) *When Knowledge Is Power*. Berkeley: University of California Press.

– (1997) *Nationalism, Liberalism, and Progress*. Ithaca: Cornell University Press.

Haas, Peter M., ed. (1992) 'Knowledge, Power and International Policy Coordina-tion.' *International Organization*. Special Issue 46(1).

Habermas, Jürgen (1998) *Die postnationale Konstellation*. Frankfurt: Suhrkamp.

Haftendorn, Helga, Robert O. Keohane, and Celeste A. Wallender, eds. (1999) *Imperfect Unions*. Oxford: Oxford University Press.

Hajer, M., and H. Wagenaar, eds. (2003) *Deliberative Policy Analysis*. Cambridge: Cambridge University Press.

Hall, Peter, and Rosemary Taylor (1996) 'Political Science and the Three New Institutionalisms.' *Political Studies* 44: 936–73.

Hall, Rodney Bruce (1999) *National Collective Identity: Social Constructs and International Systems*. New York: Columbia University Press.

Hall, Rodney Bruce, and Thomas Biersteker, eds. (2002) *The Emergence of Private Authority in Global Governance*. Cambridge: Cambridge University Press.

Haniotis, T. (2000) 'Regulating Agri-food Production in the U.S. and the EU.' *AgBioForum* 3: 84–6. Available at http://www.agbioforum.org

Hansen, John Mark (1991) *Gaining Access: Congress and the Farm Lobby, 1919–1981*. Chicago: University of Chicago Press.

Hardt, Michael, and Antonio Negri (2000) *Empire*. Cambridge: Harvard University Press.

Hasenclever, Andreas, Peter Mayer, and Volker Rittberger (1997) *Theories of International Regimes*. Cambridge: Cambridge University Press.

Haufler, Virginia (1993) 'Crossing the Boundary between Public and Private: International Regimes and Non-State Actors.' In Volker Rittberger, ed., *Regime Theory and International Relations*. Oxford: Oxford University Press, 94–111.

– (2001) *A Public Role for the Private Sector: Industry Self-Regulation in a Global Economy*. Washington: Carnegie Endowment for International Peace.

Heimer, C., and A. Stinchcombe (1999) 'Remodeling the Garbage Can: Implications of the Origins of Issues.' In Egeberg and Laegreid, eds., *Organizing Political Institutions*, 25–57.

Held, David (1995) *Democracy and the Global Order: From Modern State to Cosmopolitan Governance*. Cambridge: Polity Press.

– et al. (1999): *Global Transformations: Politics, Economics and Culture*. Cambridge: Polity.

Helleiner, Gerry (2002) 'Global Economic Governance.' Paper presented at the Conference From Doha to Kananaskis. Munk Centre for International Studies, University of Toronto, 15 May.

Hellermann, Gunther, Klaus Dieter Wolf, and Michael Zürn, eds. (2000) *Die neuen internationalen Beziehungen*. Baden Baden: Nomos.

Herbst, Jeffrey (2000) *States and Power in Africa: Comparative Lessons in Authority and Control*. Princeton: Princeton University Press.

Héritier, Adrienne (1999a) 'Elements of Democratic Legitimation in Europe: An Alternative Perspective.' *Journal of European Public Policy* 6: 269–82.

– (1999b) *Policy-Making and Diversity in Europe: Escape from Deadlock*. Cambridge: Cambridge University Press.

– (2002) 'New Modes of Governance in Europe: Policy-Making without Legislating?' in Héritier, ed., *Common Goods*, 185–206.

Héritier, Adrienne, et al. (2001) *Differential Europe: The European Union Impact on National Policymaking*. Lanham, MD: Rowman and Littlefield.

Héritier, Adrienne, Susanne Mingers, Christoph Knill and Martina Becka (1994) *Die Veränderung von Staatlichkeit in Europa: Ein regulativer Wettbewerb: Deutschland, Grossbritannien, Frankreich in der Europäischen Union*. Opladen: Leske and Budrich.

Herman, Barry (2002) 'Civil Society and the Financing for Development Initiative at the United Nations.' In Jan Aart Scholte and Albrecht Schnabel, eds., *Civil Society and Global Finance*. Tokyo: U.N. University Press, 162–78.

Herman, Barry, Frederica Pietracci, and Krishnan Sharma, eds. (2001) *Financ-

ing for Development: Proposals from Business and Civil Society. UNU Policy Perspectives, no. 6. Tokyo: U.N. University Press.

Hewson, Martin, and Timothy Sinclair, eds. (1999) *Approaches to Global Governance Theory*. Albany, NY: SUNY Press.

Hill, Martin (1946) *The Economic and Financial Organization of the League of Nations: A Survey of Twenty-five Years' Experience*. Washington: Carnegie Endowment for International Peace.

– (1978) *The United Nations System: Coordinating the Economic and Social Work*. Cambridge: Cambridge University Press.

Hinsley, F.H. (1966) *Sovereignty*. London: Watts.

Hirst, P.Q. (1999) 'Globalization and Democratic Governance.' Paper presented at the triennial meeting of International Political Science Association, Quebec City, 17 July.

– (2000) 'Democracy and Governance.' In Pierre, ed., *Debating Governance*, 13–35.

Hodson, D., and I. Maher (2001) 'The Open Method as a New Mode of Governance.' *Journal of Common Market Studies* 39: 719–46.

Holden, Barry, ed. (2000) *Global Democracy: Key Debates*. London: Routledge.

Hollis, Martin, and Steve Smith (1991) *Explaining and Understanding International Relations*. Oxford: Clarendon.

Holmberg, S., and L. Weibull (1998) *Opinions Samhallshället*. Gothenberg: SOM Institut, University of Gothenberg.

Hood, C. (1986) *The Tools of Government*. Chatham, NJ: Chatham House.

– (1999) 'The Garbage Can Model of Organization: Describing a Condition or Prescriptive Design Principle?' In Egeberg and Laegreid, eds., *Organizing Political Institutions*, 59–79.

Hooghe, Liesbet, ed. (1996) *Cohesion Policy and European Integration: Building Multi-Level Governance*. Oxford: Oxford University Press.

Hooghe, Liesbet, and Gary Marks (2001) *Multi-Level Governance and European Integration*. Lanham, MD: Rowman and Littlefield.

– (2003) 'Unraveling the Central State, but How? Types of Multi-Level Governance.' *American Political Science Review* 97: 233–43.

Horlick, Gary, and F. Amanda DeBusk (1993) 'Dispute Resolution under NAFTA: Building on the U.S.–Canada FTA, GATT and ICSID.' *Journal of World Trade* 27(1): 21–41.

Hunter, Rod (1999) 'European Regulation of Genetically Modified Organisms.' In Julian Morris and Roger Bate, eds., *Fearing Food: Risk, Health and Environment*. Oxford: Butterworth Heinemann, 196–230.

Huntington, Samuel (1996) *The Clash of Civilizations and the Remaking of World Order*. New York: Simon and Schuster.

Hurd, Ian (1999) 'Legitimacy and Authority in International Affairs.' *International Organization* 53 (2): 379–408.

International Monetary Fund (2001a) 'Assessing the Implementation of Standards – an IMF Review of Experience and Next Steps. Public Information Notice no. 01/17' (5 March) [Online]. Available at www.imf.org/external/np/sec/pn/2001/pno117.htm

– (2001b) 'Widespread Participation, Cooperation Are Key in Developing, Implementing Standards.' *IMF Survey* 30(7): 101–7.

International Monetary Fund/The World Bank (2001) 'Assessing the Implementation of Standards: A Review of Experience and Next Steps' (11 Jan.). [Online]. Available at www.imf.org

Isaac, Grant E. (2002) *Agricultural Biotechnology and Transatlantic Trade: Regulatory Barriers to GM Crops.* New York: CABI Publishing.

Isaacson, Walter (2004) *Benjamin Franklin.* New York: Simon and Schuster.

Jachtenfuchs, M., and M. Knodt, eds. (2002) *Regieren in internationalen Institutionen.* Opladen: Leske and Budrich.

Jachtenfuchs, Markus (1997) 'Democracy and Governance in the European Union.' In Andreas Follesdal and Peter Koslowski, eds., *Democracy and the European Union.* Berlin: Springer, 37–64.

Jachtenfuchs, Markus, and Beate Kohler-Koch, eds. (1996) *Europäische Integration.* Opladen: Leske and Budrich.

Jackson, Robert (2000) *The Global Covenant.* Oxford: Oxford University Press.

Jasanoff, Sheila (1995) 'Product, Process, or Programme: Three Cultures and the Regulation of Biotechnology.' In Martin Bauer, ed., *Resistance to New Technology.* Cambridge: Cambridge University Press, 311–31.

Jessop, Bob (1994) 'The Transition to Post-Fordism and the Schumpeterian Workfare State.' In Roger Burrows and Brian Loader, eds., *Towards a Post-Fordist Welfare State?* London: Routledge, 13–37.

Joerges, Christian, and J. Neyer (1997) 'Transforming Strategic Interaction into Deliberative Problem-Solving: European Comitology in the Foodstuffs Sector.' *Journal of European Public Policy* 4: 572–90.

Joerges, Christian, and Oliver Gerstenberg, eds. (1998) *Private Governance, Democratic Constitutionalism and Supranationalism.* Luxembourg: Office for Official Publications of the European Communities.

Joerges, Christian, and Ellen Vos, eds. (1999) *EU Committees: Social Regulation, Law and Politics.* Oxford: Hart.

John XXIII (1963) *Pacem in terris.* Encyclical letter. 11 April.

Jolly, Richard (1995) *The U.N. and the Bretton Woods Institutions.* London: Macmillan.

Jones, B. (2001) *Politics and the Architecture of Choice.* Chicago: University of Chicago Press.

Jones, C.O. (1982) *The United States Congress: People, Place and Policy.* Homewood, IL: Dorsey.

Josling, Timothy E., Stefan Tangermann, and T.K. Warley (1996) *Agriculture in the GATT.* Basingstoke, UK: Macmillan.

Juca, Lisa (2002) 'Belgium: EU Attempts to Soothe Fears and Boost Biotech.' *Reuters English News Service,* 23 Jan.

Kagan, Robert (2002) 'Power and Weakness.' *Policy Review,* no. 113. Available at http://www.policyreview.org/JUN02/kagan_print.html

– (2003) *Of Paradise and Power: America and Europe in the New World Order.* New York: Knopf.

– (2004) 'Die transatlantische Tragödie.' *Die Zeit,* 8 Feb. 8.

Kahler, Miles (1995) *International Institutions and the Political Economy of Integration.* Washington: Brookings Institution.

Kahler, Miles, and David A. Lake (2003) *Governance in a Global Economy.* Princeton: Princeton University Press.

Kaiser, Karl (1971) 'Transnational Relations as a Threat to the Democratic Process.' In Keohane and Nye, eds., *Transnational Relations and World Politics,* 356–70.

Katzenstein, Peter J. (1996a) 'Regional Integration Compared.' *ARENA Working Paper* 96(1). Oslo: ARENA.

– ed. (1996b) *The Culture of National Security.* New York: Columbia University Press.

– (2005) *A World of Regions: Asia and Europe in the American Imperium.* Ithaca: Cornell University Press.

Kaul, Inge, Isabelle Grunberg, and Marc Stern (1999) *Global Public Goods: International Cooperation in the 21st Century.* Oxford: Oxford University Press.

Keck, Margaret, and Kathryn Sikkink (1998) *Activists beyond Borders: Advocacy Networks in International Politics.* Ithaca: Cornell University Press.

Keene, Edward (2002) *Beyond the Anarchical Society.* New York: Cambridge University Press.

Keleman, Daniel R. (2002) 'The Politics of "Eurocratic" Structure and the New European Agencies.' *West European Politics* 25: 93–118.

Keohane, Robert O. (1984) *After Hegemony.* Princeton: Princeton University Press.

– (2001) 'Globalization: What's New? What's Not? (And So What?)' *Foreign Policy* 118: 104–99.

– (2002) 'Ironies of Sovereignty: The European Union and the United States.' *Journal of Common Market Studies* 40(4): 743–65.

Keohane, Robert O., and Joseph S. Nye Jr (1971) 'Transnational Relations and World Politics: An Introduction.' In Keohane and Nye, eds., *Transnational Relations and World Politics*. Cambridge, Mass.: Harvard University ix–xxix.

– (1977) *Power and Interdependence: World Politics in Transition*. Boston: Little Brown.

– eds. (1971) *Transnational Relations and World Politics*. Cambridge, Mass.: Harvard University Press.

Kerremans, Bart (1996) 'Do Institutions Make a Difference? Non-Institutionalism, Neo-Institutionalism and the Logic of Common Decision-Making in the European Union.' *Governance* 9: 217–40.

Kerwer, Dieter (2002) 'Standardising as Governance: The Case of Credit-Rating Agencies.' In Heritier, ed., *Common Goods*, 293–315.

Khagram, Sanjeev (2000) 'Toward Democratic Governance for Sustainable Development: Transnational Civil Society Organizing around Big Dams.' In Florini, ed., *The Third Force*, 83–114.

Kickert, W.J.M., E.-H. Klijn, and J.F.M. Koopenjan (1997) *Managing Complex Networks*. London: Sage.

King, Neil, Jr (2002) 'U.S. Ponders Next Course in EU Biotech-Food Fight.' *Wall Street Journal*. 2 Dec.

Kingdon, J. (1995) *Agendas, Alternatives and Public Policies*. 2nd ed. New York: Harper Collins.

Knight, W. Andy (2000) *A Changing United Nations: Multilateral Evolution and the Quest for Global Governance*. London: Macmillan.

– ed. (2001) *Adapting the United Nations to a Postmodern Era*. London: Palgrave.

Kohler-Koch, Beate (1996) 'Catching Up with Change: The Transformation of Governance in the European Union.' *Journal of European Public Policy* 3(3): 359–80.

– (1999) 'The Evolution and Transformation of European Governance.' In Kohler-Koch and Eising, eds., *The Transformation of Governance in the European Union*, 14–35.

– (2002) 'European Networks and Ideas: Changing National Policies?' *European Integration On-line Papers* 6 [Online]. Available at http://www.eiop.or.at/eiop/texte/2002–006a.htm

– ed. (1998) *Regieren in entgrenzten Räumen* (PVS-Sonderheft 29). Opladen: Westdeutscher Verlag.

Kohler-Koch, Beate, and Jakob Edler (1998) 'Ideendiskurs und Vergemeinschaftung: Erschliessung transnationaler Räume durch europäisches Regieren.' In Kohler-Koch, ed., *Regieren in entgrenzten Räumen*, 167–206.

Kohler-Koch, Beate, and Rainer Eising, eds. (1999) *The Transformation of Governance in the European Union*. London: Routledge.

König, Klaus, and Angelika Benz, eds. (1997) *Privatisierung und Staatliche Regulierung*. Baden-Baden: Nomos.

Kooiman, J. (1993) 'Social-Political Governance: Introduction.' In J. Kooiman, ed., *Modern Governance: New Government-Society Interactions*. Newbury Park, CA: Sage, 1–8.

Korey, William (1998) *NGOs and the Universal Declaration of Human Rights: 'A Curious Grapevine.'* New York: St Martin's Press.

Krasner, Stephen D. (1985) *Structural Conflict: The Third World against Global Liberalism*. Berkeley: University of California Press.

– (1999) *Sovereignty: Organized Hypocrisy*. Princeton: Princeton University Press.

– ed. (1983) *International Regimes*. Ithaca: Cornell University Press.

Kratochwil, Friedrich K. (1983) 'Is International Law 'Proper Law'? The Concept of Law in the Light of an Assessment of the "Legal" Nature of Prescriptions in the International Arena.' *Archiv für Rechts- und Sozialphilosophie* 69: 13–46.

– (1989) *Rules, Norms, and Decisions*. New York: Cambridge University Press.

– (2000) 'How Do Norms Matter?' In Michael Byers, ed., *The Role of Law in International Politics: Essays in International Relations and International Law*. Oxford: Oxford University Press, 35–68.

Kreher, Alexander (1997) 'Agencies in the European Community: A Step towards Administrative Integration in Europe.' *Journal of European Public Policy* 4: 225–45.

Krinsky, Sheldon, and Dominic Golding, eds. (1992) *Social Theories of Risk*. Westport, CT: Praeger.

Lake, David (1999) *Entangling Relations: American Foreign Policy in Its Century*. Princeton: Princeton University Press.

– (2003) 'The New Sovereignty in International Relations.' *International Studies Review* 5(3): 303–24.

Landfried, Christine (1999) 'The European Regulation of Biotechnology by Polycratic Governance.' In Joerges and Vos, eds., *EU Committees*, 173–94.

Lash, Scott, and John Urry (1994) *Economies of Signs and Space*. London: Sage.

Lehmbruch, Gerhard (2000) *Parteienwettbewerb im Bundesstaat*. 3rd ed. Wiesbaden: Westdeutscher Verlag.

Lehmkuhl, Dirk (2000) *Commercial Arbitration: A Case of Private Transnational Self-governance?* Bonn: Max-Planck-Projektgruppe Recht der Gemeinschaftsgüter.

Leibfried, Stephan, and Paul Pierson, eds. (1995) *European Social Policy*. Washington: Brookings Institution.

Levidow, Les, et al. (1996) 'Regulating Agricultural Biotechnology in Europe:

Harmonisation Difficulties, Opportunities, Dilemmas.' *Science and Public Policy* 3: 135–57.

Levi-Faur, David (1999) 'The Governance of Competition: The Interplay of Technology, Economics, and Politics in European Union Electricity and Telecom Regimes.' *Journal of Public Policy* 19: 175–207.

Lex Fori (n.d.) *La meilleure pratique dans le recours à des normes juridiques 'douces' et son application aux consommateurs au sein de l'Union européen.* Étude réalisée à la demande de la Commission européenne DG SANCO Brussels: Commission européene.

Lietzmann, Hans J. (1998) 'Reflexiver Konstitutionalismus und Demokratie.' In Bernd Guggenberger and Thomas Würtenberger, eds., *Hüter der Verfassung oder Lenker der Politik*. Baden-Baden: Nomos, 233–61.

– (2002) 'Europäische Verfassungspolitik.' In Hans Vorländer, ed., *Integration und Verfassung*. Wiesbaden: Westdeutscher Verlag, 291–312.

Linder, Stephen H., and Pauline Vaillancourt Rosenau (2000) 'Mapping the Terrain of the Public-Private Policy Partnership.' In Rosenau, ed., *Public-Private Policy Partnerships*. 1–18.

Lipschutz, Ronnie D. (1992) 'Reconstructing World Politics: The Emergence of Global Civil Society.' *Millennium* 21: 389–420.

– (2000/2001) 'Why Is There No International Forestry Law? An Examination of International Forestry Regulation, Both Public and Private.' *UCLA Journal of Environmental Law* 19: 153–79.

Lock, Peter (2001) 'Sicherheit à la carte? Entstaatlichung, Gewaltmärkte und die Privatisierung des staatlichen Gewaltmonopols.' In Brühl et al., eds., *Die Privatisierung der Weltpolitik*, 200–29.

Londoño, Nestor Osorio (1998) 'Implementation of the Agreement on Agriculture and the Work of the WTO Committee on Agriculture.' *Working Paper* 98(3). St Paul, MN: International Agricultural Trade Research Consortium.

Lord, Christopher (2001) 'Assessing Democracy in a Contested Polity.' *Journal of Common Market Studies* 39: 641–61.

– and David Beetham (2001) 'Legitimizing the EU: Is There a "Post-Parliamentary Basis" for its Legitimation?' *Journal of Common Market Studies* 39: 443–62.

Luhmann, Niklas (1972) 'Die Weltgesellschaft.' *Archiv für Rechts- und Sozialphilosophie* 57: 1–34.

– (1991) *Soziologie des Risikos*. Berlin: de Gruyter.

– (1995) *Social Systems*. Stanford: Stanford University Press.

– (1997) *Die Gesellschaft der Gesellschaft*. 2 vols. Frankfurt: Suhrkamp.

– (2000a) *Die Politik der Gesellschaft*. Frankfurt: Suhrkamp.

– (2000b) *Organisation und Entscheidung*. Opladen: Westdeutscher Verlag.

Lyons, Gene M., and Michael Mastanduno, eds. (1995) *Beyond Westphalia? State*

Sovereignty and International Intervention. Baltimore: Johns Hopkins University Press.

MacMillan, Margaret (2003) *Paris 1919*. New York: Random House.

Majone, Giandemenco (1994a) 'The Rise of the Regulatory State in Europe.' *West European Politics* 17: 77–101.

– (1994b) 'The Rise of the Regulatory State in Europe.' In Wolfgang C. Müller and Vincent Wright, eds., *The State in Western Europe: Retreat or Redefinition?* Ilford, UK: Frank Cass, 77–101.

– (1996) *Regulating Europe*. London: Routledge.

– (1997) 'The New European Agencies: Regulation by Information,' *Journal of European Public Policy* 4: 262–75.

– (1999) 'The Regulatory State and Its Legitimacy Problems.' *West European Politics* 22: 1–24.

– (2000) 'The Credibility Crisis of Community Regulation.' *Journal of Common Market Studies* 38: 273–302.

– ed. (1990) *Deregulation or Re-Regulation? Regulatory Reform in Europe and the United States*. London: Pinter.

Mann, Michael (1986) *The Sources of Social Power*. Vol. 1, *A History of Power from the Beginning to AD 1760*. Cambridge: Cambridge University Press.

Manow, Philipp (1996) 'Informalisierung und Parteipolitisierung -zum Wandel executiver Entscheidungsprozesse in der Bundesrepublik.' *Zeitschrift für Parlamentsfragen* 27: 96–107.

March, James G., and Johan P. Olsen (1976) *Ambiguity and Choice in Organizations*. Bergen: Norwegian University Press.

– (1989) *Rediscovering Institutions: The Organizational Basis of Politics*. New York: Free Press.

March, James G., and Herbert A. Simon (1958) *Organizations*. New York: Wiley.

Marks, Gary (1993) 'Structural Policy and Multilevel Governance in the EC.' In Alan Cafruny and Glenda Rosenthal, eds., *The State of the European Community*. Vol. 2. Lanham, MD: Rowman and Littlefield, 391–410.

Marks, Gary, Liesbet Hooghe, and Kermit Blank (1996) 'European Integration from the 1980s: State-Centric v Multi-Level Governance.' *Journal of Common Market Studies* 34: 343–77.

Marks, Gary, Fritz W. Scharpf, Philippe C. Schmitter, and Wolfgang Streeck (1996) *Governance of the European Union*. London: Sage.

Mayntz, Renate (1998a) 'Informalisierung politischer Entscheidungsprozesse.' In Axel Görlitz and Peter Burth, eds., *Informale Verfassung*. Baden-Baden: Nomos, 55–66.

– (1998b) 'New Challenges to Governance Theory.' *Jean Monnet Chair Papers*. no. 50. Florence: Robert Schuman Centre at the European University Institute.

- (2000) *Politikwissenschaft in einer entgrenzten Welt. MPIfG Discussion Paper oo(3).* Köln: Max-Planck-Institut für Gesellschaftsforschung.
- (2002) 'Common Goods and Governance.' In Héritier, ed., *Common Goods*, 15–27.

Mayntz, Renate, and Fritz W. Scharpf, eds. (1995) *Gesellschaftliche Selbstregelung und politische Steuerung.* Frankfurt: Campus.

McGowan, Francis, and Helen Wallace (1996) 'Towards a European Regulatory State.' *Journal of European Public Policy* 3, 560–76.

McGrew, Anthony, ed. (1997) *The Transformation of Democracy?* Cambridge: Polity.

McKinney, Joseph (2000) 'NAFTA-Related Institutions in the Context of Theory.' In Joseph McKinney, ed., *Created from NAFTA: The Structure, Function, and Significance of the Treaty's Related Institutions.* Armonk, NY: Sharpe, 14–24.

Mekata, Motoko (2000) 'Building Partnerships toward a Common Goal: Experiences of the International Campaign to Ban Landmines.' In Florini, ed., *The Third Force*, 143–76.

Mellon, Margaret (1994) *Comments to the U.S. Food and Drug Administration Advisory Committee on Genetically Engineered Food.* Washington: Union of Concerned Scientists.

Meyer, John M., et al. (1997) 'World Society and the Nation-State.' *American Journal of Sociology* 103(2): 144–81.

Mitchell, Ronald B. (2002) 'International Environment.' In Carlsnaes, Risse, and Simmons, eds., *Handbook of International Relations*, 500–16.

Moore, Elizabeth (2000) '*Science, Internationalization, and Policy Networks: Regulating Genetically Engineered Food Crops in Canada and the United States, 1973–1998.*' Unpublished doctoral dissertation, University of Toronto.

Moran, Michael (2002) 'Understanding the Regulatory State.' *British Journal of Political Science* 32: 391–413.

Moravcsik, Andrew (1998) *The Choice for Europe.* Ithaca: Cornell University Press.

Morçöl, M. (1996) 'Fuzz and Chaos: Implications for Public Administration Theory and Research.' *Journal of Public Administration Research and Theory* 6: 315–25.

Moynihan, D.P. (1973) *The Politics of Guaranteed Income.* New York: Vintage.

Müller, Michael (1996) 'Vom Dissensrisiko zur Ordnung der internationalen Staatenwelt: Zum Projekt einer normativ gehaltvollen Theorie der internationalen Beziehungen.' *Zeitschrift für Internationale Beziehungen* 3: 367–79.

Münch, R. (1996) *Risikopolitik.* Frankfurt: Suhrkamp.

Murphy, Craig (1994) *International Organization and Industrial Change.* New York: Oxford University Press.

Naschold, Frieder (1969) *Organisation und Demokratie*. Stuttgart: Kohlhammer.

Nassehi, Armin (2002) 'Politik des Staates oder Politik der Gesellschaft? Kollektivität als Problemformel des Politischen.' In Kai-Uwe Hellmann and Rainer Schmalz–Bruns, eds., *Niklas Luhmanns politische Soziologie*. Frankfurt: Suhrkamp, 38–59.

Nelson, R. (1968) *The Moon and the Ghetto*. New York: Norton.

Neyer, Juergen (2000) 'Justifying Comitology.' In Karlheinz Neunreither and Antje Wiener, eds., *European Integration after Amsterdam*. Oxford: Oxford University Press, 112–28.

Neyer, Juergen, Klaus Dieter Wolf, and Michael Zürn, eds. (1999) *Recht jenseits des Nationalstaates*, ZERP-Diskussions paper für Europäische Rechtspolitik (ZERP), Universität Bremen.

Noll, Roger G. (1985) 'Government Regulatory Behaviour: A Multidisciplinary Survey and Synthesis.' In Noll, ed., *Regulatory Policy and the Social Sciences*, 9–63.

– ed. (1985) *Regulatory Policy and the Social Sciences*. Berkeley: University of California Press.

Norris, P. (1996) *Critical Citizens*. Oxford: Oxford University Press.

Nurmi, H. (1998) *Rational Behaviour and the Design of Institutions*. Cheltenham, UK: Edward Elgar.

Nye, Joseph S. (2002) *The Paradox of American Power*. New York: Oxford University Press.

Nye, Joseph S., P. Zelikow, and D.C. King, eds. (1997) *Why People Don't Trust Government*. Cambridge: Harvard University Press.

O'Brien, Robert, Anne Marie Goetz, Jan Aart Scholte, and Marc Williams (2000) *Contesting Global Governance: Multilateral Economic Institutions and Global Social Movements*. Cambridge: Cambridge University Press.

Offe, Claus (2000) 'The Democratic Welfare State in an Integrating Europe.' In Greven and Pauly, eds., *Democracy beyond the State?* 63–89.

Ohmae, Kenichi (1995) *The End of the Nation State: The Rise of Regional Economies*. New York: Harper Collins.

Olsen, Johan P. (1983) *Organized Democracy*. Oslo: Universitetsforlaget.

(2001) 'Garbage Cans, New Institutionalism and the Study of Politics.' *American Political Science Review* 95: 191–98.

Onuf, Nicholas (1989) *World of Our Making*. Columbia: University of South Carolina Press.

Organization for Economic Cooperation and Development, (OECD) (2000) 'Reducing the Risk of Policy Failure: Challenges for Regulatory Compliance' [Online]. Available at www.oecd.org/puma/pubs/index.htm, accessed 28.3.01

Osiander, Andreas (2001) 'Sovereignty, International Relations, and the Westphalian Myth.' *International Organization* 2: 251–87.

Padgett, J.F. (1980) 'Managing Garbage Can Hierarchies.' *Administrative Science Quarterly* 25: 583–602.

Parsons, Talcott (1969) *Politics and Social Structure.* New York: Free Press.

Pastor, Robert (2001) *Toward a North American Community: Lessons from the Old World for the New.* Washington: Institute for International Economics.

Pauly, Louis W. (1997) *Who Elected the Bankers? Surveillance and Control in the World Economy.* Ithaca: Cornell University Press.

– (2001) 'What New Architecture? International Financial Institutions and Global Economic Order.' *Global Governance* 7, 469–84.

– (2005) 'The Political Economy of International Financial Crises.' In John Ravenhill, ed., *Global Political Economy.* Oxford: Oxford University Press, 176–203.

Pellizzoni, Luigi (2001) 'Democracy and the Governance of Uncertainty: The Case of Agricultural Gene Technologies.' *Journal of Hazardous Materials* 86: 205–22.

Peters, B.G. (1992) 'Bureaucratic Politics in the European Union.' In A.M. Sbragia, ed., *Euro-Politics.* Washington: Brookings Institution, 75–122.

– (2001) *The Future of Governing* 2nd ed. Lawrence: University Press of Kansas.

– (2002) 'Governance as a Theory of Comparative Politics.' Paper presented at the Colloque on Comparative Politics, University of Amiens, May.

Peters, B.G and J. Pierre (2001) 'Multi-Level Governance: A Faustian Bargain?' Paper presented at the Conference on Multi-Level Governance, University of Sheffield, July.

Peters, B.G., and F. Van Nispen (1998) *Policy Instruments and Public Policy.* Cheltenham, UK: Edward Elgar.

Peterson, John (1995) 'Decision-making in the European Union: Towards a Framework for Analysis.' *Journal of European Public Policy* 1: 69–93.

Phidd, R., and G.B. Doern (1978) *The Politics and Management of the Canadian Economy Policy.* Toronto: Macmillan.

Philpott, Daniel (1999) 'Westphalia, Authority, and International Society.' *Political Studies* 47: 566–89.

– (2001) *Revolutions in Sovereignty.* Princeton: Princeton University Press.

Pierre, J. (1997) *Partnerships in Urban Governance: European and American Experiences.* Basingstoke, UK: Macmillan.

– ed. (2000) *Debating Governance.* Oxford: Oxford University Press.

– and B.G. Peters (2000) *Governance, the State and Public Policy.* Basingstoke, UK: Macmillan.

Pierson, Paul (1994) *Dismantling the Welfare State?* Cambridge: Cambridge University Press.
– (1996) 'The Path to European Integration: A Historical Institutionalist Analysis.' *Comparative Political Studies* 29: 123–63.
Pollack, Mark A. (1996) 'The New Institutionalism and EU Governance: The Promise and Limits of Institutional Analysis.' *Governance* 9: 492–528.
– (1997) 'Representing Diffuse Interests in EC Policy-making.' *Journal of European Public Policy* 4: 572–91.
Porter, Tony (1999) 'The Late-Modern Knowledge Structure and World Politics.' In Hewson and J. Sinclair, eds., *Approaches to Global Governance Theory.* 137–56.
– (2001) 'The Politics of International Financial Standards and Codes.' Paper presented at the annual meeting of the International Studies Association, Hong Kong, 26 July.
Putnam, Robert (1988) 'Diplomacy and Domestic Politics: The Logic of Two-Level Games.' *International Organization* 42: 427–60.
Quaritsch, Helmut (1970) *Staat und Souveränität.* Vol. 1. *Die Grundlagen.* Frankfurt: Athenäum.
Rabkin, Jeremy (2004) *The Case for Sovereignty: Why the World Should Welcome American Independence.* Washington: American Enterprise Instutute.
Radelet, Steven (2003) 'Bush and Foreign Aid.' *Foreign Affairs* (Sept./Oct.): 104–17.
Rasch, William (2000) *Niklas Luhmann's Modernity: The Paradoxes of Differentiation.* Stanford: Stanford University Press.
Rayner, S. (1992) 'Cultural Theory and Risk Analysis.' In Krimsky and Golding eds., *Social Theories of Risk.* 83–117.
Reinhard, Wolfgang H. (2000) *Geschichte der Staatsgewalt. Eine vergleichende Verfassungsgeschichte Europas von den Anfängen bis zur Gegenwart.* 2nd ed. Munich: C.H. Beck.
Reinicke, Wolfgang H. (1998) *Global Public Policy: Governing without Government.* Washington: Brookings.
Reinicke, Wolfgang H. and Francis Deng (2000) *Critical Choices. United Nations, Networks, and the Future of Global Governance.* Ottawa: IDRC Publishers.
Reus-Smit, Christian (1999) *The Moral Purpose of the State.* Princeton: Princeton University Press.
Rhodes, R.A.W. (1996) 'The New Governance: Governing Without Governance.' *Political Studies* 44: 652–67.
– (2000) 'Governance and Public Administration.' In Pierre, ed., *Debating Governance,* 54–90.
Richardson, Jeremy (2001) 'Policy-Making in the EU: Interests, Ideas and Gar-

bage Cans of Primeval Soup.' In Jeremy Richardson, ed., *European Union: Power and Policy-Making.* 2nd ed. London: Routledge, 3–26.

– (2000a) 'Government, Interest Groups and Policy Change.' *Political Studies* 48: 1006–25.

– (2000b) 'EU Agricultural Policies and Implications for Agrobiotechnology.' *AgBioForum* 3(2/3): 77–83.

Ringeling, A. (2002) 'An Instrument Is Not a Tool.' Paper presented at Conference on Policy Instruments, McGill School of Law, Montreal, 26–27 Sept.

Risse, Thomas (2000) '"Let's Argue!" Communicative Action in International Relations.' *International Organization* 54: 1–39.

– (2002) 'Transnational Actors and World Politics.' In Carlsnaes, Risse, and Simmons, eds., *Handbook of International Relations,* 255–74.

– (2004) 'Global Governance and Communicative Action.' *Government and Opposition* 39(2): 288–313.

Risse, Thomas, Stephen C. Ropp, and Kathryn Sikkink, eds. (1999) *The Power of Human Rights: International Norms and Domestic Change.* Cambridge: Cambridge University Press.

Risse-Kappen, Thomas (1995) *Bringing Transnational Relations Back In: Non-state Actors, Domestic Structures and International Institutions.* Cambridge: Cambridge University Press.

Robertson, Roland (1992) *Globalization: Social Theory and Global Culture.* London: Sage.

– (1998) 'Globalisierung, Homogenität und Heterogenität in Raum und Zeit.' In Beck, ed., *Perspektiven der Weltgesellschaft,* 191–220.

Rokkan, Stein (1976) *Organization for Comparative Social Research.* Ann Arbor, MI: Inter-University Consortium for Political and Social Research.

Ronit, Karsten, and Volker Schneider (1999) 'Global Governance through Private Organizations.' *Governance* 12, 243–66.

Rose, Richard, and R. Guy Peters (1978) *Can Governments Go Bankrupt?* New York: Basic Books.

Rosecrance, Richard (1999) *The Rise of the Virtual State: Wealth and Power in the Coming Century.* New York: Basic Books.

Rosenau, James N. (1995) 'Governance in the Twenty-first Century.' *Global Governance* 1: 13–43.

– (1997) *Along the Foreign-Domestic Frontier: Exploring Governance in a Turbulent World.* Cambridge: Cambridge University Press.

– (2003) *Distant Proximities: Dynamics beyond Globalization.* Princeton: Princeton University Press.

Rosenau, James N., and Ernst-Otto Czempiel, eds. (1992) *Governance without*

Government: Order and Change in World Politics. Cambridge: Cambridge University Press.

Rosenau, Pauline Vaillancourt, ed. (2000) *Public-Private Policy Partnerships*. Cambridge, MA: MIT Press.

Ruggie, John Gerard (1982) 'International Regimes, Transactions and Change: Embedded Liberalism in the Postwar Economic Order.' *International Organization* 36: 195–231.

– (1993a) 'Territoriality and Beyond: Problematizing Modernity in International Relations.' *International Organization* 47: 139–74.

– ed. (1993b) *Multilateralism Matters: The Theory and Praxis of an Institutional Form*. New York: Columbia University Press.

Rugguie, John Gerard, Peter J. Katzenstein, Robert O. Keohane, and Philippe C. Schmitter (2005) 'Transformations in World Politics: The Intellectual Contributions of Ernst B. Haas.' *Annual Review of Political Science* 8.

Sabatier, P. (1988) 'An Advocacy-Coalition Model of Policy Change and the Role of Policy Oriented Learning Therein.' *Policy Sciences* 21: 129–68.

Salamon, L. (2002a) *Handbook of Policy Instruments*. New York: Oxford University Press.

– (2002b) 'Introduction: The New Governance.' In L. Salamon, ed., *Handbook of Policy Instruments*. New York: Oxford University Press, 1–47.

Sartori, Giovanni (1992) *Demokratietheorie*. Darmstadt: Wissenschaftliche Buchgesellschaft.

Sbragia, A. (2002) 'The European Union as Coxswain: Governance by Steering.' In Pierre, ed., *Debating Governance*, 219–40.

Scharpf, Fritz W. (1997a) *Games Real Actors Play: Actor-Centered Institutionalism in Policy Research*. Boulder, CO: Westview.

– (1997b) 'Introduction: The Problem-Solving Capacity of Multi–level Governance.' *Journal of European Public Policy* 4: 520–38.

– (1999a) *Governing in Europe: Effective and Democratic?* New York: Oxford University Press.

– (1999b) *Regieren in Europa*. Frankfurt: Campus.

– (2002) 'European Governance: Common Concern vs. The Challenge of Diversity.' *Working Paper* 01/6, May-Planck Institute for the Study of Societies, Cologne, Germany, September.

Schechter, Michael G., ed. (2001) *United Nations-Sponsored World Conferences*. Tokyo: U.N. University Press.

Schieder, S., and M. Spindler, eds. (2003) *Theorien der Internationalen Beziehungen*. Opladen: Leske and Budrich.

Schlacke, Sabine (1997) 'Foodstuffs Law and the Precautionary Principle: Normative Bases, Secondary Law and Institutional Tendencies.' In Joerges and Vos, eds., *EU Committees*, 169–86.

Schlichte, Klaus, and Boris Wilke (2000) 'Der Staat und einige seiner Zeitgenossen: zur Zukunft des Regierens in der "Dritten Welt."' *Zeitschrift für Internationale Beziehungen* 2: 359–84.

Schmalz-Bruns, Rainer (2002) 'Demokratisierung der Europäischen Union – oder: Europäisierung der Demokratie?' In Matthias Lutz-Bachmann and James Bohman, eds., *Weltstaat ohne Staatenwelt?* Frankfurt: Suhrkamp, 260–307.

Schmidt, Susanne K. (1998) *Liberalisierung in Europa: die Rolle der Europäischen Kommission*. Frankfurt: Campus.

Schmitt, Carl (1963) *Die geistesgeschichtliche Lage des heutigen Parlamentarismus*. 3rd ed. Berlin: Duncker and Humblot.

Schmitter, Philippe C. (1974) 'Still the Century of Corporatism?' *Review of Politics* 36(1): 85–131.

– (1991) 'The European Union as an Emergent and Novel Form of Political Domination.' *Working Paper* 1991/26. Madrid: Juan March Institute.

Schneider, Volker (2000) 'Global Economic Governance by Private Actors: The International Chamber of Commerce.' In Justin Greenwood, and Henry Jacek, eds., *Organized Business in the New Global Order*. Basingstoke: Macmillan, 223–40.

Scholte, Jan Aart (1998) 'The IMF Meets Civil Society' *Finance and Development* 35: 42–5.

– (2000) *Globalization: A Critical Introduction*. Basingstoke and London: Palgrave.

Schulze-Fielitz, Helmuth (1984) *Der informale Verfassungsstaat*. Berlin: Duncker and Humblot.

– (1998) 'Das Verhältnis von formaler und informaler Verfassung.' In Görlitz and Burth, eds., *Informale Verfassung*. 25–53.

Schuppert, Gunnar F. (1997) 'Vom produzierenden zum gewährleistenden Staat: Privatisierung als Veränderung staatlicher Handlungsformen.' In König and Benz, eds., *Privatisierung und staatliche Regulierung*, 539–75.

Scott, Colin (2000) 'Accountability in the Regulatory State.' *Journal of Law and Society* 27: 38–60.

Seidman, Harold, and Robert Gilmour (1986) *Politics, Position, and Power: From the Positive to the Regulatory State*. 4th ed. Oxford: Oxford University Press.

Sell, Susan K. (1998) *Power and Ideas: North-South Politics of Intellectual Property and Anti-trust*. Albany: State University of New York Press.

Selznick, Philip (1985) 'Focusing Organizational Research on Regulation.' In Noll, ed., *Regulatory Policy and the Social Sciences*, 363–67.

Shapiro, Martin (1997) 'The Problems of Independent Agencies in the United States and the European Union.' *Journal of European Public Policy* 4: 276–91.

Simon, H.A. (1947) *Administrative Behaviour*. New York: Free Press.

Singer, P.W. (2001/2002) 'Corporate Warriors: The Rise of the Privatized Military Industry and Its Ramifications for International Security.' *International Security* 26: 186–220.

Skogstad, Grace (1987) *The Politics of Agricultural Policy-Making in Canada*. Toronto: University of Toronto Press.

– (2003) 'Legitimacy and/or Policy Effectiveness? GMO Regulation in the European Union.' *Journal of European Public Policy* 10(3): 321–38.

Slaughter, Anne-Marie (2004) *A New World Order*. Princeton: Princeton University Press.

Smith, A. (1997) 'Studying Multi-Level Governance: Examples from French Translations of the Structural Funds.' *Public Administration* 75: 711–29.

Sorenson, E. (1997) 'Democracy and Empowerment.' *Public Administration* 75: 553–67.

Soros, George (1998) *The Crisis of Global Capitalism*. New York: Public Affairs.

Spindler, M. (2003) 'Interdependenz.' In Schieder and Spindler, eds., *Theorien der Internationalen Beziehungen*. 89–116.

Spruyt, Hendrik (1994) *The Sovereign State and Its Competitors*. Princeton: Princeton University Press.

Steinberg, Rudolf (1990) 'Kritik von Verhandlungslösungen, insbesondere von mittlerunterstützten Entscheidungen.' In W. Hoffmann-Riem and E. Schmidt-Aßmann, eds., *Konfliktbewältigung durch Verhandlungen*, vol. 1, *Informelle und mittlerunterstützte Verhandlungen in Verwaltungsverfahren*. Baden-Baden: Nomos, 295–315.

Steinmo, Sven, Kathleen Thelen, and Frank Longstreth, eds. (1992) *Structuring Politics: Historical Institutionalism in Historical Perspective*. Cambridge: Cambridge University Press.

Stichweh, Rudolf (2000) *Die Weltgesellschaft: Soziologische Analysen*. Frankfurt: Suhrkamp.

Strange, Susan (1954) 'The Economic Work of the United Nations.' *Yearbook of World Affairs*. London: Stevens and Son, 118–40.

– (1996) *The Retreat of the State: The Diffusion of Power in the World Economy*. Cambridge: Cambridge University Press.

Streeck, Wolfgang, and Philippe C. Schmitter (1985) 'Community, Market, State – and Associations? The Prospective Contribution of Interest Governance to Social Order.' In Streeck and Schmitter, eds. *Private Interest Government*, 1–29.

– (1985) 'Community, Market, State – and Associations?' *European Sociological Review* 2: 119–38.

– eds. (1985) *Private Interest Government: Beyond Market and State*. Beverly Hills: Sage.

Suchman, Mark C. (1995) 'Managing Legitimacy: Strategic and Institutional Approaches.' *Academy of Management Review* 20: 571–610.

Swinbank, Alan, and Carolyn Tanner (1996) *Farm Policy and Trade Conflict: The Uruguay Round and CAP Reform*. Ann Arbor: University of Michigan Press.

Talalay, Michael, Chris Farands, and Roger Tooze, eds. (1997) *Technology, Culture and Competitiveness: Change and the World Political Economy*. London and New York: Routledge.

Tänzler, D. (2002): 'Klimawandel: Divergierende Perzeptionsbedingungen als Ursache gescheiterter Klimaverhandlungen.' In Daase, Feske, and Peters, eds., *Internationale Risikopolitik*, 87–112.

Tarnoff, Curt, and Larry Nowels (2004) 'Foreign Aid: An Introductory Overview of U.S. Programs and Policy.' *Congressional Research Service Report*. Washington: Library of Congress, 15 April.

Tarrow, S. (1998) *Power in Movement: Social Movements and Contentious Politics*. 2nd ed. Cambridge: Cambridge University Press.

Taylor, Paul (2000) 'Managing the Economic and Social Activities of the United Nations System: Developing the Role of ECOSOC.' In Taylor and Groom, *The U.N. at the Millennium*, 100–41.

– and A.J.R. Groom, eds. (2000) *The United Nations at the Millennium*. London: Continuum.

Thatcher, Mark (1998) 'Institutions, Regulation, and Change: New Regulatory Agencies in the British Privatised Utilities.' *West European Politics* 21: 120–47.

Thomas, George (2004) 'The Sociology of World Society.' In Albert and Hilkermeier, eds., *Observing International Relations*, 72–85.

Thomson, Janice E. (1994) *Mercenaries, Pirates, and Sovereigns: State-Building and Extraterritorial Violence in Early Modern Europe*. Princeton: Princeton University Press.

Tilly, Charles (1990) *Coercion, Capital, and European States, AD 990–1990*. Oxford: Blackwell.

Tomlinson, John (1999) *Globalization and Culture*. Chicago: University of Chicago Press.

Tsing, Anna (2000) 'The Global Situation.' *Cultural Anthropology* 15: 327–60.

U.N. General Assembly (2002) 'Final Outcome of the International Conference on Financing for Development.' *UN Doc. A/CONF.198/1*.

U.S. General Accounting Office (2002) *Genetically Modified Foods: Experts View Regimen of Safety Tests as Adequate, but FDA's Evaluation Process Could Be Enhanced*, GAO-02-566. Washington: Government Printing Office.

U.S. Government (1999) 'Counterparty Risk Management Policy Group Report.' Proceedings of the U.S. House of Representatives Subcommittee on Capital Markets, Securities, and Government Sponsored Enterprises, Com-

mittee on Banking and Financial Services, 24 June [Online]. Available at
commdocs.house.gov/committees/bank/hba57791.000/hba57791_0.htm

- (2002) *The National Security Strategy of the United States of America*. Washington, White House [Online]. Available at www.whitehouse.gov
- Executive Office of the President, Office of Science and Technology Policy (1984) 'Proposal for a Coordinated Framework for Regulation of Biotechnology.' *Federal Register* 49:50856, 31 Dec. Washington: Government Printing Office.

van Crefeld, Martin (1999) *The Rise and Decline of the State*. Cambridge: Cambridge University Press.

Van Houtven, Leo (2002) 'Governance of the IMF.' *International Monetary Fund Pamphlet Series*, no. 53.

Vaubel, Roland (1986) 'A Public Choice Approach to International Organization.' *Public Choice* 51: 39–57.

Vaubel, Roland, and Thomas D. Willett, eds. (1991) *The Political Economy of International Organizations: A Public Choice Perspective*. Boulder: Westview.

Vogel, Steven K. (1996) *Freer Markets, More Rules: Regulatory Reform in Advanced Industrial Countries*. Ithaca: Cornell University Press.

Voigt, Rüdiger, ed. (1995) *Der kooperative Staat*. Baden-Baden: Nomos.

von Trotha, Trutz (2000) 'Die Zukunft liegt in Afrika: Vom Zerfall des Staates, von der Vorherrschaft der konzentrischen Ordnung und vom Aufstieg der Parastaatlichkeit.' *Leviathan* 1: 253–79.

Vos, Ellen (2000) 'Reforming the European Commission: What Role to Play for EU Agencies?' *Common Market Law Review* 37: 1113–34.

Walker, R.B.J. (1993) *Inside/Outside: International Relations as Political Theory*. Cambridge: Cambridge University Press.

Wallace, Helen (2002) 'The Changing Politics of the EU: An Overview.' *Journal of Common Market Studies*, 39, 581–94.

Wallace, Helen, and William Wallace (2000) *Policy-Making in the European Union*. Oxford: Oxford University Press.

Wallace, McClure (1933) *World Prosperity as Sought through the Economic Work of the League of Nations*. New York: Macmillan.

Waltz, Kenneth (1979) *Theory of International Politics*. New York: McGraw-Hill.

Wapner, Paul (1997) *Environmental Activism and World Civic Politics*. Albany: State University of New York Press.

Weaver, Kent R., and Bert A. Rockman, eds. (1993) *Do Institutions Matter? Government Capabilities in the United States and Abroad*. Washington: Brookings Institution.

Weber, Cynthia (1995) *Simulating Sovereignty: Intervention, the State and Symbolic Exchange*. Cambridge: Cambridge University Press.

Weber, Max (1978) *Economy and Society*. Vol. 1. New York: Bedminster.

– (1994) *Sociological Writings*. Edited by Wolf Heydebrand. New York: Continuum.

Wehling, P. (2002) 'Jenseits des Wissens: Wissenschaftliches Nichtwissen aus soziologischer Perspektive.' *Zeitschrift für Soziologie* 30: 465–85.

Wendt, Alexander (1999) *Social Theory of International Politics*. Cambridge: Cambridge University Press.

Wiarda, H. (1997) *Corporatism and Comparative Politics: The Other Great 'Ism.'* Armonk, NY: Sharpe.

Wolf, J. (2002) 'Staatszerfall: die riskante Stabilisierungsstrategie der Europäischen Union für den südlichen Mittelmeerraum.' In Daase, Feske, and Peters, eds., *Internationale Risikopolitik*.

Wolf, Klaus Dieter (2000) *Die Neue Staatsräson – Zwischenstaatliche Kooperation als Demokratieproblem in der Weltgesellschaft*. Baden-Baden: Nomos.

– (2001) 'Private Actors and the Legitimacy of Governance beyond the State.' Paper presented at ECPR Joint Session of Workshop, Grenoble.

– (2002) 'Zivilgesellschaftliche Selbstregulierung: ein Ausweg aus dem Dilemma des internationalen Regierens?' In Jachtenfuchs and Knodt, eds., *Regieren in internationalen Institutionen*, 183–214.

Woods, Ngaire (2001) 'Making the IMF and the World Bank More Accountable.' *International Affairs* 77: 83–100.

Woodside, Kenneth (1992) 'Trade and Industrial Policy: Hard Choices.' In M.M. Atkinson, ed., *Governing Canada: Institutions and Public Policy*. Toronto: Harcourt Brace Jovanovich, 241–74.

Yataganas, Xénophon (2001) 'Delegation of Regulatory Authority in the European Union.' *Harvard Jean Monnet Working Paper 03(01)*.

Young, Oran R. (1998) *Creating Regimes: Arctic Accords and International Governance*. Ithaca: Cornell University Press.

Zacher, Mark W. (2001) 'The Territorial Integrity Norm: International Boundaries and the Use of Force.' *International Organization* 55: 216–50.

Zangel, Bernhard (1999) 'Internationale Normdurchsetzung,' Institut für Interkulturelle und Internationale Studien (InIIS), Universität Bremen, InIIS-Arbeitspapier 15(99).

Zimmer, Annette (2001) 'NGOs – Verbände im globalen Zeitalter.' In A. Zimmer and B. Weßels, eds., *Verbände und Demokratie in Deutschland*. Opladen: Leske and Budrich, 331–57.

Zürn, Michael (1998) *Regierenjenseits des Nationalstaates*. Frankfurt: Suhrkamp.

– (2000a) 'Politik in der postnationalen Konstellation: über das Elend des methodologischen Nationalismus.' In Hellmann, Wolf, and Zürn, eds., *Die neuen internationalen Beziehungen*, 181–203.

- (2000b) 'Democratic Governance beyond the Nation-State: The EU and Other International Institutions.' *European Journal of International Relations* 6: 183–221.

Zürn, Michael, and K.D. Wolf (1999) 'Europarecht und internationale Regime: zu den Merkmalen von Recht jenseits des Nationalstaates.' In Neyer, Wolf, and Zürn, eds., *Recht jenseits des Nationalstaates*, 1–32.

Contributors

Mathias Albert is an associate professor in the Faculty of Sociology at the University of Bielefeld.

Ulrich Beck is a professor of sociology at the University of Munich and the London School of Economics and Political Science.

Tanja A. Börzel is chair of European integration in the Otto-Suhr Institute for Political Science at the Free University of Berlin.

Stephen Clarkson is a professor of political economy at the University of Toronto and directs the Program on the Governance of North America.

William Coleman is a university professor, Canada Research Chair, and director of the Institute on Globalization and the Human Condition at McMaster University, Hamilton, Ontario.

Burkard Eberlein is a DAAD visiting professor in political science at the Canadian Centre for German and European Studies at York University, Toronto.

Edgar Grande is a professor of political science at the University of Munich.

Michael Th. Greven is a professor and dean of social sciences at the Institute for Political Science at the University of Hamburg.

Louis W. Pauly is a professor of political science, Canada Research Chair, and director of the Centre for International Studies at the University of Toronto.

B. Guy Peters is the Maurice Falk professor of American government at the University of Pittsburgh.

Tony Porter is a professor and chair of the Department of Political Science at McMaster University, Hamilton, Ontario.

Thomas Risse is a professor in the Department of Political and Social Sciences and the Center for Transatlantic Foreign and Security Policy at the Free University of Berlin.

Grace Skogstad is a professor of political science at the University of Toronto.

Index

agriculture: Agreement on the Application of Sanitary and Phytosanitary Measures, 104, 110, 115, 116, 253; Biosafety Protocol, 111–12; biotechnology and, 103, 108–10, 116, 240, 247, 250, 252–3, 256; Codex Alimentarius Commission, 104, 109, 253, 256; common market, 100; Conference of Parties, 111; Convention on Biological Diveresity, 111–12; Creutzfeldt-Jakob disease and BSE, 246; domestic, 98–9, 104, 116; export subsidies, 99–101; food security, 109; and GATT, 98–100, 102; governance of, 95; grain prices, 100–1; import quotas, 99; international governance of, 109; policy-making, 100, 102, 108, 117; trade, 97–101, 117; transnational, 106–7, 112–13; and Uruguay Round, 94, 103–5, 107; U.S. Agricultural Adjustment Act, 99; WTO rules, 104–6, 111–13. *See also* genetic engineering

Amnesty International, 199, 201, 211, 274–5, 278

anarchy: garbage can model, 81–2; organized, 77–9, 287; perspective of privatization, 271

Ansell, Chris, 147

Arendt, Hannah, 273

Asia, 256, 289; financial crisis, 128–9, 229, 231

Asia-Pacific Economic Cooperation (APEC), 146, 188, 286, 290–1

Aust, Anthony, 280

authority: concepts of, 54, 238, 276; definition of, 276; domestic, 206; expert, 238, 240, 246–7; governance, 291; moral, 199, 211–12, 276; political (*see also* Weber), 4–8, 50, 54–5, 185, 187, 217–18, 235–6, 239–45, 291, 298; private, 19, 20n14, 63, 144n56, 206, 240–1, 243–4, 250–1, 255, 257, 271, 273, 297–8; public, 5, 7–9, 12–19, 21n25, 123, 135–6, 201–2, 206–7, 229, 244, 249–51, 273, 299n5; sources of, 278; state, 8, 196, 207; transnational, 149, 177, 188, 292–3, 297

authoritative, 20n15, 68, 121, 127, 136, 147, 196, 198, 210, 238–44, 253, 255, 276, 286, 290–5

ment, 173–6, 181–5, 187 (*see also*
WTO); enforcement of, 186; governance, 191; information forums,
179; intergovernmental committees, working groups, and profes-
sionals, 177–86; judicial function,
169, 173–5; Land Transportation
Sub-Committee (LTSC), 182; legislative capacity, 171, 176; legitimacy, outsourcing, and unemployment, 19; national treatment in,
171; new continentalism, 178–81;
peripheries, 189–90; regional integration, 286, 290; ruling on Mexican trucks, 190; and sovereignty,
185; trade in energy and basic petrochemical goods, 183–5; transna-
tionals, corporate rights, 175;
unmaking legislation, cases of
Ethyl, S.D. Myers, Metalclad, 176;
U.S. and Mexican trucking companies, 181–2
North American Free Trade Commission, 172
Nye, Joseph, 41

OECD. *See* Organization for Eco-
nomic Cooperation and Develop-
ment
Office International des Epizooties
(OIE), 104
Open Network Provision (ONP)
Committee, 159
Organization for Economic Coopera-
tion and Development (OECD),
98–107, 129, 160, 205, 212; Global
Forum on Corporate Governance,
231; Public Management and
Governance program, 222; self-
regulation of private actors, 222;

transnational policies on agriculture, 98–107
organization theory, 19, 74–6. *See also*
garbage can model of goverance
outsourcing, 19, 201, 207

Paris Convention for the Protection
of Industrial Property, 110
Pastor, Robert, 187
Patent Cooperation Treaty (PCT),
international system granting
IPRs, 110
policy decisions: bureaucracy, 81;
epistemic communities, 24; legislature, 81; network, definition of,
65n11; process, civil society, 79;
principal players, 79; transnational
politics, 45. *See also* decision-
making
political authority, 4–8, 50, 54–5, 185,
187, 217–18, 235–6, 239–45, 291,
298 (*see also* Weber); changes in,
286; European regional, 168; EU
regulatory state, 164; EU risk management of GMO or GM products,
249; global, 4, 49; global finance,
236; key component of, 137;
national society, 49; North American continental, 187; premodern,
20; problems of global transformation, 293; reconstitution of, 15, 218,
235, 255; regulatory governance in
North America, 249; role of the
private sector in governance, 217;
types of, 242; standards of legitimation, 241; transnational level,
297
politics: cosmopolitan, 45; described,
74; enablement, 26; participation:
concept of, 272, decline, 80; fluid,